# Education a

In this brief, interpretive history of American schooling, John L. Rury focuses on the evolving relationship between education and social change. This revised edition considers the impact of social forces such as industrialization, urbanization, immigration, and cultural conflict on the development of schools and other educational institutions. It also examines the various ways that schools have contributed to social change, particularly in enhancing the status and accomplishments of certain social groups and not others. Detailed accounts of the experiences of women and minority groups in American history consider how their lives have been affected by education. Changes in this new edition include the following:

- A more up-to-date discussion of several elements of social theory—human capital, social capital, and, particularly, cultural capital.
- An improved discussion of social change, a difficult concept for students to grasp.
- An expanded discussion of colonial schooling that includes new research on colonial literacy, racial and ethnic diversity, and educational exchanges between native Americans and European settlers.
- Considerations of social class in the discussions of gender, race, and ethnicity.
- Updated and expanded discussions of Black, Mexican American, Asian American, and rural education.
- Updated and expanded discussions of recent changes in educational politics, finance, and policy, and the troubles presently facing No Child Left Behind (NCLB).

**John L. Rury** is Professor of Education and (by courtesy) History at the University of Kansas. A past president of the History of Education Society and vice president of the American Educational Research Association, he has also served as a senior program officer at the Spencer Foundation, Chicago.

# Education and Social Change
## Contours in the History of
## American Schooling

Third Edition

John L. Rury

Routledge
Taylor & Francis Group

NEW YORK AND LONDON

First edition published 2002
by Lawrence Erlbaum Associates, Inc.

Second edition published 2005
by Lawrence Erlbaum Associates, Inc.

This edition published 2009
by Routledge
270 Madison Ave, New York, NY 10016

Simultaneously published in the UK
by Routledge
2 Park Square, Milton Park, Abingdon, Oxon OX14 4RN

Routledge is an imprint of the Taylor & Francis Group, an informa business

Typeset in Minion by Wearset Ltd, Boldon, Tyne and Wear
Printed and bound in the United States of America on acid-free paper by Edwards Brothers, Inc.

Library of Congress Cataloging-in-Publication Data
Rury, John L., 1951–
Education and social change : contours in the history of American schooling /
John L. Rury.
p. cm.
Includes bibliographical references and index.
1. Education —United States —History. 2. Educational sociology —United States.
3. Social change —United States.
LA205 .R67 2008
370.973 dc22                                                    2008019493

ISBN10: 0-415-99564-7 (hbk)
ISBN10:  0-415-99544-2 (pbk)
ISBN10:  0-203-88841-3 (ebk)

ISBN13: 978-0-415-99564-1 (hbk)
ISBN13: 978-0-415-99544-3 (pbk)
ISBN13: 978-0-203-88841-4 (ebk)

To Aïda

# Contents

# Preface

It is a familiar commonplace that the world is changing rapidly. We live in a time of considerable social and political turmoil, marked by violent conflict around the globe that has directly touched the lives of thousands of Americans. Deep divisions and critical problems face the nation, as a range of issues are debated fervently, extending from national and personal security to poverty and inequality to the condition of the natural environment. In many respects, we seem to be standing at a crossroads as the 21st century gets underway. If there is anything that Americans seem to agree upon, however, it is the growing importance of education for the future. Without expanding our present knowledge and abilities, it is unlikely that our society will successfully meet the challenges that lay ahead.

The heated debates of our time also reveal how far we have come, and how we often take the conditions of modern experience for granted. Technology has transformed life: we fly in airplanes, work in skyscrapers, and communicate instantly across vast distances. At the same time, our values have changed too, perhaps in more subtle terms. Today we publicly object to discrimination, celebrate principles of equality, and cherish the idea of freedom. We also hold an extraordinary belief in the transforming power of education. These facets of contemporary American life, however, have not existed for very long in historical terms. To one extent or another, each is the consequence of a vast and complex process of social change that has unfolded over several centuries. They also are the result of human sacrifice and anguish, a continuing process of conflict and struggle to achieve a better life. Such change represents a course of events that continues today, and one that has come to affect much of the rest of the world as well. This is partly what accounts for the fervor of debates we hold today. But understanding this process of social conflict, transformation, and renewal is critical to deepening our appreciation of who we are, and how we can best contend with what lies ahead. It is to such purposes that this book is committed, focusing on the question of education as a condition and manifestation of social change.

This is a history book, one that addresses a broad and complicated topic. Its purpose is both analytic and descriptive, relating what has transpired and explaining why events have taken a particular path. Finding the proper balance between these different goals has often proved difficult for me as a historian. But I trust that a book such as this is testimony to the worthiness of the goal. It is meant to be an aid for students just beginning to think about these questions, although I hope that others also will find it interesting and useful. The intent is to help generate insights into the ways that formal systems and practices of education have been related to social change. In this respect, it is an exercise in the history of education, a field of inquiry and explanation with a long and distinguished tradition of its own. Hopefully, the book will convey some of the potential of this branch of scholarship as a means of comprehending the present and contemplating the future. As John Dewey pointed out many years ago, the ultimate role of education is one of preparing for an ongoing and inescapable process of change. Understanding this aspect of life may be our best hope for posterity, and studying history can help a great deal in undertaking such a task.

# Acknowledgments

In writing a book an author incurs many debts. In the years that I have worked on this project, I have amassed a number of my own. The first is to Lane Akers, my editor, first at Lawrence Erlbaum Associates and now at Taylor & Francis, who conceived of a book such as this and asked me to write it. Lane also encouraged me to undertake subsequent revisions of the volume. I first wrote the book while working at the Spencer Foundation and at DePaul University in Chicago as a faculty member. Revisions for the second and third editions were completed at the University of Kansas, where I joined the faculty in 2003.

The preparation of this book has also benefited from the critical reading and advice of a number of other scholars, too numerous to recount by name, along with generations of students in my classes. Several anonymous reviewers also provided very valuable ideas for changes specifically for this revision. Belinda Latchford performed copyediting for this edition. All offered valuable observations for revising and improving the text. I have attempted to adopt their numerous suggestions, but many problems undoubtedly remain. Consequently, the customary academic aphorisms are certainly applicable in this case: My friends and colleagues should be held blameless for my own shortcomings as a historian, and responsibility for any errors, omissions and infelicities that remain is mine alone.

Both DePaul and KU provided stimulating environments for the research and writing required for a project such as this. Librarians at each institution were particularly helpful, especially as I learned to rely upon the numerous electronic information retrieval systems and databases available through their modern academic libraries.

To close, I especially would like to acknowledge the support of my wife, Aïda Alaka, who has been a steadfast and enthusiastic advocate of this project since its inception, extending to this new edition. Although not a historian herself, and engaged with her own demanding professional career, she has been unstinting in her willingness to endure a spouse's private fixation with obscure scholastic concerns. She also is an excellent writer and an insightful editor, and although I would scarcely hazard her appraisal of the manuscript, she has long been a discerning and persistent critic of my writing. Beyond all that, she remains a constant inspiration and an endless source of encouragement—and it is for these reasons, among countless others, that I continue to dedicate the book to her.

John L. Rury
March 2008

# 1
## Introduction
### *History, Social Change, and Education*

This book is an introduction to the history of American education. It approaches the topic by considering ways that education has been related to social change. As such, it begins with a simple query: Do schools change society, or does society change the schools? Obviously, the answer is more complicated than this rather plain question suggests. It's not hard to see that influences run in both directions: education clearly affects the course of social development, and schools also invariably reflect the impact of the larger social context. Still, the question of basic relationships remains. Can schools function effectively as instruments of social change? Or are they shaped and therefore constrained by larger cultural, economic, and political forces at play in society, reflecting and amplifying these factors but exerting little influence of their own?

History can help to answer such questions. There have been moments in the past when reformers believed that education could easily remedy social problems, and much time and energy was devoted to improving things through schooling. But this also raised nagging questions: Is educational reform a strategy potent enough to affect sweeping change? Or is it more limited in impact, perhaps destined to ultimate failure or disappointment? The answer to this is a persistent puzzle in American history, for people in this country have placed uncommon faith in the power of education. As historian Henry Perkinson noted more than three decades ago, schooling has been an "imperfect panacea" for curing the nation's ills, often promising changes it could not deliver (Perkinson, 1968). But even Perkinson did not say what the schools *could* accomplish.

As already suggested, educaton includes an extensive set of activities, so as a way of focusing the discussion, this book concentrates on schools and other institutions of formal instruction. It is not intended to be comprehensive. Instead, as the title suggests, it is thematic, identifying broad contours or patterns of change by looking at events and developments that help to illuminate general tendencies in the past. The point is to feature moments in history that were especially telling in creating the educational organizations, policies, and practices that exist today. By examining key steps in the evolution of the current school system, after all, it is possible to see some of the most important ways that education has been related to other aspects of social change.

Obviously, this book is somewhat different from other texts about the history of American education. For one thing, it does not pretend to include everything. Names and dates are hardly its major concern. Rather, the principal goal is to help you, the reader, *think* about history, and the ways that institutions such as schools change, along with the rest of society. In doing this, the book draws upon ideas from the social sciences, especially those used to explain broad patterns of social change in the past. Such concepts are critical tools to be used in thinking about processes as large and complex, and as significant as these. It is important, in that case, to devote some attention at the outset to a few of the ideas that will be encountered in the narrative that follows. At the same time, it also is necessary to consider just what we mean by terms such as "education" and "social change."

## Why Study History?

Some people enjoy reading history, others dread it. But beyond its intrinsic pleasures and difficulties, does history have any particular value? This is hardly a rhetorical question; indeed, it's undoubtedly quite common, especially concerning the history of education. After all, to grasp educational problems and their relationship to social change, the idea of studying history can seem patently ridiculous. Wouldn't it be better to simply examine pertinent issues, and devise solutions to current problems? How can the experiences of 100 years ago or more possibly help anyone today? What has history got to do with education?

Things change. It is commonplace for people to observe that society is different from not so very long ago. In fact, today we often hear the comment that things are changing faster than ever. Everyday news contributes to this impression with its constant drumbeat of reports about changing attitudes, and innovations in technology. There's a steady stream of information about "progress" in one sphere of life or another, and the ever-advancing march of science. Given this, who can doubt that we live in an era of significant social change? Why should anyone look to the past to understand it?

History poses challenges to questions such as these. Are we justified in assuming that ours is an era of unprecedented change? Because we embrace the idea of progress, we often have a tendency to believe that society today is somehow different—even better—than in the past. After all, people then were "old-fashioned" or unenlightened, and we seem to know so much more today. But this is a big presumption, and may not be true. How do we know that the pace of change is faster now? It is possible, after all, that people in earlier times experienced even greater social and economic shifts than we have today. To many of us this would come as a surprise. There is a natural inclination to see our own time as more interesting and dynamic, if only because it is so immediate and familiar—and there also is a tendency to see the future as even better. There are pessimists among us too, of course, and we are constantly reminded of the big problems that loom on the horizon. But most of us like to believe that progress has been good and we expect it to continue. This is a part of the enchanting lure of presentism, and what might best be called an intrinsic faith in social improvement (Nevins, 1938).

In fact, the present is not unique as a period of remarkable change. Things evolved quite rapidly in earlier times, in some respects at a faster rate than now. Indeed, in many ways the world today is in an era of considerable stability, even if technology and knowledge are being rapidly transformed. Truly revolutionary change on a very large scale occurred in the more distant past (Aghion & Williamson, 1998). It was those earlier processes of change and adaptation that set the stage for developments visible today. One of the great values in studying history, in that case, is to better appreciate the dynamic quality of our own time, by examining the challenges faced by those who lived in earlier periods. There is much to learn from seeing how people responded to a rapidly changing world in the past, and appreciating how their experiences have shaped our own (Tuchman, 1978).

Of course it is not easy to comprehend the scope or impact of changes in the present; social change is a slippery concept. For one thing, it is everywhere. It is the very nature of society to constantly evolve, after all, just as individuals and communities develop continuously. But all change is not the same. There are major developments and small ones, and it is often hard to distinguish between those that are enduring and others destined to have little lasting impact. This is another reason to study history, to see how things have developed over time, and to understand the ways that social change is influenced by events and circumstances, and by people. In this way too, history can help us to comprehend how we have arrived at the present, even if it can never provide a formula for solving any particular dilemma. At its best, history offers a point of comparison, to better interpret our immediate circumstances and to respond to them.

What does this have to do with education and schools? Like social change, education also is a complicated subject, even without considering its history. On one hand, education is an intricate human experience of individual growth and development, a process we all have encountered in everyday life (Dewey, 1938). In other respects, it also is the social and institutional activity of transmitting knowledge and values from one generation to the next, a process involving large segments of society and billions of dollars. And because education is linked to power and social status, it is a subject for almost constant debate. In its institutional form, education also has become a means of imparting and certifying the skills and knowledge essential to the welfare of society, a fact that has helped to make it a topic of great public interest. Understanding education in its many dimensions, in that case, can be a daunting proposition.

Because of these manifold purposes and functions, education often has been closely connected to the historical processes of social development. Indeed, in U.S. history, education has been a centerpiece of important periods of change. It has contributed to economic growth and political shifts, and it has helped to forge a national identity from the country's rich tapestry of cultural and social groups. Of course, the process of education itself also has evolved over the years, and it has been influenced by changes in the economy, the political system, and other facets of the social structure. Schools today are quite different from those in the past, and their purposes have changed from one period to another.

Consequently, we can say that education has been on either side of social change: both as a causal agent and as an aspect of life that has been transformed because of other social forces. The link between education and social change, however, is complex and constantly evolving. This makes it especially interesting as a topic of study, and as a means for reflecting on the present.

## Thinking about Social Change

In recent decades the study of history has grown rather complicated. Historians no longer have a monopoly on studying the past; they have been joined by social scientists, especially those in sociology, economics, and political science. This has been a natural development, as members of these academic disciplines have become concerned with studying large-scale social change and its effects on individual lives, as historians are. Indeed, historical study has become increasingly an interdisciplinary enterprise (Abrams, 1982; Rabb & Rotberg, 1982). These newcomers to the study of history have contributed more than just new information, however. The social scientists brought with them a number of ideas and propositions, or theories, about society, to test and refine with the use of historical evidence (Skocpol, 1984; Smith, 1991).

Some of these concepts are quite familiar, and have become everyday terms in conversation. Social critic Theodore Roszak has described the notions that help to organize our thoughts, those that precede information, as "Master Ideas" (Roszak, 1994). This is because they help us think about the problems encountered in life, by organizing facts, values, beliefs, and theories so that we can understand the world more easily. Some are commonly encountered in school; many have become a part of the conventional wisdom about how society has developed over the years. Roszak suggested that "all men are created equal" is such an idea, a notion that most Americans share as a basic proposition of social experience. Others are a bit more obscure, but include concepts that are used to interpret facts and make sense of the events in people's lives. A commonplace example is the idea of intelligence, which can be interpreted in a number of ways but often is related to technical skill, knowledge, and verbal ability. We often adopt terms such as this to describe human behavior or to understand events in particular contexts. Some of the terms that are discussed herein can play a similar role, especially with regard to understanding such complex phenomena as education and historical change. Even if they fall short of Roszak's definition of Master Ideas, these abstractions are helpful in thinking about the process of social transformation.

In the academic setting, such ideas often fall into the realm of social theory. As such, they can help us to understand large-scale shifts in society, past and present. Whatever they are called, it is important to consider just how historians and social scientists have thought of various concepts to help in understanding the history of education. Social change is difficult to define, but certain concepts can help to identify its many dimensions. A discussion of social theory, in that case, is more than a hollow academic exercise. It provides some tools for reflecting on history, and for examining the process of social change, along with ways it has affected the educational system.

The most pertinent social science ideas are those that describe vast processes of change, denoting effects on a grand historical scale. A prime instance is *industrialization*, perhaps the most familiar and significant single concept utilized in discussions of this sort. Although not as inspired as Roszak's example, it is indispensable to understanding the process of social change. Industrialization is a term used to represent a host of shifts in society and the organization of work that accompanied the rise of mass production manufacturing. Sometimes referred to as the *industrial revolution*, it describes a rapid rise in per capita output, or a sharp increase in the productivity of individual workers. This could only be accomplished, of course, by instituting other changes, such as the introduction of new technologies and organizing work in new ways. Historically, this first occurred in Great Britain, between 1750 and 1850. It appeared a little later in the United States, in the mid-19th century. And it developed even later in Japan and other countries. Wherever it happened, however, industrialization had a profound impact on the people who experienced it directly, and it produced a lasting effect on the organization of society (Ashton, 1948; Brownlee, 1979).

This can easily be seen in history. Before the industrial revolution the vast majority of people lived in the countryside and worked the land in agrarian settings. Artisans made most consumer goods, often by hand, and people purchased them locally. This changed dramatically with industrialization. After the industrial revolution large numbers of people were employed in factories and related occupations (such as transportation), and lived in cities where they consumed goods produced elsewhere. They worked longer hours, often performing relatively simple, repetitive tasks, and they had little control over their work, as it came to be dictated by machines. Altogether, people's lives changed drastically, sometimes in a relatively short time. Industrialization, in that case, meant more than just a shift in production; for many people it meant a whole new way of life (Laslett, 1965).

The process of industrialization caused many aspects of society to change. This was partly due to the sheer volume of goods and services produced. It enabled cities to be built, and fortunes to be made by a select few. For many people—perhaps most—the increased quantity of commodities meant a rising standard of living. But for others it was a time of wrenching dislocation, especially for those who left the countryside to seek work in burgeoning cities. In the United States many industrial workers came from Europe, traveling thousands of miles to seek employment. The large-scale movement of people from one part of the world to another often led to cultural conflict and political instability. It also held important implications for education, as schools struggled to prepare students for a rapidly changing world (Rabb and Rotberg, 1981).

As already suggested, industrialization also has been associated with the concept of *technology*, the use of machinery or other devices to conserve or enhance human labor. This is another important factor in comprehending historical change. Factories called for new forms of labor controlled by mechanized processes. Similar changes occurred in other settings. Even in the countryside, introducing machinery and rationalizing production helped to reorganize work. Such changes had important implications for the development of education, as new forms of knowledge and skill were called into play. Schools were expected to help train people to work under these conditions. Technological change often required new work habits, and close attention to organization and efficiency. Eventually, as a complex industrial society began to emerge, new roles for management focused on planning and the disposition of time. This too would have important implications for education, as schools were called upon to meet the requirements of rapidly changing social roles (Cowan, 1997).

Yet another concept associated with social change—along with industrialization and technology—is *urbanization*. This term refers to the changing spatial arrangement of society, particularly the growth of cities and all the myriad social questions that came with them. Historically, cities grew as markets for the exchange and distribution of goods, and the location of specialized services. With industrialization, however, cities became centers of manufacturing, requiring large numbers of workers and complex transportation networks. Expanding cities meant ever more people crowding together, sharing space and competing for power and wealth. This, in turn, entailed the development of social institutions such as schools, but also churches, reform groups, charities, and a host of governmental entities to oversee social amity. As cities grew they became more complicated, and finding new ways of managing an increasingly diverse citizenry became a major challenge (Monkkonen, 1988; Rabb & Rotberg, 1981).

These changes augmented the importance of formal education. With the growth of large cities, people's relationships appeared to evolve. Social scientists observed a pattern of social behavior peculiar to cities. It was no longer possible to know everyone in the community or on the job. In rapidly growing urban centers people were constantly coming and going, and close personal relationships became more difficult to sustain. In this context, people began to relate to one another in largely functional terms, based on their occupations and other social characteristics. Some believed that the social cohesion of communities began to weaken. Historically, it appeared that shared norms and expectations eroded, and familiar social controls lost their significance. More formal systems of socialization and discipline, such as the schools and police, gained new significance as a result. A new institutional culture began to take shape in the largest cities because of these developments (Schnore, 1965, 1974).

All of these occurrences were manifestations of social change, and they made education especially important as a way of certifying a person's knowledge, abilities, and even moral character. If it was impossible to know a man's background, for instance, or even to investigate by asking others about him, using credentials such as diplomas and degrees could at least certify a certain standard of achievement. As the social scientists have put it, *secondary relationships* were substituted for firsthand knowledge of a person's past, and as a result mediating institutions such as schools became more important in the evolution of society. Established patterns of behavior evolved significantly, and researchers noted the development of a historically new and distinctive urban culture in the largest cities (Palen, 1997).

Social scientists and historians have long noted that both industrialization and urbanization have been linked to a more highly defined *social division of labor*. Indeed, increased specialization in productive activities was almost axiomatic during the process of industrial development; it was one of the chief ways productivity gains (the production of goods and services at lower cost) have been realized historically. At the same time, as urbanization advanced, there was a sharpening division of labor in the occupational structure of cities. Larger cities developed more specialized occupations and services. This too was an important manifestation of social change, and the effects are easy to see today. For instance, we usually find the most skilled surgeons in hospitals located in the bigger metropolitan areas, along with exotic health-food stores, specialized music distributors, and costume shops. Only the biggest cities have the population base necessary to support such specialized activities and interests. Thus, the historical development of the division of labor has been linked to both industrialization and urbanization. And because the division of labor is closely tied to the need for new and different types of knowledge and skills, it has held profound implications for the development of education in American history (Hawley, 1950).

The division of labor in society is tied to yet another enduring concept in social theory: *class conflict*. This idea often is associated with social inequality and the development of the capitalist economic system. Karl Marx, the famous German revolutionary and philosopher, was probably the best-known proponent of the view that capitalism inevitably produces such inequities, but it has had many other adherents too. Today social scientists continue to debate such questions, but few dispute the importance of systematic inequality based on the type of work a person does or how much property he or she owns. And when such inequalities grow extreme, conflict can erupt. Historically, as the division between owners of capital and workers widened, Marx and others predicted that people who owned nothing but their labor—*the working class*—would come into conflict with those who controlled the means of production. There is much evidence of this in history, even though the apocalyptic vision of the Marxists has yet to be fully realized. With industrialization, and particularly the development of the factory system, differences between social classes were aggravated. This led to socialist movements, relatively small in the United States but larger elsewhere, and the development of modern labor unions. Historically, there was considerable strife over the rights and living standards of workers. This too was an important element of social change. These conflicts included battles over education and schooling, especially in the nation's growing industrial cities (Bowles & Gintis, 1976).

Industrialization, urbanization, the development of technology and the division of labor all have been important dimensions of social change as it has unfolded in the United States. They also are practical concepts, developed by social scientists and historians to explain extensive transformations in society. As such, they are vital to the task of comprehending just how education and social change have been related. But these are hardly the only ideas relevant to historical reasoning. Many additional social science concepts also are pertinent to understanding education and its shifting relationship to society. Unlike the terms discussed above, most do not deal directly with large-scale processes of change. They include ideas that have not been used much by historians, even if they are quite germane to the history of education. But these concepts also fit Roszak's definition of "master abstractions," and can be very useful in understanding social change in the past. To consider them further it is necessary to delve a bit more into the realm of social science ideas.

### History and Social Theory

One of the important goals of social science is the identification of basic categories of collective experience, expressed in terms that can illuminate human behavior in a wide variety of settings. Such conceptions are the elements of social theory, ideas or abstractions that are helpful in developing explanations of societal development. As such, they are critical to making sense of the broad processes of social transformation in American history.

A good example of a major abstraction in social science, and perhaps one of the most familiar in everyday usage, is represented by the term *culture*. Broadly defined by anthropologists as the way of life in a human society, culture can be thought of as a set of behavioral characteristics or traits that are typical of a social group. These usually include rituals or ceremonies, customs (established patterns of behavior), attitudes, and ideas that are passed down from one generation to the next. It is commonplace to think of these features of social life as especially evident in people from distant or exotic places, but they exist in contemporary American society as well. In fact, a person's own cultural traits are often difficult to recognize simply because they are so familiar. A handy definition of culture is "when you act like your mother but didn't intend to." The tricky part is identifying these traits even when they are considered normal, what anthropologists have come to call "making the familiar strange." Regardless of the social groups in question, if people exhibit the same patterns of behavior and attitudes or values as previous generations, social scientists often engage the notion of culture to describe it. Because it is so encompassing a concept, culture is a slippery term to define precisely. But it is indispensable in explaining the process of social change, particularly as it has occurred on a sweeping historical scale (Kluckhohn, 1949; Kuper, 2000).

Culture is especially useful in thinking about schooling, because education can itself be defined broadly as the process of cultural transmission. If society is to function smoothly, after all, familiar types of behavior need to be taught to each succeeding generation. This does not mean that new generations have to accept the old patterns of behavior or the ideas and attitudes that accompany them. Indeed, younger generations have often rejected key aspects of the culture of their parents. When there is a pattern of new attitudes and behaviors that develop with the young, one can speak of cultural change. And because schools are directly involved in the process of teaching ideas and shaping attitudes, they stand at the very center of the process of change in culture. A major question in the history of education and schooling, in that case, concerns the process of cultural transformation. How have identifiable patterns of behavior, customs, attitudes, and ideas changed in American history, and how have schools and other forms of education participated in these shifts (Spindler, 1963)? As suggested in the chapters ahead, the answer to this question is complicated and differs from one period of history to the next.

The question of culture gets even more complicated, however, in the realm of social theory. Some social scientists interested in education have employed the concept of culture to pose yet another abstraction: *cultural capital*. This idea is premised on the recognition that all cultures are not valued equally in modern society. In the United States, for instance, it is clear that certain patterns of behavior, values, and attitudes are more widely admired and rewarded than others. We may not all be pleased about it, but this is evidence of a dominant culture that continues to dictate and enforce many traditional values and tastes. Most of us are familiar with this through experience, regardless of whether we appreciate the cultural mainstream or not, but there can be little doubt that prevailing national values exist and exert great influence. The concept of cultural capital thus can be linked to the idea of *social status*. Certain ways of speaking, dressing, and conducting oneself, after all, are associated in many people's minds with greater standing or prominence in the social order. In this respect various cultural forms are linked to the status of different social groups. For example, an English accent is often favored over a Spanish one; suits are preferred to jeans and tee shirts. Knowledge of classical music or jazz is often taken as a sign of sophistication, as is a taste for fine wines. Knowledge of this sort is taken to represent cultural capital, a command of certain types of information and ability that are valued or respected by others with social status. Individuals who possess such knowledge and skills often have access to greater social benefits as a result. Those who lack them are frequently considered to be inferior. In this respect the concept of cultural capital is related to patterns of social inequality.

Cultural capital can also find expression in other ways, many of which are more substantial than the somewhat trifling examples above. It can take the form of more formal knowledge, such as a large vocabulary, a well-developed understanding of history, or the ability to speak a foreign language—especially a high-status tongue such as French. People possessing these skills generally are admired in the larger society because such capabilities are rare and considered a sign of accomplishment or refinement. Cultural capital can have more practical dimensions too, such as knowledge of how institutions function or understanding how to behave in certain situations, like being a good conversationalist, or even doing homework in a timely fashion. Individuals who possess these desirable traits hold advantages in social life and often enjoy greater respect as a consequence. It is in this regard that the term *capital* is fitting. Because these characteristics or conditions allow individuals to do things that they otherwise could not, yielding certain social benefits, they can be considered a tangible form of wealth (Bourdieu & Coleman, 1991; DiMaggio, 1982; Lamont & Lareau, 1988).

Schools can help to mediate the process of realizing such benefits if they reward the holders of cultural capital with greater access to credentials or other forms of social recognition. There is a considerable body of research demonstrating that various forms of cultural capital can be an advantage in school settings (Lareau & Horvat, 1999). Children with highly educated parents, for instance, have access to books, music, magazines, and media technology that may help them to impress their teachers, as well as others in the larger society. If they travel abroad, attend the theater, or frequent museums, their cultural capital could be augmented even further. Parents who understand how complex institutions function can pass this knowledge on to their offspring, affording them even more advantages. These are forms of cultural capital that are highly relevant to education today, but every historical period has been marked by one form or another of cultural advantage that can be transferred across generations. Consequently, *cultural capital* is a useful term in studying the history of education, even if the meaning of the concept is understood to shift from one historical period (or cultural setting) to another (Kalmijn & Kraaykamp, 1996; Roscigno, Ainsworth, & Race, 1999).

Another social science term that has gained wide currency in recent years is *social capital*. This idea is parallel to cultural capital, but conveys a somewhat different point. Social capital refers to advantages that individuals derive from relationships. As the sociologist James Coleman pointed out, in order for cultural capital (socially valued knowledge and skills) to be conveyed from one generation to another, it must be transmitted via positive and sustained relations between adults and children. In this connection, the existence of supportive relationships can be considered a valuable asset, and hence a form of resources or capital. Within groups, it can serve to reinforce dominant attitudes and behavior, as long as strong relations sustain them. Social capital can thus help to perpetuate the helpful dispositions, values, and bearing exhibited by communities or other social groups, insofar as they are passed along and become evident in the young. As Coleman noted, it can be especially efficacious in networks of association and influence that serve to benefit people. There are many instances of this in everyday life. Knowing the right people to secure a certain advantage, such as lawyers or bankers, can be regarded as a form of social capital. Tightly knit communities, where people help one another with all types of problems typically provide valuable social capital to their residents. As Coleman noted, it generally resides in mutually reinforcing webs of relationships. When members of these communities share values that encourage socially responsible behavior, such as maintaining a job or attending school, this can be considered a tangible benefit of social capital (Coleman, 1988).

With regard to education, perhaps the most straightforward example of social capital is the effect of local communities on school attendance. It has long been observed, for instance, that some social groups seemed to encourage school enrollment more than others. The children of Jewish immigrants in American cities had unusually high levels of school attendance in the early 20th century, even though their parents often were poor and lacked formal education. Similar patterns have been observed more recently among Asian Americans. Some of this behavior appears to have been due to attitudes in the community that attached great importance to school as a place where young people should spend their time and strive for success. This can be considered a form of cultural capital, but its realization depended on the close relationships between adults and children, ties that helped to transmit these advantageous values. Historically these groups were poor and did not enjoy many conventional forms of cultural capital, such as knowledge of American customs or command of proper English. The school was an institution that helped them to develop these traits, but their success was dependent on values gained from relationships with adults in the community. Such examples demonstrate that it is possible for a group of children to possess high levels of social capital (strong relationships), but relatively low stocks of cultural capital (socially valued knowledge and abilities). In the case of immigrant groups with comparatively little cultural capital, social capital was a resource that helped them to overcome disadvantages, and eventually acquire certain elements of cultural capital. If a community is quite cohesive and can influence the young to meet or exceed societal expectations regarding education, we can say that social capital has enhanced their achievement (Perlmann, 1988; Rotberg, 2001; Zhou & Bankston, 1994).

Of course, this also can work in the opposite direction. There have been groups that have shunned the schools, discouraging their children from attendance. Italian immigrants, for instance, sometimes told their children to leave school and find jobs so that they could contribute directly to household income. These communities were quite cohesive and successful at exerting influence, but it is possible that their relationships did not offer an enduring benefit. These relationships transmitted values that did not represent a form of cultural capital in the larger society, hence it is not clear that they represented social capital in the usual meaning of the term. As Coleman suggested, social capital is highly situational. Indeed, if community relations have a contrary impact on school participation, children may be disadvantaged in the larger society. Some social scientists have described this as *negative social capital*, as it represents relationships that may be beneficial in a limited context, but ultimately problematic for the individuals involved. In any case, a tightly knit community with broadly enforced values and expectations contributes to social capital only if it results in a tangible advantage for the individuals in question. The impact on education depends on the character of the attitudes in question and how they are conveyed through relationships in the immediate community (Perlmann, 1988; Portes, 1998).

Social and cultural capital are examples of ideas that are commonly employed to examine the behavior of individuals and social groups. In particular, these concepts are useful for explaining why some individuals and groups succeeded historically in the larger society and others did not. In this respect, both are related to the economic term *human capital*, which refers to differences in skills and knowledge that help explain why some people—and groups—are more economically productive than others. Lawyers and doctors, for example, can perform tasks routinely that would take less knowledgeable people much longer to complete, if they could do them at all. The same principle applies to nearly all jobs that require advanced levels of training.

Consequently, people who possess such abilities and knowledge typically command higher wages or salaries than those without them. This, according to economists, is the reason why people with higher levels of education generally earn more money than others. As demonstrated later in this volume, human capital has become a critical component of the modern economy (Becker, 1964). To the extent that social and cultural capital can contribute to a person's opportunities to acquire human capital—which is typically accomplished through school or other types of formal training—they can provide tangible assistance toward improving social status.

These various conceptions of capital possessed by groups and individuals are important to understanding the development of modern school systems and the way that they function in society. The concepts differ in that human capital—skills and comprehension—is usually seen as an outcome of schooling, whereas cultural and social capital—socially helpful knowledge and relationships—are typically considered factors that help account for success in school. In all three examples, however, capital is generally considered a good thing to possess, whether it is human, cultural, or social. It represents a palpable resource that can be drawn upon for social advancement. In short, the terms *cultural* and *social capital* identify resources that contribute to achievement in school and in the larger society, while *human capital* represents understanding and skills that contribute to economic advancement. Broadly speaking, culture and capital are concepts that help to characterize people and groups, and they allow greater understanding of differences in people. Together, these are ideas that have special significance in research on education today, and they are relevant to educational history as well (Rury, 2004).

People who occupy various positions in society, of course, often view the world in altogether different ways. And the manner in which they perceive problems often gives shape to their responses to them. Social scientists employ the term *ideology* to represent the systems of ideas and beliefs that people use to interpret their circumstances and to guide their actions. This is yet another critical concept in comprehending the relationship between education and social change, and it is clearly connected to the definition of culture discussed above. One useful way of distinguishing between these terms is to think of culture as principally representing patterns of behavior, and ideology as limited to beliefs and ideas, even though each influences the other. As historian Carl Kaestle has noted, in the United States ideology has been strongly linked to Protestant religion—or, in historical terms, to the Protestant Reformation—and a battery of ideas revolving around the capitalist economic system: private property, hard work, and self-denial for purposes of enrichment. These somewhat disparate ideological elements have worked together through American history to form a coherent worldview that has shaped attitudes and the development of institutions. There are other aspects of ideology that are touched on later but, as noted above, the development of values and attitudes clearly is a crucial component of schooling as a social institution. Ideology—and changes in it—consequently has been a critical factor in the development of education in the United States (Kaestle, 1983).

Like culture, ideology is a tricky concept. Because ideology also affects the way people see the world, sometimes it is difficult to recognize its impact in different aspects of everyday life. History provides a useful medium for examining the effects of ideology on familiar institutions and events. Some elements of ideology are more important than others; there are particular aspects of popular ideology that have been especially important, at least in the United States. *Racism* and *sexism* are collections of ideas that hold certain groups of people to be inferior in certain respects to others, notions that historically have had a profound effect on American society. *Racism* is an ideology that suggests African Americans and other groups should be seen as biologically different and less deserving of social status than others, particularly Whites. *Sexist* ideology holds that women are inferior to men in terms of intellect and physical stamina. Both of these elements of ideology have exerted powerful influences on popular thought and behavior in U.S. history. Obviously they also have held important implications for education, and for comprehending the development of schooling in the United States (Omi & Winant, 1994).

There is more to the question of ideology and its impact on education, however, than the distressing legacy of racism and sexism. Yet another aspect of popular ideology in this country has been *equity*—or the principle of equality of opportunity. This idea is associated with such other familiar features of American ideology as freedom and fair play, and Roszak's Master Abstraction cited earlier, "all men are created equal." These sentiments are contradictory, of course, to notions such as racism and sexism, and other ideas that would inhibit one social group or another on the basis of biological or cultural traits. It often has been noted that popular ideology in the United States is riddled with such incompatible elements. But conflict over these inconsistencies is part of what has made the United States such a dynamic society, and helps to account for the rapid pace of social and institutional change in its history. The concept of equity became a rallying point for transforming schools at various times, especially in the latter half of the 20th century. It was during this most recent period that the largest waves of reforms to make the schools into agents of change were instituted. The nation's school system continues to struggle with the legacy of those efforts today (Ravitch, 1983).

Concepts such as *culture, industrialization, urbanization, social* and *human capital, ideology,* and *equity* are useful only to the extent that they allow us to think clearly and judiciously about how society changes, and the ways that such changes have affected people's lives. In the case of education, these concepts are helpful in interpreting just why schools and related social institutions, such as families and other agencies of socialization, changed over the course of history. Schools have evolved a great deal in the past several centuries, even if certain aspects of education seem to have remained the same. As suggested earlier, studying this process can help us to see just how schools and society have interacted over time. To do this, however, it is necessary to consider just how the schools themselves developed.

## The Evolution of American Education

Schools are among the most familiar social institutions that people encounter in today's complex modern society. They have become an integral element of American culture. Nearly everyone has attended some sort of school for a considerable length of time, typically during life's most impressionable stages. And for the most part, people's experiences in school have been quite similar, at least as regards the institution itself. Hallways and classrooms are nearly ubiquitous in contemporary schools, as are teachers and principals. Almost all schools divide the day into discrete periods of activity, and follow annual schedules set by state authorities. In the main, schools pursue goals dictated by sponsoring institutions and agencies, such as state governments or churches. And all of them share a commitment to individual growth or human development and responsibility to the future of society.

For most of us, these and other aspects of schooling are so ingrained that they are virtually taken for granted, one of the most telling definitions of culture. Historians David Tyack and Larry Cuban have referred to some of these features as the "grammar of schooling," or rules and expectations that define the institution's structure and everyday operations. Because schools contain large numbers of children, for instance, they demand special attention to discipline and order, and they require adult authority in matters of supervision and training. Schools also place great emphasis on the routine transmission of formalized knowledge, and the evaluation of learning with more or less standardized methods of assessment. Of course, schools are also places where people make friends, play games, and do a variety of other things, but these features of experience do not identify the institution as a school. Rather, it is the rules and formal relationships of power and authority that form the familiar institutional parameters that most people associate with schools. Memories of these aspects of school life stay with individuals, and seem to be essential to the very concept of "school." One that lacked these characteristics would hardly qualify as that type of institution (Tyack & Cuban, 1995).

But schools have not always been this way. Indeed, many of these taken-for-granted qualities of schools did not exist in earlier times. These are aspects of schooling that have evolved historically, in response to forces of social change, and to address various social problems in the past. People like to think of schools as fixed social entities that resist change (indeed, some see social stability as a goal of schooling), but in fact they have been quite pliable and subject to modification throughout history. One of the purposes of studying the history of education, in that case, is to determine just how the familiar features of today's schools appeared. This, of course, also can be a step toward changing these structures in the future, to make better schools.

We start with some basic questions: How did schools develop in the past, and what caused them to change? These matters are central to the history of education, and critical to anyone interested in educational reform. As a prelude to the more detailed discussions in the chapters to follow, it is fitting to take a look at some of the big changes that have affected schooling, and consider how they may have been related to some of the social science concepts we have considered thus far.

Two hundred years ago schools were held in makeshift huts or cabins, or in rented rooms in urban areas. Most of the population lived in the countryside, so small schoolhouses predominated, where any schools existed at all. Children of all ages attended, and teachers conducted many different lessons simultaneously. School sometimes only lasted a few months each session, and attendance often was sporadic. Teachers did not have regular employment, working from one term to the next, and many were barely better educated than their students. Features of school that people often take for granted, such as age-grading and a common curriculum, all had to be invented and accepted as widely observed routines, as they were during the 19th century common school revival and later reforms. These changes were largely coterminous with industrialization. In fact, the first modern schools often were compared to factories. Even so, the process of change was painfully slow, and often met with stubborn resistance. It may have occurred during a time of rapid social change, but building the modern American school system was something of a protracted struggle (Axtell, 1974; Cremin, 1951).

Other features of the now familiar education system developed later. Most teachers in the United States did not receive profession training until the early 20th century, at least not in the current sense of the term, and bureaucratic systems of management became widespread even later. Schools for children of different ages, grammar schools and high schools, were introduced in piecemeal fashion. Many of these changes were driven by population growth, and ever-expanding numbers of children attending schools. This was especially true in the nation's major cities, some of which grew exponentially at the turn of the century. Urbanization, it turns out, was a central element of educational change. Without the growth of enrollments, modern, rationalized school systems would not be practical. Larger numbers of children made age-grading feasible, along with the long-term employment of teachers. Just finding rooms for all of these students was a major challenge facing educators (Tyack, 1974).

At the same time, the process of industrialization and the growing division of labor became associated with curricular differentiation in schooling, and the development of specific courses of study to prepare students for various careers. By the early 20th century, high-school students could choose between industrial education courses, college preparatory programs, and such specialized subjects as home economics and stenography. The idea of linking schools closely to the world of work became known as *vocationalism*. As schooling became associated with a host of different types of jobs, school completion (sometimes called *attainment*) became an important factor in the allocation of people to various types of employment. Schools were becoming adapted to the development of modern, urban America as it grew more diverse and forward-looking (Rury, 1991a).

Some would say that the education system at that time was becoming an important instrument for assigning people to different positions in the social order, a large-scale sorting machine (Spring, 1976). In the words of one observer, the schools helped to produce inequality (Kaye, 1973). Others would argue that the schools were engines of opportunity, allowing individuals to aspire to whatever position their talents were suited for (Ravitch, 1978). In either case, the central question was the link between schooling and the growing complexity of the social structure, an outcome of industrialization and urbanization. As the social division of labor became more complicated, the issues of schooling and training people for productive careers in the new urbanizing society grew in importance. Linked to this was the question of providing individuals and groups with the skills and knowledge required by the development of the economy, particularly in the 20th century. As technology advanced, and the tasks people were asked to perform became more complex and challenging, the demand for human capital, people with appropriate skills and knowledge, grew significantly. By the latter 20th century there was a revolution in the perceived importance of human capital, and public interest in schooling reached new heights (Goldin, 2001).

These developments, in turn, made education a potent political issue, especially in cities but in other settings as well. As schooling came to be seen as an economic and cultural advantage, it also became a point of contention. The history of American education is rife with instances of groups organizing to demand changes in the schools. Such incidents were commonplace in the 19th century, but seem to have increased in frequency with the growing importance of education in people's lives. In the latter half of the 20th century education became an increasingly thorny issue, especially as it was related to social and economic status (Ravitch, 1983; Vinovskis, 1999). Historically, much of this agitation has focused on the question of equity, and whether one group or another was being denied equal access to education. In the early 19th century there were debates about working-class children in schools, along with women in secondary and higher education. In the 20th century political conflicts often concerned new ethnic groups, along with questions of school funding. These battles were difficult, but they also contributed to important changes. As a consequence, many of the greatest inequalities in American education have been reduced or eliminated, even if important disparities still exist. Today the issue of equity in education continues to be a point of frequent partisan dissension, and schooling has become a major issue in national politics. Looking at the history of this issue can help one to understand today's conflicts over education, and imagine ways to address them (Katznelson & Weir, 1985; Peterson, 1985).

This basic outline demonstrates some of the general ways education has evolved in the United States over the past 200 years, as society has developed in response to industrialization, urban development, and the growing complexity of modern life. The educational system that exists today is the result of a long process of adaptation to changing social conditions. Most of the features of modern schools that we know so well at present were formed in response to specific historical circumstances. Given this, there can be little doubt that schools will continue to change as they adapt to shifting social forces in the future.

### Schools Changing Society

While it is clear that society has shaped the evolution of schooling, the converse question is less certain: how has the development of education changed society? There is, of course, the process of individual development that education typically entails. But what has been the cumulative effect, if any, of this sort of individual change on society writ large? This is a problem that has not received much attention, yet there are a number of telling examples one can highlight.

One is the case of women's education. Early in American history women were largely uneducated. But after the Revolutionary War new attention was given to education for females. As public school systems were established by the states in the 19th century, most were coeducational, granting boys and girls similar educational opportunities. Female enrollment grew, and by mid-century literacy rates for women in northern states were just about equal to those for men. Women also began to attend academies, high schools, and colleges in greater numbers. All of these changes preceded the movement of women into jobs requiring higher levels of skill, and the development of the first women's rights movement. Did education "cause" these latter developments? The answer is not entirely clear, but it certainly appears to have contributed to them. Given the historical evidence, it is probably safe to speculate that these large-scale shifts in female employment and political status would have occurred as they did without changes in women's education (Rury, 1991: Tyack & Hansot, 1990).

There is a parallel instance of education affecting social change in the case of African Americans. The ancestors of most African Americans came to North America as slaves, and as such were excluded from most forms of conventional schooling, even if they cultivated their own rich forms of informal education. Following the Civil War, after gaining freedom, African Americans enrolled in schools on a massive scale for the first time in history. Although their schools were inferior to those for Whites, these opportunities did contribute to the development of an educated elite that was able to articulate effective challenges to racism and discrimination in the 20th century. Eventually, African Americans made schooling a defining issue in their struggle for civil rights, with the historic *Brown* case in 1954 standing as a turning point in the movement for equality. Without the development of education as a resource for the Black community, and as an object of struggle, it is doubtful that these changes would have occurred quite as rapidly as they did (Anderson, 1988; Sitkoff, 1993).

These are just two of the most dramatic and profound changes in American society that have been affected, at least in part, by the development of schooling as a formal institution (and they are discussed in greater detail in Chapter 4). There are many others, as noted elsewhere in the book. And of course there were yet other changes, concerning ideology or the larger question of American culture, wherein schools have played a less dramatic but nevertheless important role in the evolution of such popular ideas as equality, democracy, and fair play. Ideology often changes at a slower pace than other aspects of society, so shifts such as these are more difficult to identify and attribute to the schools. But this does not mean that they did not occur. A part of the problem of education and social change, in that case, is identifying less obvious developments such as these, and making judgments about just how they fit into the more general relationship of education and society.

All things considered, there is much evidence that schools have had a substantial impact on society at particular points in time, even as they have been shaped by urbanization, political conflict, and other societal changes. All of these events have established the features of modern education that most of us take for granted today. It is the analysis of this process that makes history interesting and worthwhile as a mode of analysis, for understanding how the present has arrived, and perhaps what the future holds.

## A Final Word about History

Henry Ford once said, "History is more or less bunk." Generations of students also have declared it boring. At its worst history is a lifeless list of names and dates, or a set of formulas for describing otherwise intricate and complicated processes of social development. But at its best history is a story complete with human drama, memorable characters, political and ideological struggle, and lessons for life writ large. For historians it also is a science, one that requires scrupulous attention to getting the facts straight and testing explanations against the best available information about the past. This means that good history is reliable, at least in the sense that it cannot be disputed on basic matters of evidence. It also means that history is more than just a story, in the sense that it has to strive to achieve a higher level of verisimilitude than mere plausibility or internal consistency. History is also a matter of setting the record straight, attempting to identify what in fact occurred in the past as much as possible.

Throughout the narrative that follows, you—the reader—will find references to other works, generally contained in parentheses with the date of publication so that the full citation can be located in the Bibliography at the back of the book. The text also refers to important authors who have studied a particular topic and who have been especially influential in shaping the work of historians. These references have been included as a way of corroborating the facts in this historical account, but also as resources for readers to utilize in investigating particular topics themselves. Please follow up on any questions that may arise in reading this book by looking at some of the relevant citations provided. The book's List of References, moreover, is hardly exhaustive; there are many other studies in the history of education and related topics that readers may also want to investigate. Let this volume mark the beginning of your thinking about these issues, not the end.

Of course, history is about more than just identifying what happened. The historical record is always incomplete, and historians have to make judgments about just what is truly significant in the great mass of surviving materials. But the expectations of history as a scholarly field exert a powerful discipline: the story a historian constructs must conform to the historical evidence. The same is true, by the way, of the major ideas just outlined briefly. The use of ideas such as *industrialization* or *ideology* must fit the evidence at hand as well. Historians argue constantly about whether these terms are appropriate to describe a particular period or series of events. Constructing historical explanations, it turns out, is a complicated business, at least if one wants to be faithful to the factual record. Of course, new evidence is constantly being turned up, bringing down established explanations and theories, and posing challenges to the way people think about the past. The narrative of American education and social change that is presented in this book is informed by the most recent research, but eventually there doubtless will be new perspectives to consider and additional evidence that challenges some of the interpretations offered herein.

This means that readers have to pay attention to the details of educational history at the same time that they work to construct useful and appealing explanations of social and educational change. Names, dates, and statistical data, consequently, matter to some extent, although not as ends in themselves. They are meaningful insofar as they help to establish and to ratify the ideas and theories that are engaged to explain and understand the past. In addition to this, there is the task of straightforward historical description. A major part of the historian's task is to paint pictures of the past, to reconstruct the world of the people whose lives and behavior are under scrutiny. In doing this, the goal is to comprehend these people and their social setting in terms of their own understanding of it. It is possible to explain and comprehend; judgment is another matter. The historian aims to reconstruct history as it occurred, while offering explanations that help depict the past in terms that are familiar and meaningful today.

The task of the historian is arduous, in that case, and the challenge of reading history is to construct and test one's own understanding of patterns in the past. In the accounts of historical events presented in this book there are many names and dates. These comprise important place markers in the historical development of American education. They are not furnished for memorization, but rather to act as points of reference in developing your own comprehension of American society and the educational system that grew out of it and helped to shape it. Names and dates, in this case, are important pieces of the historical puzzle, and it is up to each reader to make use of them in the narrative that follows.

The book also features somewhat detailed accounts of certain events, or chains of events, that have marked the development of American education. These instances, descriptions of particular moments, are used to illustrate various themes in the history of education. Each one is labeled "Focal Point." These episodes are intended to help bring an issue to life, to illuminate the broad trends that a book such as this must dwell on. Education, after all, was a topic that people often became passionate about, and the struggles that they engaged in helped to create the school system—and the larger culture—which exist today. One such instance in the history of American education has been chosen to start most of the chapters, and others are sprinkled throughout the narrative. They touch on a variety of themes, but several are concerned with the changing conditions of childhood. Others afford a glimpse of conflicts that marked a particular era, or additional events that help illuminate a historical moment. In each case the intention is to offer a taste of how people experienced education, and how educational ideas and institutions appeared at different times. Although they are not highly detailed historical accounts, they may also offer some perspective for today's problems as well.

Now the stage is set. The chronicle that follows is a history of the institutions and experiences that we have come to call "education," and the way it fits into the larger process of change that has shaped modern society. Hopefully it will help to illuminate contemporary problems, and stimulate ways of thinking about them a little more clearly and expansively.

# 2

# Colonial America
## *Religion, Inequality, and Revolution*

Our narrative begins by considering the development of education and society during the colonial period of American history. Extending from the beginning of the 17th century (1600s) to the time of the American Revolution (1776–1783), this period encompassed nearly two centuries, and witnessed the appearance of a nascent Euro-American society on the North American continent. It was a time of beginnings for many aspects of what has come to be known today as American culture, patterns of behavior and attitudes distinct from those found in Europe and other parts of the world. And it was an era of sweeping social changes, even if it predated industrialization and large-scale urban development. Colonial society was agricultural, and it was cast on a small scale. But it was also a society in transition, experiencing growth and a process of change that eventually led to the Revolutionary War and the dawn of a new age in American social and political history.

A good way to start an exploration of colonial society is by considering the experiences of one of its best-known and most historically controversial figures. This will afford a glimpse of what it meant to live at this time, and the chance to learn about what has been perhaps the most essential aspect of education: the difficult process of growing up.

### FOCAL POINT: PARENTS AND CHILDREN IN A NEW WORLD

Cotton Mather, who lived between 1663 and 1728, was one of the most influential and celebrated men of his time. He was perhaps the leading cleric (minister) and intellectual in New England during the 18th century. He had been named for his maternal grandfather, the well-known English cleric John Cotton. Mather was the pastor of Boston's famous Old North Church, having followed in the footsteps of his father and grandfather in that pulpit. In short, the Mathers were a renowned family; Cotton's father Increase even served for a time as president of Harvard College. Cotton was appointed an overseer (or trustee) at the college twice during his lifetime, and is widely credited with being responsible for the establishment of Yale, later turning down its presidency. He was also a controversial figure in the infamous Salem Witch trials in 1692, having published a tract against witchcraft a few years earlier. Altogether, he authored hundreds of works, including the famous *Magnalia Christi Americana*—a history of Puritanism in America (Silverman, 1984).

In addition to all this, Mather was an inveterate keeper of diaries, and his daily reflections, unusual even for the most literate of minis-ters, provide a unique window on the society of his time. For pur-poses of this account, Mather's chronicles of his family life are very revealing, for they offer insight into the trials and tribulations of a well-known 18th-century parent (Hiner, 1979).

In 1717 Cotton Mather was profoundly troubled. The reason was his children, and his 18-year-old son Increase in particular. "Creasy," as his son was nicknamed, had been accused by a local "harlot" of father-ing her child out of wedlock. Mather was mortified, writing in his diary, "Oh! Dreadful Case! Oh, Sorrow beyond any that I have met withal! What shall I do now for the foolish youth! What for my afflicted and abased family?" Mather managed to keep the case out of the local courts, and he also kept Creasy confined at home, plying him daily with sermons and remonstrations for piety and good behavior (Hiner, 1979). But Creasy was not altogether contrite. Just two weeks after being accused, Mather wrote that young Increase had "made a worse exhibition of himself unto me ... than I have ever yet met withal."

Seemingly desperate, Mather wrote in his diary, "Oh my God, what shall I do? What shall I do?" He had harbored great hopes for Increase, consciously naming him after his own father in expectation that the child would continue the Mather tradition of conspicuous piety and religious stewardship in colonial Massachusetts (Silverman, 1984). What he found instead was a continuing source of anguish and pain, disappointment tempered by love but nonetheless humbling and humiliating. It was a telling trial of 18th-century parenthood.

Altogether Cotton Mather was father to some 16 children. This was a high number even for colonial America, where the average rate of fer-tility was about eight children per married woman (more than four times today's birthrate). But Mather also lived to see all but five of his children die, most before the age of four. He buried two wives also, and had married a third just two years prior to the accusations against Creasy (Hiner, 1979). It is possible that the large size of his family, at least in part, represented an effort to compensate for these losses. Some historians and demographers have speculated that high birth rates were a response to the terrors of death and uncertainty in the New World; if children were likely to die, a family needed more of them (Moran & Vinovskis, 1992). No doubt the revelations about young Creasy did little to assuage Mather's anxieties about his children. To a man of such acclaimed piety and faith, a wayward son was a test at least as great as the loss of an infant offspring.

Yet there is abundant evidence that Mather cherished his son deeply. Less than two years after the implications of an illicit union, Creasy was charged with "bearing a part in a night-riot, with some of the most detestable rakes in town." Once again Mather was distraught. "My miserable, miserable, miserable son Increase," he wrote in his diary, at the same time asking, "Oh what shall I do?" After pondering the situation, he decided to send Creasy to stay with his grandfather, who also was upset at his behavior, and to write him a "tremendous letter" threatening that he would "never own him or do for him or look upon him" until he earnestly repented.

Shortly after sending his son away, however, Mather found himself in tears as he asked God to help his son. "Ah poor Increase," he wrote in his diary, "Tho I spake against him, yet I earnestly remember him, and my bowels are troubled for him." A little later, in writing another pastor for help with Creasy, Mather predicted that "when you see him, you will certainly love him" (Silverman, 1984). Creasy continued to be a test to his father's devotion until his untimely death at sea in 1724. But Mather's torment upon hearing the news suggests the depth of his affection for the wayward son. "Ah vain world," he wrote, "how little is to be expected in thee and from thee ... disappointed harvests, how frequent are you ... this world will afford us no substantial happiness." In this respect Mather's feelings toward Creasy were not unusual: he grieved openly and sorrowfully when each of his children died. The fact that it occurred so frequently, or in the case of Creasy so far away, did nothing to diminish the pain these events occasioned. Youthful indiscretion, sickness, and death were all a part of life for Cotton Mather and other parents in 18th-century British North America. Yet families were bound together with genuine love and affection, even if they were separated by vast distances and for long stretches of time. And it was these sentiments that defined parenthood more than any other.

In many respects, Cotton Mather's behavior was quite contrary to what one might expect of an accomplished and didactic 18th-century cleric of his stature. He did not assert the authority of patriarchy or parenthood, and he did not command his son or threaten him with dreadful punishments (except an apparently hollow warning of banishment). Nor did he throw him out on his ear, or condemn him to damnation and suffering. Rather, he fretted like a dear friend, one who identified with Creasy's plight and cared deeply about his prospects for future happiness. Despite his conservative religious background, in this respect Cotton Mather was quite a modern parent for his time. Behavior such as his eventually would come to be emblematic of familial relations in British North America (Morgan, 1966).

Historians have suggested that the Europeans who settled in the New World acquired a distinctive view of life and social relations (Bushman, 1967; Butler, 2000). Part of this was a reaction against Old World traditions of upholding inherited authority, and hierarchical rules dictating status and delimiting opportunity. However much these European settlers may have missed their former society, the New World imposed a different set of expectations on them, and a distinctive way of life that was free of many of the constraints posed by the old order. Even though many young men observed what historian Harvey Graff has described as the "traditional pathways" of following in their father's vocation and station in life, others did not. American children did not even have the memory of European convention to constrain them, and alternative pursuits may have proved inviting (Graff, 1995).

Cotton Mather, for all of his regard of tradition and respect for authority, was a product of this new social environment. He did not dictate orders to his children as much as he educated them. In this respect it is possible to say that he attempted to transmit a high level of cultural capital to his offspring. But the transfer of these attributes was never automatic; nor was it often easy, as Mather's experience with Creasy suggests. Mather worried about his children's prospects, but all he could give them was training and wise counsel. It was up to them to make their way in the world as free, autonomous individuals. And of course there was Mather's undying affection, the source of his great pleasure in family life and his extraordinary anguish. Such is the puzzle of human development and education in the modern era: How does one prepare the next generation for the challenges of the future, while wanting to protect them from the dangers? It was a dilemma posed especially poignantly in the New World.

## Life in a New World

As difficult as it may be to imagine today, North America seemed truly a "New World" in the 17th and 18th centuries, the time and place referred to as colonial America. At least this was true for the Europeans who came to the Western Hemisphere to settle—or to profit and plunder—between 1492 and 1776. This was a vast stretch of time, of course, and much happened between the moment when the first White settlers arrived in British North America and the American Revolution. A largely English colonial society was established, and it evolved rather quickly from one generation of settlers to the next. On the western side of the continent, and in Florida and the southwest, Spanish settlements were established, and they too witnessed considerable change. Recognizing the complexity of this process of transformation, it is still possible to make certain general observations about the period as a whole. It was a time quite different from today.

Throughout this period most of North America was an expansive wilderness, inhabited only sporadically by a native population numbering just a few million across the entire continent. It was said that during the 1600s visitors to New England could smell the pine trees more than a hundred miles offshore. This was doubtless true of other parts of North America also. The first European settlements were tiny, and did not extend very far into the continent's interior. Residents of these colonies lived in close proximity to nature, and its hardships were a major preoccupation for them, especially the weather and encounters with wild animals or pestilence. Life in these circumstances was a constant battle against the elements, and dogged perseverance was required to forge a living from the wilderness.

Of course, the North American continent was already inhabited when the first waves of English settlers arrived in the 17th century. The Native Americans, or "Indians," as they had been dubbed by Christopher Columbus, were a diverse and occasionally contentious population, embracing hundreds of different social and cultural groupings. The vast majority lived in agricultural and hunting societies, cast on a scale considerably smaller than European nations of the time, even if there were exceptions in certain tribal federations. Although the American Indian population was substantial, it was spread thinly across the landscape. Divided into relatively small and isolated tribes and without advanced military technology, the Native Americans were often unable to resist the demands of these newcomers in disputes over land or other issues. As a consequence, they were eventually defeated, exploited, and pushed out of the way to make room for the expanding European population in the "New World." In educational terms, this was perhaps one of the most basic and profound lessons taught by the experience of colonial settlement: the Europeans saw Native Americans as an inferior people. When not feared, they were to be crushed and discarded if standing in the way of "progress," pitied and made "civilized" once they were defeated (Nash, 1974/2000).

The self-righteous attitudes of Europeans who felt superior to American Indians took different forms, and weren't always expressed in hostility or violence. Some newcomers found themselves beguiled by the handsome features of the natives, or by their seemingly simple, natural lifestyle. But even the "friends" of the Native Americans often sought to convert them to a particular religion, teach them Christian morality, or alter their culture in countless other ways. This early contact between two vastly different social and cultural traditions marked what was perhaps the first great process of social change in what is today described as American history. It was a transformation that proceeded largely in one direction, with American Indian society being gradually and forcefully pushed to the margins of the emerging European-based civilization in North America, even though Europeans certainly learned a great deal from Native Americans in the process (Axtell, 1985). In light of this historical turn of events, the term *New World* is both telling and ironic.

### The Different Realms of Colonial North America

The process of cultural interaction and displacement that led to European domination of the Western Hemisphere was in full bloom by the time Englishmen came to settle in the opening years of the 17th century. In time, British North America came to be a large, diversified land, extending along the Atlantic seaboard in a series of colonies, each established under different circumstances. Religious expatriates started some of these settlements; others were founded for personal or collective gain. It was a domain marked by different climates and a varied topography, and settled by people from a wide variety of backgrounds. Accordingly, it is difficult to make generalizations about the colonial population, and the various educational practices and institutions characteristic of the time. It would be wrong, consequently, to speak of a single, unitary colonial culture. Instead there were several different societies in British North America. Although they shared a number of similarities, each was quite distinctive—especially when it came to everyday culture and attendant educational customs.

Spanish colonial settlements were a bit different. The Spaniards launched exploratory missions and dispatched conquering armies in search of fortune nearly a century before the English. In North America they established outposts in Florida and Texas, but experienced the most success in establishing permanent settlements along the Pacific coast in the territory of California during the eighteenth century. Because of the great distances from Europe, California and other Spanish colonies did not attract large numbers of European settlers. Instead, it was a land of missions and ranches, with garrisons of troops to protect the interests of the Spanish crown (Rawls and Bean, 2003).

Most historians divide British colonial America into three broad regions, each representing a large contiguous territory and its corresponding population (Henretta, 1973; Main, 1965). The first, in order of settlement, was the South, which began with the settlement of Jamestown in 1607. Representing the colonies of Virginia, Maryland, the Carolinas, and Georgia, the South was characterized by specialized forms of commercial agriculture, along with a social structure and cultural tradition well adapted to its dominant commercial interests. Just to the north were the middle colonies, the largest of which were Quaker Pennsylvania and Dutch New Amsterdam, later named New York by the English. These colonies, which also included New Jersey and Delaware, featured a heterogeneous mix of peoples who had come to the New World for a variety of purposes. To the north of the middle colonies was New England, perhaps the best known and most studied of the colonial regions, and oft-noted in regard to the history of education.

A distinctive pattern of economic development and a correspondingly singular array of cultural and political traditions characterized each region. All of the colonies were preindustrial and local economies were dominated by agriculture, but climate and terrain made for considerable variation in the way people worked and lived. The South, with its relatively warm climate and long growing season, quickly became dominated by an export economy trading in tobacco and to a lesser degree rice and other cash crops. At the start of the colonial era land was plentiful in this part of the continent, but labor was not. So Southern landholders turned to involuntary labor, indentured servants at first and eventually to progressively larger numbers of African slaves. To the north, large-scale agriculture of this sort was rare, although not unknown, and the economy was characterized by small freeholder farms, usually worked by a single family. The quality of land for intensive cultivation varied a good deal. Such holdings generally produced little for the export market, although many participated in the expanding local trade, particularly near towns and cities (Henretta, 1973; Hofstadter, 1971).

Culturally, different traditions came to characterize each of these vast areas, and of course there were innumerable localized customs as well. In the South, for example, the wealthy planters (or plantation owners) represented the cultural and political leadership of local society. Even if they were a minority of the population, they set the tone for prevailing values and patterns of institutional development—including educational practices. Elsewhere, the local colonial leadership was dictated by the circumstances of each colony's founding. Religion was an important factor in the cultural identification of the various settlements, especially in the North. Of course, religion is a key aspect of culture today too, but it is imperative to appreciate just how significant it was in the 17th and 18th centuries. In many respects, religious beliefs and practices were a critical element of personal identification, much the way nationalism or ethnic identity may be today. It was an age of religious ferment, moreover, and there was considerable conflict between warring religious traditions on a world scale. The settling of British North America followed closely on the heels of the Protestant Reformation and the Catholic Counterreformation, events that shaped the way most people thought about the world and themselves (Fischer, 1989; Morgan, 1975). This was especially true when it came to the question of education.

Religious beliefs differed widely across the colonies. In the South, the wealthy planters were generally Anglican, the official Church of England, which had split from Catholicism during the reign of Henry VIII. On the other hand, dissident religious groups, hoping to practice their beliefs outside the purview of the established church, largely settled the New England and middle colonies. The Quakers in Pennsylvania were one such group, along with the Catholics in Maryland, and a little later the so-called Scotch-Irish in Pennsylvania, New York, and elsewhere. But the best known and probably the most important of the religious colonies were those established in New England. And it is there that discussions of the connection between religion and education in American history usually begin.

### Religion, Culture, and Education

Most Americans today are familiar with the story of the Pilgrims coming to the territory that eventually became Plymouth Colony in New England during the early 1600s. Like the Pilgrims, many of the first migrants to British North America came in pursuit of religious autonomy. Other groups seeking to practice their own faith settled nearby, the most important being the Puritans. They established Massachusetts Bay Colony and the city of Boston, which eventually became the most important settlement in the region. Their beliefs and ideas reflected elements of what eventually would become dominant features of American culture in the years that followed.

The Puritans—along with most other religious groups that arrived in North America—were resolute Protestants. In particular, they were followers, to one extent or another, of the French theologian John Calvin (1509–1564), who had rejected papal authority in favor of a church based on biblical interpretation and faith. They had departed England because they believed it to be a corrupt and decadent society, and they hoped to establish a more perfect social order based on moral authority and religious virtue. Like many other Protestants of the time, they rejected what they believed to be empty rituals in Catholic and Anglican religious practices. They were convinced that each person bore an individual relationship to God, based on piety and goodness, although they were hardly prudes either. This, however, did not necessarily mean that they were willing to tolerate the religious beliefs of others who differed with them. Consequently, there were occasional conflicts that marked the first century of settlement in New England (Miller, 1956, 1959; Rutman, 1977). Such clashes notwithstanding, most of the people who eventually came to live in this part of British North America were Protestants, and believed that the grace of God was manifest in the behavior of his subjects and the lives they led.

The religious beliefs of the Puritans, the Pilgrims, and other groups that settled in New England held great consequence for the development of educational practices there. It would not be wrong, in that case, to view religion as a principal component of the ideology of the age. Perhaps the most fundamental tenet of Protestantism was the belief that each person needed to form an individual relationship with God. To do this, of course, one had to be able to read and interpret the Holy Scripture, catechisms, and other religious writings; in particular it meant that every man, or person, should be able to read the Bible and interpret it himself. This required literacy, and the ability to reason from principles conveyed through a variety of socially sanctioned texts. It was a set of skills that earlier generations of Europeans had not cultivated widely. In the compelling new realm of Calvinist Protestantism, however, becoming literate and being knowledgeable were taken as highly esteemed virtues, as long as they were employed in the service of religion. Historically, this meant that new importance was attached to education.

Social theorists have long debated the historical significance of Protestantism, and Calvinism in particular, as a transforming influence in the development of Western civilization. Max Weber, the famous German social scientist of the early 20th century, argued that the Protestant Reformation was linked to the rise of capitalism as an economic system, along with its distinctive pattern of social and ideological practices. In particular, Weber suggested that Protestant, and especially Calvinist, predilections for self-denial (an ethic of simplicity and thrift), hard work, and self-improvement (education and careful investment of wealth) contributed to the development of a class of merchants, financiers, and forward-looking aristocrats who spearheaded the emergence of modern capitalist society (Weber, 1930). It was an ideological outlook especially well suited to capitalism as a social and economic system. In the New World, one might add, it shaped the thinking of thousands of small freeholding farmers and the entrepreneurs who served them as tradesmen, innkeepers, and peddlers. While the relationship between religion and economic and social development was not necessarily direct and immediate, there is broad agreement among historians that the appearance of Protestantism as a social movement in the 16th century presaged an era of unprecedented social change (Landes, 1998).

The movement of Europeans to North America, in that case, can be considered a part of a massive social and ideological shift that occurred between the 16th and 19th centuries (1500–1800). At least this can be said of the first European settlers in what became New England. The rise of Protestantism in its various forms signaled a renewed commitment to human perfectibility and moral improvement. Migration to North America also entailed a grand experiment in economic development, one predicated on creating permanent settlements and a new extension of English society. This was different from the colonies of other European powers, which often viewed the New World as a source of immediate exploitation rather than extended investment and settlement (Landes, 1969). These factors taken together helped to give residents of British North America a distinctly modern and capitalistic sensibility by the end of the 17th century. Such predilections eventually would contribute to the outbreak of revolution, of course, but they also contributed to the development of new ways to think about the organization of society.

## Education for a New World

Schools were fragile institutions in the colonial world, existing alongside older and more familiar agencies of education, the family and the church. Even though there was a high level of rhetorical commitment to formal education in some colonies, in practice it appears that schools typically were attended infrequently, and only a minority of colonial youth would have been considered "educated" by today's standards. Big changes in the economy and the intellectual life of the colonies affected education, but it is not clear that formal schooling played a significant role in these events either. To understand education in much of colonial America, in that case, it is important to consider the ideological, social, and economic forces that shaped social development.

The cultivation of skills and the transmission of culture were major concerns of English settlers in North America, evident almost immediately upon their arrival. This was perhaps most apparent in New England, where early laws called for establishing schools and for educating young men—and eventually young women too. Another early sign of the importance of education and learning was the Puritans' decision to establish Harvard College in 1636. Massachusetts Bay Colony has been described by historians as a "theocratic" society, one that placed special value on the necessity of moral and religious leadership (Miller, 1956). Given this, preparing a cadre of educated leaders was considered essential to the moral and intellectual life of the colony. Such was the principal rationale for creating early colleges. In the wake of religious debates and schisms, other institutions of higher learning were started in nearby Connecticut (Yale College, 1701) and New Jersey (today's Princeton University, 1746) to train yet more religious leaders. Eventually some nine colonial colleges were established, providing a modest but important supply of educated men for the ministry and other professional roles in the colonies (Cremin, 1970). Similar educational opportunities were furnished by various academies, which often sent students on to the colleges to complete degrees (Nybakken, 1997).

The colonial colleges and academies were small institutions, attended by only a select few of the young men at the time. At most they possessed just a few buildings and enrolled no more than a couple of hundred students, many of whom never graduated. Even the sons of colonial intellectuals, like "Creasy" Mather, often did not exhibit an interest in higher education. But for a small and tightly knit elite they were critically important institutions. The curriculum focused on Latin and Greek, languages that linked the cultivated domains of science and theology at the time. Knowledge of classical language and related subjects thus represented a form of cultural capital that distinguished the college-educated from the rest of the population. Advanced formal education may not have been as important as today, but it still commanded respect in certain circles. For the leadership of the British colonies, the development of the colleges was an essential act of investment in higher learning (Vine, 1976).

For most colonial children, on the other hand, the only opportunity for formal instruction was offered by the local schools, which were conducted under a variety of circumstances. These institutions also were quite small, and those who bothered to enroll usually did so for less than seven or eight years, often attending only four or five months each term. They studied the Bible, along with spellers, books of prayers, catechisms, and other religious texts. The famous New England Primer was the best known of a wide range of reading materials used to impart lessons in spelling and grammar, along with morality and virtue (Axtell, 1974). In these respects, the school was an extension of the home and the church, where religious instruction and reading commenced and were further developed. Families with a greater stock of formal education, and the skills and knowledge that accompanied it, could give their children an advantage in the transmission of cultural capital. But most people in colonial America did not view schooling as a route to higher social status or economic improvement. Rather, the purpose of formal education was principally to augment the development of reading and reasoning abilities necessary for active participation in the life of a society governed by religious values.

Schools were probably most common in the colonies of New England, where the theocratic and Protestant purposes of formal education were clearly invoked. In 1647 Massachusetts enacted a law requiring towns of 50 families or more to establish a school, to confound the "Old Deluder Satan" in his unending quest to lead Christians astray. Connecticut enacted a similar decree just a few years later. Although it is unlikely that most towns complied by immediately establishing a school, the appearance of such measures signaled the importance that colonial leaders attached to formal instruction (Cremin, 1970). If the idea of a perfect society, based on a firm set of religious principles, was to be transmitted from the first generation of settlers to their offspring, some form of systematic educational process had to be established.

It would be wrong, however, to assume that this legislation marked the development of a modern school system. Schooling in colonial New England was intended to supplement—not supplant—the central role of the family in transmitting religious values and basic literary and computational skills. It was left to local authorities, and the taxpayers, to decide whether formal schooling was even necessary in particular towns and villages. Consequently, the "Old Deluder Satan" law was often honored in the breach, especially if there was not a large number of families interested in supporting a school. Here it is possible to see the influence of social capital, or relationships supporting a shared set of values and behavioral norms with respect to education. If local communities did not share the view that schools were important, formal education languished. Over time, however, the logic of Protestant values regarding education proved hard to resist, especially in more developed communities. As the population of the region grew in the 17th century, the likelihood of schools being opened to serve a town increased apace. Education remained largely a voluntary affair, and it was left to individual families to decide just how much schooling their children needed, but community norms gradually exerted greater influence on such decisions (Axtell, 1974).

Schools in colonial New England—and elsewhere in this period—generally were tiny institutions, run by a single teacher, or *master*, the term used at the time. Outside of Boston, New York, or Philadelphia, schools were rarely larger than a single classroom, attended by perhaps several dozen students. Although there were a few legendary teachers, such as Ezekial Cheever of the Boston Latin School, many were college students or recent graduates waiting to be called to a pulpit or some other vocation. Yet other teachers were men of modest education who were ill suited by temperament or training for other lines of work, and managed schools for lack of better prospects (Brown, 1902). By the early 18th century, female teachers taught younger children in "Dame Schools" in some communities, usually in their own homes. Consequently, running a school was a relatively low-status occupation from the very earliest times in American history, even when schools were relatively few and education was at least nominally assigned some importance in the culture and by colonial leaders (Perlmann and Margo, 2001).

The question of schooling notwithstanding, the effort to preserve the religious purposes and the theocratic culture of Puritan New England in the 17th century was generally a failure. This was principally due to population growth and economic development; as the next generation grew older and new waves of immigrants arrived, it became impossible to maintain firm standards of religious conformity. In the 1660s religious leaders loosened requirements for church membership in order to attract the next generation of parishioners, who often lacked the religious zeal of their parents. This was the so-called "halfway covenant." Other religious changes were important too, especially revivals that periodically swept the countryside. By the end of the 1600s the original Puritan theocracy had virtually disappeared. Religion continued to be a preeminent factor in the cultural lives of most New Englanders, but church leaders were not able to command the same authority their forefathers had wielded just two generations earlier (Rutman, 1970).

These developments demonstrated just how difficult it was to transfer the values of one generation to the next; it turned out that the transmission of culture could not be legislated. Despite measures such as the "Deluder Satan" law, schools simply could not sustain the traditional religious values of the original Puritan settlers. As noted earlier, moreover, they probably reached only a fraction of the children in colonial society. The distinguished educational historian Lawrence Cremin counted just 11 schools in Massachusetts in 1650, serving some 2,339 households (or one for every 212); by 1689 the number of schools had grown to 23 and households to 8,088 (one for every 352) (Cremin, 1970). And as seen earlier, the vast majority of these schools were quite small, and colonial families were rather large. A conservative estimate, in that case, suggests that fewer than one in ten children attended school at any one time. Even if the number of schools increased significantly in the 18th century, as some historians have suggested, many children probably attended them only briefly, if at all (Woody, 1923). Clearly, these institutions were limited in their purview, even in the region with the greatest explicit commitment to education. This suggests that underlying shared community interest in formal education, a central component of social capital, often was not very strong in early New England, at least by present standards. Many families probably relied on other resources to help impart basic reading skills and other forms of knowledge deemed important (Bailyn, 1960). Schooling simply did not play the critical role that it does today.

But change was in the air. Colonial society was in a state of flux, especially in New England. By the time Cotton Mather endured the torment of observing his children flounder on the road of life, things had evolved significantly. The population of British North America expanded inexorably, from less than 100,000 in the mid-17th century to about one million by the time of Mather's death in 1728. It would grow to about three million by the time of the American Revolution. This was a big increase, even if it still was a relatively small number in the vastness of North America. This growth meant new opportunities for commerce and trade, as well as new lands to be cultivated and regions of the continent's interior to explore (Butler, 2000).

In the two decades following 1720 the volume of colonial exports to England more than doubled (Henretta, 1973). The next generations moved out of the old settlements and established new ones. As the tide of trade grew, much of it in farm and timber products, new job opportunities emerged, along with possibilities for enterprising merchants and financiers. Colonial society, although still largely agricultural and technologically primitive, began to exhibit some of the characteristics of modern capitalism. Wealthy merchants controlled larger portions of trade, and farmers produced more crops earmarked for the international markets. People at all levels of society exhibited a new level of interest in acquiring wealth. With this, old commitments to shared religious ideals and practices were weakened further. As historian Richard Bushman suggested, in cultural terms this process represented a transition "from Puritan to Yankee" (Bushman, 1967).

Perhaps the most popular single series of cultural events in colonial times represented the Great Awakening, a period of religious revivalism that occurred principally in the 1730s. British evangelist George Whitefield, a young man with extraordinary oratorical gifts, arrived in 1739 and proceeded to travel up and down the colonial seaboard, speaking (or shouting) to growing throngs. While not directly challenging traditional beliefs, Whitefield preached a doctrine of salvation based on faith and good works, a gentle revision of the views of Puritan forefathers. Where the elders had believed in an elect leadership of learned ministers, Whitefield held that conviction and commitment to God was more important than scriptural interpretation (Heimert, 1966; Hofstadter, 1971; Rutman, 1977).

Ideas such as these dealt a final blow to the Puritan orthodoxy, already weakened by in-migration and intergenerational differences in religious views and practices. But Whitefield and his many followers, including influential Puritan divine Jonathan Edwards, also infused new energy into the Protestant values that underlay colonial society. New colleges were started to train "new light" (enthusiastic) ministers, and added emphasis was placed on the importance of basic literacy skills for reading religious texts (Cremin, 1970). In a short time, religion became both more accessible and more democratic in orientation.

Yet another important source of influence on the intellectual and cultural life of colonial North America was the broad scientific and ideological movement known as the Enlightenment. Even more diffuse and variegated than the Reformation, the Enlightenment was a revolt among European intellectuals against superstition and religious dogma, an affirmation of the power of reason and scientific discovery. Its leading English figures included Isaac Newton and John Locke, but there were many others. In general, these men stood for ending artificial status distinctions based on principles of "divine right," typically espoused by the European aristocracy. We often take these Enlightenment ideas for granted today, but they constituted a revolutionary ideology at the time, a point of view sometimes referred to as *modernism.* Representing the principles of natural equality between men (people), these ideas spread with the circulation of books, pamphlets, and magazines, and often found an appreciative audience in the New World. After all, the Enlightenment thinkers represented a perspective well suited to the expansive capitalist and individualistic ethic of British North America, where solving immediate, practical problems often came to take precedence over the preservation of orthodoxy. Enlightenment ideas about social equality also were well received in colonial America, as aristocratic pretensions and claims to status had little relevance in a land of freeholding farmers, merchants, and planters. Although the direct influence of Enlightenment figures may have been limited to the most literate and cosmopolitan colonists, the ideas of these thinkers were well suited to the social conditions emerging in the New World (Butler, 2000).

British colonial society, in that case, underwent a critical process of social and ideological change in the 17th and 18th centuries. It was shaped both by the changing atmosphere of European intellectual and religious life, and by the evolving economy of the North Atlantic world. Similar forces were evident in the Spanish settlements that were growing more slowly on the west coast and in the southwest, if on a somewhat smaller scale. Schools were established, but served a relatively small segment of the population. Other children in settlements across the continent learned more practical lessons from adults who taught them in a variety of settings. Thus it is clear that the earliest schools in American history were not very effective agencies of change. Rather, the impetus came from the market economy, the arrival of new groups with values and religious beliefs different from the original settlers, and a growing populism in religion and politics presaged by the Great Awakening and the arrival of Enlightenment ideas. The changing intellectual and ideological atmosphere reflected the growing circulation of books and other reading materials in colonial society, and not the influence of formal institutions of education. If anything, schools were intended to be conservative institutions, bulwarks against change that reinforced traditional beliefs and moral virtues. Insofar as they contributed to a rising level of literacy in colonial America, schools also may have helped to lay the foundations of the period's most far-reaching process of social change: the American Revolution. But that was a later development, one to be considered in due course.

## Schools and Literacy

New England may have been the most self-consciously religious region in British North America, but it certainly was not the only collection of colonies concerned with the transmission of culture. In the West, Spanish missions and other schools provided a Catholic education to the sons and daughters of ranchers, although comparatively little is known about them. Other social and religious groups settled in the British colonies to the South, and they each had different traditions of education and cultural transfer. The Dutch brought their own religious practices with them to New Amsterdam, later called New York, and the Quakers (an English dissenting religious group) established the colony of Pennsylvania. Virginia, the Carolinas, and other Southern colonies were divided, with the coastal or tidewater regions settled by planters interested in exporting tobacco, rice, and other agricultural products, and the Piedmont or backcountry populated by yeoman farmers. The planters generally remained solidly Anglican, whereas other settlers represented a variety of Protestant denominations, although there were small pockets of Catholics in Maryland and elsewhere. Like New England, these colonies also grew substantially in the latter 17th and early 18th centuries, and, as new generations of settlers set out on their own, questions of religion and culture inevitably were raised (Greene, 1988). Even if newcomers did not challenge orthodoxy as dramatically as in New England, all were affected by the Great Awakening and the newfound enthusiasm for popular religion that it signaled. The result was a gradual lessening of religious distinctions among the various colonies with time. A more populist and liberal (or tolerant) Protestantism, and the values it represented, became a feature of many settlements in British North America by the 18th century (Hofstadter, 1971).

Even so, in the colonies outside New England the schools numbered fewer than in Massachusetts and its neighbors. By Cremin's estimate, in 1689 Virginia counted only eight schools for more than 7,000 households (or about one for every 900); and New York had 11 for about 2,200 families (one for every 200) (Cremin, 1970). For most colonial children, schooling was not a major element of life, although it appears to have been more important in Northern colonies than in the South. This, of course, points to the connection between religion and education. Children went to school to learn to read for largely religious purposes, and not to prepare for work or for other aspects of life. In New England, the local theocratic authorities had tried to mandate the provision of schooling for religious purposes, and families there clearly valued schools more than in other colonies. Governments rarely advocated schooling elsewhere, especially in the Southern colonies. In a famous statement, Lord

Berkeley of Virginia stated in 1671, "I thank God that there are no free schools nor printing, and I hope that we shall not have these [for a] hundred years." Berkeley, who was governor at the time, echoed the view of many aristocrats and wealthy planters, saying that "learning has brought disobedience, and heresy and sects into the world" (Fischer, 1989). As a corollary of attitudes such as this, there was less interest in schooling in the Southern and middle colonies.

Statistics on literacy, the ability to read and write, seem to bear this out, although it is not clear that literacy was always linked to schooling. The region with the highest rates of literacy, measured by counting signatures on wills, was New England. Historian Kenneth Lockridge estimated that about three-quarters of the male population there was literate in the mid-18th century, and nearly 90% by the time of the Revolution. Literacy rates appear to have been somewhat lower in the middle colonies, New York and Pennsylvania, but they were the lowest in the South. Lockridge placed the male literacy rate in Virginia at about 70% by the end of the 18th century. Interestingly, literacy levels in England were comparable to those observed in Virginia. Indeed, historians have noted that schooling and literacy practices in the areas of England that colonists migrated from appear to have been similar to patterns noted in the various colonial settlements. There does seem to have been a general correspondence, in that case, between the amount of schooling provided in the colonies and the levels of literacy observed by historians, an association no doubt linked to cultural practices carried over from the Old World (Fischer, 1989; Lockridge, 1974).

It is uncertain, however, whether literacy was simply derived from formal instruction, particularly in schools of the sort counted above. Lockridge attributed much of the growth of literacy to changing "functional demands of society." By the latter 18th century, he wrote, "land was obtained by purchase, often from an entrepreneur, and deeds were registered in the county court" (Lockridge, 1974). In other words, reading and writing skills became increasingly important for the performance of essential commercial tasks, such as transferring property and keeping accounts. Here again, economic growth appears to have been a source of social change, along with the development of the legal system and the advent of public record-keeping. In this case, the expansion of commerce and government made basic literacy skills indispensable. And once there was a clearly recognized need for these abilities, people began to find ways of attaining them, including formal instruction of one sort or another.

As it turns out, there were multiple avenues to the attainment of literacy in colonial America. The wealthy often hired private tutors to teach their children to read, especially in the South, and others were taught at home or in other settings, as apprentices, for instance. No doubt there was considerable "on-the-job" learning of requisite skills, and bright, enterprising boys (like young Benjamin Franklin) picked up knowledge from their employers and fellow workers. There was more specialized training for certain jobs also. In the larger cities it was possible to gain essential skills in "writing schools" and commercial classes run by entrepreneurial masters, providing lessons in a variety of subjects deemed important in the growing world of mercantile commerce (Cremin, 1970; Kaestle, 1973a). As literacy became more important, new routes to its achievement became available. And in the most commercially expansive regions of the country, particularly in the cities, literacy rates among both men and women rose sharply in the 18th century.

Literacy statistics are interesting, in that case, but difficult to interpret. Not surprisingly, in all colonies literacy was highest for those with property and wealth, and it was generally higher for men than it was for women. But rates among the poor were highest in Puritan New England, a fact that seems to support arguments for the importance of religion and schooling. There is evidence that women in certain parts of New England had attained high levels of literacy as well. It was probably the case, moreover, that individuals with more schooling possessed greater mastery of literacy. Simply put, they could read better. There is little historical evidence about proficiency in reading, however, apart from the general circulation of books, newspapers and other forms of reading material. And on this score there seems to have been only a little variation among the colonies, some of it a function of population size. By and large, British North America was a literate society, even if schools were better developed in one region than another (Moran and Vinovskis, 2007).

Literacy of one sort or another was essential, of course, to the development of colonial society. It aided the transmission of information and knowledge, matters that became increasingly important with the growth of commercial enterprise and political affairs. In general, the circulation of printed materials was quite wide and the number of published items rather large throughout colonial America, especially in towns and cities (Cremin, 1970). Newspaper and magazine circulation figures and book sales (press runs), on the other hand, were generally modest. This suggests that reading materials were often not kept or discarded by individuals, but were rather passed from one group of readers to another. In this way, a relatively small volume of printed material probably reached a wide audience. In this respect literacy appears to have had a strongly communal flavor in 18th-century America. Given this, uniformly high levels of literacy proficiency may not have been very important, as long as at least some members of colonial society were relatively good readers. If a man was unable to read something, after all, he may have been able to have it read aloud or the contents described (Brown, 1989). This was done with all types of reading material, from the Bible and religious sermons and commentaries to the hundreds of political tracts and pamphlets that circulated in the years preceding the Revolution (Bailyn, 1967; Hofstadter, 1971). Thus the benefits of literacy probably were spread quite widely, and much informal literacy instruction undoubtedly was conducted in the every-day exchange of information on a wide variety of topics.

It is likely, consequently, that the levels of literacy that historians have identified in the various colonies were caused by a number of factors, including the availability of schooling, religious values, the volume of reading materials, and overall levels of trade and information exchange. As a consequence of these influences, literacy was considerably more widespread in the New World than in the Old, and the highest levels were to be found in New England, which also had more schools than any other region (Bailyn, 1960; Fischer, 1989; Lockridge, 1974). The precise relationship of literacy and schooling remains something of a historical puzzle, but schools alone probably did not produce the high levels of reading in some of the American colonies.

Literacy is an intriguing problem in itself, but it also raises a number of questions about colonial education. If so few children attended school at this time, and schools played such a small and uncertain role in the educational process, just how was culture transmitted from one generation to the next? How were skills developed, and information imparted about the facts of life in the New World? To answer these questions and others, it is necessary to consider the realm of informal education, or the ways people learned and lived on a daily basis in colonial society. It is this set of processes that may have constituted the most important educational activities of the age.

## Education by Other Means

Society in the New World was cast on a very small scale. As indicated earlier, this was a preindustrial time, when most things were made by hand and people rarely traveled long distances, even if commodities increasingly did. Cities were small by modern standards, and the vast majority of the population seldom set foot in them. Most settlements numbered no more than several dozen families, and visitors were few and fairly far between. Even in such relatively densely populated regions as New England there was a pervasive sense of isolation in many places. Most people in other colonies did not even live in towns or villages. Instead, they were on farms scattered across the countryside. Even though there was a growing commerce in agricultural produce, lumber, and other goods, these folks lived in worlds circumscribed by their immediate families and neighbors (Butler, 2000; Main, 1965).

For typical colonial settlers comforts were scant, at least by modern standards. Their dwellings were small and cramped, lighting was sparse, and other amenities were rare. Virtually every household chore, even one as simple as drawing water, was performed by some measure of human labor. There was little of what one could call manufacturing on a large scale in colonial America; there was limited economic development. Most things people owned, consequently, were produced by hand, often not far from where they were used. Skilled labor, necessary to produce many items of utility and value, was at a premium. Although the New World certainly offered abundant resources, long hours of hard work were required to produce the goods that people needed to survive and prosper (Demos, 1970).

Even if life was difficult in colonial North America, however, it was better in many respects than what people endured in Europe. Although there was a great deal of variation on this score, life expectancy was greater in New England than in most parts of the Old World, and there was considerable social stability as well. Compared to Europe, land was abundant, and a man only needed to toil hard to make a living and, with a little luck, to succeed. These favorable conditions also contributed to the lessons of life in the New World (Fischer, 1989; Vinovskis, 1979). People began to feel that hard work was eventually repaid with tangible rewards. In the face of abundant resources, on the other hand, poverty came to be seen as the consequence of an inability or unwillingness to work. Ideas such as these, reinforced by the resource-rich environment of a sparsely settled colonial society, eventually would become a cornerstone of traditional American beliefs.

Given the wealth of natural resources and the small but growing population, labor quickly became the most critical element of the colonial economy. This had profound implications for the social structure of different colonies, depending on the types of workers needed and commodities produced. Shortages of labor in the Southern colonies, where unskilled workers were needed for clearing land and harvesting tobacco (the chief export of the region until after the Revolution), led to the widespread use of white indentured servants and black slaves. In the North, where agriculture was dominated by subsistence products and local markets rather than export crops, these forms of labor were less prevalent. From the very beginning, in that case, the differing economic circumstances of the various colonies, dictated in large part by climate and agricultural conditions, created distinctions between the principal regions of European North America (Main, 1965).

In sparsely settled colonial settings there were few institutions, educational or otherwise. By and large, life revolved around the family, the central unit of productive activity. As a rule, families were large in British North America, averaging about eight children per household through most of the 18th century. This was a higher level of fertility than found in England at the time, and reflected the premium attached to labor in a society where land was acquired relatively easily. Economic historians have suggested that family size was greater with abundant land and scarce workers because children became potential helping hands. They also have noted, however, that high birth rates were sustained even when certain colonies became densely populated. Like Cotton Mather, settlers in British North America valued their children, and many had large families even when circumstances seemed to dictate otherwise (Demos, 1986; Henretta, 1973). In terms of population, early American society was expansive, and the New World conveyed a sense of optimism about the future that often was less evident in European settings.

About nine out of ten European settlers in the colonies were farmers of one sort or another. Although there was considerable variation in the types of crops they cultivated and the ways they made a living from them, the majority consumed much of what they grew or traded it locally for goods and services. This meant that most of their time was taken up with daily tasks of caring for crops, with the busiest times at planting and harvest; and minding animals; preparing food from raw produce and meat; and maintaining the tools, farm implements, and other meager elements of technology at their disposal. They also built and maintained their houses, barns, and other structures necessary for life in relative isolation, although many tasks also were shared with neighbors. Added to this were innumerable other household chores, such as cleaning, childcare, and making and repairing clothing.

For the men of these households, this way of life usually meant caring for ten or 12 acres of crops, the most that could be planted and harvested with a family's manual labor, along with tending draft animals (horses, oxen, or donkeys), working on buildings, and performing other tasks counted as heavy labor. For the women it meant food preparation, cleaning, mending clothes, and childcare. The latter was especially important, given the high fertility rate. With eight offspring, a colonial woman could be pregnant or nursing a baby almost continually for as many as 24 years. Given the fact that the women typically married in their early 20s, this meant that their years of greatest strength and vitality were preoccupied with childbirth and caring for young children (Henretta, 1973; Mintz & Kellogg, 1988; Norton, 1980). And this was accomplished in a setting with few modern comforts and conveniences. For most families, prospering in conditions such as these required hard work and perseverance. It also called for a special type of education.

With so much to be done, and so much dependent on accomplishing these largely manual tasks, children contributed a great deal to the success of most colonial households. This, of course, constituted a strong incentive for having large families, but it also dictated a peculiar form of socialization. Children were raised with the expectation that they would contribute their share of responsibility for the family as a whole. Hard work was not to be shirked; indeed, it was considered a virtue. Relevant skills and bodies of knowledge, ranging from farming, carpentry, husbandry, and hunting to food preservation, soap making, cooking, and sewing, had to be imparted along the way, so that children could perform these tasks and be ready to maintain their own households upon reaching majority. By and large, these were not topics associated with schooling. At the same time that families worked to survive, consequently, a continuing process of education and training unfolded in most colonial homes. It was a system of education that was well suited to the conditions of the New World; indeed, it was essential for survival (Demos, 1970,

1986; Morgan, 1966). And it set the stage for subsequent developments in the history of American education.

Contrary to some stereotypes of harsh colonial ideas about children, parents in British North America exhibited great affection for their children. The anguish Cotton Mather suffered over the fates of his own children was doubtless felt by many other parents whose offspring were beset by similar catastrophes. Historian Jay Fliegelman has observed that the most popular books of the era often dealt with childhood and the transition to adulthood. Colonial Americans appear to have been especially drawn to stories that emphasized the independence of children and the effects of lessons learned away from parents and family. This literature was influenced by the ideas of John Locke and other Enlightenment thinkers, who suggested that individuality and reason were characteristics parents should foster in children, rather than obedience and obsequious loyalty. Colonial fathers were advised, consequently, to forge relationships of friendship and mutual respect with their offspring, and not to assert their power or exert undue control over their households. The result, Fliegelman suggested, was an "American revolution against patriarchal authority" in the 18th century, which defined distinctive patterns of childrearing (Fliegelman, 1982). Colonial parents loved their children, but they also wanted them to grow up to be free and independent members of the larger society.

Historians of the colonial family have noted a peculiar custom among many households, particularly in New England and other Northern colonies: sending older children away to board with other families, especially neighbors or relatives. Historians have surmised that this practice served as a form of training, a sort of apprenticeship in a variety of tasks that would prove useful around a colonial household. But why send them away when there was so much work to do at home? Children were sent out, it is speculated, so that they could be disciplined more effectively. It undoubtedly also served as a way of imparting independence, helping children to pull away from their immediate family and to form relationships in the larger world (Norton, 1980; Rury, 1988a; Smith, 1980).

Parents worried about pampering their own children, or giving in to their tendencies to resist the regime of hard work in colonial society. They also were concerned about children becoming overly dependent on their parents or each other. So they sent their children to other households, at the same time that they took in teenage children from other families. This practice principally affected young women, but boys were occasionally boarded out as well. In this way the family served as an institution for somewhat more formal expectations about education. The critical task of imparting knowledge and skills relevant to the challenge of maintaining a household in the New World made this a necessity.

Of course, there also were traditional forms of apprenticeship for young men interested in learning a trade. This was a practice with deep roots in European history, and it was widely observed in the colonies. In many respects, boarding children out to other families comprised a special form of apprenticeship. In both cases formal contracts were drawn up, periods of service were outlined, and lessons to be learned were agreed on. It was typical for the host household, or the master in the case of an apprentice, to provide food, lodging, and other necessities of support in exchange for work, and to train and educate the child in the period specified by agreement. As colonial society grew, concerns were expressed about the quality of education and training received by apprentices. Benjamin Franklin, for instance, railed against cruel masters who summarily ordered their charges about and who did not take their education seriously. Franklin himself had endured such an apprenticeship for a time, as did many others (Cremin, 1970). Such controversy was testimony to the importance that this form of education came to assume in colonial society.

Thus, even if relatively few of North America's European settlers attended school, all of them received an education. They learned from their parents and from the churches that they attended, along with the apprentice and "boarding out" arrangements that were so ubiquitous at the time. This was true in the Spanish settlements that took shape in California and Texas during the 18th century, as well as in the British colonies on the eastern seaboard. Given this, it is hardly a wonder that so few institutions of formal learning existed during much of the colonial period. Education was largely an informal affair, embedded in a host of other social relationships and guided by the necessities of life and work in a New World. This would change—somewhat remarkably—in the years to come.

## FOCAL POINT: EDUCATION AND SOCIAL BETTERMENT

The most dramatic change in 18th-century British North America, of course, was the Revolution waged by the colonies for independence. As in most political upheavals, a larger process of social change accompanied this war, and education was profoundly affected. The American Revolution brought new ideas about schooling and its role in the social order, and these notions eventually led to the appearance of new educational institutions and practices. One example of this new way of thinking about education appeared in New York City in the years immediately following the Revolution.

In the year 1785 the American war against King George of England had just ended. Members of the newly formed New York Manumission Society came together in a large room for their second meeting. Comprised of many of the city's most prominent citizens, including such famous figures as Alexander Hamilton and John Jay, the group had been formed to protect recently freed slaves from being kidnapped and shipped to the South, where they could be sold back into slavery. The war had visibly changed New York's population. The city had grown, and it had become the temporary capital of the new nation, but there had been social changes too. Among other things, the war had increased the number of ex-slaves in New York, as many had escaped servitude when their Tory masters fled the country, and ruthless slave traders were rumored to be preying on them. There was the danger of anarchy, as violent abductions of innocent freedmen (ex-slaves) were reported. It was a situation that called for an organized response on the part of New York's leading lights (Rury, 1985).

The men of the Manumission Society were 18th-century liberals, influenced by the ideas of Locke and other Enlightenment figures. Given this, they were opposed to slavery and considered it a violation of basic human rights. Yet, being men of means themselves, they were also concerned about the enormous investment that existing slaves represented. Here the ideals of the Enlightenment encountered the hard realities of property relations that underlay the capitalist economy of the New World. Consequently, these men supported a "gradual abolition" of slavery, whereby the children of slaves would be granted freedom upon reaching the age of majority, 21 years old. This, of course, would eventually lead to the end of slavery, when adult slaves all passed away. It was not personally beneficial for slave parents, but it did promise to eliminate slavery in the future, as was later accomplished in New York and other Northern states. The wealthy and influential members of the Manumission Society, after all, were interested in social reform, but they did not advocate radical measures that would threaten property. While they hardly wished to overturn the existing social order, especially after the chaos of the war, they did feel strongly about the principles of freedom and republican democracy articulated in the Revolution (Zilversmit, 1967).

At their second meeting, however, members of the Manumission Society were presented with some disturbing news. It was reported that freed slaves had been involved in a series of disturbances in the city. In particular, there were reports that they had become associated with sailors and other individuals of questionable repute, and that they had been observed "playing music" and dancing "in their homes" into the late hours of the night. This information was not happily received, and the conversation quickly turned from the issue of saving ex-slaves to questions of proper behavior and propriety among the freedmen. It was resolved that the society would make its concerns known, and that it would "withhold the benefits" of its association from those parties engaging in such activities. Clearly, the good men of the Manumission Society did not approve of the behavior attributed to certain members of New York's free Black population. At subsequent meetings they considered measures intended to forestall reports of this sort of behavior in the future. They voted to establish two new institutions for New York's free Black residents: a church and a school (Rury, 1985).

The New York African Free School, the Manumission Society's

"charity school" for free Black children, opened its doors in 1787, the same year that the Constitutional Convention met to discuss a legal framework for governing the new nation. From the beginning the school was intended to deliver an education in traditional morality for the children of ex-slaves. Its purpose was to see that they did not "inherit the vices of their parents acquired in slavery or to learn similar ones through want of a proper education." As historian Carl Kaestle has noted, the school was intended in this regard to intervene between these children and their parents, whom the Manumission Society did not believe were capable of teaching properly traditional values. Here the purpose was different from the town and district schools of New England and other colonies, which were intended to supplement the education that children received at home. Charity schooling, largely confined to the cities, was supposed to reform the poor, not necessarily to reinforce and extend the values of their parents. And the key to this was teaching them how to behave properly (Kaestle, 1983).

Protestant religion and morality dominated the curriculum of the African Free School, as in similar institutions established elsewhere. The school was not large, enrolling just 100 students at the start. Many members of New York's free Black community doubtless greeted it with an understandable suspicion. But before long it had succeeded in one of its principal aims: identifying a core of respectable families within the free Black population who could be called upon as leaders. It was the members of this group, the Manumission Society hoped, who would serve as examples to others, and who could exert pressure on less reputable members of their community to behave properly (Rury, 1985). The men of the Manumission Society were liberals, after all, and believed that even the most stubborn and disreputable individuals were subject to improvement. It was their considered opinion, however, that the best course of change was in one direction—toward greater conformity with the norms of Protestant rectitude and the values of mercantile capitalism. For them, schooling was an instrument of reform, a way of changing individuals and groups—and ultimately society—for the better.

This was a form of 18th-century education that went well beyond the confines of the family and immediate community for certain groups of children. The Revolution signaled a distinctive set of attitudes about society and the role of education in changing it. But the ideas and approaches adopted by reformers were not altogether new either. The New York African Free School was a prominent example of a certain type of schooling that had deep roots in the evolution of British North America. As historian Gary Nash noted, European settlement had created a diverse society by the mid-18th century (Nash, 1974/2000). The institutions and methods developed by the Europeans to train and educate other groups, especially Native Americans and Africans, were distinctive, and quite different from those established for their own children. This too was a vital part of the development of education and the transmission of culture in the New World. And it was one that would have important implications for schools as they took shape in the decades following the colonial period as well.

## Education for Civilization

The issues facing the New York Manumission Society were not entirely new ones in the 18th century. One of the central questions that emerged with the growth of colonial society, one that did not concern the "Old World" of European society, was just how people from vastly different racial and ethnic groups were going to coexist. The answer, by and large, was on terms dictated by the White Protestants who comprised the leadership of the various British colonies. This held important implications for the education of non-Europeans, who represented the majority of North America's inhabitants in the 18th century.

By the mid-1700s British North America was home to people who historically had come from three different continents. As noted earlier, they included European settlers and American Indians. The third group comprised Africans, who were brought to resolve the labor crisis, especially in the South but in other colonies as well. Each of these groups represented a substantial portion of each colony's population, even if Native Americans generally were pushed to frontier areas, on the fringes of European society. Africans grew significantly in number as the slave trade picked up after the 17th century, and a host of new laws solidified their status as slaves, a category of bondage that had not existed in English law prior to that time. By the second half of the 1700s, Blacks constituted about a fifth of the colonial population, almost double their proportion in the United States today. In some parts of the South, such as South Carolina, they outnumbered both Europeans and Native Americans; in the words of historian Peter Wood, they were a "Black majority" (Wood, 1974). Even in such Northern cities as Philadelphia and New York, Blacks amounted to nearly a quarter of the residents—about the same proportion as today. All things considered, in that case, colonial America was a multiracial society. Statistically it was not unlike parts of the United States today, even if the various groups interacted less frequently. This raised questions about acculturation and socialization that were impossible to ignore.

The Europeans who settled in North America were acutely aware of the social and cultural diversity posed by the New World. In the South, elaborate legal barriers were erected to separate Whites and Blacks during the 17th century, among them widely different provisions for education. It took time for the institution of slavery to develop completely, but by the early 1700s there could be little doubt that Africans occupied a distinctly inferior social position, even compared to the most destitute European indentured servants (Morgan, 1975). Explanations were constructed to account for these racial differences in social and legal status, with the early development of a racist ideology that would hold non-Whites inherently subservient to Europeans, and to Englishmen in particular. In some quarters there was greater sympathy for the Native American population. Schools were established to accommodate the education of American Indians, including Dartmouth College, although this feature of the institution was short-lived. Most such experiments ended with very few non-Whites receiving an education, however. For the most part, the schools established by European settlers were for Whites only (Cremin, 1970; Hofstadter, 1971).

While colonists established schools for themselves, missionaries undertook the education of others. This form of education was especially important in Spanish California, where more than 20 Catholic missions had been established by the late 18th century. Many of these outposts made the education of native people a focal point of activity, with special emphasis on teaching Spanish and the Catholic catechism. The Spanish authorities believed that educated Indians would make pliable leaders, who could act as intermediaries between the Europeans and indigenous peoples. American Indian children selected for schooling were separated from their families, and required to learn the traditional curriculum brought by their missionary teachers. It was a model of obligatory education that would be utilized extensively during a later period of American history (MacDonald, 2004).

The most important British missionary campaign was launched by the Anglican Church. Concerned about the growth of the colonial population in the closing years of the 17th century, a group of influential Anglicans started the Society for the Propagation of the Gospel in Foreign Parts, or SPG, as it came to be known. The founders of the SPG worried that God-fearing Englishmen would drift away from the church in the relative isolation of the colonial wilderness, or that they would fall under the influence of the dissenting groups prevalent in the colonies, such as the Puritans, Pilgrims, and Quakers. There were yet other religions to worry about also, with the Presbyterians and the dreaded Catholics being the most prominent. And of course there was also the question of non-Christian residents of the colonies: Native Americans and Africans. Over the next eight decades, the SPG dispatched hundreds of ministers and teachers to the New World, with the aim of "saving" the English population, and converting the non-English people of the colonies to the glories of Anglican faith (Calam, 1971).

The SPG encountered a good deal of resistance to its plan, as one might expect, and in the end it probably accomplished relatively little in the way of conversion. Outside of the cities and large towns, its preachers and teachers found it difficult to find sufficient numbers of Anglicans to support churches and schools. Native Americans and Africans presented troubling educational dilemmas that proved largely intractable in the end. Perhaps the biggest problem, however, was the failure of the SPG to consider its mission in terms of an educational exchange between cultures. Instead, the SPG believed its duty was one of proselytizing and conversion. In particular, its role was to make good Anglicans of the uneducated Native American and African (slave) populations (Cremin, 1970).

Not surprisingly, the SPG campaign of education for conversion engendered relatively little interest on the part of Native Americans, who generally found the religious content of the SPG schools to be irrelevant to their interests. Slaves, although interested in the skills to be gained in school, were often not allowed to participate by their masters. Indeed, a slave revolt in New York was blamed on a church school. Both groups, moreover, had their own traditions of socialization, and doubtless preferred to teach the children their own values, customs, and beliefs. Thus, although the SPG did open many schools, most of them did not last very long, and their cumulative impact was slight. The SPG probably exerted greater influence in the area of publishing. The group printed many books and religious tracts, and thousands of Bibles, which circulated throughout colonial society, an effort that almost certainly reached many more people than the schools (Calam, 1971).

However ineffective the SPG may have been as an educational force in colonial America, it did represent a model of a different kind of educational institution that would become more prevalent in the latter 18th century: urban charity schools like the African Free School described earlier. Often operating in a single classroom, sometimes in the evening or on Sundays, these schools would serve groups that could not afford other types of schooling. As American cities grew, especially in the years following the Revolution, this type of schooling became more commonplace. It is little wonder, in that case, that the Manumission Society decided to create a charity school for the children of freed slaves when given reports of troubling behavior in the city's Black population. They were drawing on a tradition in American education with deep roots in the colonial era. It was a practice that would be put to new uses, however, in the years to come.

### Building a New Nation

It is an old axiom that political and social upheaval is often accompanied by a transformation in education. The American Revolution, which started nearly a decade before the Constitution was finally drawn up, produced widespread social and political change in British North America. The Revolution was influenced by the ideas of such Enlightenment thinkers as John Locke and Baron Charles Louis Montesquieu. As stated prominently in the Declaration of Independence, it was premised on an assumption that "all men are created equal." Notwithstanding the question of slavery and racial inequities, this view of the social order held profound implications for the political future of the new nation (Bailyn, 1967; Morgan, 1975). It also led to a number of telling changes in the educational arrangements of colonial society.

Among the most important challenges facing the newly formed United States of America was establishing a system of education that would prepare its people for citizenship in a new social and political order. The ideals of the Revolution, informed by Enlightenment notions of equality and democratic governance, suggested a political system of popular rule through periodic elections. This was a new and untried idea, however, so when the new government of the former colonies was being debated in the 1780s, many were pessimistic about the prospects for a truly representative form of government. The men who drafted the Constitution included some astute students of history; and experience suggested that republics were doomed to failure. Ancient Rome was often cited as a prominent example. The difficulty seemed to stem from the problem of popular control by elections. Could the common man, poorly informed and subject to manipulation by elites, be relied on to uphold the principles of fairness and honesty that were vital to the country's future? Prevailing theories of government held that the aristocracy was naturally suited to rule, even if it needed the guidance of representative assemblies, such as England's Parliament. The very idea of a popularly elected government, without the stabilizing influence of a landed aristocracy, was dismissed by many contemporaries as potentially disastrous (Brown, 1996; Tyack, 1967).

Because of these sentiments, Jefferson, Madison, Franklin, and the other leaders of the emerging republic felt that if the new nation was to succeed, education was essential. Voters in a representative democracy, after all, had to be well informed, and prepared to critically assess the arguments and opinions of the day. If democracy was to take root as a political tradition, popular education had to become an American institution. This became a rallying cry of the movement to establish a government for the United States, and a point of departure for the elite men then forging a new political culture in the former British colonies (Cremin, 1970). The question remained, however, of whether such a system of education could succeed in a country as large and diverse as the United States.

A modest number of proposals and recommendations for establishing an educational system accompanied the Revolution. Education and schooling became topics of discussion and debate, the subject of speeches, addresses, articles, and pamphlets. Seven of the new state constitutions made reference to education, and this too prompted controversy. Jefferson proposed his famous plan for establishing publicly supported schools throughout Virginia, in a "Bill for the More General Diffusion of Knowledge" in 1779, even before the Revolution finally ended. Characteristically, he believed that widely distributed and free schooling would lead to the rise of a "natural aristocracy" of talent and accomplishment, which would provide leaders for the new nation. Jefferson's plan was never adopted, even after he reintroduced it later, but it reflected the significance attached to education in the minds of many Revolutionary leaders (Brown, 1989, 1996).

One of the most prominent advocates for improved education after the war was Benjamin Rush, a well-known Philadelphia doctor, professor, and signatory to the Declaration of Independence. Rush called for establishing schools across Pennsylvania, supported by taxes and land grants, citing "fewer pillories and whipping posts and smaller jails" among the chief benefits to society. In a famous statement, Rush advocated making American children into "republican machines" through improved systems of schooling. Noah Webster, author of the first American dictionary and speller, also advocated universal free education to foster national unity. Webster called for schools to establish "an inviolable attachment to their country" in the minds of children, and urged Americans to "begin with the infant in the cradle; let the first word he lisps be Washington" (Rudolph, 1965; Welter, 1962).

As quaint as these ideas may sound today, they represented a radical break with the prevailing educational views and practices of colonial North America. They stand in stark contrast, for instance, with Lord Berkeley's utterances against popular education 100 years earlier. They also helped to make education a national concern. These new proposals and others like them called for an end to schooling as a purely localized set of practices, undertaken largely for religious purposes or for the transmission of community values. In the wake of a political revolution, schools suddenly assumed new importance as agencies of political socialization, even though this term— a product of 20th-century social science—was never used at the time. National leaders believed an educated citizenry was essential to the future. The United States has been described as the world's "first new nation," and in the context of forging a new national identity, especially during the years immediately following the Revolution, the idea of schooling gained new significance (Lipset, 1979).

On the other hand, these were merely proposals offered by elite and well-educated national leaders, and the question of whether American schools would in fact come to perform these functions was a different matter. In fact, none of the radical calls for new statewide or national systems of education were adopted in this period. Schooling, after all, was largely a local matter, and most Americans at the end of the 18th century had far more pressing concerns to occupy their attention—such as making a living. The creation of systematically organized, state-controlled systems of public education dedicated to purposes of mass socialization would have to wait for another generation of visionary leaders. But a new way of thinking about schooling had been broached by the Revolution, and yet other changes were set in motion that had a more immediate impact on educational practices.

## Republican Motherhood

Among the most important and underappreciated effects of the American Revolution was its impact on the lives of colonial women. Like most early modern societies of the Western world, British North America was quite patriarchal. Women had few publicly accorded rights inside or outside of the family structure, rarely worked outside of the home (unless widowed), and usually had little formal education. As noted earlier, statistics on literacy in the 18th century, collected by studying signatures, indicate that the majority of women were illiterate. New England was an exception, as female literacy may have exceeded 60% by the latter 18th century. But even there, large numbers could not read. Women, it was widely believed, did not need to be literate, because they were not formal members of many colonial churches, a status reserved for men, and were expected to rely on their husbands for moral guidance and the conduct of business affairs (Brown, 1989; Kerber, 1980).

But circumstances were changing. This was partly due to the liberal atmosphere of family life in colonial America, seen earlier in the discussion of Cotton Mather. Women were also affected by the fact that they had been relatively few in number through much of colonial American history, a demographic trait typical of many colonial or frontier societies, which are usually settled first by males. This helped to raise their status informally, because men came to value them in light of their scarcity. Added to these factors was the impact of the Great Awakening, with its sweeping liberalization of traditional religious views and practices. Even if George Whitefield and other leaders of the Great Awakening were not proponents of women's rights, their criticisms of traditional churches may have created more openness towards women's participation in religious life. Developments such as these were part of a more gradual reaction against patriarchal views and practices in colonial society, leading up to the Revolution in the last quarter of the 18th century (Norton, 1980).

There was also evidence of changes in women's education during the colonial period. Lockridge noted a significant shift in female literacy, growing from the later 17th century through the time of the Revolution. In New England, the proportion of women able to sign their wills increased from less than one-third to nearly one-half in this period. Other historians have argued that these figures underestimate the extent of female literacy there, and that it was probably considerably higher. All of this suggests a growing openness to female learning, and perhaps increased involvement by women in formal education (Lockridge, 1974; Perlmann, Siddali, & Whitescarver, 1997). The "dame schools" appeared in this time frame, with classes conducted by women for young children—both boys and girls—in basic literacy skills along with lessons in morality and good behavior. Some girls may also have been introduced to domestic arts, sewing, embroidery, and the like, and manners in special schools, particularly in the larger towns and cities. As the number of schools increased in more commercially developed parts of the countryside, new opportunities for women's education emerged there also. For example, girls were allowed to attend the short summer sessions in New England schools during the latter 18th century. This may account for some of the observed improvements in literacy, along with greater openness towards women's involvement in religious affairs (Perlmann and Margo, 2001; Sklar, 1993).

Historians suggest, however, that even more sweeping events affected colonial women with the advent of the Revolution. This was due in part to the disruptions of daily life that generally accompany war. Many women, for instance, found themselves alone when their husbands left or were killed in the conflict. As a consequence, women ran businesses and conducted household affairs in their absence, or longer in the case of those who became widows. They negotiated contracts, paid debts (often without prior knowledge of their existence), managed employees, and conducted correspondence (despite poor literary skills). In short, women were required to fill a variety of male roles, and in doing this they implicitly—and sometimes explicitly—highlighted the question of female capabilities (Kerber, 1980; Norton, 1980).

Beyond the upheaval in gender roles occasioned by the war, there was the ideological impact of the Revolution, especially its broadly egalitarian rhetoric and Enlightenment intellectual roots. The words "all men are created equal" in the Declaration of Independence, after all, inevitably raised the question of women's status too. Abigail Adams urged her husband John, "do not forget the ladies," and leaders began to weigh the roles of women in the emerging social order (Norton, 1980). Even though the weight of popular opinion probably did not change much regarding differences between men and women, the possibility that women deserved more rights and greater social recognition became a subject of wider debate. The later 18th century also saw the development of a nascent movement for women's rights internationally. This was the era of Mary Wollstonecraft's call for women's equality, and other treatises on equality of the sexes. A new view of women's status was emerging (Rendall, 1985).

There was a shift in thinking about women's education as well, even if it was largely unrelated to more radical propositions for women's rights. Revolutionary leaders, faced with the question of educating citizens for the new republic, came to view American women as a vital resource. Benjamin Rush was probably the best-known proponent of women's education following the Revolution, but there were many others as well. The reasoning was straightforward: If children needed to be trained in the virtues of republican government, the task of early education would fall to their mothers. Hence it followed that American women had to be educated, at least enough to read, write, and teach their children moral precepts and principles of American democracy. This is a view of female roles that historians have labeled "republican motherhood," and it became the rationale behind a surge of interest in women's schooling during the later decades of the 18th century (Brown, 1989; Kerber, 1980).

Benjamin Rush's celebrated "Female Academy" in Philadelphia was only one of perhaps scores of similar institutions established in the United States in the decades following the Revolution. Unlike Rush's school, however, many others were apparently coeducational. These schools were not large, and many of them probably only lasted a short time. But the very fact of their existence pointed to a new set of attitudes concerning women's education. These institutions generally did not teach the classical languages, the curriculum of the era's more prestigious male academies. Instead, they typically offered a course in literature, history, languages, and the "domestic arts," subjects deemed appropriate for young ladies (Woody, 1929). These were also subjects well suited for preparing women for the task of educating their own children, particularly their sons, and rearing them for citizenship in the new republican social order. Thus the new female role of "republican motherhood" was ultimately quite conservative, and was tied more closely to the theme of nation building than to ideas of women's liberation. At the same time, however, it marked a radical break with the status of previous generations of women, and set the stage for yet other developments in the history of American education (Nash, 2001).

The movement to establish schools for women in the closing years of the 18th century was important, but it would be wrong to suggest that it represented a change in the experiences of most American women. These small and largely ephemeral academies, despite their numbers, could educate just a tiny fraction of the female population. As noted earlier, even in New England women probably attended school only during the summer sessions, and elsewhere few women attended any kind of school at all. In a largely agricultural society, where wealth was accumulated slowly and through painstaking effort, it is hardly surprising that relatively little energy was devoted to women's schooling. Yet the idea that women should be educated, once broached, would prove impossible to suppress for long. In the years to come it would have a transforming effect on the development of the nation's school system (Nash, 2005).

### Education and Social Change in Colonial America

There can be little doubt that British colonial society evolved significantly during the 17th and 18th centuries. As noted earlier, this was partly due to simple population growth; new patterns of behavior appeared as the numbers of Europeans multiplied more than threefold in the century prior to the Revolution. But there were other forces at play too. The value of land increased and the volume of trade surged forward, fostered by an expansive capitalistic ethic that eventually eclipsed the religious and cultural conservatism of the original settlers. This was a gradual process of change, but it was punctuated by such dramatic events as the Great Awakening and the Revolutionary War. British North America remained preindustrial and rural in character, but change was inexorable. By the end of the 18th century many aspects of an emerging national culture, embracing the values of individualism and self-determination, were beginning to be evident. Colonial society was giving way to what is known today as America.

This was not an easy process. It entailed displacement of the Native American population and the movement of millions across the Atlantic to the "New World." As many as a fifth of these people were Africans, the vast majority slaves. Many Europeans, moreover, worked as indentured servants, often with little realistic prospect of freedom. In other parts of North America, Spanish settlements maintained the interests of the Spanish Crown and the Catholic Church, vouchsafing land to favored noblemen and missions, and ruling the native population with veiled despotism. Despite its growth and relative prosperity, in that case, colonial society was marked everywhere by great inequity. This too would become a telling characteristic of American life.

For most of this period, education played a minor role in the transformation of colonial society. Schools were small and usually reinforced traditional values, and they touched the lives of a fraction of the colonial population. The various avenues of informal education that existed at the time, ranging from apprenticeship to literary circles, may have done more to transmit essential skills than the schools.

The biggest changes in colonial society, however, came with the approach of the Revolution. The movement to sever ties with England, culminating in the Declaration of Independence and the war that followed, gave birth to a new republican sensibility in British North America, a development with enormous implications for education. In the ferment to establish a new nation on principles of popular rule and representative government, great significance was attached to education as an instrument of political socialization. At the same time, the purview of popular education was widened to include women and certain members of racial minority groups, even if such changes were isolated and episodic. A new vision of civil society was emerging, albeit in fits and starts, one holding great moment for the future of American schooling.

# 3
# Emergence of a Modern School System
## *The 19th Century*

The dawn of a new century in 1800 was a momentous time in the United States. The new nation was brimming with optimism and hope for the future as its citizens contemplated the vast continent that they had begun to settle. It was a land of great abundance and natural wealth, and immense challenges too. The decades to follow marked a time of important transitions in the development of American society, and the history of American education. The United States expanded across continental North America, and national systems of transportation and communication began to take shape. This period also saw the creation of state-supervised systems of public education, beginning with common (or primary) schools and eventually extending to high schools and universities. The reach of formal education expanded considerably as a result, with greater numbers attending school for even longer periods of time.

Perhaps the most basic changes in 19th-century America were economic and social: It was a time of manufacturing development and urbanization. This era brought the industrial revolution to the United States, a process that had started decades earlier in England. As suggested in Chapter 1, there were important links between industrialization and the evolution of American schools. Economic development contributed to the expansion and improvement of education; as income grew and the economy became more complex, people attached greater value to schooling. Industry also provided important models for the growing school system. Like most forward-thinking Americans of their day, school leaders were impressed by the power and efficiency of early factories, and they lauded the virtues of a disciplined and orderly workforce.

Industrialization stimulated sweeping social change, and this too influenced the development of schooling. Educators worried about the waves of immigrants that industrial growth attracted to American cities, and they devised new educational schemes to prepare children for changing work roles and citizenship. Guided by an emergent ideology of Protestantism and republicanism, these men and women sought to utilize schooling to impart traditional values. Poverty also became a problem of large proportions in rapidly expanding cities. Changes linked to urbanization and inequity caused considerable uncertainty, and the 19th century was also a time when many Americans started worrying about maintaining social order and stability in their lives. This made some cling even more anxiously to the beliefs and practices that had characterized an earlier era, and it sharpened debates over the future course of education in this young, rapidly evolving society. It was in this context that a foundation for the nation's modern school system was established.

The 19th century was also a time of ferment in American culture. It was marked by lively debates over questions of childrearing and how best to educate children both in and out of school. Gradually the attitudes and practices of earlier times, emphasizing tradition and authority, gave way to more liberal views of education and the rights of children. But the process of change was slow and halting. The newly created American republic was large, and was undergoing rapid—if uneven—social and economic development. Old ways died hard, and new ones struggled to gain acceptance.

## FOCAL POINT: PARENTS AND CHILDREN IN AN AGE OF TRANSITION

No matter the period, ideas about schooling are inevitably influenced by social norms and expectations regarding the behavior of children. This is an important aspect of ideology as it has affected education. Schools, after all, came to comprise an important element in the experiences of children. It stands to reason that these institutions would exhibit many of the same concerns that affect parents and other adults interested in the growth and conduct of children. Looking at debates about childrearing in the 19th century can thus reveal much about the ideological context of American education during its formative years.

Francis Wayland was an important figure in the history of American education. The fourth president of Brown University and an advocate of reform in higher education, he was probably most famous as an author of textbooks on ethics and political economy used widely in high schools and colleges. In 1831, however, he published an anonymous letter in a local Baptist newspaper about an incident in the rearing of his own son, Heman (McLoughlin, 1975/1985). It is a revealing account, because Wayland both described his course of action in this case and attempted to justify it on religious grounds. It affords a rare glimpse into the thinking of a middle-class American parent concerned with the proper upbringing of a child, in a case that also engendered a bit of controversy.

The incident in question occurred when Heman was just 15 months of age (terms in quotations are Wayland's own). Wayland observed that his son was unusually "self-willed" and that he had a quick temper. One morning when Wayland took the young boy from his nurse, Heman began to cry "violently." Determined not to let the child have his way,

Wayland decided to hold him until he stopped, and took away a piece of bread the boy clutched in his hand. When Heman stopped crying, Wayland offered him the bread, but the child threw it down. At that point Wayland resolved that Heman would not eat until he accepted food from his father and voluntarily welcomed his affection. Moreover, he was to be restricted from contact with other members of the household. Thus began a test of wills that would last more than 30 hours.

Wayland kept the child in a room by himself during the entire ordeal, and only allowed him to eat when he accepted food from his father. When Heman took the bread but refused to embrace his father, the food was taken back. The boy was obstinate throughout the first day, despite Wayland's regular visits, "every hour or two," and his speaking "in the kindest tones." Wayland described the boy "hiding his face in the bedclothes" and crying "most sorrowfully," but he refused to approach or embrace his father. Finally, in the late afternoon of the second day, young Heman finally relented, after nearly two days without eating. In the end he "repeatedly kissed" his father and "obeyed his every command."

Wayland clearly believed that his approach in this case was appropriate, perhaps even exemplary, and wrote about it as a lesson to others. In justifying his actions, Wayland reasoned that if he had not confronted the child's will, "I must have obliged my whole family to have conformed in all their arrangements to his wishes." He noted that Heman's disposition toward other members of the household also changed as a result of the incident. Describing Heman as now "mild and obedient," he commented approvingly that "my whole family has been restored to order." In drawing principles from the incident he declared, "there can be no greater cruelty than to suffer a child to grow up with an unsubdued temper" (McLoughlin, 1975/1985). Wayland believed he had performed a great service in this case, both to his son and to society at large, and he wrote to provide a lesson to other parents confronted with similar challenges.

This incident warrants examination because it captures a set of attitudes about parental responsibility and child development that were quite common among American Protestants in the 19th century. Willfulness in children often was considered a special kind of vice, parallel if not equivalent to original sin, which had to be overcome by learning obedience and respect for authority if the child was to become a useful member of society, a point in Wayland's letter. The childrearing stories and advice books of the age, such as the popular works by Jacob Abbott and Lydia Sigourney, constantly warned of the dangers of children disregarding their parents, or engaging in selfish or self-centered behavior. The purpose of discipline was to teach the child a particular kind of self-control and conformity to the expectations of adults, especially the child's parents. Bad children were those who ignored the wishes and commands of adults, and such children ran the danger of becoming poor citizens, adults who ignored the rules of society and religion. Making the young conform to the expectations of adults was seen as being in their best interests, and representing the best possible course for society as well (Kaestle, 1983; Mintz & Kellogg, 1988).

It is important to bear in mind that Francis Wayland probably was not a typical American parent, insofar as it is possible to identify one. He was a man of intense religious convictions, and as a college president he was accustomed to exerting authority over the young. Being an educator, moreover, he probably was more didactically motivated than most parents. He deliberately seized on the use of feeding as an opportunity for confronting Heman's temper, even if he did not anticipate the ordeal that ensued. Although Wayland's account of the episode was published, not everyone thought that it was an example of good parenting. A second local newspaper published two responses criticizing the course of action described in Wayland's letter, one characterizing it as starving an "infant boy ... into a state of passive obedience" (McLoughlin, 1975/1985). Even in the 19th century, not all agreed with adult domination of children and the need to curb the "willfulness" of their spirits. Various parental advice books of the era cautioned against breaking the spirit of young children, instead urging that their natural playfulness and curiosity be nurtured and allowed to flourish. But few questioned the need for children to respect their parents and ultimately to adhere to paternal authority (Wishy, 1967).

In many respects the case of young Heman Wayland probably did represent traditional American conventions about children and education, despite the severity of his father's instructional mode. Most Americans at the time certainly would have agreed with the proposition that children must obey adults, and should learn self-control at an early age. Many would have imparted such lessons quickly and roughly with one form or another of corporal punishment, a course of action Francis Wayland pointedly rejected. And the belief that children should be taught obedience and respect for authority clearly dominated much of American education at the time. It was telling in this connection that Wayland's critics compared his actions to those of schoolmasters accused of flogging their pupils, yet another point of controversy in the 19th century. Wayland doubtlessly disagreed with this analogy, for he was opposed to corporal measures. Critical commentaries about such abuses notwithstanding, however, most American schools were founded on the principle that adult authority was paramount, and that children were supposed to learn compliance before all else (Finkelstein, 1989; Hogan, 1990).

Social theorists since Max Weber have suggested that the ability to exercise self-control, to repress one's emotions and desires, was a key component of the development of capitalism. An ideology of self-denial, one that held various forms of deprivation in high esteem, was important to the process of capital accumulation and economic development. This is one of the reasons that pietistic Protestantism of the sort practiced by Wayland is thought to have been among the foundation stones of modern society. Good capitalists, after all, did not dispense their riches by following base impulses; they saved and reinvested them to advance the greater glory of Protestant civilization. Francis Wayland, in addition to restoring order to his own household, was teaching young Heman to exercise restraint, to control his feelings, and to heed the influence of virtuous adults in his life. These were the lessons of middle-class American childrearing in the 19th century, however they might be imparted, and they were the ideological wellsprings of much of the nation's formal system of schooling. The ethic of improvement through self-denial and deprivation, glorified in Wayland's confessional and yet didactic letter, contributed to a gradual reformation of American education and life (Greven, 1977; Rodgers, 1978).

## An Age of Expansion

The 19th century was a time of national growth, as the United States spread steadily across the North American continent. It also was an era of accelerating change in the nation's economy and its social structure. Industrialization came to the United States during the 1800s, along with the manifold social changes associated with that process. As the volume of goods and income produced by the economy increased rapidly, a hallmark of industrialization, the extremes of wealth and poverty across the country widened. In sheer numbers, the population grew geometrically, increasing from 5.3 million to about 75 million over the span of the century. At the same time, the English-speaking populace extended to the west, establishing new towns and cities, along with such larger entities as deemed appropriate, principally counties and states. Geographically, the continental United States came to assume its now familiar shape, reaching from Atlantic to Pacific and forming one of the largest nations in the world. Even more significantly, this territory was rapidly filling with fresh waves of settlers and came to represent an expansive network of markets, and thus a powerful inducement to the development of industry. By the end of the 1800s the United States was no longer a slender string of settlements extending along the Atlantic coastline; instead, it was the largest economy and perhaps the most powerful nation in the world (Brownlee, 1979).

Even with rapid settlement, industrialization did not happen overnight. Factories capable of manufacturing vast quantities of goods needed access to markets for the sale of their products. They also required manpower, eventually in large numbers. The United States was a big country and its population was widely dispersed, making labor a scarce commodity. At the start of the industrial age American cities were small and most of the country's population lived in the countryside. The development of a national transportation network was a necessary precondition to industrialization, a means of moving products and people. This would become the infrastructure for the development of national markets, both for goods and for labor (Cochran, 1981).

The building of this network was the principal task of the opening decades of the 19th century. It was an age of large-scale projects, building roadways, canals, and eventually railroads to link the various cities and regions of the country together. Historians have variously dubbed this period the "transportation revolution" or the "market revolution" (Sellers, 1991; Taylor, 1968). In either case, it was a time when the distances that separated people seemed to shrink. It became easier to travel from one place to another, and, more important, goods produced in one part of the country became more widely available in other areas.

The transportation revolution held important implications for the social and political life of the nation as well. News and information traveled with people and merchandise, and hence were communicated more effectively as well. Political parties could wage national campaigns more practically, and public figures could travel more widely to promulgate political or religious views. With the growing national transportation network of roads, canals, and railroads, a national consciousness of shared concerns and values emerged, spurred by federal debates and conflicts such as the War of 1812. Disputes over territorial expansion and the divisive question of slavery also contributed to this. People found themselves less preoccupied with local issues, even if the problems of daily life continued to occupy much of their attention. Now a shared set of concerns and controversies gave new meaning to the term *American* as a source of identity and pride. The transportation revolution helped to hasten the evolution of a national identity (Sellers, 1991).

The transportation or market revolution picked up the pace of economic life and contributed to the process of industrial development. Access to markets made the building of factories, already a central element of the economy in England, a practicable step in the United States. As it became cheaper to transport merchandise, the economies of scale in producing larger quantities of goods in factories made industrialization even more viable. With the New England textile industry leading the way in the 1830s and 1840s, the United States underwent a lengthy process of industrial growth that extended well into the following century. Between 1820 and 1860 the volume of cotton cloth produced annually in New England mills increased from less than 14,000 yards to nearly one million. And the pace of change increased even faster after the Civil War. Between 1860 and the turn of the century, the value of manufactured goods produced in the United States jumped nearly eight-fold, from less than $900 million to more than $6 billion, without inflation. Textiles continued to be important in the later phases of industrial expansion, but new industries led the advance, particularly iron and steel, paper, petroleum and chemicals, machine tools, and the processing of agricultural products, especially meat (Brownlee, 1979).

Over the course of the 19th century, manufacturing grew from less than 5% of the gross national product to more than half. Altogether, this process led to an unprecedented expansion of the economy, with the volume of manufactured goods growing more than four times faster than the nation's population. Per capita income, a figure that included children, increased at a similar rate. The impact of these changes was uneven, yielding great fortunes for some and creating impoverished pockets of industrial workers in the shadows of bustling factories. At the same time, however, it contributed to the wealth of most other Americans by enabling them to acquire a widening array of commodities (Dalzell, 1987). The foundation of what often is described today as the American way of life was established during industrialization in the 19th century.

The growing wealth produced during this early age of industrialism was accumulated at considerable cost. The development of the factory system resulted in a loss of autonomy and independence for many workers. It also contributed to a devaluing of skills, and the replacement of skilled labor with machines. Apprenticeship, long an integral element of the educational experience of American youth, especially boys, gradually disappeared during the 19th century. As the scale of industrial production increased, thousands of workers were crowded together in drab factory towns or industrial cities, often living in conditions most of us would consider miserable today, as contemporaries did then too. Beginning in the 1840s and escalating quickly during the decades following the Civil War, millions of European immigrants came to the United States, many to take jobs in the burgeoning industrial economy. Industrialization appeared to have produced a new class of unskilled, impoverished workers, and a high degree of cultural and social diversity. Cities and towns grew larger and dingier; even the countryside was changed, as mechanized farming and large-scale agriculture slowly became more commonplace. The Industrial Revolution altered the face of America, but not everyone felt it was a change for the better (Laurie, 1997).

### Industry, Cities, and Education

Even if many did not recognize it at the time, the impact of economic development on education was pervasive. Schooling became an increasingly significant social issue as the industrial revolution unfolded. The nation's total investment in education grew dramatically, as larger segments of the population attended school for greater lengths of time. Economic historian Albert Fishlow estimated that the average American received just 210 days of formal education in a lifetime in 1800. By 1850 that figure had more than doubled and by 1900 it had jumped to 1,050 days, about half of what it would be in 2000. Because these figures represent averages, it is important to note that some children, especially the well-to-do, received more schooling than this, while others got less (Fishlow, 1966a). In the course of these changes, however, formal education began to assume the familiar dimensions of school experiences as they are known today.

Apart from the sheer quantity of education, the character of school began to change as well. For many children, especially in cities and towns, schools became associated with preparation for life, and for work in particular. This is not to say that education became vocationalized, or focused on training for specific occupations, even if attention to preparation for employment increased a good deal. Rather, schooling increasingly was directed at the cultivation of proper "habits" of industriousness and responsibility, along with essential skills of literacy, numerical calculation, and knowledge of history, geography, and other subjects. This was education for citizenship, of course, but it was also preparation for the emerging industrial order, a society increasingly characterized by formal economic relationships and the rule of the clock and efficiency. It was only in the latter decades of the 19th century that vocational education became a concern of educators interested in preparing workers for various industries. Prior to that, industrialization provided a milieu for educational development, and perhaps some organizational models. If the 19th century was the age of the factory, the school became a parallel institution concerned with preparation for industrial life (Nasaw, 1979).

It would be wrong to assume, however, that there was a direct and immediate relationship between the rise of factories and the development of schools. In many instances the advent of industrialization meant that fewer children attended school in a given community. Early factory owners generally were interested in reducing costs, and it was not unusual for them to recruit child labor, especially in Northeastern and Southern towns and cities. In such instances the factory became a school by default, even if the lessons taught were quite harsh. Although some states had laws requiring factory owners to provide instruction in reading and other subjects, such measures were often honored in the breach. In cases when factories did not hire young children, they drew large numbers of teenagers and young adults, both male and female. These youthful workers had the strength and stamina of adults, along with energy and a willingness to work for lower wages. The availability of work in factories with few skill requirements created an alluring alternative to attending school. The immediate and direct effect of industrial development, consequently, may have been to reduce educational attainment for children in these areas, typically the offspring of poor industrial workers who found factory wages attractive (Faler, 1981; Thernstrom, 1964).

In other respects, however, there was a tangible connection between the growth of the factory as an institution and the evolution of schools. Many 19th-century leaders were fascinated by industrial development, and viewed it quite differently than we may today. The factory was seen as an engineering marvel, a wonder of efficiency and practical ingenuity. Some even suggested that it offered visions of an ideal social order, premised on technological innovation and a harmonious division of labor. Exemplars of enlightened manufacturing enterprise existed outside of the cities, and many observers believed it possible to build factories that were clean and even morally uplifting to the youth that worked in them. The famous textile mills of Lowell were perhaps the best-known case of this, and their workforce of seemingly demure young women seemed to suggest that industrial development could be made wholesome. As industry expanded, however, and the demand for labor increased, conditions deteriorated. When larger numbers of poor immigrants came to dominate the industrial labor force, the character of even the most progressive experiments in industrialization changed dramatically (Dawley, 1976; Dublin, 1979; Marx, 1964).

Other reformers rejected the idea of industry altogether, and attempted to establish ideal agrarian societies in isolated communities, far removed in the countryside. The best known of these communal experiments was Robert Owen's socialist cooperative in Indiana, called New Harmony. Established on principles of shared work and property, and an education system predicated on performing useful tasks without the imposition of discipline, New Harmony was a challenge to the emerging industrial order. Its practice of schooling was equally radical. Drawing on the work of European educational theorists, Owen and his followers were sharply critical of existing schools in the U.S. Unfortunately, Owen's idealism did not suffice to insure the success of New Harmony, and the venture ended amid acrimony and misunderstanding. Although other communal experiments persisted considerably longer, they exerted little influence on the larger process of social development or on the educational system (Kaestle, 1983; Tyler, 1962).

Despite questions raised by Owen and other critics, many educators believed that industrial development represented the future. As historian David Tyack (1974) has observed, "the division of labor in the factory, the punctuality of the railroad, the chain of command and coordination in modern businesses ... aroused a sense of wonder and excitement in the men and women seeking to systematize the schools" (p. 28) With little direct experience in industry, after all, it was relatively easy to focus on its virtues. To reformers, like other middle- and upper-class observers, the manufacturing process was a marvel of rationality, efficacy, and speed. Workers were required to conform to the demands of production, to be prompt, to follow orders, and occasionally to solve problems encountered on the factory floor. In other words, they needed self-discipline and attentiveness, along with deference for authority. Such expectations appealed to the Protestant values of early school reformers. They sought similar goals for children in their institutions, claiming outright in some instances that the duty of the school was to prepare students for the demands of the emerging industrial order. Even as some factory owners pulled children away from schools, many educators emulated the industrial system as a model for their new organizations. It was a powerful metaphor for the future social order (Kasson, 1999; Pollard, 1965; Vinovskis, 1970).

As noted in Chapter 1, the industrial revolution was also accompanied by rapid urbanization. The poet Carl Sandburg once quipped that America grew up in the country and moved to the city. This was an observation applicable to most of American history, but it was especially true of the 19th century. In 1800 fewer than 1 in 50 Americans lived in towns or cities; by the end of the century the number approached 40%. Industrialization was a major part of this story. Cities had been established and prospered during colonial times as nodal points of trade and essential services, but their growth accelerated significantly with the onset of industrial development. Many cities became centers of manufacturing activity and processing points for agricultural products, while others became distribution hubs for the rapidly growing volume of fabricated goods. The new urban industrial economy attracted millions of workers from the countryside and across the Atlantic, prompting unprecedented growth in the major cities. The 19th century also was a time of mass immigration, as the first large groups of destitute immigrants arrived in North America since the slaves and indentured servants of the 17th and 18th centuries. Successive waves of immigration were tied directly to the demand for industrial labor (Pred, 1966; Sharpless, 1977).

It was in the cities that the social impact of industrialization was most readily evident. The population of leading cities surged in the 19th century. Starting with fewer than 50,000 in 1800, New York became the first city in the country to surpass one million by 1860. Others, such as Boston, Philadelphia, Pittsburgh, and Cincinnati, grew nearly as fast, along with port cities in the South and West. With immigration the cities also became increasingly diverse socially and culturally (Blumin, 1976; Chudacoff, 1975; Ward, 1975).

As cities grew, a host of institutions was established to cope with new social problems. Poorhouses, asylums, police departments, and jails appeared at this time. Questions of poverty and destitution, crime and social conflict, along with greater cultural variety, seemed to call for institutional responses. Education also was viewed in this light. Although not a new institution, the school did take on added social functions. In petitioning the city council for public support of their schools in 1828, for instance, a group of New York philanthropists declared that better schools were necessary to forestall the need for more prisons. In their view, education was a vital necessity in the campaign to assure social stability. Similar arguments were made in other cities. For these leaders, schooling was a means of collective restraint, preventing youth from embarking on lives of crime and deviance. In conjunction with such problems as poverty and criminal behavior, the era's urban centers gave rise to many important changes in American schools. It is fair to say that the cities, particularly the larger ones, were incubators of innovation in education, but a peculiar form of it: schooling to foster social order and control (Boyer, 1978; Mohl, 1971; Schultz, 1973).

The earliest publicly supported, non-church schools in 19th-century cities were called "charity schools" and were designated for the children of the poor. Similar in most respects to the New York African Free School established in the 1780s, these schools were intended to impart acceptable norms of behavior along with basic lessons in literacy, mathematics, geography, and other subjects. Started by civic-minded members of the urban elite, much like the Manumission Society, these schools started as small-scale institutions, but eventually were taken over by boards of education or similar governmental bodies entrusted to govern the public schools. By the mid-1800s most large cities possessed the rudiments of a public school system, many of them having started with privately sponsored charity schools. With its New England roots, Boston boasted the most venerable public schools, but New York and Philadelphia also developed large-scale systems in the opening decades of the 19th century (Boyer, 1978; Kaestle, 1973a). Other cities followed suit.

Given the problems they faced, it is little wonder that these urban centers became sources of educational change. It was in the nation's larger cities that one of the first comprehensive systems for school organization and operation was adopted: Lancastrian education. Joseph Lancaster was an English schoolmaster who perfected a system for organizing schools efficiently and inexpensively. Lancaster posited that a single teacher could manage the education of hundreds of children by using older students as "monitors," or teaching assistants, to oversee the lessons of their schoolmates. Because the knowledge of these assistants was quite limited, most of the "instruction" consisted of "dictation," wherein the monitors pronounced words, phrases, or numerical problems that were written down en masse by the students and then inspected for accuracy. Monitors also listened while children recited reading selections or presented answers to exercises (Kaestle, 1973b).

In employing these methods, the Lancastrian system of school organization demanded strict discipline and order among the students. Monitors, consequently, often did little more than exert control to insure quiet while recitations and reports were delivered. Students were given medals or other minor prizes for achievement, and the resulting competition provided motivation and another means of pinpointing errors, while students monitored their peers. With pupils divided into "classes" supervised by a small number of monitors, a single adult teacher was capable of conducting a school with hundreds of children spanning many age groups. It was a system well suited to the demands of the rapidly growing cities and the low budgets of the charity-school sponsors.

Lancastrian education was also well designed for the demands of the new industrial age. Exhibiting a preoccupation with order and efficiency, highly structured routines and uniformity of expectations, these schools represented a factory-like approach to mass education. This, of course, heightened their appeal among certain reformers, who believed that this approach promised to teach poor children proper habits of behavior, and a respect for order and discipline that would serve them well. Making children familiar with the routine and drill of daily recitations and exercises also promised to ready them for life in new work settings, where tasks were often repetitive and demanded a high tolerance for monotony. These schools also taught punctuality and respect for authority, attributes especially important in an age when fewer children were likely to become independent artisans or masters of their own trade. If the factory and the industrial city were the heralds of a new era, Lancastrian schools for the children of the poor were institutions well suited to the future (Hogan, 1989, 1992; Mohl, 1971).

Lancaster's system was adopted in many urban school systems, including New York, Boston, Philadelphia, Baltimore, Pittsburgh, Cincinnati, and other large cities. Most of these schools were not publicly supported at first; instead, philanthropists interested in improving the lot of the poor and addressing the growing problems of poverty, crime, and disorder sponsored them. The New York Free School Society was one such organization, chartered in 1805 and comprised of many of the same individuals who had formed the Manumission Society two decades earlier. The Free School Society employed the Lancastrian system in its schools almost from the start, and helped to promulgate its virtues to education groups elsewhere. About five years later, the Manumission Society hired an English schoolmaster, Charles Andrews, to utilize Lancastrian methods in its African Free Schools as well. Such prompt adaptation of the system to a variety of different schools was symptomatic of its popularity among urban school leaders at the time (Kaestle, 1973b; Rury, 1983).

The prevalence of Lancastrian schools continued through the first several decades of the 19th century. When Joseph Lancaster came to the United States in 1818, he was greeted with acclamation everywhere, and even spoke before Congress. A runaway New York horse cart killed him during another visit in 1838, just as his method of school organization approached its peak of popularity. Following his death it came under criticism from a number of sources, and by the middle of the century it had fallen decidedly out of favor. Even so, the urban school reformers' preoccupation with order and routine remained inviolate elements of big-city school systems, long after Lancaster's peculiar method of monitorial instruction became a distant memory. As new generations of poor and unruly children poured into city schoolhouses, the basic purposes of urban education changed little, even if methods of instruction had evolved considerably (Boyer, 1978; Kaestle, 1983).

Charity schools were primary (or elementary) schools, but it was also in the 19th century that American secondary or high schools became popular institutions. These too represented a largely urban phenomenon, as a sizeable population base was required to generate enough students for such advanced instruction. It is widely acknowledged that the Boston Latin School was the first secondary institution established in the New World, in 1629, about a decade before Harvard, even though the modern concept of "secondary education" (existing between primary schools and colleges) was not fully developed at the time. Public high schools appeared much later. Because private tutoring and tuition-based academies prepared many young men for college and few occupations required secondary education, there was relatively little demand for high schools until well after the American Revolution. When these schools finally appeared, however, they quickly became the dominant form of education beyond the primary level. Beginning in 1821, with the first Boston high school distinct from a grammar school or academy, American secondary schools prepared students for a host of commercial and educational purposes. Although attendance was low at first, high schools would eventually become one of the most significant educational innovations of the 19th century (Reese, 1995). The growth of secondary education is discussed in greater detail later.

The most important educational developments of the early 19th century, however, concerned the common school, the primary institution that became a symbol of American education at the time. Urbanization and economic development helped to spawn a movement to improve the common schools and expand their purview. But the rise of urban industrial society also entailed the appearance of other institutions to help mediate the process of economic growth and social differentiation. These included public agencies for building and maintaining the transportation system, government offices for managing natural resources and industrial waste, and agencies for prisons, asylums, and similar institutions. These all were supported by the modernizing segment of 19th-century society, middle-class social reformers (Boyer, 1978).

The spread of school reform beyond the cities also was abetted by the growth of political parties, particularly those dedicated to national development through enhancing the institutional infrastructure. The early decades of the 19th century were a time of growing electoral participation in the nation's political system. Although the vote was still limited to white males, it was liberally extended to members of virtually all social classes. In light of these changes, politics was becoming an increasingly important aspect of life in the United States. Reformers, consequently, often worked through the national political parties then taking shape, and the corresponding state and local organizations. In terms of their general affiliation, these individuals usually were linked to the Whig Party, or later with the Republican Party. Such groups were a driving force behind the development of common school reform. They found support in workingmen's parties and early labor organizations in the cities, long-time advocates of free public schools. But most reformers were middle class in orientation, and animated by visions of a more perfect republican social order. It is possible to think of them as modernizers, helping to build the institutions that have become so familiar today. They faced a daunting task in the early 1800s, for there was considerable resistance to these efforts. Despite their lofty goals, the process of building a coherent and uniform system of schools was marked by a good deal of uncertainty (Kaestle, 1983; Kaestle & Vinovskis, 1980).

## A Gradual Transformation: Education in the Countryside

Not everyone agreed that schools should change, or that new institutions were necessary for social advancement. There was opposition to the logic of urban industrial development and to the institution-building activities of reformers throughout the 19th century. This may seem surprising from today's vantage point, when urban industrial social institutions appear to be quite natural, as though they always existed. But 19th-century society was in a state of transition. Although industrial development was the principal engine of change, most of the nation's population remained rural and agrarian, remote from the cities and other centers of industrial development. Consequently, many were uncomfortable with the changes that industrial society brought with it. Historian Charles Sellers has characterized this large segment of 19th-century America as a "subsistence" society, one that spent much of life outside the rapidly growing national economy associated with industrial development (Sellers, 1991).

People living in this largely rural social setting generally were self-sufficient, although they were drawn inexorably into the market economy as time passed. By and large, many were suspicious of the urbanite champions of industrial development and the institution builders who sought to transform and "improve" the United States. They wanted to keep taxes low and preserve the way of life that they had carved out of the land, or the livelihood their forefathers had started generations earlier. While not opposed to education, these people were hardly champions of a new and improved system of schooling, and therein lay the source of discord over reform. In very general terms the question at the heart of the matter was this: Would education be utilized as an instrument of social and economic development, or would it remain a prerogative of individual families and local authorities? For the locals, it served personal tastes for improvement and literacy, and provided an introduction to Protestant values. Reformers approved of this, but wanted the schools to do more (Cremin, 1951; Graham, 1974; Sellers, 1991).

The answer to this question was by no means certain for people living at the time. And its terms of debate were not always clear either. In comparison to today, formal schooling did not occupy much of people's lives, and their futures did not hinge decisively on possession of educational credentials. Most made a living, and developed careers, in one line of work or another without reference to education or prescribed training. Money spent on education, although high in comparison to other nations, was well below the levels of today as a fraction of the nation's economy (Goldin, 2001; Solomon, 1970). So it would be wrong to suggest that it was an issue that predominated in everyday public discussions. Rather, it was a facet of life that became an object of dispute when reformers suggested making it a larger, more important, and expensive aspect of the social infrastructure. By and large, the critics of the schools were intent on expanding and improving popular education, and they met resistance from people who believed change was unnecessary or undesirable. The changes being debated were hardly monumental; examples might be a longer school year or a state exam for teachers. Wholesale reform in the educational system did not occur overnight. But disagreements occasionally became bitter just the same. In this way, schools evolved by degrees, with each step in the process marked by varying degrees of resistance, as well as a good deal of apathy, from a public too preoccupied by the uncertainties of daily living to worry much about changes proposed in education (Larkin, 1988; Lasch, 1991).

The most controversial issue was taxation of local property to support the schools. In many districts, long-standing custom dictated that parents contribute to the school fund to support their children's education, or that all households offer assistance based on willingness to maintain the schools. Reformers argued that a tax on property across the districts would provide a more stable financial foundation for the schools, and allow the poorest children to attend without having to be labeled as "charity cases," a proposal often met by sharp retorts. In 1849 a New York state law calling for such a duty was decried as allowing individuals "to put their hands into their neighbors' pockets." Another critic declared that the legislation "takes A's property without his consent and applies it to the benefit of B, which is unconstitutional, arbitrary and unjust." Similar complaints were registered across the country in response to other property tax proposals. The New York law was overturned within a year, demonstrating the pitfalls of educational reform in an age when finding additional resources for schools was not always a major public concern. Educational reformers decried the poor condition in many rural districts, and inequity in schooling, but it took considerable time and effort to persuade many people that improving their local institutions was an important priority (Binder, 1974; Kaestle, 1983, p. 150).

There certainly appeared to be much room for improvement in American education in the early 1800s. The schools that existed throughout much of the rural United States had changed relatively little since colonial times. They were isolated, small in size, conducted for relatively short periods of time, and taught by itinerant masters with little formal training. They had also become quite ubiquitous. By and large, the typical rural district school served an area of 2–4 square miles, accessible by walking, and was populated by some 20–50 families. Thus by the 1830s they literally dotted the countryside, mainly in the Northeast, serving millions of children in small, intimate settings bound by an immediate community. Levels of enrollment, attendance at any type of school for any part of the year, were already quite high in the opening decades of the century, over 70% for children aged 9 to 13. Americans clearly valued some form of formal education, as overall attendance figures were higher than in other major countries; only Germany had higher rates in 1830, and by 1880 the United States led the world. Following the Revolution, growing numbers of girls attended school along with the boys, at least in the Northeastern states and upper Midwest, marking yet another unique feature of American education (Fishlow, 1966b; Larkin, 1988; Vinovskis, 1972).

Large regional disparities marked American education, with enrollments consistently lowest in the South, where industrialization did not take root until the latter 1800s. Indeed, public schooling was slow to develop as a popular institution across the Southern states, especially those dominated by a plantation economy specializing in cotton or other export crops. By and large, the wealthy planters who controlled the political and financial life of the region did not favor education for common folk. Their own sons and daughters were taught by itinerant tutors, or attended expensive private schools, but they saw little need for educating other children. Instead, these men were interested in keeping wages and taxes low, and assuring an abiding respect for traditional class distinctions. Above all, they worried about the possibility of literacy spreading to the slave population, and the attendant dangers of widespread insurrection. The Nat Turner rebellion in 1831 demonstrated the possibility of violent revolt by educated slaves, and led to extensive prohibitions on education for them. Because of these tensions and large differences in wealth and social status in many Southern communities, it was difficult to establish a consensus about the importance of schooling, or to spur interest in reform. Despite the efforts of a small number of intrepid reformers, investments in public education remained meager. As a consequence, children across the South exhibited low levels of literacy and other school-related skills, with the exception of the sons and daughters of planters, who often received an even better education than their Northern counterparts (Kaestle, 1983; Rury, 2006).

Schools were considerably more popular elsewhere, of course, especially in the Northern tier of states where attendance by 1840 often exceeded 90% of school-aged children. Even with high enrollments, however, it was not always clear just what most children learned in the commonplace district schools. The circumstances of formal education differed from one part of the region to another, indeed even from town to town in the same area. The residents in some districts took the question of education quite seriously, while those in other districts did not. The length of school terms varied a good deal, as did the condition of schoolhouses, and there was often considerable inconsistency in day-to-day attendance. Such variations were especially vexing to reformers of the time. For them, the issue was not one of persuading more Americans to send their children to school, but rather improving the quality of educational arrangements that had long existed (Rury, 1988b).

The rural common schools probably were not very effectual educational institutions, at least by modern standards. Indeed, they often just reinforced and expanded on lessons children had already learned at home and in church, the other two institutions that dominated the lives of Americans in the 19th century. No doubt, such schools helped to impart and enhance basic literacy skills, but they built on a foundation established by Protestant family values. Reading and writing were skills highly prized in most devout Protestant households, simply because they were considered essential to piety and to basic communication. Consequently, most rural children probably were introduced to reading at home and in church before they were asked to read anything in school. This was an early expression of cultural and social capital at work in the history of American education. A modicum of reading skill was a behavioral norm conveyed at home and upheld in most local communities, particularly in the North. It was reinforced by the local church, a central community institution. In a similar fashion, schools also conveyed basic mathematical and computational principles, along with a smattering of history, geography, and "moral philosophy" (Fuller, 1982; Gilmore-Lehne, 1989; Soltow & Stevens, 1981).

The success of these efforts hinged decisively on the attitudes of parents regarding the education of their children. The chief instructional technique was recitation, requiring students to repeat portions of text memorized through reading either at school or at home. There were contests and games, such as spelling bees or multiplication tournaments, which served to break up the monotony. Friday-night gatherings of children and adults made such competitions prized community events. Storytelling, both in and out of school, helped impart memorable history and geography lessons. But there was scarcely any advanced instruction in a particular field, as most teachers knew little beyond the basic elements of the "three Rs," the usual school subjects. On top of that, there was little continuity of instruction, because teachers seldom remained in a single district longer than a year or two. The schools were generally ungraded, which meant that children of all ages sat in the same room, and they often endured the discomforts of poor ventilation and threadbare accommodations. Added to this, there was a heavy emphasis on discipline, with rules typically enforced by means of harsh physical punishments (Finkelstein, 1989; Gulliford, 1991; Kaestle, 1983).

In short, much of the schooling in the countryside was boring, repetitious, uncomfortable, riddled with conflict, and held little prospect of sustained intellectual stimulation. Without a great deal of parental support for the goals and objectives of such schools, it is unlikely that anyone would have undertaken such an onerous and disagreeable road to learning. The parental interest in these institutions was generally reinforced by the attitudes and values of other adults in the immediate community, whom children saw regularly at church and at other public gatherings. These networks of relationships supported local schools. Thus it is probably accurate to say that the success of 19th-century rural schools was significantly dependent on the level of social and cultural capital possessed by students and imparted by their families and immediate communities. The importance of learning basic reading and mathematical skills was widely agreed on, and the necessity of mastering their lessons was impressed on children by a dense web of association in all aspects of their lives. The schools undoubtedly did serve important socialization functions, especially for the children of Midwestern immigrant families, who may have been less aware of community norms and expectations. But even this purpose had to be upheld by the parents and other adults who supported the school in its everyday operations. Given their rudimentary character, the rural schools of the 19th century could hardly have succeeded without a high level of community support (Brown, 1989; Cohen, 1982; Gilmore-Lehne, 1989; Rury, 2006).

The process of change in rural schools followed a generally similar pattern in much of the country, particularly in the North. Reform advocates, most representing the urban or market sector of 19th-century society, were intent on building institutions that could certify reliable criteria for achievement and impart a common understanding of moral principles and standards of behavior. Some historians have suggested that it was the commercial farmers and local merchants, those most closely connected to the market economy, who led the process of change in the rural districts. They could more easily afford the costs associated with the reform agenda. They were also influenced by educators who articulated a set of parallel goals concerning new methods of instruction and humane treatment of children. But even these ideas were ultimately predicated on the expectation that more liberal forms of pedagogy would improve the outcomes of instruction: producing better-educated and morally superior citizens. This appealed to parents who realized that their children were unlikely to spend their lives as farmers, and would have to make their way in a rapidly changing society. Some even suggested that investment in schools could make communities more attractive, and possibly raise property values. Such arguments undoubtedly helped open the door to reform in innumerable local districts. From this, school leaders worked assiduously to build a system of educational institutions that worked efficiently and effectively. Although reformers often employed idealistic, even messianic language, ultimately their task was a profoundly practical one (Kaestle, 1983; Parkerson & Parkerson, 1998).

The idea of a coherent system of education was an important theme among reformers, to counter the problem of disparities from one locality to another. Even in the countryside, many promulgated a vision of schooling that drew parallels to the industrial system. In this respect their concerns were similar to those of the charity-school founders in the large cities; they shared an interest in greater efficiency and increasing the productivity of local schools. But from the standpoint of the time, there was another issue that made common-school reform different: a concern with improving the quality of education. Here too, ideas were influenced by the example of industry. Another virtue of factory production, after all, was uniformly high standards of quality. Not only were products manufactured with greater efficiency, but they were also often better in terms of their appearance, function, and reliability. This was a result of standardization in multiple phases of production and the superior technology of industrial enterprises. It was a logic that reform-minded educators came to apply to systems of education (Hogan, 1990).

It was in this sense that industrialization may have been most influential as an example, or perhaps a metaphor, for education. After all, the effects of manufacturing development were plain for everyone to see, and were hardly limited to the cities. They also became ever more evident as time passed. Mass-produced farm tools and a wide range of other products gradually came to replace the clumsy, makeshift items that had characterized the subsistence economy for generations. This was true of clothing, eating and cooking utensils, and a vast array of other products used on a daily basis. Consequently, for many forward-thinking people, particularly those most directly connected to the growing national economy, the living image of an integrated system of production represented by industry exerted a powerful influence. This and the nation's rapidly developing transportation network, and improved communications, were symbols of progress and the superiority of American civilization. Reformers wanted to depict schools in the same light: They would improve each succeeding generation, uniting the country in a common set of values and forging a national identity (Cowan, 1997; Kaestle, 1983).

Given the close association between home and school in the lives of most rural American families, it is little wonder that there was resistance to the efforts of reformers to change the educational system. The United States still was largely a pastoral nation, and many people felt quite distant from the urban centers of innovation and change. From their standpoint, the existing schools functioned quite adequately, and there was little or no need for costly changes, especially those that might threaten local control of education. In many places, the traditional practice of requiring families to pay tuition for the common schools persisted for decades (Beadie, 2008). But the logic of reform was difficult to oppose. A growing drumbeat of calls for improvement in the schools, and for eliminating tuition, issued forth from the ranks of reform advocates. In their minds education was linked irrevocably to a larger process of social and institutional change, and free schools were necessary to insure universal participation. Even if the outcome of debates over school reform appeared uncertain at times, in the end resistance to the general logic of reorganization proved ineffectual.

**Common-School Reform**

The time roughly between 1830 and 1860 is considered the first great period of school reform in American history. It marked the beginning of efforts to create a uniform system of mass public education, governed largely by the states, spanning the nation. It would take more than a century for this to be achieved, but it was the dream of a generation of reformers who started their work in the decades preceding the Civil War. Animated by a Protestant commitment to social perfectibility and the republican spirit of national advancement, along with the model of the factory system, these men and women presented the school as a solution to a host of social problems, and as a tool of economic and political development. As reformers, they were hardly unique in this respect. But they did articulate a number of ideas that might be classified as among the founding myths of the modern American educational system.

To grasp the motivation of reformers, it is important to consider the problems they saw. As suggested above, school reformers were troubled by the enormous variability that existed as a consequence of the highly localized arrangements in American education. They also fretted over the haphazard training of many schoolmasters, the short terms that characterized rural education, often squeezed between harvest and planting seasons, and the chance provision of such basic school supplies as books and firewood. They dreamed of a school system with consistent standards of teacher preparation, long and uniform school terms, and generous supplies of books and other essential educational materials. They worried that without such a system, American schools would prove inadequate to the task of educating the nation's children for the demands of the industrial and urban age then dawning. They were concerned too about the growing diversity of American society, and the possibility of widespread social conflict in the absence of common values and a shared identity. For these reasons, school reformers proclaimed the cause of public education across the land. Consequently, historians have referred to the years between 1830 and 1860 as the "age of the common school" (Binder, 1974; Cremin, 1951).

The most famous proponent of common-school reform was Horace Mann, an indefatigable lawyer and former state legislator who accepted the newly created post of Secretary of the State Board of Education in Massachusetts in 1837. Working with a modest salary and virtually no budget for his new position, Mann crisscrossed the state speaking to anyone who would listen to his message about the virtues of common schools. Mann explored a wide range of issues in education, some of them still points of controversy today, and lobbied incessantly for the passage of new laws establishing the first elements of a modern educational system in Massachusetts. His annual reports, published by the state and distributed widely, became influential statements of educational reform. Other reformers across the country drew inspiration from his example (Curti, 1959; Messerli, 1972).

Looking around him at the changes occurring in 19th-century society, Mann was especially concerned about the divisions beginning to become evident in the social fabric. Early in his career Mann had witnessed an ugly mob attack a Catholic orphanage in a fit of anti-Irish hysteria in Boston. There were many other instances of bigotry and intolerance in his time. He recognized that religious sectarianism and cultural conflict posed a big challenge to the future of American institutions, especially the principle of democratically elected government. This made the idea of a common school, attended by children of the different groups in society and without affiliation with any particular religious viewpoint, essential to the future development of the republic. Mann advocated a nonsectarian form of Christianity for the public schools, and was roundly attacked by Calvinist church leaders in Massachusetts, who felt that schools without connection to churches were Godless and immoral. Catholics also objected to the principle of nonsectarianism, seeing the religious and moral content of non-Catholic schools as essentially Protestant. Bedeviled by seemingly endless debate over these issues, Mann eventually prevailed in separating the public schools from the churches. In doing so he helped to establish the idea that publicly supported education was intended to serve children representing the full range of religious beliefs and cultural practices in society. This became one of the principal meanings behind the term *common school* (Binder, 1974; Messerli, 1972; Welter, 1962).

As indicated earlier, this inclusive vision did not result in growing numbers of children in the schools. The common-school movement, led by Mann and scores of like-minded men and a few women across the Northern tier of states, and by a few intrepid pioneers in the South, did not dramatically affect enrollments. These had crept up in the opening decades of the century, and common-school attendance was near universal among children aged 7 to 12 by the 1840s, at least in the North. Instead, Mann and his fellow reformers focused on other problems, related to issues like those touched on above. In addition to nonsectarian instruction, they urged longer school terms, advocating eight- or nine-month sessions instead of the four- or five-month terms common in many rural areas. They pressed for systematic examinations and minimum training requirements for teachers, to raise the level of instruction and to help establish a professional identity for teachers. In particular, Mann succeeded in persuading the Massachusetts legislature to establish the nation's first publicly supported teacher-training institution, called a normal school, derived from the French word *normale*, in Lexington in 1838. Other such schools appeared in the wake of common-school reform, supplying modest numbers of professionally trained teachers to staff the nation's schools (Curti, 1959; Herbst, 1989; Kaestle, 1983).

Changes such as these required money, and much of Mann's time was spent in convincing the state's varied political and social constituency groups that public education was a cause worth supporting. Because schools were wholly controlled and supported by the districts, usually defined by towns and villages and not by the state, Mann had little alternative to exhortation as a reform strategy. He and other reformers worked largely in the realm of ideas, and it was in this domain that the mythology of modern public schooling was born. Local school authorities had to be convinced of the need for longer school terms, professionally trained teachers, more and better supplies, and other facets of school reform. Mann could get the legislature to pass laws requiring lengthier terms and exams for teachers, and even these steps occasioned political infighting, but without financial support for such measures, and sanctions to enforce them, there was little immediate impact. Mann and other reformers waged protracted battles against opponents of taxation to support the schools. As noted earlier, property taxes proved particularly vexing, as reformers were accused of undermining the very sanctity of private property. Childless adults also objected to school taxes, because they claimed to have no direct interest in education. But Mann argued that schooling was a public responsibility, a stewardship incumbent on all members of society, regardless of one's personal circumstances. Reformers also successfully fought against "rate bills" and other forms of partial tuition occasionally charged by the schools. Public education was to be free to all, and open to everyone. These were lofty—and expensive—principles, and it took time to resolve the debates they engendered. Consequently, school reform was a slow and difficult process (Cremin, 1951; McCluskey, 1958; Welter, 1962).

Horace Mann was an astute reformer, however. He recognized the most important opponents to reform, and concentrated his efforts on winning them to the banner of change. In particular, Mann was concerned about the wealthy, who often did not send their own children to the public schools and may have been prone to thinking popular education equivalent to charity schooling. Consequently, Mann devoted effort to convincing the state's most affluent citizens, along with those who did not have children in school, that support for public education was clearly in their best interest. Taking a page from the philanthropic proponents of urban charity schools, for instance, he argued that moral education was the most important element of popular schooling, emphasizing the importance of a nondenominational Christian foundation to public schooling. Such an education, he maintained, would impart norms of proper behavior, teach respect for property and hard work, and help to prevent irresponsible behavior (Hogan, 1990; Messerli, 1972).

Beyond the question of morality, however, Mann also argued that educated workers were more productive, and that schooling could add to the value of Massachusetts's growing industrial output. In his fifth annual report, published in 1842, Mann quoted industrialists who preferred educated workers for their reliability and tractability. Elsewhere in his writings Mann suggested that schooling could also help bridge the widening gulf that separated the wealthy from the laboring classes, promoting social harmony in an era of increasing disparities in social status. Using an oft-cited industrial metaphor, he argued that education could thus serve as the "balance wheels" of society, preventing inequality from leading to destructive conflict and helping all the varied groups in society contribute to social and economic progress. This reasoning became a cornerstone of the common-school tradition (Curti, 1959; Vinovskis, 1970).

Mann did not campaign for school reform simply to advance a political cause or an economic agenda, however. He fervently believed in the power of education to resolve a wide range of social problems and to enhance the perfectibility of civilization. He viewed public schools as essential institutions of the emerging American republic. His annual reports, published in each of the 12 years he served as the state's Secretary of Education, were circulated and reprinted widely by his contemporaries. Consequently, Mann became the most prominent national leader of the common-school reform movement, even though he rarely left Massachusetts while engaged in his campaigns. In the mid-1840s he visited Europe to inspect the national education systems there, and returned with reports of schools he observed. In Prussia he noted a state-run system of education with uniform standards of instruction, well-trained teachers, and child-friendly instructional materials and practices. Mann's description of these institutions helped generate great interest in foreign models of education, and the Prussian schools in particular. Eventually, this was a further impetus to educational reform in the United States: Educational competitiveness would become a source of national pride. Only the Germans had higher enrollment levels than the United States, and eventually even they would be surpassed. American schools had to be as good as anyone else's (Binder, 1974; Kaestle, 1983).

Mann was also a great believer in women's education, and a strong proponent of the theory of republican motherhood first articulated in the Revolutionary era. True to his time, he did not necessarily think that women's schooling should be the same as men's, or that women ought to aspire to male roles in adult society. Rather, he believed that women had a special role to play in the development of the modern educational system as teachers. Mann thought that women were naturally suited to serve as teachers, as he believed a maternal disposition of patience and affection helped them to work effectively with students—especially small children. Women teachers also cost less than men, even when professionally trained, so their employment could help to restrain the expense of improved schooling. Thus, recourse to women teachers held benefits in terms of both their quality as instructors and the expense of educational reform (Bernard & Vinovskis, 1977; Brown, 1996; Rury & Harper, 1986).

Women had been teaching for decades in Massachusetts when Mann became Secretary of the Board of Education, so his ideas did not represent a major innovation in educational practices. In this case, too, it was Mann's role as a popularizer and advocate for reform that was most important. Mann's vigorous testimonies in support of women teachers helped to make school leaders elsewhere amenable to hiring them, particularly in the cities. During the latter half of the 19th century the nation's teaching force feminized rapidly, especially in the Northern tier of states, areas where common-school reform took root most rapidly. This was a critical aspect of social change, for it also altered the character of a major category of employment at the same time that it opened a new line of work for women. Some historians have even suggested that the job of teaching came to be seen as a uniquely female form of work during the 19th century, and that these views accounted for the rapid feminization of teaching. In this respect, common-school reform left a particular stamp on American education; by 1900 the vast majority of teachers were women. This is a pattern that has changed relatively little in more than a century (Perlmann & Margo, 2001; Rury, 1989; Vinovskis & Bernard, 1978).

At the same time that Mann was campaigning for reform in Massachusetts, a generation of school leaders who shared his vision of a uniform and professionalized system of education began their work in other states and cities. Many of these men also were Protestant New Englanders, committed to social perfection and concerned about the growing divisions in American society. Like others in their generation, they had migrated to newly settled regions in search of opportunity, and in the years following Mann's Massachusetts reforms they conducted similar campaigns elsewhere. They corresponded with each other, creating a network of earnest school leaders who helped to fashion a national pattern of public school organization across the United States (Kaestle, 1983; Tyack & Hansot, 1982).

Henry Barnard was a famous contemporary of Mann who held similar appointments in Connecticut and Rhode Island but did not enjoy the success Mann experienced in building state school systems. Barnard was an editor and scholar who eventually became the first U.S. Commissioner of Education in 1867, but he endured a peripatetic career simply because political support for reform measures was always subject to change. Other leading reform figures had similar experiences. They included men such as John Pierce in Michigan and Calvin Stowe in Ohio, who struggled to expand the purview and raise the quality of public schools in their states. There were many others. These reformers did not have a definite career path to follow. Instead, they made exhortation and inspiration their stock in trade. They were institution builders, but they were also engaged in a grand crusade to advance a particular vision of American civilization through education (Curti, 1959; Lannie, 1974; Soltow & Stevens, 1981; Warren, 1974).

Common-school reformers shared a similar set of values and assumptions about life and learning, and this also helped to give continuity and force to the movement. Historian Carl Kaestle has catalogued this mélange of viewpoints, and described it as the ideology of common-school reform. Much of this worldview was derived from the Protestant upbringing of these men and faith in the moral superiority of their own cultural orientation. For example, Francis Wayland, whose childrearing practices were guided by his Protestant convictions about human nature, also exhibited many of these ideas in his writings and public utterances. Politically, school leaders shared a common set of concerns about the future prospects of the American republican form of government, which was still a recent experiment on the stage of world history. They all believed in the central importance of individual character development as a key element of social progress. Without virtuous people, in their opinion, society was doomed, so proper moral development—through families, churches, schools, and other institutions—was seen as essential to national survival. Personal industry and self-discipline were deemed key to moral development, as was private property. This was an ideological perspective well suited to the capitalist social order, and the common schools everywhere trumpeted the virtues of American capitalism as a superior economic system. There was a widely shared belief that women should occupy a respected but largely delimited domestic role in the social division of labor, although one might add that non-White women often were expected to perform hard labor. And there was widespread commitment to employing education to unify the American people, so that the nation could realize its manifest destiny of world leadership (Hogan, 1990; Kaestle, 1983, Chapter 5).

Most of these ideas were not controversial in the United States during the 19th century, as they were espoused by the majority of middle-class, White Protestants—the nation's cultural center of gravity. Those that disagreed with one or more of these propositions—Catholics, immigrants, Blacks or other racial minorities, and feminist activists—were widely believed to be aberrant, part of the problem that common schools were intended to resolve—a fact that eventually led some to form their own schools. Most of the institutions established under the aegis of common-school reform, moreover, were for Whites only. This shared set of values and purposes lent the common-school crusade a clear direction and a distinctive goal: the unification of American culture, defined in narrow terms, through the mechanism of universal schooling (Brown, 1996; Lannie, 1968; Welter, 1962).

The success of common-school reform did not rest wholly on the shoulders of crusading reformers, however, nor on their messianic ideology. There was widespread support for education as a general principle in American culture. Even if there sometimes were heated debates over specific features of school reform, such as local taxation, the resolution of such conflicts often were quite similar from one state to another. Historians have noted the effusive language in support of publicly supported education in many state constitutions, and constitutional conventions, during the 19th century, particularly in the Northern tier of states extending west from New England and the mid-Atlantic. Most of these foundational documents allowed for some degree of state support for education, along with a measure of supervision, making it one of the few areas of public life to receive such attention at the time. As a consequence, some historians labeled the schools a "fourth branch of government" in the 19th century (Tyack, James, & Benevot, 1987).

In certain respects this was a legacy of the enthusiasm over education evident immediately after the Revolution. Beginning in 1797, the federal government passed the famous Northwest Ordinance, which provided for the sale of public (federal) lands to support education, as a condition for admitting new states to the union. Consequently, education was widely recognized as a legitimate and important function of governmental authority almost from the very beginning of the republic. It was on this base of broad public and historic commitment to education as an activity of the government that common-school advocates built their campaigns. And it was a critical foundation for their ultimate success. The republican ideology of the new nation, holding that citizenship entailed responsibility and knowledge, dictated that schooling be made universally available, at least for those groups deemed eligible to be citizens (Meyer, Tyack, Nagel, & Gordon, 1979). These sentiments helped advance the cause of reform, and lent it a particular social and cultural orientation.

By the time of the Civil War the logic of reform had nearly swept its opposition from the stage of popular discourse over education, starting in the Northern states. There was a great deal of work to be done, to be sure, but the ideas that schools should be supported by property taxes, should have greater uniformity, should be nonsectarian, should last for more than six months, and should be taught by trained, professional teachers were no longer sources of widespread controversy. This does not mean, of course, that all of these goals had been achieved. Great variation on all of these counts existed in virtually every state of the union, even more significantly in the South and the West than in the Northeast. But instituting these reforms gradually became a matter of enforcing standards that had become accepted by the political establishment. The cause had been aided by the ascendancy of the Republican Party and presidential candidate Abraham Lincoln, inheritors of the modernizing mantle of earlier reformers, and by union victory in the Civil War. These historic developments represented the supremacy of the reform-oriented, institution-building ethos of the urbanized northeast. Struggles to establish the first compulsory school laws in the latter 19th century marked the closing stages of this campaign. By then, the common-school wars had been largely won, even if some battles remained unsettled; now it was time to turn to new challenges facing the nascent public school system of the United States (Graham, 1974; Tyack, 1978).

## FOCAL POINT: REFORMING PEDAGOGY

Horace Mann was an idealistic and tireless advocate for pedagogical reform; he was also a complex historical figure. Among other things, he held a compassionate belief in the inherent goodness of children and their natural proclivity to learn and grow in the proper environment. In this respect his views departed from more conservatively minded educators, even if he shared many other aspects of the period's dominant Protestant ideology. Historians speculate that his own unhappy childhood experiences with the strictures of traditional Calvinist beliefs led him later to reject educational theories that emphasized submission to authority as a fundamental principle. No doubt he would have been a critic of Francis Wayland's tactics in the case described earlier (Messerli, 1972).

As seen earlier, the conviction that children needed to learn obedience and respect for authority was widely held in 19th-century America, although there was a growing debate over how such lessons should be imparted. One of the primary issues was the matter of how children should be treated. The controversies aroused by Francis Wayland's public airing of his own approach to childrearing was indicative of public interest in these questions. A much larger dispute raged during the 1840s over the question of corporal punishment in the schools. At issue was a basic question about pedagogy: Did children require fear to learn properly, or did such emotions make learning even more difficult to achieve (Hogan, 1990; Wishy, 1967)?

On returning from his first tour of Europe, Mann extolled the virtues of schools in Prussia. Although autocratic Prussia evoked images of authority and iron discipline, Mann found the schools there to be quite humane. Teachers actually presented the subject matter rather than demanding that students memorize and recite their lessons, and they employed a variety of teaching aids to help stimulate student interest and assist learning. Most significantly, Prussian teachers eschewed any form of physical punishment, arguing that fear and pain inhibited learning rather than encouraging it. They were trained in special institutes, featuring the ideas of such humanistic thinkers as Swiss educator Johan Heinrich Pestalozzi and the German philosopher Friedrich Froebel, originator of the kindergarten. Mann found himself drawn to this perspective, and suggested in his Seventh Annual Report that American educators had much to learn from their European counterparts. In contrast to schools in Massachusetts and elsewhere in the United States, the Prussian educational system was also quite centralized and well funded (Messerli, 1972; Cremin, 1980).

Mann's report was well received in many circles, but drew a negative reaction from one of the most prestigious and powerful groups of educators in Massachusetts: Boston's grammar-school masters. These 32 men were the headteachers, equivalent to principals today, in the city's public grammar schools, which drew pupils from the primary or common schools and sent the best students off to high schools or academies. Most of the masters had gained their positions by virtue of long experience in the public schools, and they were widely held to be among the most knowledgeable and influential educators in the state, if not the nation. Their reaction to Mann's report represented a serious challenge to his authority, but it also offered a rare occasion for public discussion about pedagogical principles and differing views of children and education (Binder, 1974; Schultz, 1973).

In a lengthy response to Mann's report, the masters challenged many aspects of Mann's work as Secretary of the State Board of Education, but devoted special attention to the Pestalozzian principles he had advocated and his condemnation of corporal punishment. They dismissed the idea that children could learn through natural curiosity, and maintained that physical punishments were necessary to "focus" and "discipline" the minds of students. "Duty should come first," they argued, "and pleasure should grow out of the discharge of it." As long-time veterans of the public schools, they asserted that it was foolishly sentimental to believe that order could be maintained without the threat—and actual use—of physical coercion. As a matter of principle, they were strong believers in "faculty psychology," which held that the mind is like a muscle in need of exercise and training. The study of dead languages like Latin and Greek, for instance, was widely considered a virtue among 19th-century educators, because it helped to train powers of concentration and disciplined the mind to overcome difficult or wholly foreign subject matter. In this spirit, the masters affirmed the central importance of memorization and recitation as pedagogical techniques essential to "forming the habit of independent and individual effort." To them, upholding the long tradition of teachers exercising fearful authority over students, forcing them to train the "faculties" of observation and memory through sheer willpower, was of paramount importance (Katz, 1968; Messerli, 1972).

The masters may have had the force of tradition on their side, along with discipline-minded parents, but Mann seized on the opportunity afforded by their response to advance his agenda of reform in pedagogy. The central thrust of his reply to the masters was to charge them with base self-interest, and with defending their own privileged positions at the expense of children. He demanded that the regime of discipline based on unquestioned authority and fear be replaced by an education motivated by mutual respect, affection, and the love of knowledge. Mann also advocated authority in the classroom, but believed it best achieved by observing courtesy and compassion. In defense of his office he listed the steps he and others had taken to establish a more comprehensive and effective school system throughout the state, and the salutary effects of the state's fledgling normal schools, which the masters had also attacked. In particular, he rejected the suggestion that physical force was necessary for the success of modern schools (Hogan, 1990; McCluskey, 1958).

There were additional volleys of responses and replies over the next several years, with each side repeating many of the essential points without affecting the course of debate. The masters resolutely refused to budge on the issue of corporal punishment, declaring that "all authority is of God and must be obeyed." In the meantime, however, several of Mann's allies in Boston gained seats on the Boston School Committee, the body charged with conducting inspections of the schools. Although such inspections were usually just ceremonial, Mann's friends turned the annual grammar-school examinations into real tests of what students had learned, and the results were devastating to the masters. It turned out that the students had actually gained very little through fear and recitation, and that the haughty masters were almost totally dependent on textbooks and time-worn exercises in their teaching. As a consequence, the students performed poorly on the exams, and those that did the worst were in schools controlled by the most domineering and abusive masters (Messerli, 1972).

A report issued by the inspectors revealed that some masters had engaged in various forms of corporal punishment as many as 50 times per week. This led to a public outcry. It was a decisive turning point in Mann's battle to change attitudes about pedagogy. Even though some Bostonians continued to defend the masters, the tide of public opinion clearly started to swing against the traditional pedagogy of fear and authoritarianism (Katz, 1968; Schultz, 1973; Wishy, 1967).

As a result of the investigation of the Boston Grammar Schools, four masters were dismissed from their positions. Others were transferred to other duties in the school system, a dramatic loss of face. In the wake of the controversy, a large group of civic and cultural leaders in the Boston area raised thousands of dollars to establish yet another normal school, concrete testimony of public support for Mann's ideas about children and pedagogy (Messerli, 1972). Although the weight of tradition would continue to make corporal punishment, recitation, and authoritarianism basic elements of popular schooling for decades to come, there were signs of change. The pace of reform was slow, but it also began to gain speed as the 19th century drew to a close.

## The Rise of Secondary Education

The high school is sometimes said to be an American invention. An institution designed to teach the graduates of the primary and grammar schools, at about age 13 or so, it was virtually unknown until the early 19th century. Historians agree that Boston's English Classical High School was the nation's first such institution. Founded in 1821 to provide a more practical and accessible alternative to the famous Boston Latin School, it came to serve youth interested in acquiring certain of the "higher branches" of learning without undertaking a classical (Latin and Greek) education. It was not long before other large cities along the Atlantic coast and the major transportation arteries to the North and West came to establish similar schools. These institutions taught the growing number of primary-school graduates who sought a well-rounded but practical education to prepare them for the urban world of commerce and industrial development. Consequently, the popularity of high schools grew. By the end of the 19th century they existed in one form or another in every type of city or large town in the United States. Even though the high school did not directly affect most Americans, as formal education typically ended at the elementary level, it nevertheless had become an important element of the nation's institutional culture (Brown, 1902; Herbst, 1996; Reese, 1995).

The high school started as an innovation in urban school systems with large numbers of students and expansive tax support for public education. Popular demand for instruction in such advanced subjects as history, mathematics (algebra and geometry), literature and writing, political economy, science (or "natural philosophy"), and geography led to its rapid spread. Most high schools also featured instruction in some classical subjects, especially Latin, long considered a sign of achievement and standing. From the beginning, however, there was little expectation that most children would attend these institutions; rather, they were intended to teach the very best graduates of the primary and grammar schools. The early public high schools represented something of a contradiction, in that case. They were a part of the popular education system, yet they were designated to serve an academic and social elite. This accounted for both their great attraction and the controversies they engendered (Krug, 1964; Reese, 1995).

Most of the early large public high schools admitted students by examination, and many prospective entrants were turned away because their scores were not high enough. As one might imagine, students in the primary schools and their teachers frequently anticipated such tests with dread. In many respects, these exams represented a 19th-century equivalent of standardized tests in today's educational system. It was a rare form of assessment that was extended to children from a number of schools, or even across an entire community. In time, the high-school admission exams became important indicators of how well a particular primary or grammar school was performing and provided a convenient standard of comparison for parents interested in choosing a school for their children. In this way the high schools helped to establish and enforce uniform academic standards throughout the nation's large urban school systems, simply by virtue of their position at the pinnacle of many children's (and parents') ambitions. Consequently, the development of the high school did much to help create better-integrated and more unitary school systems in the cities (Beadie, 1999; Labaree, 1988).

The high school, however, also was a controversial institution. It competed with private or semipublic secondary institutions, many of them called academies, which had developed in response to demand for higher levels of education in earlier years, some dating back to the 1700s. High schools eventually eclipsed these institutions altogether, but the process of change was fraught with conflict. The academies were rather numerous, especially in the Northeast where they represented a dense network of institutions and had many influential supporters who were not happy to see them displaced. Furthermore, the early public high schools were quite costly, often occupying palatial buildings erected at great expense and with considerable fanfare. Critics decried the expense, noting that relatively few students were educated and that tuition-charging academies provided more or less the same services at considerably less cost and with little public funding. The fact that high schools turned away many students because of low examination scores or poor grades did not help matters. They were attacked as little more than finishing schools for the elite, paid for with public monies (Beadie and Tolley, 2002; Herbst, 1996).

Such criticisms came to a head in 1874 in Kalamazoo, Michigan, where opponents of the local public high school unsuccessfully sued the school board to have it abolished, a case widely cited in later disputes. As a rule, courts did not sanction the argument that only the common or elementary schools qualified for public support. Legal challenges notwithstanding, there was the larger question of popular perceptions. By and large, educational leaders succeeded in persuading the public that the quality of public high schools was generally much higher than most private academies, and that the high schools helped set proper academic standards for the rest of the educational system. They also argued that high schools conferred economic and social benefits on talented students, providing them with reliable credentials, and that these students became local leaders. The high school was depicted as a valuable asset for a community to maintain, a resource well worth the cost (Goldin & Katz, 1999a; Reese, 1995).

This latter argument pointed to the high school's principal source of success. Probably more than anything else, the future of the high school hinged on its popularity with the relatively small but growing urban middle class. Parents in this social stratum, perhaps less than one-tenth of the population at mid-century, increasingly were concerned with passing advantages along to their children in the form of social, cultural, and human capital (even if they did not use such terms). They were the beneficiaries of industrial growth and the market revolution, but there was great uncertainty about how their offspring would gain positions in the burgeoning commercial culture of the cities. Apprenticeship and other informal modes of training were rapidly disappearing. The establishment of public high schools with rigorous and exclusionary entrance requirements provided a clear and legitimate way for such families to accord status to the next generation. The rhetoric of the high school, free and open to all, gave the appearance of a meritocratic system of performance-based evaluations, whereby the talented succeeded. This clearly carried great appeal to middle-class urbanites, who instinctively eschewed the open display of social advantage or favor based on anything but ability and accomplishment. Competitive high schools, sitting atop the growing public system of education, proved irresistible to this social group. This attraction accounted for much of the initial success of the high school and its rapid spread in the later 19th century (Hogan, 1996; Labaree, 1988).

For most working-class children, on the other hand, high-school attendance simply was not a viable option, because they were expected to start working at about 14 or 15. Unlike their middle-class counterparts, poorer families typically could not afford to send children to school once they could contribute to the household income. Thus, although the rhetoric of public education made the high school appear meritocratic, it was disproportionately enrolled with middle- and upper-class students throughout the 19th century, even if enough working-class students attended to lend the appearance of fairness. In this regard the critics were correct: It was a largely elite institution conducted at considerable public expense. The high school's popularity among urban society's most influential social classes, however, usually rendered such criticisms moot (Katz, 1968; Reese, 1995).

There was a great deal of variation in the size and character of high schools in the 19th century. In the big cities, where there was a ready supply of students and a large middle-class constituency, high schools could be sizeable, and often were widely admired for their academic standards. Philadelphia's Central High School, for instance, enrolled hundreds of students and was among the most famous in the country; its graduates commanded considerable prestige. Advanced instruction in this setting imparted cultural capital, and local networks of graduates represented a potent source of social capital for career advancement. Such urban high schools had large teaching staffs and attracted the best-qualified faculty, with high salaries and opportunities to specialize in particular subjects. It is little wonder that they proved so attractive to the aspiring urban middle class. Institutions such as these, however, constituted less than one in five high schools in the country (Labaree, 1988).

On the other hand, in smaller towns the high school generally was little more than a single class where one or two teachers taught advanced subjects to older students. The quality of education was much lower in these settings, and the credentials graduates received were frequently questionable. In 1873 the U.S. Commissioner of Education remarked that many such schools were offering instruction barely above the primary level. But these classes often were the start of much larger and more comprehensive secondary institutions, built in later years as the community grew. In time, high schools came to reflect local ambitions, and many boosters dreamed of institutions closer in size and function to the highly regarded flagship high schools in the cities. If the high school was becoming instrumental in conferring middle-class status, after all, it stood to reason that every growing community would harbor ambitions to have one (Goldin & Katz, 1999a; Reese, 1995; VanOverbeke, 2008).

Yet another important feature of 19th-century high schools was the widespread practice of coeducation. Secondary education traditionally was a largely male preserve. Almost from the very start, however, high schools in many parts of the country enrolled male and female students together. For ambitious educators, this was partly a strategy for finding the students to support these expensive institutions: Admitting girls meant twice as many potential enrollments, and it widened the base of support among middle-class families. Coeducation also conformed to the logic of meritocracy: If girls could pass the exams and receive good grades, how could they be refused admission? Additionally, female high-school graduates constituted an important source of teachers for the rapidly growing urban school systems of the later 19th century. Educators predicted dire shortages of qualified teachers if women were not encouraged to enroll in the high schools. As a consequence, most American high schools in the 19th century served both genders, a practice not observed in other countries. Exceptions occurred in the largest cities and in the South, where separate schools for boys and girls often prevailed as a policy. But in most localities coeducation was the norm. Altogether, by the end of the century, female students outnumbered males in the nation's high schools, in practically all regions of the country. The growth of secondary education and the rise of the high school helped usher in a unique era of (relative) gender equity in American education (Rury, 1991; Tyack & Hansot, 1990). This issue is discussed further in the next chapter.

At the end of the 19th century over half a million students were enrolled in secondary institutions in the United States, most in public high schools. This meant that the high school had become a pervasive form of popular education, even though it served less than one-tenth of the nation's teenage population. Despite the populist rhetoric of the high-school's supporters, it still served a fairly select clientele. And even if most high school students were women, almost none were Black or Native American. Its inherent elitism notwithstanding, however, there was no denying the power of the high school to attract students once it was established. In the decades to follow, high-school enrollments would climb even faster than they had in the 1800s. After years of struggle and debate, the high school had finally arrived and there was no turning back. Even though these institutions served a small fraction of the nation's school-aged population, they had come to be seen as an indispensable feature of the educational landscape (Herbst, 1996; Krug, 1964).

## The Age of the College

The 19th century was also a time of rapid expansion among the nation's higher-education institutions. The period prior to the Civil War, in fact, is sometimes referred to as the "age of the college," although only a tiny fraction of the nation's population engaged in post-secondary studies. Instead, it was a time when many collegiate institutions were established, most with high hopes for the future but little else in the way of either students or resources. These colleges generally prepared students for careers in the ministry or as educators. Other professions usually did not require a college education in the 19th century, although some students did attend college before studying medicine or law. Horace Mann, for instance, graduated from Brown University before standing for the bar, as did many other leaders in various callings. It was not until the closing decades of the century that modern universities began to develop with a focus on science and research, dedicated to preparing students for a wide range of careers. Even then, however, the collegiate sector of the nation's educational system was tiny, enrolling less than 5% of the relevant age cohort. Despite their rapid proliferation, 19th-century colleges were concerned with only a small fraction of the nation's students, something of an academic elite, even if not necessarily the best or brightest students (Ogren, 2008).

As noted in the previous chapter, the United States had a handful of collegiate institutions at the close of the 18th century. In the next 50 years, several hundred others were established, most of them by religious denominations interested in training candidates for the ministry. These institutions fought for survival, competing bitterly over students and financial contributions, and some were eventually forced to close their doors. Many enrolled only a fraction of their students in college-level courses, with the rest taking "prepatory" classes equivalent to those offered in academies or high schools. Even the early state universities were small and religious in character, and they too had sizeable preparatory departments. Because the higher education system was not clearly linked to the nation's changing occupational structure, and because there were relatively few secondary schools to send them students, the colleges struggled through much of the 19th century. They proliferated because of religious zeal and the idealism of their pioneering founders, but few prospered until well after the Civil War. By then the fundamental purposes of higher education had started to change (Burke, 1982; Rudolph, 1962).

Through much of the 19th century American collegiate institutions were dominated by a classical curriculum and an academic culture shaped by traditions handed down from the colonial period. English models of higher education influenced these institutions, particularly the colleges of Cambridge University, which emphasized classical preparation as the foundation of higher learning. Latin and Greek represented the core of the curriculum, and most classes were conducted by recitation. Knowledge of these subjects was a source of considerable cultural capital for students at these institutions, and this was a part of their appeal. Curricular reform ideas circulated from an early date. There were efforts to introduce more scientific, historical, and literary studies; Francis Wayland, for example, advocated such innovations at Brown, and they were taken up elsewhere too. But the Yale Report of 1828, a faculty document defending classical studies, helped to slow widespread change during the antebellum period. Simply put, tradition held that a classical emphasis was indispensable; without it no course of study could be said to represent collegiate standards. This, of course, helped to insure that most of what was taught in the colleges would be irrelevant to developments in the economy, or in society at large. It was a powerful means of transmitting cultural knowledge, but collegiate education had few immediate or practical uses outside of that (Hofstadter, 1955a; Rudolph, 1978).

Things began to change, however, in the closing decades of the century. Passage of the first Land Grant College Act in 1862 was a harbinger of the future. Drafted by Vermont Congressman Justin Smith Morrill, this legislation set aside federal lands for the support of institutions devoted to practical and scientific courses of study, particularly in the fields of agriculture and "mechanics" (A & M), today's engineering. A second Morrill act in 1890 provided even more support for "A & M" state universities, including many that had been founded in earlier decades. Meanwhile, visionary leaders such as Harvard's Charles Eliot broke the stranglehold of tradition in the collegiate curriculum. Eliot introduced a liberal elective system that allowed students to choose courses themselves, with few requirements—a reform that was later modified to feature a required core. Scientific research institutes had been opened at Harvard, Yale, and other institutions even before Eliot's reforms, and new research-oriented universities were established afterward, with Johns Hopkins, Cornell, and Chicago leading the way. As a matter of principle, the German model of higher education, which emphasized research-based learning instead of classical training, influenced the leaders of these institutions. Flagship state universities, such as Michigan, Wisconsin, and California, also exhibited German influences, and attracted leading professors dedicated to social and technological advancement through scholarship and research. The result was a newfound degree of social relevance in higher education, and enrollments began to climb sharply (Eddy, 1957; Hawkins, 1972; Veysey, 1965).

Of course, rising high-school graduation levels also helped to fuel collegiate enrollment, but many of the brightest students clearly were drawn to the leading centers of innovation. University leaders such as James Angell at Michigan and Eliot at Harvard campaigned to make the secondary-school curriculum correspond to collegiate entrance requirements. In this way, links between the high schools and the emerging universities were strengthened. Many other institutions, especially those with strong religious ties, were slow to change, and classical studies continued to be a staple of collegiate study for decades to come. Traditions rarely die easily, but the direction of change ultimately would prove very difficult to resist. Colleges were gaining new currency, and there was excitement in the air. A stronger connection had been made between collegiate life and the larger social and economic world, and that would bode well for the future of American higher education (Goldin & Katz, 1999b; Lucas, 1994; Ogren, 2008; VanOverbeke, 2008).

## Conclusion: The Shaping of a National System of Education

The 19th century was a time of profound transformation in American life, and important changes in the nation's educational system. Industrialization and the market revolution helped to expand the economy, raising standards of living at the same time that employment was transfigured for thousands of workers. Rapid urbanization brought a host of new problems to the nation's cities, along with fresh waves of immigrants from other lands. Reformers puzzled over the best ways to respond to these developments, and devised a host of new institutions to address the challenges posed by the emerging urban industrial order. Not the least of these were the schools, which were supposed to inculcate proper middle-class values and work habits at the same time as they helped to forge a new national identity. In particular, the common-school reform movement aimed to make education the linchpin of social, political, and economic development. It was a means of sustaining republican values in an age of considerable ferment. If society was changing rapidly, schools would help to ease the passage to a brighter future.

School reform brought many changes to the education system, most of which reformers would count as progress. Common schools were improved, and high schools were established, most of them open to all members of a community, even if many still required an entrance exam. Following the Civil War, growing numbers of schools outside of the South conducted annual sessions of 160 days or longer, close to today's standards, with urban areas leading the way. Professional standards had been established for much of the nation's teaching force, with normal schools and teacher-training departments existing in scores of high schools, colleges, and freestanding institutional forms. Hundreds of colleges and universities beckoned to students finishing secondary schools, and even if only a small minority attempted collegiate study, the potential for higher education becoming a normal step in the process of American education was firmly established (Cremin, 1980).

Of course the United States remained a largely rural nation at the end of the 19th century, and most Americans did not even attend a secondary school, much less graduate from one and enter college. But the basic elements of the national system of education had been created. Corporal punishment and traditional views of childhood and adult authority prevailed everywhere—although probably most definitely in the countryside—but there were voices of dissent, and new perspectives on children and pedagogy were slowly gaining favor. The process of change, although speedy in many respects, was also painfully slow in terms of its dispersion to all corners American society. With some 75 million people stretched across millions of square miles, the United States was a vast land, with great unevenness in social and economic development, and considerable cultural and social diversity. As significant as the reforms launched in the 19th century were, the process of shaping the modern educational system had only started.

What about the direction of change—the question posed at the start of the book? In the 19th century there can be little doubt that industrialization was the driving force in the transformation of the economy and society at large. One can say the same thing about its impact on education. Clearly, industrial development and urbanization dictated the general thrust of reform in education. The basic organizational form of schooling was shaped by the central institution of the industrial era: the factory. Schools were organized to increase efficiency, to raise the quality of a standardized product, and to produce more compliant and dependable workers. This was most plainly evident in reforms such as the Lancastrian schools, but was apparent in other aspects of common-school reform as well. Industrialization also produced a growing commercial middle class, whose members clamored for secondary institutions, especially the public high school. These schools made secondary curricula more practical, bringing education in line with the requirements of the economy and the expectations of the newly emerging entrepreneurial and professional social strata. The same could be said of higher education, although it took somewhat longer for these changes to be realized. By the end of the century, however, a definite hierarchy of educational credentials was emerging for ambitious youth striving to find a secure niche in the modern social order.

By and large, changes in the larger economy and society drove the process of change and development in American education during the 19th century. As in the colonial period, the schools appear to have responded to the changing demands of the rapidly evolving social and economic system. In a certain sense, this is what one would expect: Schools, after all, must provide society with individuals prepared to address the ever-changing needs of economic and social life. On the other hand, education clearly worked to the advantage of some people and not to others. Examining the question of how the nation's schools may have helped certain members of society, and effected social change in new ways, the story now turns to the issue of education for the nation's excluded or "outsider" groups in the next chapter.

# 4

# Ethnicity, Gender, and Race
## *Contours of Social Change in the 19th Century*

In previous chapters we have seen some of the ways that education was shaped by larger social forces during the 1800s. There can be little question that industrialization, urbanization, and other broad processes of social change historically influenced the development of schooling in the United States. But there is the opposite relationship to consider as well. How has the evolution of schooling affected the process of social development?

As it turns out, this is a complex question. As noted earlier, the connection between education and the larger society is multifaceted and subject to a wide range of factors and conditions. Historically, some lines of influence were fairly straightforward. Rising literacy rates, for instance, generally have been attributed to the growth of formal education. Greater skill levels of this sort in the nation's population, moreover, have been thought to be linked historically with economic growth. This is an aspect of *human capital*, the productive capacities of a given populace. Consequently, schooling generally is believed to represent a direct contribution to improved proficiency, and hence general social advancement. But in other respects the role of education in social change is more difficult to perceive. There is the question, for example, of how schooling affected the social structure, or the relative standing of various groups in American history. Clearly it helped some to advance, but did its benefits extend to everyone? Did the general contributions of schooling to economic growth serve the interests of some groups better than others? This question addresses a particularly sensitive feature of the social change process: who succeeded in history and who did not? Expressed a little differently, it speaks to a key issue in the history of education: Did schooling help to change the prevailing social structure, or did it simply reinforce existing patterns of inequality?

This chapter considers some of the most basic elements of inequality in American history. To address these issues, it is necessary to examine several different social groups, and the impact of education on their social status during the 19th century. In many respects, the members of these groups lived at the margins of society throughout much of American history. The groups to be considered include immigrants (mainly from Europe, but from elsewhere too), White (native-born) women, African Americans (slaves and freedmen), and Native Americans (or American Indians). As noted earlier, these groups all occupied positions of dependency or inferiority in North American society at large. Each was subject to discrimination and exclusion in various forms, justified by an ideology defined and fostered largely by native-born White males, although even its victims sometimes harbored such ideas as well. All of these groups came to attach differing degrees of importance to education in challenging the terms of their subordinate social status. The successes and disappointments they experienced speak to the transformative power of education as an instrument of social change, and to its limitations.

There are many other tales to tell in assessing the contributions of schooling to social change in the United States during this time. For instance, it is clear that children from working- or lower-class families did not benefit from school to the same extent as their counterparts from middle- and upper-class backgrounds. This was pointed out in the discussion of the high school in the previous chapter. Over time, consequently, education came to demarcate broad social class distinctions in American society. These were differences that existed throughout the country, across regions, among women, and within the various ethnic and racial minority groups. But even going beyond these nearly universal class-based variations in schooling, it can be quite revealing to examine the categories of gender, ethnicity, and race. To many children in these groupings the question of education was especially poignant. For some, schooling proved to be a potent vehicle of reformation and social mobility, and for others it ultimately became a grim reminder of failure and a source of frustration. Taken together, their stories point to some of the contours of education, or its boundaries, as an instrument of social change, and as an indicator of it, during the 19th century.

## FOCAL POINT: CONFLICT OVER RELIGION AND CULTURE IN EDUCATION

The late afternoon meeting of New York's Common Council on October 29, 1840, was a momentous occasion. Attended by a standing-room-only crowd in the City Hall chambers, this gathering was convened to consider a petition by the city's Catholics to receive public funds for the support of schools linked to their churches. Emotions ran high on both sides of the debate that ensued. Bishop John Hughes, a fervid and articulate champion of New York's Irish community, presented the Catholic position. Opposed to Hughes stood the Public School Society, the semi-private corporate entity that had managed the city's charity schools for decades (successor to the Free School Society mentioned in Chapter 3), represented in this case by two well-known New York lawyers. In the course of the dispute that unfolded over almost 15 hours in two evenings, practically all of the 19th-century arguments regarding the development of common schools were heard, pro and con. Of particular importance, however, were the Bishop's pointed objections to the idea that a common, nonsectarian form of education was desirable, or even possible to attain. The Catholic petition represented a serious assault on the principle of public education as espoused by Horace Mann and other champions of public schooling. Even though it ultimately was unsuccessful, this challenge revealed much about the tensions that underlay 19th-century American society. In this instance, cultural conflict threatened to overturn public education just as it barely was starting. Ethnicity, and all of its varied cultural and religious complications, made the task of defining a common-school experience in the United States especially difficult.

Hughes and his followers objected to the Public School Society's institutions on a number of grounds. The first, and most important, concerned the question of religion. Nonsectarianism, according to the Catholics, was simply another form of religion, and in the case of the city's public schools it took the shape of a general distillation of Protestant precepts and maxims, along with readings from the King James Bible. This, declared Hughes, posed the danger of Catholic children turning against their own faith, while gradually being captivated by the inveiglement of Protestant culture that prevailed in both the schools and American society at large. Even worse was the threat of students losing religion altogether. "To make an infidel, what is it necessary to do?" demanded Hughes. "Cage him up in a room, give him a secular education from the age of five years to twenty one, and I ask you what he will not come out, if not an infidel?" (Ravitch, 1974). To the minds of Hughes and other Catholics, this was a most pernicious sectarianism.

Added to this were numerous slights and slanders against Catholicism and the Irish that marked the popular textbooks and readers of the day, and reportedly characterized the conduct of many teachers in the public schools. It was little wonder, reasoned Hughes, that New York's Catholic children were so poorly represented on the rolls of the Public School Society's institutions. These schools were deemed hostile to the beliefs and cultural heritage of the immigrant Catholic population, and particularly the Irish. Textbooks related appalling accounts of the Inquisition, equating "papists" with intolerance and oppression. Other accounts praised Martin Luther, the founder of the Protestant Reformation, as a heroic figure, leading "mankind" away from the "ignorance and superstition" of the Catholic Church (Lannie, 1968). One book declared that immigration would make the United States the "common sewer of Ireland" (Kaestle, 1983). Instances such as these confirmed the belief of Hughes and other Catholics that the Church's parochial schools were entitled to tax monies to support their operations. The existing public schools were discriminatory and culturally intolerant, and fairness demanded that Catholics be allowed to run their own public institutions.

Bishop John Hughes was an unusually ardent champion of Catholic and Irish causes, and he quickly rose to a position of national prominence among American Catholics. In this instance, however, he did not succeed in winning public support for the parochial schools. Instead, the controversy over religion in the schools of the Public School Society was resolved by establishing New York's first publicly elected Board of Education in 1842, and within a decade virtually all of the city's tax-supported schools were brought under its control. Offensive passages in textbooks were gradually expunged, and eventually new books were purchased that were more even-handed in their references to religious themes and immigrants. For his part, Hughes became a champion of separate Catholic schools, and spearheaded the development of parochial school systems in cities across the country. These institutions were especially popular in certain larger cities with significant immigrant populations. For members of these groups, the parochial schools offered a way to maintain the religious traditions of their various nationalities and subcultures, and also a safeguard for native languages and other traditional values and social practices. In short, they represented a means for the preservation of culture, long-observed beliefs, and customs that were threatened by the prospect of assimilation into a larger, assertive American civilization (Lannie, 1968; Ravitch, 1974).

A part of Hughes's fervor can be explained by the circumstances of his immigrant, largely Irish constituency in the mid-19th century. Most immigrants were quite poor, and they often were subjected to blatant discrimination at the hands of native-born Whites. This was especially true of the Irish, who often arrived almost directly from the impoverished countryside of their native counties, with all of the rough-and-tumble manners and proclivities of their traditional folkways. In the years following 1845, when the infamous potato famine drove more than 2 million Irish abroad, tens of thousands of destitute and desperate immigrants poured into New York and other coastal cities each year. Crime rates went up dramatically, as did the numbers of individuals and families applying for poor relief (financial assistance) and other forms of public aid. Overcrowded and dirty, the Irish wards of the cities often were rife with sickness and disease. Many native-born Americans reacted quite negatively to these newcomers, labeling them heathens, criminals, and drunkards. Anti-Catholic sentiments were inflamed also, especially in light of the rapid growth of the American Catholic Church in the wake of immigration. Nativist (anti-immigrant) fears were fueled by the perception of growing immigrant voting power as their numbers swelled in certain cities. Cognizant of these inhospitable sentiments, leaders of local Irish communities, especially the priests and bishops, continually felt embattled. Even though the numbers of immigrants were increasing, they still formed a relatively isolated population in a land that frequently appeared to be quite hostile (Archdeacon, 1983; Kenny, 2000).

Sometimes the threats were more than the loss of culture and religious traditions. In the mid-1840s nativist mobs in Boston, Philadelphia, and other cities attacked Catholic establishments, burning churches and other buildings in fits of anti-Catholic and anti-immigrant hysteria. These episodes were fueled by anxieties about competition for jobs and political influence that the foreigners often represented, and by the growing problems of crime and public disorder that many associated with immigrants in general and the Irish in particular. In Philadelphia the fighting began after nativists accused the Catholics of scheming to remove Protestant Bibles from the public schools (Wainwright, Weigley, & Wolf, 1982). Violence was also linked to a deeply rooted hostility to Catholicism in American culture, which held the Pope to be a despotic foreign authority who threatened native traditions of democratic self-government. The growth of the Catholic Church, with the spread of parochial schooling and other institutional manifestations of its influence, was sometimes seen as a direct challenge to ancestral American institutions.

Incidents of mob violence certainly did not make members of immigrant communities feel very welcome. Indeed, these events tended to reinforce the idea that the foreign-born needed to develop their own institutions and other sources of support, and to actively resist efforts to bring them into the mainstream of American society. For many immigrants in the 19th century, assimilation was scarcely a cheerful thought. The United States seemed an antagonistic land, one that posed particularly great dangers to their children (Archdeacon, 1983; Jacobson, 1998).

Given these facts of life in the 19th century, it is hardly surprising that relatively few Irish children attended school, especially those children from the poorest families. In his comments before New York's Common Council, Hughes estimated that fewer than half of the city's Catholic children were enrolled. He cast the blame for this at the intractability of the Public School Society, and the hostility of its wealthy, Protestant patrons toward poor immigrant students. Even though Hughes did not succeed in getting tax monies for his own schools, he did manage to impair the reputation of his principal adversaries. Eventually, the imperious Public School Society was displaced, and the public schools became somewhat more hospitable establishments for the city's Irish students, along with other immigrants. Hughes's expanding system of parochial schools also offered greater educational opportunities to Catholics. But the question of whether significant numbers of indigent foreign children would be educated remained a critical one throughout the 19th century. These students posed a telling challenge to the schools, especially those of the newly formed Board of Education. Could the children's diverse cultural and social backgrounds be accommodated by institutions dedicated to assimilation? Or would ethnic groups stand apart from the educational system, creating a parallel community replete with its own institutions, separate from the rest of American society?

## Ethnic Struggles and Success Stories

The ultimate fate of most European immigrant communities, of course, is well known. The descendants of the Irish and other groups eventually came into the mainstream of American civilization, and it appears that schooling played an important role in this extended process of assimilation. It was not accomplished easily, however, and the ethnic struggle for success in the United States unfolded over several generations for the various groups that came to the United States in the 19th century. For the Catholics that Bishop Hughes represented, this was an interval marked by considerable conflict, but one also ultimately characterized by progress. Faced with daunting obstacles when they first arrived in North America, even the poorest European immigrants could look hopefully toward the future, especially as it concerned their children (Olneck, 2008).

Not everyone came from Northwestern Europe, however, and for other groups the question of acclimation proved even more painful. While immigration was predominantly European on the East Coast, elsewhere Hispanic (largely Mexican) and Asian communities represented ethnic alternatives to the cultural mainstream. Their numbers were limited in the 19th century and concentrated in the West, but members of these groups often were forced to attend segregated schools, where any were provided, with inferior academic offerings. Like the Irish, they encountered hostility to their native culture, and disdain for their religious traditions. They too waged battles for equal treatment in the schools, but usually found it difficult to achieve lasting progress. Not all ethnic groups experienced the schools as uplifting, in that case, and much depended on the circumstances of attempting social and economic integration into American life (Gonzalez & Fernandez, 2003).

With respect to European immigration, the Irish represented a telling case. As noted already, most arrived destitute in the years following the 1845 potato famine. Crowding into Eastern coastal cities, particularly New York and Boston, they had few marketable skills and little cultural capital to help secure a foothold in the local economy. Consequently, many Irish were unemployed, whereas others worked as unskilled laborers, living in abject poverty, and fueling stereotypes of shiftlessness and irresponsibility. They occupied the lowest tiers of the working class, often competing with African Americans for jobs, a situation that led to considerable social tension. Irish women worked as household domestics, cleaning the homes of middle-class urbanites and further reinforcing popular impressions of their servile standing. As Bishop Hughes noted, Irish children were less likely than others to attend school; most ceased formal education before their teens in order to find jobs and help support their families. The Irish were more likely than any other major group in New York to land in the city's jails, and they constituted a disproportionate share of the homeless. Theirs was hardly a plight that offered promise of redemption (Kenny, 2000).

With time and much hard work, however, the living conditions and social status of the Irish improved. Although most of the famine generation was unskilled and impoverished, their children often were able to find opportunities for advancement. The second generation moved into the skilled trades, becoming bricklayers and carpenters, plumbers and masons. These were jobs requiring skills learned on the job, or in an apprenticeship, rather than demanding study or knowledge derived from books. The same could be said of posts as factory foremen or skilled operatives. They afforded a higher standard of living, however, and entry into the lower reaches of the middle class. For the enterprising Irish lad who was willing to work hard and learn from experience, it was possible to get ahead. This was the first step in a much broader process of social mobility and adaptation (Archdeacon, 1983; Thernstrom, 1973).

The Irish also benefited when they left the crowded cities of the East, as did other immigrant groups. In the mid-19th century, New York newspaperman Horace Greeley advised his readers to escape the congested urban areas, famously declaring, "Go west young man!" Those heeding his admonition often did quite well; historians have determined that the Irish and other immigrants tended to do better in the cities and communities to the West. These were rapidly growing areas where opportunities abounded, and immigrants and their offspring were less likely to encounter discriminatory stereotypes where large ethnic enclaves did not exist. Accordingly, it was not long before the social profile of the Irish in places such as Chicago, Detroit, and St. Louis came to closely resemble that of the native-born population. Economic good fortune contributed to social and cultural integration (Sanders, 1977; Vinyard, 1976).

The gradual success of the Irish eventually led to better school attendance for their children, and further occupational mobility as a result. As more Irish families gained middle-class status, educational attainment levels improved. By the end of the 19th century, enrollment rates for students of Irish heritage were practically the same as for those of long-settled American natives. The sons and daughters of Irish Americans often attended parochial schools, including Catholic high schools, but the scholastic standards and moral tone of these institutions gradually became quite similar to their public counterparts. As a consequence of greater educational accomplishment, second- and third-generation Irish Americans began to achieve a degree of occupational parity with the general population. This was evident in the reduced numbers of Irish Americans employed in manual labor with each new generation. In the cities, they took positions in the growing civil service, as policemen, and in the rapidly expanding field of office employment. By the beginning of the 20th century, nearly 30% of all public-school teachers in New York were of Irish descent, making them the largest single European ethnic group among Board of Education employees. The teaching forces in other large cities exhibited similar ethnic profiles. The Irish, once noted for their poor school attendance, had come to oversee many urban schools and classrooms. This was a telling measure of attainment (Kenny, 2000; Perlmann, 1988).

The Irish possessed a number of advantages that no doubt helped them to succeed in 19th-century America. They spoke English on arrival, and were rapidly integrated into the domestic political system. New York's first Irish mayor was elected in the 1880s, and Irish politicians were successful elsewhere. They were also the first major immigrant group to arrive in the United States, starting in the 1840s, placing them in a position to benefit from the decades of rapid industrialization and urban development at the close of the century. Even though they clung closely to the Catholic Church and established their own schools, hospitals, and other institutions, economic success eventually helped them to feel comfortable in their new homeland (Archdeacon, 1983; Kenny, 2000).

Other immigrants faced similar challenges, and some took considerably longer to achieve the success realized by the Irish. But in the end, all the major European groups followed a path at least broadly similar to that marked by the Irish and their offspring. In a careful analysis of the experience of several different ethnic groups, historian Joel Perlmann has argued that some immigrants exhibited a greater proclivity toward schooling than others. As noted in Chapter 1, for instance, Russian Jews sent their children to school in unusually high numbers, and experienced considerable occupational mobility as a consequence. Italians and Poles, on the other hand, had lower rates of enrollment, and manifested slower advancements in social status. Over time, however, school attendance increased for all such groups, and this ultimately contributed to their acclimation to American life. For most, this was a process that extended well into the 20th century. In some cases it was a painstaking, step-by-step struggle, but the evidence of progress was undeniable as the years and decades passed (Hogan, 1985; Perlmann, 1988).

With respect to non-European "alien" groups, the situation was both similar and different. As the U.S. added the territories (later states) of Texas, California, New Mexico, and Arizona, following the Mexican–American War, it also acquired a substantial number of what would later be called Mexican Americans. Like the immigrants described earlier, much of this population was quite poor and retained its own distinctive cultural, linguistic, and religious traditions. Even though they were a majority in some places, and had lived there a century or more, these people generally were treated as colonial subjects. Their language and religion was denigrated, and schooling was sparse, much of it supplied by the Catholic Church or Protestant missionaries. When available, public schools usually were segregated, with inferior institutions for Spanish-speaking children. Conditions were especially harsh in Texas, where the Hispanic population was subservient to the "Anglos" who controlled the region's political and economic resources (San Miguel and Valencia, 1998).

In New Mexico, where the native population was called "Hispanos" and numbered more than 50,000, it was able to exert considerable political power. But even there it was a constant struggle to assure equity, and the schools were poorly funded, if not sharply segregated. Discrimination and exclusion, rooted in struggles over land and economic status, remained predominant themes. Consequently, the experience of Mexican Americans was ultimately quite different from that of the Irish and other immigrant groups in the 19th century. For them, social and economic integration into the mainstream proved an elusive goal. The same was true of the small number of Asian families that came to the Western U.S. in the 19th century. For these Americans, the struggle for equality would not begin to bear fruit until another era (Getz, 1997; Tamura, 2001).

The gradual but eventually successful assimilation of European immigrants into the mainstream of society is the centerpiece to one of the nation's great parables. It is widely known today as the American Dream, a story of success against great odds. Of course, the experience of Spanish-speaking communities in the Southwest was quite different. But like the Irish, most European immigrants ultimately did find success. Arriving with little more than a capacity for hard labor, they made their way in the booming industrial economy, while their children attended school in ever-greater degrees. As rising numbers entered the middle class, their children attained even higher levels of education. There was considerable variation in these trends, but the effects of growing enrollment inevitably affected the changing occupational profile of successive generations. Schools also helped to accommodate these children to their new American identities, inculcating national pride and loyalty along with community values. These institutions added human capital, conveying new skills and knowledge, at the same time that they imparted valuable cultural capital. In this respect it is possible to say that the school system contributed directly to the process of social change. In many ways, after all, education was integral to a grand process of social, economic, and cultural integration that marked the growth of American society in this era. This seems to have been true for many immigrants, even if not for all of them. The ideal of education contributing to social success and integration into the larger society is a legacy that continues to the present. Whether or not it has worked equally well for everyone, however, is still an open question.

### Gender and Education: A Quiet Transformation

As noted in earlier chapters, American women had a mixed educational legacy at the start of the 19th century. In most parts of the new nation they historically had been excluded from the usual forms of formal education. Female literacy rates lagged behind those for men, even in New England, where girls probably received more education than in other regions. The period following the Revolutionary War saw a flurry of activity in female education, but it is not clear just how many women were affected by these developments. Although some female academies may have been established, no colleges admitted women in the 18th century. In 1800, despite evidence of growing female enrollment in common schools, at least in the North, most American women were poorly educated compared to the men of their time (Nash, 2005; Sklar, 1993; Vinovskis & Bernard, 1978).

All of this changed profoundly in the next 100 years. By the end of the 19th century, female literacy rates exceeded those of males, women outnumbered men in high schools, and they were gradually gaining on them in the nation's colleges and universities. Even if it was a process largely restricted to Whites, the magnitude of change was striking. At one time excluded altogether from the higher branches of education, women now threatened to dominate them, causing alarm among certain male educators. As seen in the previous chapter, the majority of the nation's teachers were women by the end of the 19th century, and other educated job categories were becoming feminized as well. Altogether, a revolution of sorts had occurred in American education, at least with regard to gender, a process of change no less remarkable when viewed from the perspective of today (Nash, 2008; Tyack & Hansot, 1990).

A shift of such proportions raises a host of questions for historical consideration. How did this happen? What were the implications of such a change? How did it affect women's status? Did it signal a diminishing of sexism, or did it curb the effect of patriarchy in the larger society? Just how did the rapid growth of female education change the ideological construction of gender in North American society? To answer these questions and others, it is necessary to examine the growth of 19th-century women's education a bit more closely (Rury, 1991).

The process of change in women's schooling occurred in fits and starts, and was marked by a series of struggles by visionary leaders, both women and men. Perhaps the best-known early figure was Emma Willard, founder of the Troy Female Academy, near Albany, New York, today known as the Emma Willard School. In 1819 Willard wrote a treatise on female education to help persuade legislators in New York to support her planned school. She was not successful, but did raise money elsewhere. Decrying the poor state of female schooling, especially at the secondary level, Willard argued that women deserved and needed an education similar in quality—if not exact content—to that provided for "young gentlemen." She called for schools established with endowments—hence her plea for support—so tuition charges would be moderate, and such institutions would not be overly dependent on students for income (Scott, 1979).

Willard did not envision training young women for work or careers outside the home. Rather, she argued that higher-quality education was necessary "to form the character of the next generation, by controlling that of the females who are to be their mothers." In other words, she subscribed to a form of the ideology of "republican motherhood," first articulated in the years following the Revolution and discussed in Chapter 2. Willard was among the first women to espouse this view publicly, however, marking an important step in the development of female education. Historian Anne Firor Scott has argued that this was an early expression of feminism, an effort to create a sphere within which women could grow intellectually and develop their capacities without threatening male status. Other scholars described this impulse as "domestic feminism," an especially apt designation given the concerns expressed by Willard and other educators. Whatever its label, it was an idea that became the underlying rationale for White women's education during the remainder of the 19th century (Scott, 1978; Sklar, 1973).

Domestic feminism, premised on the proposition that educated women made better wives and mothers, was the entering wedge for a generation of reformers championing the advancement of women's schooling. It was an argument closely tied to the idea that women made good teachers. Prominent female figures such as Mary Lyon and Catharine Beecher also made careers by founding schools, training teachers and writing about improving women's education. Common-school reformers like Horace Mann, whose efforts on behalf of women teachers helped to promote the idea of extended schooling for women too, abetted the cause. Mann later pioneered collegiate coeducation as the first president of Antioch College. All of this helped to create an atmosphere conducive to higher levels of female education. As public high schools were opened, in that case, they typically were coeducational. In some larger cities separate schools were established for girls, to maintain an appearance of decorum in segregating the sexes. This was especially true in the South. But even in the most conservative settings, few arguments were offered to challenge the logic of educating women for the responsibilities of domesticity. In opening the city's female high school in 1854, the Boston School Committee declared that women have "the most fearfully responsible duties which can be assigned to human beings: to form and give direction to human character." The purpose of the school, in other words, was to prepare young women to become "competent mothers and teachers," as well as "fit companion(s) of high minded and intelligent men." If American civilization was to prevail, according to this line of reasoning, the nation's women needed the best possible preparation for marriage and motherhood (Clinton, 1984; Rury, 1991; Welter, 1966).

Once the door was open to female enrollment in secondary education, the nation's high-school population soon was marked by a preponderance of young women. By 1870 they were a majority in public high schools, and at the century's end there were almost twice as many girls as boys enrolled. The large number of female students was due both to relatively low male attendance rates and the fact that young middle-class women liked school. Boys could find jobs more easily and at younger ages, leading many to curtail their education. On the other hand, going to high school got the young women out of the house and into a setting where they could make friends and learn about the larger world. They excelled in a range of subjects, including those normally associated with males, such as the sciences. It also helped many of them prepare for jobs in teaching, working in an office, or even going on to college. About one-fifth of the collegiate student population was female by 1900. The high school, in that case, proved to be quite alluring to teenage girls, especially those from "middling" households, and this represented a major shift in American culture. Given the growth of high-school enrollments, and the gender-neutral character of many other educational institutions, White, native-born women probably were better educated than their male counterparts by the 1890s, a notable shift in American history (Tolley, 2002; Tyack & Hansot, 1990).

Not everyone participated equally in this process of change. As might be expected, women from certain backgrounds were better represented in the high schools at this time. By and large, the teenage daughters of white-collar workers, the emerging middle class, were more likely to enroll in school than other girls their age, and young women with parents born in the United States outnumbered those from immigrant families. For young women of the working class, the necessity of employment often made advanced schooling impossible. In this pattern of attendance it is possible to see once again the effects of social and cultural capital at play. It was young White women from stable, older communities, and with relatively well-educated parents, who possessed clear advantages when it came to availing themselves of advanced forms of education. Other women also enrolled in high schools, including some from immigrant and working-class backgrounds, but they faced obstacles that middle-class students did not. Typically, poorer women were required to work to help support their families, and they often married at earlier ages. Consequently, they did not graduate at the same rates as their middle and upper cohorts. Domestic feminism, it seems, favored the education of women most easily disposed to pursue schooling beyond the primary grades, and those comfortable with the role of transmitting American cultural traditions to the succeeding generations. Well-educated women were appealing as potential spouses, as they could prepare their children for success in school and life beyond it. In this respect, the growth of women's education was the very embodiment of cultural capital, a means of transferring valuable skills and knowledge consistent with social class differences in family roles and expectations (Hunter, 2002; Rury, 1988a, 1991).

The expansion of women's education, consequently, was a quiet revolution. The ideology of domestic feminism held that the new skills and knowledge acquired by educated women were not a threat to their traditional social roles. Higher levels of education did not mean that women were going to compete with men for positions of authority and leadership in society at large. Women's education, in that case, posed little challenge to traditional patriarchy. Because the numbers of women attending high schools and colleges were still relatively small, less than 10% of the relevant age cohort, female educational attainment hardly jeopardized the place of most men. Although there was some debate over women's education at the time, it generally did not concern a change in women's standing. The success of women's schooling, in the end, may have hinged on educators' inability—or unwillingness—to seriously challenge the status quo in gender relations.

## FOCAL POINT: EDWARD CLARKE AND THE DANGERS OF FEMALE EDUCATION

Not everyone was pleased with the development of female secondary and higher education in the late 19th century. Some conservatives were troubled by the prospect of coeducation, which seemed to imply that young men and women should receive precisely the same education. Others worried about the morality of teenage male and female students even mixing in the same building, and feared an epidemic of promiscuity. Catholic leaders, for example, denounced coeducation on these grounds. But perhaps the biggest uproar was occasioned by the publication of a slim volume in 1873 by physician Edward Clarke, titled *Sex in Education, or a Fair Chance for the Girls.* This book, which went through some 11 printings in just six years, claimed that extended academic and physical exertion was dangerous to young women, and that schooling during the teenage years threatened their health and prospects of fertility. The controversy that Clarke's book spawned revealed much both about Victorian beliefs concerning women and sexuality, and about popular attitudes regarding female education. It also underscored the magnitude of change in women's education (Zschoche, 1989).

Clarke was a one-time member of the Harvard medical faculty, and his modest academic pedigree added to his book's notoriety. The fact that he was from Boston, where conservative morality often prevailed in public discourse and institutional practice, no doubt contributed to the national debate that followed the book's publication. But Clarke did not ground his arguments in tradition and morality. Instead, he maintained that scientific evidence clearly indicated that exertion of the kind associated with school often presented the danger of infertility—or sterility—in young women. He argued that adolescence was a critical time in the physical development of women, when their reproductive organs took shape. During that period, he wrote, a young woman "accomplishes an amount of physiological cell change and growth which nature does not require of a boy in less than twice the number of years." The book featured a series of cases that Clarke claimed to know firsthand, discussed in a clinical fashion, which described high-school-aged girls suffering from anemia due to over-strenuous study. Such accounts were no doubt shocking to the sensibilities of most Victorian parents, and the aura of scientific respectability that Clarke lent to them gave the book credibility. To many families, the mere possibility of young women losing their ability to beget children was a specter too terrible to contemplate. It was this question that lay behind the book's considerable public appeal (Rosenberg, 1982).

The threat of infertility struck at the very heart of women's education, particularly as it was supported by the ideological formulation of domestic feminism. If schooling threatened to compromise a woman's capacity to bear children, after all, what was the point of being educated in the first place? The very object of female education was to become better mothers. If schooling somehow put motherhood itself in jeopardy, the logic of domestic feminism would seem to obviate the need or desire for education. Clarke's argument thus appeared to pose a dire hazard to the prospect of reform and growth in women's schooling (Rothman, 1978).

The challenge to women's education represented by Clarke and his book, it turned out, was a rather empty one. The response to his argument was swift and compelling. Within a year of its publication at least three other volumes appeared in print, challenging the idea that schooling was a danger to women's health. Educators across the country clamored to protest Clarke's suggestion that women should be discouraged from pursuing higher education. Several argued that women's health problems were the result of poor exercise and too much confinement indoors at home. Young women, they maintained, needed to get away from the house during the day, and to be stimulated intellectually and physically. They were able to cite dozens of cases of women flourishing at school, instances that seemed to directly contradict the evidence in Clarke's book. Echoing the arguments of others, former normal-school principal Anna Brackett argued that young women needed intellectual stimulation to thrive, and that boys and girls were "wonderfully alike" in their search for knowledge and understanding. To deny women the opportunity for education, she reasoned, would leave them "dwarfed and crippled," physically developed but "mentally a child." Statements such as these left little doubt where most of the nation's educators stood on the question. Although some conservatives rallied to Clarke's defense, his argument found relatively little support within the educational community. Despite the book's many editions and the attending public outcry, it ultimately did not exert much influence on the development of women's schooling (Rury, 1991; Tyack & Hansot, 1990).

This episode is telling, however, on a number of counts. Clarke's book sparked controversy because it touched on Victorian anxieties about female fragility and sexuality. At the same time that domestic feminism opened the door for greater female education, it also put women on pedestals in the name of virtue, morality, and motherhood. As suggested in the previous chapter, the idea of a revered but highly delimited role for women was an important component of 19th-century common-school ideology. Middle-class Americans thus often harbored contradictory feelings about women's education. Although they welcomed the growing opportunity for girls represented in the coeducational high schools and colleges, they also worried that new patterns of schooling might serve to compromise traditional gender roles. This partly accounted for the great public interest that Clarke's book provoked. In addition to this, 19th-century medical theories placed inordinate emphasis on the reproductive organs in explaining women's health, a by-product of the Victorian preoccupation with sexuality and motherhood as the preeminent female role. Consequently, the very fact that Clarke suggested that schooling could be linked to infertility was bound to draw attention to women's education (Degler, 1980; Hunter, 2002).

Nevertheless, in the end there were too many factors in support of women's education for critics like Clarke to stem its development. Among the many responses engendered by *Sex in Education* in the year following its publication was a thoughtful critique by William Torrey Harris, then superintendent of the St. Louis public schools (he eventually became U.S. Commissioner of Education). Harris noted that teaching boys and girls together seemed to be a natural arrangement, similar in practice to the ways they worked together in other settings, like the family and church. "It is in accordance with the spirit of institutions," he declared, "to treat women as self determining beings, and less in want of those external artificial barriers that were built ... in past times." In addition to this, Harris suggested that the girls exerted a positive influence on the boys, making them less unruly and acting as models of good behavior. "The rudeness and abandon which prevails among boys," he wrote, "at once gives place to self restraint in the presence of girls." Of course, Harris also appreciated the value of women teachers, and the importance of educated mothers, the major tenets of domestic feminism. But his principal motivations may have been quite practical, if not even penurious. Harris realized that without young women, high schools like the ones his own district had spent so much money building probably would not have been feasible. Female enrollments made these institutions viable; male students were too few in numbers and they tended to have lower graduation rates. Female high-school graduates also insured a supply of new teachers for the burgeoning urban districts. Given these considerations, it is little wonder that educators across the country vociferously rejected Clarke's arguments. Women's education was a key component of the emerging public school system, especially the rapidly expanding secondary schools (Reese, 1995; Rury, 1991).

Perhaps the most important element in the debate, however, was the experience that young women and their families encountered in the schools. For the most part, American parents who permitted their daughters to go to high school and college did not observe them getting sick or becoming sterile. Indeed, there is little systematic evidence that women's experiences in this regard were any different than those of young men. Female attendance in St. Louis, for instance, averaged only 2 percentage points less than boys over a 15-year period (94% vs 96%). Clearly, girls were not missing school in large numbers because of illness, and they also had lower dropout rates than the boys. If Clarke's book was intended to give parents some pause about female schooling, the experiences of their daughters were cause for reassurance. The vast majority of American high-school students were quite healthy, and the girls apparently were no more sickly than their male classmates (Rury, 1991).

Still, the old Victorian anxieties did not die easily. Popular beliefs about inherent differences between men and women were deeply ingrained, and were reinforced by the professional utterances of ministers, physicians, and a host of other pundits. Even if educators believed in the virtues of coeducation, they also took pains to insure that female students would not become overexerted, nor find themselves exposed to any unseemly influences. Consequently, it was commonplace for schools built in this era to feature separate doors and staircases for male and female students. Some educators warned against scheduling too many classes on higher floors for young women, as too many stair-climbing requirements might pose a danger. Others urged regular programs of exercise for female students, to help build stamina and combat anemia. Even the most outspoken advocates of coeducation continued to see women as frail, and in need of special attention to guarantee their health and vitality. The ideology of domestic feminism was pervasive, and it linked schooling inexorably to female roles of domesticity and motherhood. The very same ideas that served to expand women's education also defined the limits to which it might develop. This was the contradiction inherent in the controversy over Edward Clarke's otherwise unremarkable little book (Tyack & Hansot, 1990).

Coeducation and women's higher education continued to be points of contention for decades in the United States—and they still manage to get into the news today. Clarke's book, after all, was published just as the rapid expansion of female secondary and higher education began in the later 1800s. At the turn of the century, Teddy Roosevelt and other national leaders expressed concern about the low rate of marriage among college-educated women. Others worried about morality, especially as greater numbers of women began appearing on college campuses and images of "flappers" and dating began to appear in the 1920s. Such concerns, like Clarke's, represented the push of women's education against the boundaries of patriarchy and the ideology of domesticity that had defined women's lives through most of the history of American civilization. It was a tradition and set of cultural expectations that would change only slowly in the years to come (Gordon, 1990; Solomon, 1985).

## Education and Women's Roles

The foregoing begs an obvious query: what were the effects of these changes? If the quiet revolution in women's education did not challenge traditional gender roles, and the purpose of women's education was to prepare better wives and mothers, how did changing patterns of female schooling affect social change? This is a knotty issue, and a difficult one to address. One way to assess the impact of changes in women's education, however, is to consider its relationship to other areas of women's lives, such as work and social activism. Another way of posing the question, then, might be this: How did shifts in female education affect women's engagement with the larger world outside their immediate families? Did the revolution in women's education stimulate any appreciable change in other areas of women's lives?

There is a widespread consensus among historians that gender roles were shifting significantly in the later 19th century. This was the era of the early women's rights movement, of course, and activists such as Susan B. Anthony and Elizabeth Cady Stanton became nationally renowned, and also rather controversial. Much attention has focused on this group of women, especially in light of their campaigns for women's suffrage. There can be little doubt that expanding options for women's schooling contributed to the growth of this movement, as its most active members were themselves usually rather well educated. But the women's rights campaign was relatively small in spite of its notoriety. More significant were the thousands of women, most of them middle class, who became involved in other reform causes of the day. On issues ranging from temperance to universal peace and ending child labor, these women became immersed in a wide array of "social improvement" activities. They were in the forefront of the social settlement movement in the cities. Jane Addams's work at Hull House in Chicago is perhaps the best-known example, but there were scores of other women who worked in similar settings. They became active in local politics, and some were even elected to school boards and other offices in Western states, where liberal voting legislation permitted female participation. Women's clubs flourished across the country, and became vehicles for local reform campaigns on a host of issues. Female readers supported the first mass-circulation magazines focusing on social issues, and helped to make "muckraking" a potent political influence in the 1890s. In all of these respects, women contributed to the moral leadership of the nation, even if they were denied formal political power at the national ballot box. This also was a new development in American history, and by and large it was educated women who provided the leadership and the most active participants in these endeavors (Rendall, 1985; Rosenberg, 1982; Sklar, 1995).

Cultural historian Ann Douglas has suggested that the cumulative effect of the many changes that occurred in the later 19th century marked a "feminiza-tion of American culture." As middle-class women became more involved in social reform, they wielded a type of moral power that drew on their delim-ited but nevertheless exalted status as mothers and wives. If they were sup-posed to be inherently nurturing and virtuous in personal and family matters, after all, it followed that women should also represent a high ethical standard in social affairs. In the public mind, consequently, female reform activities became associated with the amelioration of social ills. But their intrinsic virtue, real or imagined, was only a part of the story. To function as effective reformers, these women needed highly refined organizational skills, advanced literacy and analytical capacities, and a cultivated sense of history and social change. Given this, it is little wonder that educated women played such a prominent part in the development of social reform. Schooling afforded women the skills and expansive viewpoint necessary to become effective agents of social improvement. They became capable speakers, good writers, and sharp-eyed social critics, examining a wide range of public problems and advocating any number of reforms. And at the same time they were denied conventional careers, more than a few women became outspoken reform figures and leaders of informal advocacy groups. In this regard, education contributed materially to the process of social change, even if female schooling was delimited and tended to reinforce traditional gender roles (Douglas, 1977; Harris, 1978; Sklar, 1995).

Social activism was just one area of change in White women's lives during the later 19th century; yet another quiet revolution was just getting underway in women's work. As noted earlier, girls and young women had been employed in factories since the early 19th century, and women teachers were commonplace in New England and elsewhere. But, beginning in the 1880s and 1890s, women started finding employment in offices and on the sales floors of early department stores. The invention of the typewriter in the 1880s spurred this development, a device some found inherently suitable for women by comparing it to piano playing, a presumably feminine talent. Even more important, however, was the rapid growth of office employment, stimulated by the development of large-scale industrial and retail enterprises serving national markets, and the governmental agencies created to supervise them. These new, massive firms required extensive correspondence and record-keeping, functions that called for legions of skilled workers. High-school-educated women constituted a ready pool of recruits for these positions, typically at a lower cost than men. The same tendency existed in the employment practices of the big department stores and catalogue houses then beginning to appear, such as Sears Roebuck and Montgomery Ward. The result was a new field of work for educated women: employment in a store or office. This was a respectable alternative to the factory, one that generally was clean, well lit, and involved contact with the upstanding public. The vast majority of women who took such positions were young and unmarried, and most left the labor force in a few years after they found a suitable marriage partner. The newly feminized workplace, it turned out, often provided a convenient setting for meeting potential suitors. This made such occupations all the more alluring in many instances. Without the changes in women's education, however, it is questionable whether the transition to female employment in these jobs would have occurred so quickly and easily (Davies, 1982; Kessler-Harris, 1982; Powers, 1992; Rotella, 1981).

Women moved into a number of other professions in the closing decades of the 19th century, most of them requiring one form or another of advanced education. The new research-oriented universities and professional schools admitted women, and eventually trained some to be professors, medical doctors, and lawyers. Although their numbers were tiny at the start, this indicated the beginning of a gradual transformation of women's work that would continue through the 20th century to the present. At the same time, the teaching profession underwent rapid feminization, and thousands of women found employment in the nation's schools. Many districts preferred unmarried female teachers, believing wives should be devoted to their families, and most left work after several years to be wed. This created an almost constant demand for new teachers, and young women eagerly answered the call. Even though their educational backgrounds varied, most had graduated from secondary school and a growing minority had attended colleges and normal schools. Thus, as the 19th century drew to a close, women began to appear in the ranks of what we would today call professional employment—another new development in American history. A key step in this process, of course, was women gaining access to higher education, and enrolling in colleges and professional schools, including normal schools, in ever-larger numbers. Here too, shifts in female education marked a prelude to changes in women's work (Goldin, 1990; MacDonald, 1999; Rothman, 1978; Solomon, 1985).

Changes in women's schooling, in that case, led to a number of subtle but important adjustments in female roles in the closing decades of the 19th century. It is important to recognize that only a minority of women participated in these developments, and for many others traditional role expectations and overt sexism continued to constrain their life opportunities. Most of the women who benefited from education were White and from middle- or upper-class backgrounds. But for those who had access to schooling, a transformation was underway. Women became active in public affairs and moved into new, higher-status fields of employment. Higher levels of education made these changes possible. And they would continue well into the next century, especially in the evolving workforce. In this regard, it is possible to say that education contributed directly to the process of social change, at least as regarded gender roles. In providing White, largely middle-class women with critical skills, knowledge, and credentials, it enabled them to challenge many of the restrictions that their mothers had faced, even if most of them eventually left the labor force to become mothers themselves. It certainly did not spell an end to patriarchy, and it marked a rather modest step in the long and continuing struggle over gender roles. But it was important nonetheless. This was a telling process of transition, one that appears even more significant in light of the experiences of other groups (Blackwelder, 1997).

## African American Education: Hope and Despair

If White middle-class women benefited from their commitment to education, other groups were not so fortunate. Like women, African Americans also have been subject to discrimination and exploitation throughout American history. As noted in Chapter 2, the very first schools for Blacks were intended to teach them morality and proper behavior, attributes White leaders thought they lacked. Of course, such schools served only a tiny fraction of the nation's African American population; the vast majority of them were slaves in the 18th and early 19th centuries. This meant that opportunities for education were extremely limited, although it would be wrong to assume that a significant degree of learning did not occur in slave communities. This created a great thirst for knowledge, and helped to make schooling an important priority for Black Americans.

Education has long been a major theme in African American culture. Dating from the early 19th century, Black leaders emphasized the significance of schools as instruments of social uplift. Even in slavery, when most African Americans were denied access to all forms of formal education, enterprising individuals made valiant efforts to acquire literacy and other skills. Virtually all Blacks recognized that lack of education was a mark of inferiority, one that seemed to legitimate their servile status and insure their political impotence. It is little wonder, in that case, that when slavery was formally abolished during the Civil War, African Americans rushed to educate their children in the schools opened during the conflict's aftermath. Schooling was seen as the road out of Canaan, the way to salvation.

Themes of resistance and redemption predominate in the history of Black education in the United States. During the slavery era and afterward, Blacks worked to maintain a cohesive cultural identity in the face of racist oppression. Formal education typically was denied to slaves, except for training afforded by masters interested in owning skilled workers, or lessons learned in church or from friendly Whites, often children. However, after the bloody and much sensationalized rebellion by the messianic slave preacher Nat Turner and his followers in 1831, and the rise of the abolitionist movement at about the same time, several states outlawed instruction of any sort for slaves, and such prescriptions were informally observed elsewhere. To be caught merely in possession of a book was cause for severe, even cruel punishment (Bond, 1966; Bullock, 1967).

But laws and brute coercion could not halt the process of acculturation within the slave community. Important lessons were passed from one generation to another, representing a rich cultural tradition that has left a lasting imprint on the South. Storytelling was a venerable tradition and a highly refined craft in the quarters. Slave children were taught from an early age to honor and respect their elders and to preserve family and community traditions, and at the same time they had to resist the efforts of Whites to exploit and abuse them. While doing this, they had to display deference to Whites, and to be sure not to openly transgress the many unwritten rules that governed race relations in the antebellum South. Many managed to gain literacy illegally, and passed these skills along to others. They struggled to assert their humanity in spite of Whites' efforts to rationalize slavery by comparing them to animals. In doing this, they cultivated a set of beliefs asserting the moral superiority of African Americans over their insensate oppressors, and a folklore emphasizing the exceptional resourcefulness and prowess Blacks demonstrated as a result of persecution. Above all, they expressed the desire for freedom, and the ability to determine their own destinies. Education—to attain self-improvement—was a central element of this tradition, and hence a major theme in African American culture (Blassingame, 1972; Mintz, 2004; Webber, 1978).

In the Northern states, where slavery had been ended earlier in the century, free Blacks worked assiduously to establish schools for their struggling communities, or to modify those handed down from philanthropic Whites, such as New York's Manumission Society. They often were assisted in these efforts by the growing abolitionist movement, visionary Whites and free Blacks demanding an immediate end to slavery. In the larger cities, such schools—the legacy of the Manumission Society's African Free Schools—eventually became vital Black community institutions. With support from philanthropists, these schools served a largely destitute population, as even educated Blacks struggled to gain middle-class status in the face of pervasive discrimination. A generation of Black leaders received their formal training in this way, and they provided a foundation for higher levels of schooling for African Americans chartered by White abolitionists and other humanitarian patrons. By mid-century the basic elements of an educational system for Blacks were being assembled in the North, with separate colleges and manual training schools just being founded or planned, although some African Americans were educated at White colleges too. These institutions, along with a tiny but earnest cadre of well-educated Black leaders, became models for the development of an educational system to serve the much larger African American population of the South after the Civil War (Curry, 1981; Litwack, 1961).

Despite these positive developments, 19th-century African American education was quite different from that catering to other groups. In this respect it reflected the powerful influence of racist ideology during this era. First, it was almost always segregated, and it often encountered fierce resistance from Whites, who recurrently felt threatened by the prospect of a skilled and knowledgeable African American population. Although school leaders argued that boys and girls should attend the same schools, even the most liberal reformers shrank from the suggestion that Blacks and Whites should be educated together. Even Horace Mann, champion of the common school and an outspoken opponent of slavery, would not endorse it. Popular reactions sometimes were violent; schools for Blacks were burned and their teachers run out of town. This was a contrast to the response to women's education, which prompted bitter debates but never led to such violent outbursts. Second, when Black schooling was provided, it typically had strong moralistic or vocational overtones. This was a tendency evident from the beginning, as in the Manumission Society's school in the later 18th century. Generally speaking, few Whites believed that African Americans could benefit from advanced academic study. Instead, they usually were given a curriculum that emphasized good behavior and preparation for a life of manual labor. From the very start, then, Black schooling was separate and unequal (Horsman, 1981; Moss, 2006; Rury, 1983, 1985; Schultz, 1973).

Soon after the Civil War ended in 1865, the victorious North set about changing the social and political order of the South, a process referred to as *Reconstruction*. This was no small task, and there was much debate and conflict about just how to accomplish it. But even before hostilities had ended, the federal government created the Freedman's Bureau, an organization charged with supervising the transition of former slaves to their new status as free citizens. A major aspect of the new agency's task was to provide schools for the freedmen, to give them critical literacy skills and citizenship education. Over the next several years thousands of these schools were established, staffed by idealistic teachers recruited from the North, along with some White Southerners and a growing number of Blacks. Local African American communities donated hard-earned cash and labor to establish still more schools, and to expand upon the government contributions. Tens of thousands of Black families eagerly enrolled their children in these institutions, delighted at the opportunity to receive even a modicum of formal education. The high degree of consensus in their communities no doubt represented a potent stock of social capital, shared values regarding schooling. Throughout much of the South, enrollment of African American students matched or exceeded those of Whites, eventually reaching a quarter million students of all ages. Although the circumstances of these schools were not always stable, and attendance fluctuated as African Americans struggled in a changing Southern economy, Black literacy rates began to improve significantly. In 1860 only a small fraction of the region's then mostly slave Black population could read, but by 1890 more than two-thirds were literate. Reconstruction truly marked a revolution in the lives of former slaves, and education was an important aspect of this process of change (Butchart, 1980; Fairclough, 2007; Foner, 1988; Morris, 1981).

The rise of Black schooling during Reconstruction was accompanied by a remarkable period of political empowerment and activism for the former slave population. With their basic rights affirmed by passage of the 14th and

15th Amendments to the U.S. Constitution, and enfranchised by the new state constitutions required for reentry to the union, African Americans found themselves able to vote and hold office for the first time. The result was a glorious moment of political potency, when former slaves came to occupy critical positions of leadership across the region. Black leaders led a movement to form new, liberalized state governments. Education provisions were written into new constitutional documents, and additional support for public schools was legislated. Such changes were especially galling to Southern Whites, who complained bitterly about occasional improprieties or excesses in the wake of these events. The most die-hard racists plotted a counterrevolution, and launched a violent war against the Reconstruction regimes in various states (DuBois, 1935; Foner, 1988; Franklin, 1961).

Unfortunately, the progress made during the decade or so of Reconstruction was not enduring. Northern Whites lost interest in reforming the South following the economic recession of 1873, and the federal military occupation ended, permitting a resurgence of White supremacist rule. The change was not altogether abrupt, for the Ku Klux Klan and other White racist groups had rained terror on Blacks and reform-minded Whites all during Reconstruction. But by the late 1870s there were abundant signs of the old order returning to power. With the great compromise of 1877, when presidential candidate Rutherford B. Hayes agreed to withdraw the last federal troops from the South in exchange for political support, an arrangement leading to his election, Reconstruction finally came to a close. This meant changes in many areas of life, but it also marked an end to the rapid expansion of Black schooling experienced in the years immediately following the war (Foner & Mahoney, 1995).

Without the protection of federal soldiers Blacks were gradually stripped of many basic rights. At the same time, African American political power was dramatically curtailed. By the end of Reconstruction more than 300 Blacks had been elected to state legislatures or to Congress. There was one U.S. senator and a governor too. It was these leaders who had spearheaded the development of Southern school systems, and they played key roles in drafting new state constitutions to support public education. By 1880, however, their numbers had dropped by two-thirds, and shrank even further in the years that followed. The result was an abrupt change in the region's political culture, with liberal influences sharply circumscribed. Black leaders, especially those who sought political power, and the Northern Whites who assisted them, came under pointed attack from the resurgent White Southern power structure. From the earliest days of Reconstruction, Northern Whites were called "carpetbaggers" and sympathetic Southern Whites "scallywags." It was after these struggles, during the 1890s, that Southern states initiated poll taxes or other devices to limit Black voting rights, and the region's African American population was reduced once again to a state of dependency on the local

White establishment. It was not a historical situation that held much promise for advancing the cause of Black rights, and schooling suffered accordingly (Ayers, 1992; Williamson, 1984; Woodward, 1974).

Southern Whites were never enamored of Black education, and even if they did not dismantle the schools established for African Americans, they were not about to provide them with anything more than the most basic resources. The more bigoted among them believed that "Anglo-Saxon" Southerners were the most "cultivated" race, and therefore deserved the vast bulk of school resources (VanOverbeke, 2008). As a number of historians have documented, the decades following Reconstruction marked a time of widening disparities in Black and White education throughout the South, many linked to differences in state funding. Although there is evidence that Black schooling continued to flourish for a time, differences began to grow when Southern Whites finally became interested in education. Term lengths in Black schools had stagnated by the 1890s, whereas those in the White schools began to increase, even approaching the standard of the Northern states, 150 days or more per year. Black teachers were paid much less than their White counterparts, and were permitted only tiny allocations for textbooks and other supplies. Where there had been some measure of parity in the past, school districts came to spend as little on a typical Black student as one-fifth the amount that they expended for an average White student. Public secondary schools for African Americans were relatively scarce in the South in the later 19th century, the very time when secondary schools were starting to be built in greater numbers elsewhere—and for Southern Whites. Consequently, Black schooling was generally limited to the most rudimentary forms of elementary education, with short sessions and paltry assistance. Except for a tiny group of middle-class African Americans who could afford to send their children to the handful of private Black high schools and colleges, the vast majority of the Black population was provided with no more than basic skills in reading and calculation. Even if this helped to boost overall rates of literacy among Blacks, it did little to assist their political or economic advancement (Anderson, 1988; Harlan, 1958).

As historian James D. Anderson has pointed out, the underlying problem facing African Americans was their ongoing role of servitude in the political economy of the South. In a region still dependent on a cash-crop agricultural economy, the Black population's arduous physical labor was essential to the wealth of the White elite. African Americans were no longer slaves, but they still had to make a living within the existing economic order. Radical proposals to give the freedmen land after the war, expressed in the slogan "forty acres and a mule," were never endorsed by the federal authorities, so Blacks were forced to return to the plantations many of them had abandoned upon attaining freedom. Various forms of indentured servitude replaced slavery, usually under the guise of "sharecropping." For African Americans who tried to escape to the cities, as many did, new forms of occupational segregation were devised, relegating them to the most menial forms of unskilled labor at the lowest wages. For women in the towns and cities, domestic service became a near universal form of employment, as they kept the homes of middle- and upper-class Whites throughout the South. In short, the old order was restored, albeit in a somewhat new bearing. After the heady experience of Reconstruction had passed, the familiar Southern status hierarchy reemerged in a different form, with Blacks on the bottom rung and wealthy landowners and other Whites on the top (Anderson, 1988; Margo, 1990).

It is important to acknowledge the critical role of racist ideology in offering a set of justifications for these changes. Racism reinforced the servile status of African Americans, and helped to mobilize poor Whites against political challenges to the old order. Theories and myths of Black inferiority abounded, often in even more virulent form than during slavery. Still smarting from the experience of Reconstruction, when Blacks enjoyed basic rights and a modicum of political power, many Whites were determined to prevent any such changes from occurring again. As a consequence, Southern Whites were rarely proponents of Black schooling. Rather, their interests lay in maintaining the abject status of African Americans, as it insured a ready source of labor for harvesting cotton and tobacco. Schooling, it was said, only ruined a good field hand or servant, making him or her less willing to perform menial tasks and endure long hours of labor. Because most Southern Whites wanted a compliant and reliable Black workforce, they resisted efforts to improve African American education (Fredrickson, 1971; Higgs, 1977).

By and large, education remained underdeveloped throughout the region. Schools of any kind had rarely been a priority in most Southern states, and plantation owners generally were inherently suspicious of the idea that common folk—White or Black—should be educated. Many found the very idea of popular democracy to be abhorrent, and believed that the spread of education threatened to undermine the region's traditional economic and political order. Even during the common-school era, reformers waged uphill struggles to establish even the most basic rudiments of statewide school systems—and they were far less developed than in the North and West. This changed somewhat after the Civil War, as Southern states were forced to adhere to Northern expectations in order to regain admission to the union. In the period when African Americans enjoyed a brief period of political influence during Reconstruction, they spearheaded the creation of systems of public schooling across the region. But with the end of Reconstruction, most states cut back drastically on spending for education, and granted much smaller subsidies to Black schools than to White ones. African American education, despite the ferment and accomplishments of the Reconstruction period, was stillborn. It would not be until the 20th century that new advances would be evident (Bullock, 1967; Harlan, 1958; Leloudis, 1996).

## FOCAL POINT: THE GREAT DEBATE ABOUT BLACK EDUCATION

In the decades following the Civil War there was much discussion and conflict over the direction and role of African American education. As indicated earlier, there was a long-standing tradition in the United States of focusing Black schooling on issues of moral development and vocational education. These were important themes in schooling for Whites too, but for them there also was an emphasis on intellectual development, citizenship education, and the cultivation of future leaders. Proposals for Black schooling often downplayed these latter considerations, because either Whites found such ideas threatening, or racist ideology dictated that African Americans were unlikely to benefit from them. Whatever the rationale, avenues for advanced intellectual training remained severely limited for Blacks throughout much of the 19th century, even after other educational opportunities—such as common schooling and manual training—had become more commonplace. Still, new prospects for advanced academic preparation did begin to appear in the South just before the close of the period, with many of them started and financed by African American communities. Through these efforts, an articulate class of well-educated Blacks gradually emerged on the national stage, offering new ways of thinking about African American education. As a consequence of this development, one of the great educational debates of American history began to unfold.

The principal antagonists in this conflict were two of the towering African American figures of the age: Booker T. Washington and W. E. B. DuBois. Washington was the older of the two, and without doubt the more prominent at the close of the century. Raised as a slave during his childhood in Virginia, he had been educated in the 1870s at Hampton Institute under the tutelage of its first director, General Samuel Armstrong. Reflecting the singular influence of his mentor, Washington was an avid proponent of the virtues of manual and industrial training for African Americans. In his own experience at Hampton, he had been deeply impressed by the power of physical labor to impart self-discipline and a spirit of self-improvement in students, and in himself in particular. When he became principal at Alabama's Tuskegee Training Institute in 1881, Washington had acquired a vehicle to develop his own educational philosophy, and a platform from which he could proclaim it to the world. Within a decade he was the nation's leading proponent of industrial education for African Americans. It was an idea that was hardly new, but one that was to receive fresh prominence as a result of his influence (Harlan, 1972, 1983).

DuBois's experience could scarcely have been more different from that of Washington. Born free in the North, DuBois was educated in the Great Barrington, Massachusetts, public schools before attending Fisk University in Nashville and pursuing graduate studies in Europe. He also studied at Harvard, earning a B.A. degree and becoming the first

African American in that university's history to receive the Ph.D. in 1895. Himself the beneficiary of a classical education, DuBois was an advocate of advanced academic preparation for African Americans. He felt that Blacks needed thoughtful and articulate leaders to assess and express the injustices that they had suffered and to formulate strategies to improve their status. To his mind, the traditional emphasis on manual training in African American education was an indignity, and an obstacle preventing Blacks from realizing meaningful gains in their political and economic standing. Accordingly, DuBois recommended the education of a "talented tenth" to provide an inspired and socially conscious leadership for the nation's African American population. These individuals would constitute an intellectual vanguard, challenging racist oppression with the ideals of democracy, legal principles of equity and fairness, and appeals to the nation's moral conscience. It was a visionary and in some respects a naive proposal, but DuBois believed it absolutely critical to the future (Lewis, 1993; Meier, 1963).

Between the two men, Washington was more widely recognized and celebrated during his time. This was partly due to the accommodating quality of his public utterances, which made him especially popular among many influential Whites. In his most famous public address, at the opening session of the Atlanta Exposition in 1895, Washington invoked the metaphor of a ship searching for fresh water to represent African Americans. He called upon them to "cast down your bucket where you are—cast it down in making friends in every manly way of the people of all races by whom we are surrounded." He urged Blacks to look to Southern Whites for economic opportunity, and to accept their place in society, seeking improvement through honest hard work. He emphasized the loyalty and familiarity of Blacks over immigrant workers, and endorsed acceptance of Jim Crow segregation, declaring, "in all things that are purely social we can be separate as the fingers, yet one as the hand in all things essential to mutual progress." Characteristically, Washington dispensed ridicule on African Americans who sought higher learning. "No race can prosper," he declared in Atlanta, "till it learns that there is as much dignity in tilling a field as in writing a poem," adding, "it is at the bottom of life that we must begin and not at the top." Elsewhere he offered biting caricatures of lazy Blacks seeking education as a way of avoiding hard labor, or educated African Americans who lacked the character imparted by work of any kind. In his widely read autobiography, *Up from Slavery*, Washington noted the high level of interest in schooling among Blacks, but suggested that it posed a problem. "The idea ... was too prevalent that, as soon as one secured a little education," he wrote, "in some unexplainable way he would be free from most of the hardships of the world, and, at any rate, could live without manual labor" (Harlan, 1972; Luker, 1991). While such sentiments may have reflected Southern realities, they certainly did not urge greater attainment for African Americans.

Washington could not voice too much opposition to education, however, as he ran a school himself and was known internationally as an educator. But he represented a certain kind of schooling. In describing his own institution, Washington emphasized the practical lessons imparted through manual labor, declaring, "We wanted to teach them to study actual things instead of mere books alone." In this respect, the Tuskegee model of African American education conformed closely to that advocated by prominent Whites for decades, one intended to teach Blacks good work habits and sound moral principles. Interestingly, Washington's critique of educated Blacks also echoed the sentiments of many other Whites, who believed that schooling only made African Americans less willing to perform menial labor. Perhaps to avoid this, he was always careful to point out the centrality of work to every aspect of his educational philosophy. It is little wonder, in that case, that Washington was so popular among the nation's White leaders; his stature among African Americans, however, was another matter (Anderson, 1988; Kliebard, 1999; Litwack, 1999).

DuBois was finishing his Harvard training at the time of Washington's famous address in Atlanta. He spent the next decade teaching at various Black colleges in the South and conducting research on the conditions of African American life in the United States. In 1903 he published *The Souls of Black Folk*, in many respects a response to the appearance of Washington's autobiography just two years earlier. In direct opposition to the views expressed by Washington, DuBois argued that higher education was the most pressing task facing African Americans. Without the broadest and most intellectually challenging academic preparation, he asked, how would Black leaders be prepared to provide guidance and raise up their brethren? With no colleges and universities, he wondered, where would the faculty for Black secondary schools—or even Washington's Tuskegee—come from? No educational system, DuBois declared, "ever has rested or can rest on any other basis than that of a well equipped college and university." Without higher education, in other words, there would be no advanced learning, and no prospect of general improvement for the South's Black population (Lewis, 1993).

To DuBois's mind, the time to focus attention on industrial training of the sort practiced at Tuskegee had long passed. Sharply critical of Washington, DuBois described his views as "a gospel of Work and Money to such an extent as apparently almost completely to overshadow the higher aims of life." If the African American population was to change its status of servitude and political impotence, a new form of education would be necessary. "The foundations of knowledge in this race, as in others," he wrote, "must be sunk deep in the college and university if we would build a solid, permanent structure." This, of course, was a direct contradiction of Washington's oft-repeated view that higher education for Blacks was a waste of time and resources. But it was only through the leadership of university-trained Black men and women that DuBois thought real advancement was possible

(Meier, 1963). He would eventually shift his perspective, when it became clear that college-educated Blacks were not always helpful in the struggle for social justice, but at the turn of the century DuBois was among the nation's most outspoken proponents of African American higher education (Alridge, 2008).

As DuBois noted in *The Souls of Black Folk*, Washington's most outspoken critics were members of his own race, particularly those who had been trained in universities and were involved in Black higher education. His most glowing admirers were wealthy Whites, especially philanthropists eager to help advance the cause of education in the South. As a consequence, Tuskegee and other institutions representing Washington's philosophy of industrial education received a steady stream of contributions from wealthy Northerners, amounting to millions of dollars in the years following Washington's ascendancy. Other African American institutions also received assistance, but explicit pressures to conform to the Tuskegee model of manual training often accompanied it. In time this became an important source of resentment among African American educators across the region. There also was a perception that Washington was widely hailed as a Black leader even though he did not represent any particular African American constituency, apart from his own institution. When Washington was extolled in the White press, many Blacks naturally felt pride that an African American was being praised, but others came to resent his statements advocating a delimited form of education and accommodation to the existing Jim Crow social order. Even if Booker T. Washington was held up as a role model, he was hardly universally admired (Anderson, 1988; Anderson & Moss, 1999; Hawkins, 1962; Moss, 1981).

In terms of the educational system of the day, there is no question about the winner of this debate over the future of Black education. Tuskegee was the most widely emulated and influential African American institution of its time. Until his death in 1915, Washington was the most famous and powerful Black man in the United States. Tuskegee-trained teachers fanned out across the region, spreading the gospel of industrial education through Black high schools and teacher-training institutes. DuBois dubbed this the "Tuskegee Machine," but it was not enduring. Instead, another legacy eventually came to shape the future of African American education and Black social and political aspirations. Almost from the beginning, many Black educators and institutions resisted the Tuskegee model of vocational training, preferring to focus on academic subjects and preparing ministers and other professionals. Even Tuskegee shifted its curriculum in this direction in the 20th century. Frustrated by the impotent political vision of Washington and accommodationist Black leaders of the time, DuBois and other reform-minded African Americans formed the Niagara Movement in 1909, representing a series of meetings to discuss the problems of race and inequality in the United States and potential solutions. Within a few years, these forums gave birth to a new civil rights organization, the National Association for the Advancement of Colored People (NAACP). DuBois served as the first editor of its magazine, *The Crisis*. Though not as well known, nor as influential as Washington's "Tuskegee Machine" at the time, this new association would eventually hold the keys to advancement for African American social and political status in the 20th century. And this made the question of who "won" the great debate over Black education a telling example of abiding change in policy and politics (Fairclough, 2007; Harlan, 1983; Lewis, 1993).

## The Degradation of Black Education

By the end of the 19th century the lives of most African Americans in the South had reached a low point. The gains that they had made during Reconstruction had been largely wiped out. Most were poor agricultural workers living in a state of virtual serfdom. The educational advances of the 1860s and 1870s had been rolled back. Even more important, Blacks had been stripped of even the most basic of civil rights. The 1890s were a time of political turmoil in the South, as the populist movement, an alliance of poor farmers and sharecroppers, challenged the established regime. In the wake of these tumultuous events, thousands of African Americans were murdered—most of them publicly lynched—for a variety of purported reasons, ranging from the petty to the profane. Lynching was a practice that dated back to the days of Reconstruction, but it reached new levels of severity as the century drew to a close, and it continued for decades in the 20th century. The effect was palpable in the lives of African Americans. Echoing many other such observations, the novelist Richard Wright wrote "the safety of my life in the South depended upon how well I concealed from all whites what I felt." Whatever the circumstances, these developments offered a powerful lesson in political education, viciously affirming the region's doctrine of White supremacy. It helped to create an ideological milieu that hardly boded well for the development of African American education (Ayers, 1992; Mintz, 2004, p. 116; Williamson, 1984).

As historian Louis Harlan has documented, the period around 1900 and immediately afterward witnessed a dramatic expansion of White education in the South, much of it accomplished at the expense of the region's Black population. Disparities between the schooling of children from the two races reached historic highs, with White children receiving as much as ten times the local expenditures on Black education. In the most heavily populated Black regions, the so-called "Black-belt" where big plantations and the cotton economy still held sway, White education was subsidized by Black taxpayers. More high schools were established, but by 1910 just 65 such institutions had been established for a Black population numbering more than ten million, and many were small. Apart from schoolteaching and the ministry, there were few professional jobs that young African Americans could aspire to. By and large, the education system for Southern Blacks was designed to enforce their servile status and to insure political and economic impotence. Apart from a handful of private or otherwise elite institutions largely supported by Northern philanthropy, it primarily offered education for degradation (Anderson, 1988; Anderson & Moss, 1999; Harlan, 1958).

The relatively small Black population of the North, only one-tenth of all African Americans, had access to considerably better educational opportunities. Studies indicate that African American school enrollment was equivalent to that of most Whites, and often higher than that of recent immigrants. Their school terms were as long as those for Whites, probably longer on average because most Northern Blacks lived in cities, where the most advanced school systems existed. And in a growing number of places, public schools were formally integrated, even if residential segregation made true racial diversity difficult to find. But despite their relatively elevated levels of educational attainment, African Americans encountered great trouble in gaining employment commensurate with their credentials. In his intensive study of social mobility in a Northern city during this period, Joel Perlmann discovered that Blacks benefited the least from education, even though their overall levels of enrollment were higher than those of the Irish, Italians, and a number of other European immigrant groups. Racism permeated the job market, and served to dramatically counteract the benefits of schooling for African Americans. In many cities they competed with the Irish and other immigrants, sometimes encountering violent resistance, but failed to advance as much as the various White ethnic groups. And while this was true in the urban North, discrimination was especially pernicious in the South, where White supremacy was even more thoroughly ingrained in the popular consciousness (Franklin, 1979; Ignatev, 1995; Mohraz, 1979; Perlmann, 1988).

All things considered, frustration and disappointment stalked the educational experiences of African Americans in the latter 19th century. Blacks flocked to schools in the years following the Civil War, only to see their opportunities circumscribed after Reconstruction. They fought to establish modern educational systems across the South, and then witnessed a resurgence of White supremacy that denied them basic civil rights and elevated White schools over their own. They encountered racism at almost every turn, but especially in the labor market, where their training was often considered irrelevant, if not an impairment. Where Black education did succeed, it was often designed to train students for menial employment, or to provide preparation for a very narrow range of professional positions. Altogether, it was not a happy story. African American schooling in the later 19th century represents an instance when hard work and investment in education did not result in meaningful social change. Virulent racism effectively negated any potential gains in cultural and human capital that formal education offered, and sharply restricted the benefits to be realized from social capital to the meager resources of most Black communities. In the end, the school could not materially improve the status—nor change the basic social roles—of most of the nation's Black population. A considerably more prolonged process of social and political change would be necessary to accomplish that end (Litwack, 1999).

## Schooling American Indians

If African Americans were subject to servitude, the American Indians (or Native Americans) were assaulted by military force, driven from their territories, and compelled to adapt their cultures and traditions to radically new circumstances. Perhaps the central series of educational events for this diverse assortment of groups in the 19th century was their collective experience of loss at the hands of Whites (or European Americans), who forcibly relocated them to isolated reservations. This was accompanied by a series of campaigns by Whites to change the lifestyles and beliefs of American Indians, to eradicate their traditional culture and replace it with the Christian and capitalist values of the nation's dominant groups. The principal vehicle enlisted to accomplish this was the school. The story of Native American education in the 19th century involved a deliberate crusade to fundamentally alter an indigenous way of life, utilizing instruction as a means of instilling new values and behavior on a scale not exercised with other groups. As historian David Wallace Adams poignantly observed, it was "education for extinction" (Adams, 1995).

By the end of the 19th century the era of open warfare against the American Indians had drawn to a close. Battered by almost constant conflict with European settlers, and steadily losing land and resources, the Native American population in the United States had dropped from perhaps 2 million in 1800 to about 250,000—its lowest point in modern history. In the meantime, the countryside had been settled by Whites, who eventually came to outnumber the indigenous peoples by more than a 50:1 ratio. Once the period of active conflict on the frontier had started to wind down, and the bulk of the American Indian population was settled on reservations, sympathetic Whites began to comment on what became widely termed "the Indian Problem." As they saw it, American Indians were not adjusting well to their future roles as potential citizens, and as parents of upright, responsible offspring. Instead, they were seen as living in "filth" and "squalor," without appreciation of the virtues of private property, individual responsibility, and decent standards of cleanliness and personal hygiene. The answer was an aggressive campaign of education to teach American Indians the advantages of modern civilization (Hoxie, 1984; Prucha, 1976).

Native Americans had long practiced their own forms of education, of course, a process of acculturation that varied from one tribal group to another. American Indian children traditionally learned while working alongside adults, accompanying them to the fields and hunting grounds, and being allowed progressively greater responsibilities in adult tasks. Given the rather sharp division of labor along gender lines in most tribal societies, education also usually differed for males and females. Children were told stories of their ancestors and learned legends about the history of their tribes. Elderly members of the tribal group often served as great repositories of wisdom, furnishing explanations for complex natural phenomena and suggesting solutions to difficult social and political dilemmas. With a few prominent exceptions, such as the Cherokee, however, Native Americans rarely organized separate, formal institutions to educate the young, and illiteracy was usually a norm. Instead, education was a largely informal process, conducted within the everyday events that defined life, and was not intended to impart such academic skills as reading and writing (Axtell, 1985; Fuchs & Havighurst, 1972).

Protestant and Catholic missionaries, intent on converting them to Christianity and introducing basic literacy and commercial skills, established the earliest schools for American Indians. As noted in Chapter 2, a number of experiments in indigenous education were conducted in the 18th century, most with limited success. These efforts gradually intensified in the next century. The Bureau of Indian Affairs (or BIA) was established as a branch of the War Department in 1824, and helped to supervise efforts to deliver education to the Native American population, most of which were conducted by religious groups. By the mid-19th century dozens of missionary schools had been started, but they reached only a tiny fraction of the American Indian school-aged population, less than a couple of thousand per year. It was not until the period after the Civil War, however, when hostilities between Native Americans and the federal government reached a peak, that interest in broadening indigenous education began to take hold (Berkhofer, 1965; Szasz, 1988).

Starting with the presidency of Ulysses S. Grant in the 1880s, educational programs were run directly by the BIA, rather than through missionary groups, as a part of the federal government's "Peace Policy" toward American Indians. Thereafter, appropriations increased rapidly, climbing from $20,000 in 1870 to nearly $3 million in 1900. Schools and enrollments multiplied quickly too. In the mid-1970s there were about 150 schools enrolling several thousand students, but by the end of the century the number of institutions had more than doubled and enrollments exceeded 20,000. This represented roughly half of the age-eligible indigenous population. These changes in federal policy constituted a massive intervention into the lives of American Indian children (Coleman, 1993; Hoxie, 1984).

The statistical growth of these schools, however, was only part of the story. The goals of this educational program were even more ambitious than previous reform ventures, including the schools for African Americans established during Reconstruction. The vast majority of these American Indian students, more than 80%, attended special boarding schools intended to separate them from the influence of their families and tribal customs. Others attended day schools. The first boarding institution, and most famous, was in Carlisle, Pennsylvania. Established in 1879 in an abandoned military barracks by Richard Henry Pratt, a former army officer and veteran of the "Indian Wars," the Carlisle school became a model for similar institutions across the country. Modeled after residential schools for African Americans, especially the Hampton Institute where Booker T. Washington had studied, it was dedicated to inculcating proper work habits and apposite manners. It also became quite famous for its football teams, which competed successfully against top colleges (Adams, 1995; Coleman, 1993).

Pratt fervently believed in the superiority of modern civilization over indigenous cultures, and predicted that Native American children could be changed for the better if placed in the right environment. "Transfer the savage-born infant to the surroundings of civilization," he declared, "and he will grow to possess a civilized language and habit." The goal of the government-funded boarding schools, in that case, was to obliterate any traces of American Indian traditions and identity in their students, and to inculcate the virtues of patriotism and Christian propriety. In the words of Pratt, they were intended to "kill the Indian in him and save the man" (Adams, 1995).

Clearly, one intention of this new direction in federal policy toward American Indians was the pacification of a potentially hostile indigenous population. A major problem, however, was devising ways to get their children into the schools. As suggested by the early enrollment figures, not many indigenous parents initially were eager to send their children to Carlisle or other boarding schools. But large numbers eventually were convinced to give the schools a try. Some of these parents wanted their children to learn the ways of Whites, while others felt pressured to conform to what they believed was a government policy of mandatory schooling. Through a combination of active recruitment, gruff coercion, and personal persuasion, thousands of American Indian students eventually did attend these institutions, most of them for terms of less than a few years. Despite its limited appeal, the federal network of American Indian boarding schools became one of the largest experiments in deliberate cultural revision in the nation's history (Szasz, 1977).

While on campus, Native American students were offered a course of study focused on manual training and moral development, not dissimilar to the curriculum at Booker T. Washington's Tuskegee Institute. Pratt even initiated a program that allowed Carlisle students to live with White families for a period of months, gaining work experience while learning firsthand mainstream standards of living. The reaction of students was mixed. Many learned to read and calculate, while gaining valuable insight into conventional American customs, and even recalled their experiences with pleasure. Others rebelled and returned as soon as possible to the reservation, some running away in the middle of the night. But whether they graduated or not, and regardless of how they felt about their experiences, very few indigenous students became assimilated into the larger Euro-American society as a result of their boarding-school experiences. The duration of schooling was too brief, and barriers to assimilation too great, for education alone to accomplish such a purpose (Adams, 1995).

The failure of its assimilationist goals was only partly the result of the shortsighted policies of the BIA. Apart from the narrowly vocational quality of the schools, and their strong moralistic overtone, White attitudes toward American Indians proved to be perhaps the greatest barrier to acclimation. This was especially evident when the schools attempted to place Indian students with White families to encourage acculturation. Although they did occasionally encounter hostility, Native Americans often were treated as aliens and objects of curiosity. Most had not yet been granted citizenship. Many were exploited by ruthless or racist Whites, forced to work long hours in demeaning jobs with little pay. Not feeling welcome in the larger society, the vast majority returned to the reservations, where they assumed the lifestyle of their families and neighbors. In this respect the boarding-school experiment was a failure, and Richard Pratt's vision of a "civilized" American Indian was ultimately unrealized. The cultural identities of indigenous children, it turned out, were considerably stronger than Pratt and other educators had imagined. And most other Americans were not interested in making them comfortable as participants in the nation's mainstream culture. Indeed, racist ideology was so pervasive that it proved a formidable barrier to integration even for American Indians, a group that had never been widely enslaved or economically exploited. It would take more than a few years of schooling aimed at intentional assimilation to effect change on this scale (Coleman, 1993; Gould, 1981; Horsman, 1981).

The boarding-school movement eventually lost its momentum, shortly after Pratt's generation of educators passed from the scene, and ultimately a more comprehensive and culturally sensitive set of policies was adopted. This occurred after the famous Merriam Report of 1928, which marked a major shift in thinking about American Indians. It was clear that the boarding schools had done little to acculturate indigenous students to traditional Protestant culture in the United States. BIA education expenditures also did not change the social and political standing of American Indians. In the hands of overbearing and misguided reformers like Pratt, and backed by the political will and resources of the federal government, schooling was intended to alter the values and behavior of a significant element of the Indian population. Of course, many such measures were undertaken in goodwill, with the belief that assimilation represented a distinct improvement in the lives of most Native Americans. But unlike the case of African Americans during Reconstruction, reformers did not take account of the wishes of the proposed subjects of this educational experiment. With a few exceptions, American Indians were not clamoring for schools, and they attached relatively little value to the formal instruction offered in the institutions established for them. Consequently, the effect of education on the values and social standing of this group was minimal (Szasz, 1974, 1977).

The case of American Indian education constitutes one of history's clearest examples of schooling being used consciously to effect social change—indeed, to effect dramatic cultural modification. But in this case education did little to alter the role or status of a marginal group in American society—in this instance yet another racial minority. With regard to indigenous education, reformers had clearly overestimated the power of schooling to effect change. Yet it is not clear that they ever seriously recognized the possibility of failure; nor did they understand the limits of education as an agent of social transformation. Cultural chauvinism, abetted by racism and nationalism, blinded these would-be reformers to the enormity of the task that they had undertaken and the larger problems associated with assimilation into American life. In the end, social change of this magnitude was more than schools alone could achieve, even under the most enlightened circumstances. Given the paternalistic and intolerant quality of the BIA schools in the 19th century, it is little wonder that they did not prevail.

### Schooling and the Contours of Social Change

The latter part of the 19th century was a time of accelerating change in American life. Guided by the principles of the common-school era, educational reformers proposed to use education as a means of social amelioration and assimilation. This idea certainly applied to the destitute immigrants then beginning to fill the cities of the Eastern seaboard. During Reconstruction these sentiments led to a massive campaign to educate recently freed African Americans, driven largely by Black aspirations for schooling, and a little later they contributed to a government-led crusade to "educate" American Indians. At about the same time, the offspring of European immigrants started entering the schools in greater numbers, pursuing the promise of success in their new homeland. White women began attending public high schools, buoyed by common-school ideals of inclusiveness and a political ideology that assigned women a special role in rearing future generations of citizens. Each of these episodes in educational history imparts a lesson about schooling and social change in the American experience. Together they demonstrate the limits and possibilities of education as an agent of societal transformation, revealing some of the contours of social change.

To begin, these examples allow comparison of the effects of schooling on different groups of people. This is one of the insights afforded by historical analysis, permitting one to examine patterns of inequality in the past that may not be evident today. For instance, during the 19th century, European immigrants and White women benefited substantially from the increased educational opportunities available to them, whereas other groups did not. True, the pace of progress that various ethnic groups and women experienced in entering many professional fields and in assuming larger roles in public life often was quite slow. And the benefits of schooling accrued most readily to children from middle- or upper-class households. But school enrollment rates for immigrant children gradually increased, and tens of thousands of young White women graduated from high school in the decades following the Civil War. Over time, a growing number of both groups continued on to college. The educational advance of women was especially dramatic, particularly those from the middle class. This lent them considerable cultural capital, a degree of social standing and credibility not available to other groups. Even if they lacked formal economic and political power, in that case, White women received tangible benefits from formal schooling, advantages that would eventually help them in other realms of social life. For the descendants of the major European immigrant groups, the school also became a potent instrument of social and economic integration. It was a part of the "American Dream," the idea that upward mobility was possible, even assured in the United States.

The story was quite different for the other groups discussed earlier. African Americans flocked to schools in the period after the Civil War, supporting them with hard-earned cash and donations of materials and service. They displayed enthusiastic support of education, and this contributed to rapid enrollment growth and dramatically improved literacy rates. After a brief period of expansive eagerness, however, Blacks entered an era of frustration and disappointment in their educational history. Once freed from federal oversight, Southern states reduced their support for Black schools, and sharply curtailed African American power in other spheres of life. The Southern economy depended on a servile labor force, and Whites were not ready to allow Black education to alter the existing social structure. The result was a bare-bones curriculum with meager resources for learning, hardly a recipe for social advancement.

The problem of race and social status went far beyond schooling, however. African Americans who did manage to acquire an advanced education faced severe discrimination for the rest of their lives. Even someone as distinguished as Harvard-educated W. E. B. DuBois, acknowledged today as one of the great social scientists and writers in American history, was unable to gain an appointment at a White university. Indeed, he would not have been even considered for a position in a Southern White high school. But plain discrimination was only part of the story. By the end of the century Black education in the South was under attack, and as scores of African Americans were lynched each year, the prospects for further advances in the social standing of this group appeared quite bleak indeed. Even in the North, educated Blacks were rarely able to find work commensurate with their credentials. Although African Americans clearly valued schooling, and made education an important priority in their communities, the impact on their status was quite limited. Apart from a very small minority, Black Americans did not benefit materially from schooling in this period. In this case, the promise of education to effect social change went largely unrealized.

The experiences of American Indians were similar to those of African Americans, at least regarding the effect of education on their social standing. Even though the federal campaign to educate Native Americans eventually reached many of them, the effects on their relative status and assimilation in American life were negligible. American Indians did not lobby for the educational opportunities that they were offered, and many doubtless sent their children off to the government schools grudgingly. But even if Native Americans had wanted to use the school as a vehicle of social advancement, it is unlikely that they would have succeeded. The institutions provided for them were not intended to encourage social mobility, and most Americans were unwilling to accept American Indians as their equals. For groups such as these, assimilation and social improvement required more than schooling alone.

These historical episodes point to the pervasive power of race as a factor in American life in the 19th century. Racist ideology, which held non-White peoples to be socially and morally inferior, prevented most White Americans from even contemplating the premise of social equity for Blacks and American Indians. Discrimination against European immigrants, although often expressed in racial terms at first, turned out to be quite different. Even if the Irish were despised when they first arrived, for instance, the fact that they were White eventually served to ease their assimilation. As the offspring of European immigrants became economically successful, learned to speak English properly, and began to intermingle with the larger White populace, the old ethnic antagonisms gradually began to fade away. Indeed, as some historians have suggested, the Irish and other foreigners "became White," partly by exhibiting virulently anti-Black behavior themselves (Ignatiev, 1995; Jacobson, 1998). In the case of European immigrants, racist ideology may have hastened the process of social integration by helping to identify a shared set of physical and cultural characteristics.

For non-European minorities, on the other hand, the story was quite different, including Hispanic residents of the Southwest and Asian immigrants in the West. Distinguished by physical appearance and hampered by ubiquitous discrimination, assimilation was not an option for these groups. Despite

the experience of the Civil War, and the antislavery campaigns of the abolitionist movement, racism remained a powerful ideological force in American
culture. It made the idea that simple vocational instruction was the appropriate education for children from these groups seem natural and logical. It was
also used to justify the gross inequalities in funding levels and the quality of
materials employed in Black and White education throughout the South, and
in much of the North also. Most Americans simply accepted such inequities
as inevitable facts of life, dictated by the social and biological differences that
they felt distinguished the country's various racial groups. Many decades
would pass before a significant number of American Whites would even begin
to question such assumptions (Takaki, 1979).

Gender, of course, was an important factor in the nation's social life as
well. Sexist ideology, which dictated a subservient status for women, was
also quite prevalent at this time. Sexism led most Americans, including
many women, to assume it quite extraordinary that women would even
dream of seeking social equality, or aspire to careers other than motherhood. The sexual division of labor was pervasive, and it restricted women to
a relatively narrow range of work roles in society at large. Despite the pernicious effects and omnipresent quality of this ideology, however, Americans
generally accepted the idea that White women should go to school, and
study more or less the same subjects as men. These views had deep roots in
the idea of republican motherhood, mentioned in earlier chapters. There
were those who took exception to this, of course, as the controversy over
Edward Clarke's book demonstrated. But such views were in a minority by
the latter 19th century. The vast majority of American schools were coeducational, and most people found it quite natural that boys and girls would
attend classes together on a daily basis, with proper supervision, of course.
Despite its baneful influence in other spheres of life, in that case, sexist ideology appears to have left much of the educational system open to women,
at least among Whites.

Even if women could go to school, sexist discrimination remained an
important fact of life in the United States, and change in women's status
unfolded incrementally. The fact that thousands of women could receive an
education did not necessarily mean that they would compete with men for
higher-status jobs, or choose to be socially and economically independent.
Conservative social conventions continued to dictate well-proscribed roles
for women, despite the level of their education. Still, as noted earlier, the
range of jobs open to women did begin to expand in this period, at least
partly in response to the growing numbers of well-educated women ready to
fill them. Historians have pointed to the development of clerical work and
female positions as sales clerks as evidence of such a shift, and small
numbers of women began to make inroads into the professions as well. On
top of this, hundreds of thousands of White women became schoolteachers,

constituting some 80% of the profession by the end of the century. These were occupational roles that allowed women to utilize the cultural and human capital that they gained from formal education. Beyond employment, educated White women could employ their schooling in raising their own children, a fact that appealed to many potential marriage partners, especially within the aspiring urban middle class. Although their social roles were circumscribed, in that case, women do seem to have realized certain benefits from their rising levels of educational attainment. This was one case where schooling does appear to have functioned as a lever of social change, even if a relatively modest one.

Gender and race, therefore, appear to have differed in their impact on education, and the ways that groups and individuals were able to make use of schooling in society at large varied as well. Racism was an especially virulent obstacle to the aspirations of African Americans and to the prospects of Native Americans. Blacks in particular exhibited very high levels of group cohesiveness, an expression of community social capital, which ultimately proved to be of limited value to their collective social and economic improvement. While many of them may have acquired cultural and human capital in school, it was of limited value in the larger society. American Indians may not have possessed quite the same set of values, but they too were given few opportunities to utilize the benefits of their schooling. Thus it seems that race proved to be an especially formidable barrier to advancement, a telling contour of social change. Sexism, on the other hand, limited the opportunities of White women considerably, but left certain avenues open to those who dared to utilize them. Progress was slow, and the sexual division of labor proved quite formidable, as it continues to be today, but enterprising women were able to realize gains that were largely unavailable to other groups in the 19th century, even if these advances were exacted with a struggle. Gender was a different sort of contour, robust yet also permeable, allowing women to advance in the face of hostility and to contribute in important ways to the shape of societal development.

Differences such as these, products of historical vagaries affecting the American ideological landscape of the time, clearly shaped the impact of education during the 19th century. There were some groups that found schooling to be a vehicle of social advancement, such as the European immigrants mentioned earlier, and others who encountered discrimination similar to that experienced by Blacks and Native Americans, such as Mexican Americans or Asian immigrants. For some Americans, consequently, the school was a potent instrument of improvement and opportunity, and a source of hope for a better life. For others it proved a false hope, a vision that ultimately failed to deliver on its promises. In this respect it was, as Henry Perkinson (1968) suggested, an "imperfect panacea." Ideological constructs such as racism and sexism clearly affected the ability of schools to improve the social standing of the people that they served. It would take time for these circumstances to change, but education eventually would prove to be a powerful instrument of social change for yet other groups. In short, the relationship of schooling and society would itself change as history moved ahead and education became an even greater concern for everyone.

# Growth, Reform, and Differentiation
## The Progressive Era

On January 1, 1901, Americans enthusiastically greeted the 20th century, proclaiming it a time of dramatic transformation. Although many of their predictions proved to be far-fetched, the general sentiment was well founded. From the standpoint of social change, the opening decades of the new era were among the most momentous in American history. It was a time of tremendous economic development and widespread reform. The modern urban civilization that came to characterize the 20th-century United States burst decisively into view, bringing with it a host of new social questions. It was then that many elements of today's public institutions and policies were established, including the modern school system.

The years between 1890 and 1920 are often referred to as the progressive era in American history. This term conveys the sense of advancement that many felt at the time, and typically is associated with the reform activities of political figures such as Teddy Roosevelt and Woodrow Wilson, and the muckraking journalism of Ida Tarbell, Jacob Riis, and Lincoln Steffens, among others. But it has also been used to characterize a wide range of other reform campaigns, touching on virtually all facets of life at the time. Among the more important aspects of progressivism was educational reform, and the period was marked by many different educational ideas and innovations. In fact, a major current of reform propositions and practices in schools has been self-consciously labeled "progressive education" in the last century or so. This broad reform impulse has also been a source of ongoing controversy and debate, and it continues to inspire considerable disagreement today. Understanding progressivism in education thus is an important reason to study this period in the history of American education (Goldman, 1952; Hofstadter, 1955b; May, 1964).

Education and political reform, however, did not render the basic tenor of the historical period. Rather, the forces of industrialization and urban growth defined it, the very same factors that had shaped the course of social transformation in the age of the common school. The difference between the two periods was largely a matter of magnitude and pace. By the start of the 20th century, the degree of industrial development and the rate of urbanization had reached a point scarcely imaginable just a few decades earlier. Business enterprises came to be organized on a mammoth scale, serving far-flung national and international markets, and utilizing new technologies for mass production and the rapid deployment of resources. Cities grew at a dizzying rate, as millions of immigrants arrived to seek jobs in the booming industrial economy. Cultural diversity, a matter of growing concern in the antebellum period, became a fact of life in the largest cities by 1900, where dozens of languages could be heard on downtown streets on any given day. American society was becoming more complex, and it seemed at the time to be making a sharp break with the past, in response to forces that were difficult to understand or control (Hays, 1957/1995; Higgs, 1971; Rodgers, 1998).

The disjunction posed by large-scale industrialization and urbanization proved quite distressing, to say the least. After all, the newly emerging metropolitan society of the 20th century was a far cry from the bucolic and relatively uncomplicated farm life that previous generations of Americans had enjoyed. This discontinuity became a source of new anxieties, and eventually was the focal point of innumerable campaigns for social amelioration. As noted by Robert Wiebe, it was an era marked by a "search for order," and this probably more than anything else helped to characterize it as a new stage in American history (Wiebe, 1967).

Progressivism, in short, represented an effort to respond to a startling new era of dramatic industrial development and urban growth. In the words of Lawrence Cremin, it was "a vast humanitarian effort to apply the promise of American life ... to the puzzling new urban-industrial civilization that came into being during the latter half of the nineteenth century" (Cremin, 1961). Whether or not it was entirely humane or benevolent is open to question, but there can be little doubt that education was an integral part of this reform impulse. It was an age that called for new approaches to schooling, designed to serve a multitude of different purposes. As society became more complex and variegated, so did its educational system. Much of what is discussed here, consequently, examines the response of reformers and schools to the dynamic social forces that shaped the period. But first it is instructive to consider some of the challenges of growing up in this new urban industrial milieu.

## FOCAL POINT: COMING OF AGE IN URBAN AMERICA

As one might expect, the social environment of big cities had a profound effect on American children. Among other things, contemporaries believed that it loosened traditional sources of authority and mechanisms of control that adults had engaged to manage the behavior of youth. The growth of cities was seen as ushering in a time of greater freedom and open-mindedness, when the young were allowed a new measure of latitude in how they chose to conduct themselves. These changes were hardly abrupt, as most children and youth continued to be deeply affected by prevailing social and cultural norms. But novelty was definitely coming into fashion, and it was especially palpable in the big cities.

Anzia Yezierska (1889–1970) was an immigrant to the United States in the early 20th century. She was Jewish, and came with her family from Poland to New York, where she lived on Manhattan's bustling lower East Side. Like thousands of other young women in her circumstances, she struggled to understand the strange, complicated, and often contradictory world she found herself in. She eventually became a writer, and her work focused on the immigrant experience; she was also a social activist, and had a brief but ardent relationship with the educational reformer John Dewey. In 1925 she published a partly autobiographical novel titled *Bread Givers, A Struggle between a Father of the Old World and a Daughter of the New World*, vividly portraying several of the biggest challenges she had faced. It is a moving work, and it captures the dilemmas many immigrant women encountered as they came of age in the new urban world of the 20th century (Henriksen, 1988; Westbrook, 1994; Yezierska, 1925).

The central character of Yezierska's book is Sarah Smolinsky, the youngest daughter of a rabbi who, like other devout Jewish men, was dedicated to studying the Torah. Even though her father had little income, and the family lived in dire poverty, Sarah and her sisters found themselves subjected to his paternal domination. A man of tradition, he expected the women of the house to respect his every whim and to provide most of the family's livelihood. This was a way of life for many Orthodox Jewish families in the immigrant ghetto. As Yezierska noted sardonically,

> Only if they cooked for men, and washed for men, and didn't nag and curse the men out of their homes: only if they let the men study the Torah in peace, then, maybe, they could push themselves into heaven with the men, to wait on them there.

In the book Yezierska described the miserable, crowded conditions of her family's life in New York. They shared a tiny apartment, with poor lighting and ventilation and barely adequate plumbing. They rarely left lower Manhattan, where they inhabited a world of towering tenements and congested streets. There was precious little beauty in their daily existence, and there were few prospects for hope in the future. Sarah was a bright student, but in the view of her Orthodox father, women were not supposed to be scholars. She was expected to help support the family and to obey her parents, particularly her father. As Sarah grew older, however, it became more difficult to conform to her father's demands.

A turning point came after young Sarah saw her three older sisters bound into marriages arranged by their father, to men they neither loved nor much admired. Even though her father received cash payments for agreeing to these unions, a traditional practice known as a "bride's price," the prospective husbands were hardly well-to-do. They too were struggling, and expected their wives to abide by conventional expectations for women. Indeed, Sarah became gradually more horrified as she watched her sisters enter into lives with little hope of improvement, subject to the dominance of their seemingly cloddish spouses. "I began to feel I was different than my sisters," she announces. "If they ever had times they hated Father, they were too frightened of themselves to confess.... But could I help it what was inside me? I had to feel what I felt even if it killed me." She became determined to avoid the fate of her sisters, and to escape her father's authority.

The closing chapters of the book describe Sarah's flight from both the control of her family and the cultural and physical confines of the ghetto. Fed up with her father's hypocritical and self-serving pronouncements about wanting only the best for his family, and frightened by the prospect of an experience like her sisters', Sarah left home abruptly. She found a job ironing clothes at a cleaning establishment and rented a room of her own. Even though the space was small and her furnishings quite modest, she felt a new sense of independence and self-esteem. In examining the room, she remarked on the fact that it had a door, a feature missing in the rooms of her family's apartment. "This door was life," she declared. "It was air. The bottom starting-point of becoming a person. I simply must have this room with the shut door." Thus Sarah Smolinsky began to define herself anew, with the ability to shut out those parts of her world she no longer wanted to identify with, and to define herself with a modicum of personal control over her destiny.

Education was a telling agent of change in Yezierska's book. Always bright and enterprising, the newly independent Sarah found that she was able to qualify for a college scholarship. Winning it, she decided to go away to study, an option that would have been unthinkable for a woman in the patriarchal tradition of her father's Orthodox Jewish beliefs. She found college exhilarating, even if she was painfully aware of her status as a cultural outsider in a milieu dominated by Protestant and middle-class sensibilities. Moved by her own experience of growth, Sarah decided to focus her studies on education, to become a teacher. Eventually she graduated, and took up the life of an educated, independent woman, dedicated to her profession and finally able to look dispassionately at her family's experiences. It was a tale of success against great odds, and redemption from the trials of challenging tradition and finding one's own way in the world. It was also a story that captured many themes of immigrant achievement in the United States during the early years of the 20th century. In this respect it was a continuation of the parable of uplift and assimilation derived from the experience of the Irish and other groups in earlier decades.

Anzia Yezierska was an astute observer and a compelling writer. She experienced many of the events described in *Bread Givers*, but also shaped the story to represent the lives of other young women like her. Millions of immigrant children grew up in the teeming ethnic ghettos of New York and other Northern cities. Even though their parents often clung to traditional values and Old World customs, the younger generation was unavoidably exposed to the rapidly evolving mores of the city, and to the ever-changing fashion of youth. They lived hard lives under crushing conditions. Crowded tenement apartments, similar to the one Yezierska described in *Bread Givers*, were a fact of life for many families. But the dynamism of the city, especially its atmosphere of continuing change, always seemed to offer the prospect of a better future. So long as the urban industrial economy continued to expand rapidly, there would be opportunities for improvement (Binder & Reimers, 1995; Kessner, 1977).

As a work of historical fiction, *Bread Givers* captures the theme of conflict between different generations within immigrant families, but it also highlights the difficulties facing immigrant women who found themselves caught between old and new value systems. These women loved their families, but often felt constrained by traditional expectations that sharply restricted their options in life. Of course, many willingly conformed to the wishes of their parents, marrying within their immediate ethnic communities and striving to pass traditional values on to their children. But others, like Sarah Smolinsky, rebelled in one way or another, making a break with the older generation and defining a new life for themselves. Most of these women probably did not experience as sharp a rupture with tradition as Yezierska's Sarah, but the rapidly evolving culture of the urban environment made it difficult not to challenge at least some of the tenets of parental authority. There was a big, bright world outside of the crowded ghetto communities, and the new generation of immigrant children was bound to discover it sooner or later. And for immigrant women, the lights often shone even more brightly and alluringly (Gabaccia, 1994; Harzig, 1997; Olneck, 2008).

Education was an important part of this story as well. It is no accident that Yezierska's principal character found college to be an effectual vehicle of escape from the prisons of her past life. For thousands of immigrants and their children, formal education turned out to be a potent means of social improvement. This was especially true for Jewish immigrants, as their children attended schools in unusually high numbers. Schooling endowed them with skills that they could utilize in the job market, and it also gave them a better command of English and other aspects of mainstream American culture. In other words, education afforded access to better employment opportunities and it served as an agency of assimilation. For bright young immigrant women like Sarah Smolinsky or Yezierska herself, various forms of higher education—whether in normal schools, colleges or specialized training institutes of one kind or another—proved a means to professional status and a degree of independence unimaginable to their mothers' generation.

By 1920 the daughters of immigrants represented the largest single group of teachers in New York City, and they comprised a similarly large fraction of the teaching force in other Northern cities as well. To be educated meant that assimilation was well underway, and it also suggested a greater degree of independence for American women, even if most left the schools upon marriage. In this respect, schooling helped to break the chains of tradition (Markowitz, 1993; Rousmaniere, 1997).

The emergence of a dynamic urban civilization during the early 20th century signaled a new era in the history of American childhood. The rapid growth of cities, greater ease of transportation, and seemingly boundless opportunities made many young people impatient to leave home and start life on their own. It was harder for parents to exert strict controls over their children in these circumstances, even if many continued to try. Other changes also affected family life in these years. The average size of American households became smaller, and an atmosphere of greater tolerance and compassion eventually came to characterize familial relations (Mintz, 2004; Mintz & Kellogg, 1988). This is discussed in the next chapter, but such developments marked the advent of greater independence and freedom of expression for children and youth in the United States. As one historian has suggested, teenagers especially began to move to "the beat of different drummers" in this era (Graff, 1995). Expanded educational opportunities, with new forms of schooling, also were a part of this story. It was a time of rapid change and exciting possibilities; it was the 20th century.

**Growth and Differentiation: An Age of Uncertainty**

As noted in Chapter 3, the closing decades of the 19th century were a time of unprecedented economic growth in the United States. It was the height of the industrial revolution, a period when manufacturing output, urban development, and immigration from abroad all expanded at a faster pace than in any other time in the nation's history, including the present. It was also a moment of great societal and political turbulence, much of it stimulated by rapid shifts in the nation's economy and its social structure. New scientific developments changed the way people lived, and revolutionary theories about nature and society challenged the precepts of religion and traditional ideology. International contacts grew also, and ideas from abroad influenced the way that Americans thought about the new social order. As suggested earlier, it is probably safe to say that there was a greater degree of social change at that point than during any other, simply because of the magnitude of economic expansion and population movement. Even from today's perspective, when the pace of innovation seems ever faster, it is difficult to comprehend the scale of change experienced by people who lived at the turn of the 20th century (Crunden, 1982; Hays, 1957/1995; Rodgers, 1998).

This is evident in simply examining basic social and economic indicators. In the three decades between 1870 and 1900, for instance, the size of the nation's rail system grew fourfold, from 50,000 to more than 200,000 miles, sharply reducing the time of travel and transport of goods for the vast majority of the nation's population. At the same time, the proportion of the labor force engaged in nonagricultural employment approached 60%, a sharp difference from the farm economy of the early 1800s. As industrial output grew, some cities expanded almost exponentially. Chicago, one of the boomtowns of the era, roughly doubled its population every decade between 1870 and 1910, until it finally exceeded two million people, second in size only to New York among U.S. cities. Other metropolises grew at a similar, if somewhat less frenetic, pace. Altogether, the proportion of Americans living in urban areas reached 40% by 1900, and it had become a majority by 1920. The time when the typical American experience was growing up on a farm had clearly passed. The social milieu of the 20th century was decidedly urban, and this represented a new stage in the nation's development (Brownlee, 1979; Chudacoff, 1975; Higgs, 1971).

With the development of cities came a subtle but important series of changes in the social order. The increasing volume of trade and a widening division of labor led to ever-greater tendencies toward specialization in the production of goods and services. This became a well-known and widely studied process among social scientists, and has been described by use of the term *differentiation*. Because of this general pattern of development, as urban settlements grew ever larger, a wider range of roles was available for people to play in the local economy and in the social order. In very large cities, highly specialized economic functions appeared, and there was a vast array of social and cultural groups for individuals to identify with. For instance, it was possible for young women to find employment in a wide array of jobs, from laundries to hat shops to dance halls, depending on their backgrounds and predilections. New professions developed for men also, from particular engineering fields (such as civil or industrial) to streetcar operators and police detectives. These were social and economic roles that did not exist in smaller communities, simply because such specialized occupations could not be sustained there. Overall, the number of people working in professional positions increased nearly fivefold between 1870 and 1910. This multitude of new opportunities yielded city dwellers a measure of freedom and choice in their work and careers that had been unknown to earlier generations (Hershberg, 1981; Schnore, 1974; VanOverbeke, 2008; Zunz, 1982).

This was the good news, but there also was another side to these changes. Rapid population growth and social differentiation helped to loosen social bonds and weakened the long-standing modes of identification that gave smaller places much of their social cohesion. Chicago sociologist Louis Wirth noted that life in the biggest cities was characterized by a loss of community.

People no longer knew their neighbors and other community members. Social relations became more impersonal. Given this, it is conceivable to say that social capital was dissipated. In highly urbanized areas people were known by their social roles rather than as individuals. Although urban growth offered greater liberty and options, it also entailed a degree of social detachment and isolation that was a new feature of American life. This was a critical dimension of societal change in the United States: As the cities expanded, it was possible for the individual to feel lost in a sea of humanity (Hogan, 1985; Reiss, 1964).

There were yet other features of social change that marked this era as distinctive. Fueled by demand for industrial workers, immigration surged, peaking at more than one million per year by the early 20th century. The vast majority of these newcomers were drawn to the industrial cities, where they often formed distinctive residential enclaves, conspicuous for various social and cultural links to their respective homelands. This was yet another dimension of differentiation: The city landscape became a patchwork of culturally unique communities. Distinctive religious or national districts often highlighted the new urban geography, each with its own traditions and ethnic-based neighborhood organizations. And the numbers were monumental. By the time of World War I, when immigration began to subside, about one-quarter of the nation's population comprised immigrants or their children. In the urbanized states of the Northeast and upper Midwest, the foreign-born and their children represented an even larger segment of the populace (Archdeacon, 1983; Bulmer, 1984).

The first waves of immigrants were from such Western European countries as Germany, Ireland, and England; by the turn of the century large numbers arrived from poorer areas in Southern and Eastern Europe, especially Italy, Poland, and Russia. Most of these new immigrants were Roman Catholic, and a significant minority was Jewish, two religions historically viewed with considerable misgiving in the United States. In cities with populations over 100,000, immigrants and their children represented two-thirds of the residents, defining a variegated cultural milieu that was virtually unprecedented in American experience. For once, native-born Protestants found themselves in the minority in these settings, even if they continued to command considerable prestige and cultural capital. This new, culturally diverse urban scene had emerged in a span of just several decades, and it made traditional relationships of status and authority suddenly appear a bit topsy-turvy (Barton, 1975; Gleason, 1992).

In addition to cultural diversity, there also was a problem of widening inequality in the nation's major industrial areas. Industrialism and the factory system brought thousands of workers together under harsh conditions, often for meager pay and little job security or other benefits. A 60-hour working week was commonplace, and workers had no recourse if they were injured or laid off. Understandably, these conditions contributed to festering resentments and the period witnessed large-scale protests against the industrial system. There was a growing prospect of class warfare in the face of inequity and exploitation. Treated like pawns in a gigantic competition for industrial riches, industrial workers eventually revolted in massive strikes that were met by violence from capitalists and state authorities. During industrial downturns, when large numbers of workers found themselves unemployed, such labor clashes peaked in dramatic episodes of conflict, sometimes pitting thousands against the police or the military (Stowell, 1999).

Beginning in the mid-1870s, the nation witnessed a series of such confrontations each decade. For instance, national attention was drawn to labor conflict in 1886 following a riot at Haymarket Square in Chicago that resulted in ten deaths, and in 1894, when the federal agents arrested labor leader Eugene Debs to forestall a national railway workers' strike. These widely publicized events contributed to public anxiety about the pace and direction of change in American life. Even relatively small instances of disorder over these issues were seen as cause for concern, adding to fears that labor conflict could pose a threat to the nation's social and political stability. To many middle-class Americans, unaccustomed to civil strife on this scale, such thoughts were hardly comforting (Babson, 1999; von Waltershausen, 1999).

At the same time that labor battled for basic rights and better pay, wealth became ever more concentrated in the hands of a relatively small group of industrialists and bankers. This was the age of the "robber barons," men such as Andrew Carnegie, Henry P. Morgan, and John D. Rockefeller. Today these names are associated with philanthropy and culture, support for famous libraries, museums, and schools. In fact, these men did establish such institutions, along with sizeable foundations that eventually came to play a prominent role in education and social reform. But at the turn of century they were widely considered to be notorious for ruthlessly amassing huge fortunes through monopolistic business practices, brutally stamping out competition in their respective industries, and rejecting the pleas of reformers for regulation of markets and improved working conditions (Wiebe, 1967).

These much criticized attributes, however, did not account for the success of this new breed of big-business leaders. Their financial accomplishments were largely a by-product of the logic of large-scale industrial production: immense enterprises serving national markets and wielding economic power to overcome local competition. Such achievements reflected the advantages of capital, technology, and economies of scale possessed by monopolistic national firms. In the eyes of many, however, these companies and the upstart millionaires who ran them were embodiments of greed and unbridled hegemony. To contemporaries, they threatened to become a source of power even stronger than the federal government. The idea of seemingly amoral business tycoons running the country also helped to make many people quite anxious about the future (Crunden, 1982; Goldman, 1952; Hofstadter, 1955b).

It was an age of unrest, and political turbulence extended beyond the cities. Farmers in the Midwest and South were buffeted by dramatic swings in prices for the crops and other products they brought to market, much of which was caused by the ups and downs of the new urban industrial economy. Increasingly, they felt themselves at the mercy of railroads, commodity brokers, packing companies, and a host of other middlemen who reaped large profits from the revenue from agricultural products. During the industrial depression of the 1880s, when farming prices were severely undervalued, farmers began to organize. A radically new organization emerged from this experience, the Farmers Alliance, and it grew rapidly in the following decade. Eventually, the populists, as these farmers and their supporters were called, became the political foundation for the presidential candidacy of William Jennings Bryant in 1896. Although Bryant failed to win, this episode demonstrated that farmers were not immune to problems engendered by the new urban industrial civilization. To many middle-class Americans, these too were unsettling events, and contributed to the sense that reform of the social and political order was inevitable (Goodwyn, 1978).

The closing decades of the 19th century also marked a time of dramatic technological and scientific advancement. A host of inventions and scientific discoveries began to transform everyday life, beginning with electric lights, the telephone, gas furnaces, and the internal combustion engine. Figures such as Alexander Graham Bell and Thomas Edison became national heroes, and their laboratories produced a host of technological innovations to make life easier and communication faster. Eventually the development of the automobile, and the advent of mass-production techniques to make autos widely available, would mark the dawn of a new era in transportation and in American popular culture. Henry Ford became yet another national icon in the early 20th century. Each one of these technical achievements was important; taken together they marked a sharp break with the past. Technology was no longer confined to the factory, nor was it limited to simply making goods less expensive. Now inventions had an immediate and palpable impact on daily existence, and this too contributed to a public perception that change was accelerating rapidly (Cowan, 1997).

Yet other scientific developments contributed to the climate of change. Many of the most significant intellectual events of the era followed from Charles Darwin's promulgation of evolutionary theory in 1859. Grounded in careful field studies and the development of an imaginative hypothesis about the origins of species, Darwin's work revolutionized biological thinking by suggesting that living organisms were shaped by their immediate environment. Taken at face value, Darwin's theory of natural selection appeared to challenge traditional religious explanations for the beginnings of life and the place of humans in the natural order. As a consequence, it profoundly changed the way that many people viewed the world and their own situation, lending even greater significance to the realm of science and higher education (Moore, 1979; Russett, 1976).

The influence of Darwin's ideas extended far beyond the natural sciences and religion. It also led to the development of a host of parallel explanations for other phenomena, especially human behavior. Perhaps the best-known instance of such influence was the rise of *social Darwinism*, a variant of mainstream ideology which held that attempts to assist the poor were misguided and contrary to the laws of nature. The social Darwinists reasoned that, if the poor suffered harsh working and living conditions, it was a natural outcome of their inferior abilities and inadequate work ethic. Thus the logic of natural selection was exploited to justify the advantages of wealth and social and cultural capital: The superior status of the rich was depicted as inevitable. Although Darwin's ideas challenged some aspects of the dominant ideology, they also reinforced or augmented others. In this and many other ways, the dramatic impact of new ideas contributed to the sense that the traditional world of the 19th century was rapidly giving way to a new one, where new scientific discoveries about both nature and society promised to change the way people viewed themselves. To use a Shakespearean term Aldous Huxley later helped popularize, it was a brave new world indeed, one that created a good deal of uncertainty about the future (Bannister, 1979; Hawkins, 1997).

Change abounded as the 19th century drew to a close and the 20th began. For Americans who had grown up on the farm and moved to the city, whether literally or figuratively, the pace of transformation in the economy, politics, technology, and social mores was almost too much to comprehend. It led many to question the future of traditional values, and to wonder about the prospects of the next generation. This comprised the inspiration for a wide range of reforms, most of which came to be grouped together under the banner of *progressivism*. For those concerned with the broadest array of changes, however, one reform stood out among all the others. Following a proud and long-established American tradition, the people concerned with saving modern industrial society from its own worst excesses turned naturally to the schools.

### Progressivism in Education

Reform touched on many aspects of life in the opening years of the 20th century, but few issues were affected by it as much as schooling. It was a characteristically American response to the tidal wave of change then washing over the country: inventing new institutional mechanisms to mediate the impact of social transformation. In this case the institution was the school, and the response was an explosion of new ideas and programmatic innovations aimed at making education better attuned to the needs of society. Of course, there were many ways of defining social needs at the turn of the century, just as there are today, so it should hardly be surprising that progressive school reform included many different types of innovation, some of them quite contradictory in spirit and intent. Consequently, there was considerable debate and disagreement about school reform during this era, even more than in earlier periods. In fact, the volume of argument about educational issues increased audibly, as schooling became an ever-bigger public concern. Such conflicts notwithstanding, there can be little doubt that progressive education, in all of its various guises, left an indelible imprint on American schools. Like progressivism writ large, it was a broad and diverse movement, embracing many different viewpoints as it sought to make education a central element of the new social order (Cremin, 1961).

As a general principle, historians have identified two broad impulses that characterized educational reform during this period. The first was a humanitarian disposition toward making education more responsive to the needs of children, and integrating the school more closely with its immediate community. Identified with such renowned reform figures as John Dewey, Francis Parker, and William Heard Kilpatrick, this movement has influenced a relatively small but highly visible cadre of educational reformers throughout the 20th century. Historian David Tyack has described this band of educators as "pedagogical progressives," an apt title for the men and women who historically were primarily interested in changing instructional practice. A second group of educational reformers was less idealistic by temperament and more concerned with issues of efficiency and carefully aligning the purposes of schooling with the needs of the economy. Tyack dubbed these individuals "administrative progressives," because they were especially interested in improving the organizational structure and functions of educational institutions. Historically, even though they did not produce heroic reform figures to point to, the administrative progressives came to exert enormous influence on the development of American schools. Accordingly, terms such as *efficiency*, *management*, and *vocationalism* have become important watchwords in education during the 20th century. These too were part of the legacy of progressivism (Tyack, 1974).

As one might imagine, the differences in perspective and basic values embraced by these two wings of progressive educational reform were vast. At various times, representatives from these rather diffuse groups engaged in sharp debates over particular educational issues. For the most part, however, they managed to coexist, largely because they generally were interested in different spheres of the educational enterprise. As suggested earlier, pedagogical progressives were most concerned with matters of instruction, and related issues of how children learn and links between the school and its proximate community. Their primary focus was inside the classroom, and on kindred issues of personal growth and understanding. It is also probably accurate to say that their greatest influence was on primary education, especially for younger children. Theirs was a fundamentally compassionate impetus, one that aimed to make schools better attuned to children's needs and interests.

The administrative progressives, on the other hand, chose to devote most of their attention to matters outside the classroom, on questions related to the organization of schools, the purposes of various curricula, and the large-scale measurement of student learning. Of course, many of these questions can, and did, have a direct bearing on what occurred inside of classrooms across the country. But the administrative progressives, by and large, did not concern themselves directly with issues of teaching practice, at least not during the first half of the 20th century. Instead, they were content to set the parameters within which most American teachers performed their instructional tasks, whereas the pedagogical progressives tried heroically to inspire teachers to improve their methods of teaching. In this way, the two sides of progressive reform managed to coexist, even if neither could claim complete mastery of the entire field (Kliebard, 1986).

Of course, the lived reality of most educators at the time was considerably more complex than suggested by these broadly divergent categories. Many probably took inspiration from both wings of progressivism in education, without seeing them as necessarily at odds with one another. It was a time of frenetic change in schools, and reforms of one stripe or another were considered modern innovations intended to improve education. Consequently, elements from both sides of the reform impulse often were adopted pragmatically to move school systems forward. The result was a rather disjointed process of change, one that pushed and pulled the educational system in different directions, often producing a confusing and contradictory array of outcomes. This was progressive educational reform in all its disparate and paradoxical glory, a process that helped to shape many features of the current American school system (Graham, 1974; Zilversmit, 1993).

## Pedagogical Progressivism

Like the progressive movement in American politics, historians have linked progressive education to the rhetoric of crusading journalists bent on challenging the nation to recognize the problems that it faced. Joseph Meyer Rice was a pediatrician who toured the country in the 1890s examining children and classrooms in big-city school systems. He wrote about his findings in a widely read series of articles in *The Forum*, one of the nation's premier muckraking (or reforming) journals. Rice's discoveries were shocking. He reported children required to recite lessons in machine-like order, maintaining silence in large classes in cramped spaces, and subject to educators who took pride in punishing even the most inconsequential infractions. As a medical doctor who treated children, he questioned the pedagogical and physiological effects of such approaches to education. Was it possible for children to learn when all of their inborn, natural propensities to exercise their bodies and minds were denied by these repressive school regimes? Was it healthy for children to sit in silence for hours on end in crowded, poorly ventilated school buildings? As big-city school districts scrambled to find classroom space for their rapidly expanding populations of immigrant children, often ignoring building codes and pressing substandard facilities into service, many other people started asking similar questions. Most importantly, a growing number of reformers became interested in the way children were being asked to learn in schools, and they began to consider alternatives to the prevailing models of memorization and recitation. It seemed to be time for a change, a new way of thinking about teaching and learning (Cremin, 1961).

As noted earlier, the reform figures who advocated more humane and child-friendly practices in schools were described as *pedagogical progressives.* These individuals challenged the logic of faculty psychology, which argued that memorizing and reciting school lessons helped to build greater mental capacity and discipline. Instead, pedagogical progressives suggested that children learned best by following their own interests, expressing themselves, and actively investigating the world around them. In this regard, these reformers represented the legacy of such well-known 19th-century European educational thinkers as Friedrich Froebel, Heinrich Pestalozzi, and Johann Herbart, men whom Horace Mann and other 19th-century American educators had admired from afar. Their ideas also reflected the influence of Edward Sheldon, who trained teachers at the Oswego, New York, normal school and was the chief American proponent of Pestalozzian ideas. Sheldon introduced the use of objects to teach school subjects, the origin of today's widely used phrase "object lesson," and lectured extensively on "new" methods of instruction. Pedagogical progressives were also influenced by William James, a Harvard professor and pioneer of modern psychology who emphasized the importance of experience, and who was also the brother of novelist Henry James. These men and like-minded thinkers downplayed the notion that human beings had inborn proclivities and strengths that required isolation to be developed, and instead argued that engagement with the larger realm of human endeavor was the key to individual growth and learning. Education was supposed to be fun, they suggested, as the child eagerly pursued a natural curiosity to know and understand the world of experience. Schooling did not have to be all a matter of drudgery and restraint; it also could represent a process of liberation, one that allowed children to express their inherent proclivity to learning (Cremin, 1961; Curti, 1959; Reese, 2001).

The most famous of the pedagogical progressives was John Dewey, although there were certainly many others. Dewey was born in Vermont in 1859, just a few months after Horace Mann's death. He attended local schools and worked briefly as a teacher until he went to Johns Hopkins University for graduate studies in philosophy during the early 1880s. Gradually embracing a far-reaching philosophy of experiential learning, Dewey eventually went on to become the preeminent American philosopher of his age and perhaps any other. Dewey also became well known for his work with the University of Chicago Laboratory School, which he founded when he joined the university's faculty in the mid-1890s. It was Dewey's work at the Lab School, as it soon became known, that led to his early writings on education and learning (Dykhuizen, 1973; Ryan, 1995).

Unlike more traditional educators, Dewey believed that education was a process of interaction between the child and the curriculum, and between the school and society. But Dewey was not a radical reformer; he did not advocate doing away with traditional academic subjects altogether, and letting children follow their every whim and fancy. Instead, he felt that school lessons should be taught differently, utilizing the larger world of experience to impart critical material in history, biology, geography, and other fields. Accordingly, students at the Lab School learned about the past by visiting museums and historical sites, they toured factories to learn about the economy; and they conducted biological experiments in parks and nature preserves. In these and many other ways, Dewey and the Lab School faculty (his wife Alice served as director) experimented to learn more about the process of education and ways of improving the conditions of teaching and learning. It was a relatively small school, and benefited from a talented and dedicated staff of teachers, who were able to give students a great deal of individual attention. It was not immediately clear, in that case, what lessons it offered to the burgeoning public schools, which often struggled with classes of 50 or more. Still, Dewey wrote extensively about the insights he and others gained from this experience, providing the intellectual tutelage for a growing movement to transform the school (Cremin, 1961; Kliebard, 1986; Tanner, 1997).

John Dewey eventually came to believe that the school was the central organization in a modern democratic society. It was this institution, he reasoned, that afforded citizens the skills and knowledge necessary for political participation, an argument Horace Mann had articulated 70 years earlier. But Dewey also believed that schools should convey the scientific sensibility necessary for membership in a rapidly changing urban industrial social order. As a result, his conception of the school's role in society went well beyond Mann's ideas. For Dewey, the concept of democracy embraced more than a properly informed polity; rather, it was a way of life that allowed for the fullest possible development of every member of society. Democracy, in that case, embraced a range of ideas, such as tolerance, fair play, critical discussion of social issues, and respect for the rights of others. Ultimately, he felt it was nothing less than the highest form of collective intelligence. If a democratic society was to succeed, he argued, the school's role was to help cultivate these and similar values, and the key to imparting them was experience. In short, Dewey believed the school should model these values, and should represent itself as a microcosm of community in order to help teach democratic values experientially, in a way that children would be unlikely to forget. The school was the first place where most children encountered the larger world outside of their immediate families on a sustained and intensive basis, and because of this Dewey felt it essential that these institutions exemplify the very best values and practices of democratic society (Westbrook, 1991).

The atmosphere of rapid social transformation that characterized this period also contributed to Dewey's conviction that schools had a critical role to play in sustaining a democratic civilization. Like many others of his time, Dewey was alarmed by the magnitude of the social and economic shifts then evident, especially in places like Chicago and New York, the cities where he spent most of his professional career. He was concerned about the growing social divisions between the rich and poor, about conflict over labor issues, and about the fragmentation of society due to religious and ethnic distinctions. People's work lives were also increasingly dictated by forces beyond their control. Industrialization, he declared, threatened to turn individuals into "mere appendages of machines." Because of these tendencies, he suggested that the school had an even more important role to play in teaching democratic principles than during earlier periods of American history. Where Horace Mann had invoked an industrial metaphor in declaring the school a "balance wheel" of society, Dewey saw it as a refuge from the ravages of the factory and commercial life, a place for children to learn essential values of democracy and principles of reasoning (Dykhuizen, 1973).

Unlike Mann, Dewey did not dwell on combining various elements of the population in a single institution, the central idea of the common school. While he certainly was in favor of bringing people together, Dewey recognized the reality of growing social and economic differentiation in urban society. He also realized that that nearly all children attended school in his day, at least in the primary grades, so he focused more on the construction of community within the walls of the institution. Consequently, he argued that the role of the school was to impart the tenets of democratic life and the principles of scientific reasoning, so that democracy could flourish in spite of rapid societal change, even if the schools might not immediately bridge the widening civil divisions. As the social distance between various elements of the nation's population increased, the role of education would become ever more important in sustaining these core elements of American civilization. Dewey's basic concern, in that case, was not simply a more humane and sensible form of pedagogical practice; it was nothing less than the preservation of essential American values in the face of sweeping social change (McCluskey, 1958; Westbrook, 1991).

Dewey was hardly the first pedagogical progressive, and he drew many of his ideas from the work of other educators with similar concerns and interests. Chicago became something of a hotbed for these ideas after Francis

Parker arrived in the early 1890s to head the Cook County Normal School, one of the city's teacher-training institutions. Parker had acquired a national reputation for innovation in education as superintendent of schools in Quincy, Massachusetts. While there, he had done away with traditional drill and memorization approaches to instruction, and emphasized the cultivation of children's natural curiosity and propensity to learn through direct experience. The Quincy schools drew visitors from around the world to see new methods of learning through the study of objects, taking field trips, and allowing children to devise answers to problems that they encountered. After leaving Quincy, Parker spent a frustrating period of time as superintendent of the Boston schools before moving to Chicago. Once there, he established a practice school connected to the city's normal school, one that demonstrated his principles of education in action. It was hardly coincidental that when John Dewey arrived in Chicago, he enrolled his own children in Parker's school. Eventually the two men became collaborators in forging a new approach to schooling. Parker represented an important progressive educational influence, one whose ideas found expression in many of Dewey's writings (Curti, 1959; Ryan, 1995).

Parker's school, however, represented just the early stage of a movement that gradually gained momentum in the opening decades of the 20th century. Inspired by his example and by Dewey's Lab School and writings, and by the work of other educators, dozens of visionary individuals established schools embracing progressive pedagogical principles. In 1915 Dewey and his daughter Evelyn published *Schools of To-Morrow*, a description of a number of exemplary progressive schools in different parts of the country. These cases provided evidence that schools embracing the progressive ideals of nurturing individual interests, fostering expression, learning through experience, and upholding democratic values could be established in a wide range of settings and circumstances. Thousands of other like-minded educators took heart from these and other such examples, and the ideals that they represented found their way into countless schools and classrooms across the country and around the world (Cremin, 1961; Zilversmit, 1993).

While in Chicago, Dewey had been profoundly influenced by his friendship with the famous progressive social reformer Jane Addams, and he was a strong proponent of gender equity in education. Women were especially prominent in this reform movement, founding and leading new schools with progressive principles and occasionally lending leadership to school districts. For example, Caroline Pratt, Marietta Johnson, and Flora Cook were prominent leaders of innovative private institutions, and Chicago's Ella Flagg Young was among the nation's most important progressive superintendents of the era. Perhaps even more important, the principles of pedagogical progressivism proved to be especially significant among teacher-educators, both women and men, who were deeply influenced by Dewey and other progressive intellectuals. In this way, progressive ideas lived on for generations in many of the nation's colleges and university schools of education, as they do today (Blount, 1998; Lagemann, 1979, 1985; Semel & Sadovnick, 1999).

After Dewey joined the philosophy department at New York's Columbia University in 1904, his influence became particularly strong at that institution's affiliated education school, known as Teachers College. A number of faculty members at Teachers College became widely known as advocates of curricular reform strategies designed to introduce a stronger experiential and problem-centered approach into traditional schools. Perhaps the most famous was William Heard Kilpatrick, who developed an instructional reform approach known as the "project method" in the early 1920s. Kilpatrick's approach was a way of circumventing traditional curricular structures, such as the disciplines of English, history, and mathematics, by allowing students to undertake projects that were linked to their own interests and experiences. His intention was to devise a way to infuse opportunities for children to study topics that appealed to them, often focusing on social issues outside of the school, while developing such traditional skills as reading, writing, and numerical analysis. Often defined without regard for traditional subjects, these "projects" were supposed to be carefully planned and evaluated. Dewey was critical of Kilpatrick for breaking so dramatically from the academic disciplines, but this had little effect on the popularity of his ideas. In a relatively short time, Kilpatrick's techniques were being tried in school districts across the country, spreading the doctrine of progressive education as they proceeded. In addition to this, thousands of students were influenced by Kilpatrick and his progressive-minded colleagues at Teachers College, which quickly became the nation's most prominent and influential school of education. Many of these individuals eventually became important educators in communities across the country. These developments, along with the founding of the Progressive Education Association in 1919, helped to give the movement an institutional voice, a stronger identity and greater visibility (Graham, 1967; Kliebard, 1986; Westbrook, 1991).

It was not long, however, before criticisms of the pedagogical progressives began to surface. Traditional educators complained that experiential methods did not teach children basic reading and computational skills. Students who learned history on field trips, critics charged, often did not know essential names and dates from the past. Older English teachers suggested that an aversion to drill and memorization resulted in a marked increase in spelling and punctuation errors. More perceptive critics noted that progressive methods of instruction seemed to work most readily with affluent children, whose plentiful resources of cultural and social capital yielded a ready stock of educative experiences to draw on. It proved a greater challenge, however, to convey essential skills and knowledge to children from impoverished families, especially when their immediate home environments offered relatively little stimulus for intellectual growth. Classes with these students often demanded more direction and control by teachers, especially if they were quite large, which typically was the case in public schools. It was little wonder, then, that many of the most famous progressive schools were smaller private institutions serving a middle- and upper-class clientele. Critics were quick to point this out, occasionally lampooning progressive education as a trendy fad among the social and intellectual elite (Cremin, 1961; Ravitch, 2000; Zilversmit, 1993).

These and similar comments came to resonate with large segments of the adult public, many of whom equated discipline and traditional forms of achievement with their own experiences in the schools of the 19th century. A majority of American parents probably continued to believe in the importance of controlling children, and were inherently suspicious of educational doctrines that seemed to celebrate self-expression. School, after all, was supposed to entail strict authority and command of factual knowledge. To many observers, progressive schools appeared to be little more than children running amok. Such perceptions were not always unfounded, of course, and there also was a good deal of criticism of various excesses within the movement itself. Dewey and other reform figures often struggled to prevent the misrepresentation of their ideas, and attempted to distance themselves from educators who eschewed any support for traditional subjects at all. By 1938, when Dewey published *Experience and Education*, his major corrective statement, the progressive education movement had lost a great deal of its creative energy and originality. Too many educators had come to interpret progressivism as simply the replacement of books with life experience, instead of Dewey's conception of utilizing experience to enrich and expand traditional sources of learning. Despite their early promise and broad appeal, the pedagogical progressives could only fundamentally transform a small portion of American education. Yet they left an indelible mark on educational thought and practice, one that continues to influence educators right down to the present (Cremin, 1961; Cuban, 1984; Ravitch, 1983).

## Administrative Progressivism

At the same time that the pedagogical progressives were seeking ways to bring a new appreciation of democracy to the nation's classrooms, other educators sought to make the schools better attuned to the widely different social roles demanded by the new urban industrial order. As noted earlier, historians have labeled this group of reformers *administrative progressives*, but it would be wrong to consider them part of a movement comparable in terms of unity and coherence to the pedagogical progressives. Rather, the term *administrative progressivism* encompasses a wide range of educators, most of whom were simply striving to make the schools function as smoothly and effectively as possible (Tyack, 1974).

By and large, the administrative progressives were not committed to using education to alter society or overcome such social problems as inequity or safekeeping democracy. They worked instead to adapt schools to the rapid evolution of urban society, especially the increasingly complex labor market. Although the pedagogical progressives included significant numbers of women, educators who fit the administrative profile were mostly men. Business and other fiscally conservative elements in society often supported their efforts, and they frequently were opposed by organized labor. The administrative progressives probably greatly outnumbered their pedagogical counterparts, and as such they represented the principal direction of change in American schools at the time. They saw themselves working to build a modern educational system for the 20th century, and many features of today's school systems can be traced to their efforts (Tyack & Hansot, 1982).

If one word were to express the principal bearing and object of administrative progressivism, it would be *efficiency*. Most of the nation's leading educators were particularly interested in building an educational system that was both rationally organized and cost-effective. This was partly due to the immediate historical experience of the larger school districts, especially those in the leading cities. As noted earlier, this was a period of rapid expansion in the nation's educational systems. Major cities like New York, Chicago, Detroit, and Los Angeles were growing especially fast, and their schools received tens of thousands of new children each year. The need to constantly build new schools, train additional teachers, buy textbooks and other supplies, and devise new curricula placed an enormous strain on district resources. This in turn led to greater public interest in the use of tax funds earmarked for education, and concern about inefficiency and corruption in the disposition of the rather large budgets of urban school systems. In the closing decades of the 19th century, when city schools were often controlled by ward (local or even neighborhood) politicians, it was not unusual for public education funds to find their way into the pockets of political machine bosses, along with money earmarked for other municipal services. Widely publicized cases of corrupt politicians and school administrators being caught accepting bribes to assign jobs, or demanding cash payments in return for construction or textbook contracts, heightened public awareness of the need for greater professionalism in the administration and governance of public education. As urban school systems faced even greater demands, and budgets grew ever larger, such questions loomed significantly for school leaders (Callahan, 1962; Drost, 1967).

These concerns led to a general movement to create new, centralized, and highly efficient school systems in cities across the country between 1890 and 1920. This was a part of a sweeping reform campaign in municipal government, one that attacked the corruption associated with ward-based political regimes. By 1920 hundreds of municipalities had changed from ward-level school boards and city councils to centralized and bureaucratic forms of governance and administration. It was one of the principal accomplishments of the administrative impulse in progressive educational reform, creating a new ethos of urban educational leadership. Instead of localized directors selected by politicians, urban school systems came to be run by boards elected from across a community or municipality, and administered by superintendents selected for their experience and professional competence. It marked a new era in urban schooling, one that emphasized separation between local political organizations and the supervision of schools. School leaders were supposed to be above corruption, expert at effective management of resources, and knowledgeable in the educational methods necessary to accomplish their goals. Efficiency was the modern watchword in school leadership, and a growing number of educators were committed to making it a principle that permeated public education (Hays, 1964; Reese, 1986).

A related type of reform that engendered considerable conflict was rural school consolidation, the process of joining smaller districts together to form larger administrative units. Despite rapid urbanization, millions of children attended one-room schools at the turn of the century. Thousands of tiny country districts still dotted the countryside, with the largest numbers in the Midwest. Once a staple of American education, these schools were denounced as ramshackle structures that lacked the benefits of larger, more modern facilities. Even when well maintained, they were criticized for not delivering a comprehensive curriculum and social activities for children of different ages. Bigger schools were deemed more efficient in many respects, from building maintenance to curricular development and record-keeping. It was a hard argument to refute, but many rural communities fought bitterly to retain their schools. Between 1912 and 1922 Iowa consolidated more than 2,000 country districts, but nearly 10,000 remained. Consolidation proceeded faster in other states, but encountered resistance wherever local residents perceived the loss of their school as a blow to the community. For these folks, efficiency was a poor substitute for the shared traditions and sense of belonging that these schools often represented. Consequently, school consolidation was an aspect of administrative reform that took a while to achieve widespread acceptance. Eventually, the development of gasoline-powered school busses, allowing children from a widely dispersed area to be brought together, speeded the consolidation of countless walking schools districts into larger units (Reynolds, 1999; Zimmerman, 2008).

As important as these changes were, however, there was more to administrative reform than just efficiency. If a second word were to characterize the ethos of the period it would be *differentiation*. This term was encountered earlier in describing the changing social organization of cities during this period. In the larger society, differentiation of roles was associated with the widening division of labor, and with the growth of specialization in the labor market and the professions. Although this process was a source of deep concern to pedagogical progressives like Dewey, other educators embraced it as an inevitable feature of modern social organization. Administrative progressives felt that the schools could help to make the general process of specialization and differentiation unfold more rationally and smoothly, by allocating individuals to different social roles based on their natural interests and abilities. To this end they adapted the term *differentiation* itself to represent the school's commitment to distinguishing between different goals for students. This was a departure from earlier generations of educators, who had emphasized themes of commonality and fellowship in public schools. With the arrival of the administrative progressives, specialization and distinction were newly accentuated, making the school a place where students began to work toward their separate destinies (Krug, 1964; Violas, 1978).

A prime arena for these developments was the secondary education system, the network of public high schools that developed rapidly between 1890 and 1920. Basically, administrative progressives sought to make the high school into an instrument for helping young people prepare for the labor market and the widening array of occupational and social roles available to them. Accordingly, vocational education became more important during this time, including curricular innovations such as home economics, commercial and clerical training, and the manual arts. Programs of study like these were designed to prepare young men and women for strikingly different purposes (Kliebard, 1999). It is also noteworthy that the rise of high schools in rural districts was a powerful impetus to school consolidation. If towns were to offer their children the advantages of these new curricular developments, and the opportunity to compete for academic honors, local resources had to be marshaled to bring students together in a single institution (Goldin and Katz, 1999a).

Eventually, however, even grammar schools became concerned with classifying students according to their academic success. As several historians have noted, special classes were created in urban school systems for "retarded" students or "laggards," those who failed promotion from one grade to the next. The extent to which the institutions were able to perform such tasks was expressed in the term *social efficiency*. This phrase was perhaps most prominently associated with David Snedden, a former Massachusetts education superintendent who became a faculty member at Teachers College. It was intended to represent the ability of schools to endow students with appropriate knowledge and skills, and to sort students according to achievement. This was a somewhat different dimension of efficiency than that sought by the new, expert superintendents then running the big-city school systems. It referred to the degree to which the schools aided and abetted the process of social differentiation, and thus contributed to the growing range of roles and economic functions people would play in the social order. It was a novel task for public education at the time, and one that engendered a good deal of controversy and debate (Drost, 1967; Tropea, 1987).

The development of this new direction in school policies was not entirely without precedent, but it certainly became more commonplace during the progressive era. Differentiation was hardly a new concept in urban education. In the nation's largest districts there had been evidence of specialization and marking distinctions for decades before social efficiency became a buzzword for the administrative progressives. In Boston and New York, for instance, manual high schools had been established as early as the 1880s, and they existed elsewhere as well. As suggested in Chapter 4, a significant number of cities had long maintained separate schools for male and female students, believing them fundamentally different in interests and aptitude. Many cities also had elite institutions that specialized in preparing students for college or the business world; Philadelphia's Central High School was a well-known example. What was different after the turn of the century, however, was the new weight attached to practices such as these. As the public high school grew in importance, and enrollments mounted quickly, the question of how the schools would prepare students for employment proved impossible to ignore. Consequently, vocational education and related curricula appeared in schools all over the country, not just in the big cities, and the doctrine of social efficiency spread accordingly. Concern about how young people would be prepared for work was a sign of the growing complexity of society, and of modern social relations, and the administrative progressives believed it was the responsibility of schools to respond in kind (Fisher, 1967; Kantor, 1988; Krug, 1964).

Developments such as these gave rise to a new form of school management and control: *bureaucracy*. In many respects, this was a historical corollary of differentiation and the drive for greater efficiency. As the social theorist Max Weber noted, bureaucracies developed as systems of rules and regulations, monitored by individuals empowered to apportion resources according to increasingly elaborate codes of behavior. Such forms of organization allocated power and resources in ways that appeared rational and objective, representing values of impartiality and efficiency. In the late 19th century, this was believed necessary to forestall corruption and political interference in the schools. As urban education systems grew larger and more centralized, bureaucratic forms of administration became ubiquitous. When specialized programs and schools appeared, following the dictates of differentiation, they were governed by the new bureaucratic ethic, including rules dictating who was eligible to attend and graduate from various types of programs. Bureaucratic rules also came to govern system-wide purchasing and distribution practices, implementing economies of scale in providing uniform and efficient services to schools throughout a given area. The administrative progressives who designed these logical systems of resource allocation and control believed that they were creating a model for realizing the greatest possible good from a limited set of assets. In the words of David Tyack, they attempted to build the "one best system" of educational organization, believing that the bureaucratic mode of school administration and governance was the optimal choice for efficient management (Katz, 1971; Tyack, 1974).

Of course, the newly rationalized ethos in education called for measures that would allow judgments to be made about various elements of the school system. This need was answered in part by new schemes of bookkeeping and accounting, and by the legions of clerks and managers who later became known as bureaucrats. The corollary to this on the instructional side was the development of standardized or psychological testing, and a generation of professionals trained in a new subfield of psychology eventually labeled *psychometrics*. This was a natural accompaniment to the themes of social efficiency, differentiation, and preparing students for an assortment of social and economic roles. It was also well suited to the bureaucratic impulse for clear, numerical criteria on which to base rules and decisions about the disposition of resources. French researcher Alfred Binet devised the first general test of mental aptitude at around the turn of the century, and after a short time psychologists in the United States had adapted his methods for use with American subjects. Lewis Terman of Stanford University and Edward Thorndike of Teachers College were among the best-known proponents of this new technology for measuring abilities, and they quickly gained international reputations for their work in the emerging field of psychometrics (Joncich, 1968; Lagemann, 2000; Minton, 1988).

During World War I the practical application of such measures was demonstrated when the U.S. Army administered I.Q. tests to millions of draftees to help determine their eligibility for various types of training. By the later 1920s thousands of school districts employed standardized tests to judge students' suitability for particular programs, to justify curricular decisions, or simply as points of information for teachers and parents. Test construction and publication became a burgeoning business, and hundreds of university-trained psychologists were employed in producing and evaluating them. Perhaps most importantly, the use of these various testing instruments lent legitimacy to the idea that the abilities of students differed widely, and that certain roles simply were not appropriate for everyone. Thorndike, Terman, and others advanced a seemingly scientific justification to the principle of differentiation, and the new discipline of testing helped to heighten the allure of administrative progressive viewpoints (Brown, 1992; Cravens, 1993; Rury, 1988c; Gould, 1981).

The rise of the mental-testing movement held especially important implications for the education of children with special needs or learning difficulties. Children who were blind, deaf, or impaired in speech had been educated in special institutions since the mid-19th century. Most of these schools were residential and served only a small fraction of the pertinent population. Following the Civil War, similar institutions were established by various states for retarded children, often called "imbeciles" by experts. Other types of learning disabilities were not well understood at the time. For families unable or unwilling to send their children away, there often was little recourse: These children were educated in the common schools with other students or they simply stayed home. This was not considered a big problem in rural communities, where the incidence of such cases was relatively rare, but in larger cities the numbers of children with these conditions could become quite significant. As urban school systems began to grow rapidly, special classes were established for students with various categories of learning impediments. In 1879, for instance, Cleveland established a special course for "feebleminded" children; Boston followed suit in 1898, as did many other cities at about the same time. By the early 20th century a fairly wide range of such programs existed, supported by the incipient testing movement. This was a new degree of differentiation, and the standardized tests vouchsafed an added degree of legitimacy to decisions to place children in these various types of classes (Franklin, 1994; Winzer, 1993).

As it turned out, this was a domain the testers were only too happy to claim. Early psychometricians charged headlong into the task of diagnosing various categories of mental ability, coining such technical terms as *idiot* and *moron* (each representing a different level of mental retardation), and suggesting that these conditions were hereditary in nature. Public concerns were raised about the prospect of children labeled in these ways intermingling with the "normal" population, sentiments fueled by pseudoscientific advocates of *mental hygiene* and *eugenics,* a term for human perfectibility. Zealous proponents of these ideas issued racist bromides against immigration and the assimilation of various minority groups, and even urged the sterilization of "feebleminded" couples. Such concepts led to even greater efforts to segregate children with learning problems, as it was widely believed that they posed a threat to other students and that they could not learn much anyway. This was differentiation taken to a hateful extreme, reflecting the influence of racialist ideology in its preoccupation with segregating people based on biologically linked criteria. Given these origins, mental tests would come to cast a long shadow over the subsequent course of American education (Gould, 1981; Lemann, 1999; Selden, 1999; Trent, 1994).

Administrative progressivism thus had a flavor quite different from that of its pedagogical counterpart. Concerned with efficiency and fitting the educational system to the needs of society, the administrative progressives were preoccupied with finding rational solutions to the various educational and organizational problems that they encountered. Unlike the pedagogical progressives, their efforts could hardly be described as an altruistic impulse in school reform. And certain features of the administrative progressive ethos, such as mental testing and bureaucracy, soon proved to be quite controversial. Although there were some urban school regimes that pursued reforms in the name of humanizing the schools, especially in cities like Toledo and Milwaukee with progressive-minded mayors, most others sought to impose a rationality that distanced these institutions from everyday public involvement. What is more, administrative progressives eschewed the idea that education should uplift and transform children, preferring instead to devise school programs that would reproduce the social division of labor (Reese, 1986; Tyack, 1974).

Like the pedagogical reformers, the administrative progressives managed to stir up opposition to their ideas in the general public. Organized labor was often in the forefront of campaigns to stop certain efficiency measures, especially those that threatened the livelihood or working conditions of teachers. Unions, socialist groups, and neighborhood associations resisted reductions in school expenditures when they believed the quality of education was being compromised. And large numbers of working-class Americans remained suspicious of vocational education, fearing that it was a tool that employers would use to undermine trade unions. It would be wrong, in that case, to imagine that the administrative progressive strand of reform swept into prominence by universal acclamation. These ideas were at least as controversial as those of the pedagogical progressives but, unlike other reformers, the administrative progressives received the support of powerful political and financial interests. For this reason, it is easy to believe that their success was preordained. But at the time it was by no means a certainty that their agenda of efficiency and differentiation ultimately would triumph (Kliebard, 1999; Reese, 1986).

The administrative reformers inevitably prevailed, however, and most believed that they were improving the ability of the schools to address important social issues. They claimed, for instance, that in helping schools to serve the diverse purposes of an increasingly variegated student population they were upholding the democratic aims of public education. Identifying the differing abilities of students, they argued, allowed the schools to be of the greatest assistance to individuals as they sought to identify their roles in the larger society. Administrative progressives also managed to achieve their goals of consolidation in thousands of rural districts. Although they may have lacked the fervor and messianic vision of a Francis Parker or William Heard Kilpatrick, they believed that they were making the schools of the 20th century far better than their 19th-century predecessors. In this regard, administrative progressivism was an important strain of modern school reform. Simply because so many elements of the program it represented continues to inform the administration and governance of public education, it is sometimes difficult to recognize the originality in the accomplishments of its adherents. They managed to impose a certain type of order on the entire nation's schools, one that highlighted the bureaucratic norms of efficiency and differentiation. This was a prodigious task, and the fruits and consequences of their many achievements are evident as a new century in the history of American education begins today.

## The Rise of the Modern High School

As noted earlier, the opening decades of the 20th century were a time of very rapid growth for the American high school. Enrollments had expanded quickly through the latter half of the 19th century, and stood at about 300,000 in 1890 (public and private schools combined). By 1930 the number of secondary students had increased more than 15-fold, to nearly five million, a figure representing almost half the nation's eligible teenage population. Much of this was accomplished by a remarkable increase in the number of institutions: On average, a new secondary school was established nearly every day between 1890 and 1930. By the 1920s, in that case, most American communities outside of the South had access to some form of secondary education, typically through a nearby public high school (Goldin & Katz, 1999a; Herbst, 1996).

This was a big change from the 19th century, when common schools represented the universal standard for mass, publicly supported schooling in the United States. Now most Americans had relatively easy access to an even higher level of academic achievement. Although a slight majority of teenagers still did not attend high school, and many more never graduated, the mere fact that secondary schooling was available to such large numbers marked a new stage in the development of the nation's educational system. If the 19th century was the age of the common (or primary) schools, the opening decades of the 20th represented the era of the high school. In the words of one historian, the rapid increase in enrollments reflected a popular "movement" for secondary education embracing most of the country (Goldin, 1998).

As one might imagine, the rapid growth of secondary education gave rise to a good deal of controversy about ways it was to be conducted and its larger purpose in American society. Historians traditionally have focused on two public reports about the high school to characterize these debates, both commissioned by the National Education Association, a broad-based professional group for all educators at the time (and today a union). The first of these was the "Report of the Committee of Ten," published in 1893. The group that produced it was comprised mainly of university officials and national education leaders. It was chaired by Charles Eliot, president of Harvard University, and included William Torrey Harris, U.S. Commissioner of Education. Their purpose was to establish order and uniformity in a secondary-education sector that included high schools, academies, private and religious schools, and sundry other institutions beyond the primary level. There also was the problem of coordinating secondary schools with the expanding colleges and universities. Given the rather haphazard development of these various aspects of American education, it was an important task indeed (Van Overbeke, 2008; Angus & Mirel, 1999).

Eliot, Harris, and other members of the committee were traditionalists, and represented a somewhat conservative perspective on the question of how secondary education ought to be organized, and how it ought to linked to the colleges. By and large, they felt that the high school should remain squarely academic in orientation. Although they were open to a degree of flexibility regarding curricular matters and the objectives of students, they did not intend to substantially expand the high school's purview. They were willing to relax the traditional emphasis on classical languages to allow greater emphasis on more modern academic subjects. But they envisioned relatively little variation in secondary curricula, regardless of whether students intended to attend college after graduation. Basically, they felt that all students should take a rigorous program of English, history, mathematics, science, and language study, with the "collegiate" course offering the classical languages, along with modern languages or advanced mathematics and science courses. Vocationalism was not much evident in their thinking. As proponents of a psychology of discipline, the committee's members believed that the powers of concentration, memory, and communication gained from such a plan of studies would be appropriate for any career a student may choose. This was a point of view that would be roundly criticized in subsequent years (Cremin 1961; Krug, 1964).

The second famous document in the history of the high school was the "Cardinal Principles of Secondary Education," the report of the Commission on the Reorganization of Secondary Education, often called the "Kingsley Commission" after its chair, Clarence Kingsley. Issued in 1918, the Cardinal Principles report offered a new vision for American secondary education: the comprehensive high school. Unlike the Committee of Ten, the Kingsley Commission advocated a differentiated secondary curriculum, but it also called for bringing students from all backgrounds together within a single institution. In other words, differentiation would be achieved by groups of students pursuing distinct courses of study while attending the same school. Some pupils would follow vocational programs, for instance, while others might pursue a pre-collegiate course of study, and yet others might opt for a general or commercial diploma. Certain classes, however, would provide an opportunity for these students to mingle, particularly in such courses as citizenship, physical education, and health and hygiene (Angus & Mirel, 1999).

In advocating a comprehensive vision of the high school, the commission hoped to encourage secondary education to follow the logic of differentiation, considered by many to be necessary for the institution's growth, while preserving an element of commonality and shared community among its increasingly diverse constituencies. The Cardinal Principles report attempted to preserve the democratic character of American public education, addressing a major concern of the pedagogical progressives, while acknowledging the importance of differentiation, one of the themes of administrative progressives. Whether the commission succeeded in charting a truly new course for secondary education is an open question, but its formulation of the high school's various purposes clearly reflected the influence of both wings of progressive education. In this regard it was a uniquely American response to the challenges posed by secondary schooling. With such an outlook, the high school could remain a distinctive national institution (Cremin, 1961; Herbst, 1996; Krug, 1964).

These two reports offer an interesting contrast, and because of this they have fascinated generations of historians. One perspective advocated a largely academic high school, with only minor differences between the various programs students could take. The other allowed for considerably more diversity in curricula, but also emphasized the school's role in socializing young people for their shared future in a democratic society. In reality, the schools of the early 20th century probably did not embody either of the ideal types portrayed in these documents. There certainly was substantial evidence of growing vocationalism in secondary education at the time of the Committee of Ten; indeed, differentiation was increasingly the order of the day, especially in the major cities. Conversely, there still was a good deal of traditional academic work in high schools following publication of the Cardinal Principles. In fact, the institution's largest constituency continued to be middle-class students interested in academic courses. Comprehensive high schools eventually did become more commonplace, but only after the secondary-student population increased even more following 1930. Other developments in the high school's history may have been just as important as these documents, particularly measures establishing universal requirements for graduation, accounting for various types of credit, and setting criteria for different curricula. Additionally, pressures from the colleges to better prepare students for admission, facilitated by establishment of national entrance exams, helped to foster greater regularity in standards. Sheer growth, of course, also was a major impetus to change. It would be wrong, in that case, to suggest that either of these reports changed the course of American educational history. They do, however, represent telling commentaries on the concerns of the day and the ways that progressivism may have shaped the thinking of secondary educators (Angus & Mirel, 1999; VanOverbeke, 2008).

Regardless of its curricular orientation, perhaps the most striking features of the high school during this period were its remarkable expansion and its impact on the economy. The high school evolved from a rather elite institution to one open to the vast majority of American adolescents. Economic historian Claudia Goldin has described the rise of secondary schooling as the "second transformation" of United States education, placing educational attainment far ahead of other nations for much of the 20th century. The geographic areas that led this secondary-school expansion were in the Northern, Midwestern, and Western states, regions with relatively high levels of income and little inequality. Enrollments tended to be higher in communities with fewer jobs in manufacturing and low numbers of immigrants. In other words, homogeneity of economic conditions and social stability of community, given a modicum of income or wealth, seems to have fostered the extension of education to the secondary level. In areas where factory employment did not lure teens away from school, and where investments in additional education seemed reasonable, the high schools flourished (Goldin, 1998).

Goldin and other scholars have also argued that the growth of secondary enrollments added significantly to the nation's economic growth after 1920. She suggested that human capital and technological change were to the 20th century what the factory was to the 19th: an engine of development. This was reflected in the rapid increase in white-collar employment in the 20th century, growing from less than one-tenth of the national labor force to more than one-quarter in the space of a few decades. People in such positions were necessary to coordinate the nation's increasingly complex industrial production and distribution system, which was quickly becoming the most sophisticated in the world. This called for a massive national investment in human capital, achieved through ever-higher levels of schooling. Advances at the secondary level accounted for most of the increase in total of the nation's educational attainment, a general measure of human capital formation. In other words, the skills that individuals gained in high-school contributed to greater productivity and efficiency in the economy, expanding the capacity for growth considerably (Goldin, 2001).

For young men and women in certain areas of the country this meant that there was a substantial economic return (or payoff) to education, especially early in the century, a condition that doubtless affected their decisions to enroll in the first place. Analysis of data that Goldin gathered from the 1920 Iowa census, for instance, indicated that the income of individuals who attended high school was significantly higher than those who did not. Many found jobs in the rapidly expanding white-collar sector of the economy, as managers, bookkeepers, and clerical workers. Even high-paying, skilled jobs in certain manufacturing industries were increasingly reserved for high-school graduates. It is not surprising, in that case, that the reasons for attending secondary school at the time included the belief that a secondary diploma could improve opportunities for economic security and well-being. The high school was seen as a way to get ahead, and this perhaps more than anything else accounted for its rapid growth (Goldin & Katz, 2000).

The link between secondary education and the economy was a critical element in the evolution of American society. Eventually, a gradual decline in the wage premium to high-school graduates appears to have set in, after the initial boom in enrollments in the 1920s and 1930s. With the expansion of the high school, larger numbers of Americans competed for coveted white-collar positions, exerting downward pressure on wages for such jobs. But this took a while to occur. During the opening decades of the 20th century, the economic impact of the high school appears to have been quite substantial. Secondary education contributed to an important process of growth and change in the American economy, a gradual shift away from industrial employment to white-collar jobs in management, planning, and record-keeping. It was the early glimmering of a postindustrial society, and at the center of this shift was the development of the nation's educational system. This was indeed tangible evidence of a strong connection between education and social change.

All things considered, the opening decades of the 20th century represented a momentous time for American secondary schools. These institutions experienced dramatic expansion, enrolling nearly half of the adolescent population by the 1930s. Although high schools were mostly traditional academic institutions in the later 19th century, by the 1920s they were slowly evolving into somewhat more comprehensive entities, embracing a variety of different curricula and vocational purposes. Perhaps more important, secondary education was becoming a significant factor in the national economy, contributing to large-scale development of the stock of human capital at the same time that it increased the earning power of its students. In this respect the high school had come to fulfill the purposes that many administrative progressives had expressed for it. These institutions became the key link between the nation's education system and the labor market. This was the leading edge of what eventually could be described as the "human capital revolution," a time when skills and knowledge would become primary factors in the country's economic growth. When this began to happen, education would never be looked on as inconsequential again. The contributions of the school system to the economy will be considered further in the next chapter.

## FOCAL POINT: INDUSTRIALISM AND PROGRESSIVE REFORM IN GARY, INDIANA

Creating ever-closer links between the economy and the schools was an important theme in progressivism. Of course, this aspect of reform had many sides in the early years of the 20th century, some of which did not conform neatly to the categories historians have devised to describe them. One such instance occurred in the case of the schools in Gary, Indiana. Under the leadership of William Wirt, a charismatic and enterprising superintendent, this city's education system became a famous example of progressive reform at work in an industrial setting. It was seen as a case that demonstrated the possibility of uniting many of the contradictory elements of progressive education reform, and it showed the potential for controversy that schooling engendered during this period. School reform in Gary also provides an interesting lesson about the fate of educational ideas and practices once they were removed from the settings in which they were originally conceived.

Gary, Indiana, was an unusual city. Founded in 1906 by the U.S. Steel Corporation to house the workers for its giant blast furnaces and mills on the southern shore of Lake Michigan, it was named for the company's founder, Judge Elbert H. Gary. Like other industrial company towns at the time, it grew quickly as the population of workers and their families, many of them immigrants, began to settle there. A key part of the new city's planning was the establishment of a school system, and in 1908 William Wirt arrived from nearby Blufton, Indiana, to begin his tenure as its first superintendent. Wirt was a one-time student of John Dewey and held great admiration for the ideas of pedagogical progressivism, and he had started experimenting with ways of implementing progressive principles while in Blufton. The call to lead the establishment of a new city's school system in Gary afforded him the scope to develop these ideas even further. Within a relatively short time, in fact, Wirt had helped to make Gary a showcase of progressive educational policy and practice (Cohen, 1990).

Like Dewey, William Wirt was a strong believer in the importance of learning from experience about the larger world outside of the everyday lives of children. Like the managers at U.S. Steel, he also aspired to greater efficiency in the enterprise he supervised. Given these predilections, he devised a series of reforms in the organization of schooling, such that both sets of purposes were addressed. Because Gary was a brand new school system, Wirt had the opportunity to design almost everything from scratch. Instead of requiring children to remain in one classroom throughout the day, as was common in primary schools of the time, Wirt rotated children between periods of academic instruction and various types of activity learning, including laboratories, gym periods, and assembly sessions. Wirt labeled his system the "work-study-play school" but it quickly became known as the Gary Plan. This approach allowed the schools to accommodate larger numbers of children, as only half the student body required seats in classrooms at a given time. The other children would be in the gymnasiums, the auditoriums, on the playgrounds, or in labs. Utilized in this way, no major resource of the school was idle at any time, and children were exposed to a wide variety of different learning situations. Wirt also emphasized learning from the larger community and he encouraged field trips and visits by various representatives from business and civic life. He made provisions for some schools to be open to the community throughout the year, giving substance to the progressive stipulation that the school should be a center of neighborhood life. His was a practical and energetic brand of progressive reform, and it was not long before it achieved wide acclaim (Cohen & Mohl, 1979).

As one might imagine, the Gary Plan proved appealing to both wings of the progressive impulse in education. Dewey praised it for the emphasis on activity learning outside of class and the imaginative ways in which the Gary teachers utilized instructional time in the schools. The degree of public involvement in the schools, and the willingness of Wirt and his teachers to embrace the local community, impressed him and other pedagogical progressives. Administrative progressives, on the other hand, were struck by the system's efficient use of resources. School leaders in other rapidly expanding urban districts marveled at the idea that schools could serve as many as twice the number of children contained in classrooms simply by utilizing other spaces for different types of activity learning. With enthusiastic endorsements from educators on both sides of the great divide in American education at the time, the Gary Plan was widely seen as the best example of progressive ideas put to practical use. After Dewey featured the Gary schools in his book *Schools of To-Morrow*, and other writers commented on the system's efficiency, Wirt became an important figure in educational reform (Callahan, 1962; Cremin, 1961).

A key element of the success of Wirt's plan in Gary was his own commitment to the principles of progressive pedagogy. Teachers who supervised children outside of classrooms had to be carefully selected and trained in activity learning. Wirt recognized the dangers of these periods becoming little more than supervised play, or costly babysitting sessions. Even though it was a rapidly growing city, Gary was small enough so that responsible and well-trained teachers could be recruited for such duties, at least in the beginning. Making field trips, lab experiments, and other activities a regular part of the curriculum required a good deal of coordination, and considerable cooperation from local businesses, government offices, and a host of other agencies. Wirt strove to supply the resources necessary to make such planning possible, and his personal magnetism and reputation helped to assure goodwill toward the schools. As the system grew larger, however, and Wirt's personal attention was diverted to other matters, the details of such preparation increasingly were left to others. Eventually, the educative value of these alternative forms of learning became open to question. Despite the emphasis Wirt and others placed on progressive pedagogy in the system's early years, as time passed it seemed that educators were most intrigued by the Gary Plan because of the potential it held for cost savings. Even if the great appeal of Wirt's system was its ability to combine the different aspects of progressive reform, it gradually became clear that one side or the other of the period's educational debates would predominate (Cohen & Mohl, 1979).

In 1914 Wirt was called to New York City, where the mayor and local school officials asked him to help implement a variant of the Gary Plan, also called the "platoon" system, in the city's schools. Wirt came into town with great fanfare, declaring that he could save the city thousands of dollars by organizing the schools to utilize their resources more efficiently. After setting up a small number of demonstration projects, Wirt claimed to be ready to implement his ideas on a wider scale when he found himself in the middle of a controversy. The platoon school became an issue in the city's mayoral election, with labor and teacher groups protesting the movement of children from one activity to another, declaring that quality education was being sacrificed in the name of cost savings. As a result of this uproar, the New York schools eventually rejected Wirt's plan, and he returned to Gary chastened but unapologetic. Even though the Gary schools continued to be the subject of considerable attention well into the 1920s, Wirt focused his energies on matters closer to home. The New York experience had taught him just how difficult it was to transplant a complex set of educational ideas and practices into a new and different social and political context (Cohen, 1990; Ravitch, 1974).

The basic concept of the platoon school, however, proved very appealing to district administrators faced with rapidly expanding enrollments and a fixed stock of classroom spaces. Eventually more than 200 cities adopted some form or another of this method of school organization. Much of the platoon school's popularity can be attributed to the work of Alice Barrows, Wirt's idealistic and enthusiastic assistant in the ill-fated New York experiment. Barrows subsequently took a position in the U.S. education office and became an untiring advocate of Wirt's ideas. It is open to question, however, whether school administrators agreed with the progressive pedagogical predilections of Barrows as much as they were interested in the greater efficiency the platoon plan afforded their districts. Children moving around the school to use laboratories, art rooms, and gymnasiums eventually would become a staple of American education, but it is not clear that such activities were linked to a progressive conception of teaching and learning. Like so many other educational ideas, Wirt's platoon system was adapted by local educators to serve their own purposes, and to help the schools achieve their traditional goals in a more efficient manner. As David Tyack and Larry Cuban have noted, most educational reforms have ended up in producing only slight alterations to the existing modes of school organization, as they were adjusted to suit the needs of teachers and principals in particular settings. The Gary Plan, however appealing at the start, was no exception to this general rule (Cohen, 1990; Tyack & Cuban, 1995).

William Wirt's approach to progressive reform was one of dozens of similarly localized efforts to improve schools both in terms of pedagogy and efficiency. The schools of Winnetka, Illinois, under the leadership of Carlton Washburn, were another prominent example, along with Helen Parkhurst's "Dalton Plan," which originated in the high school at Dalton, Massachusetts. Parkhurst later was associated with a private institution she founded in New York City, the Dalton School. Not all of these reform regimes were as schematic as Wirt's; most were located in relatively affluent communities and emphasized individual expression and a break with traditional curricula. By the end of the 1920s, however, many of them were on the defensive. In the case of Gary, a survey of the schools headed by Abraham Flexner, the famous critic of higher and professional education, found that students performed poorly on tests of traditional knowledge and that Wirt's highly touted efficiency was not evident in all of the district's schools. Similar criticisms were leveled at other districts identified with pedagogical reform. Perhaps findings such as these were inevitable, given the hyperbole that often accompanied the work of educational reformers in this era. Despite its great fervor, progressive reform seems never to have fulfilled its promise of a fundamental transformation in American schooling. Even with visionary leaders, and an abundance of local resources and goodwill, the pace of change in schooling was ultimately quite incremental. This is a lesson from history that most would-be reformers seem all too eager to overlook even today (Semel & Sadovnik, 1999; Zilversmit, 1993).

### Outsiders: Gender, Race, and Equity in Education during the Progressive Era

Progressive school reform was rooted in humanitarian principles, and Dewey and other reformers were concerned about democracy, but the movement's record on questions of race, gender, and social equality was hardly a sterling reflection of these values. Despite the interest that school leaders expressed in serving all the various elements of society, there is evidence that inequity in education grew worse during the progressive era. The benefits of progressive reform were not available to everyone. Large segments of the American population were left untouched by pedagogical change, and administrative reforms—guided by the dictates of efficiency and differentiation—probably served to hamper the educational prospects of students from certain social groups. Even though there was a growing national debate about these questions, ideologies of racism and sexism were still widely propagated at this time, even by educators. It was an era of sharp differences in social status, and this was reflected in the nation's schools. Put simply, equity was not a major focus of reform.

One example of this was women's secondary education. In Chapter 4 it was noted that the later 19th century was a time of remarkable gender equity in American high schools, notwithstanding the efforts of Edward Clarke and other opponents of coeducation. Girls outnumbered boys by a two-to-one margin in secondary schools during the 1890s, and outperformed them on most measures of academic accomplishment. More important, they appear to have taken generally the same courses as the boys; there was little evident curricular differentiation according to gender. This would change in the early 20th century, partly because some educators became uncomfortable with the idea of relative equality for women. They expressed anxiety that the high school was becoming feminized by all of the young women in attendance, and that male students were in jeopardy of losing their masculinity. These fears were voiced by the prominent psychologist G. Stanley Hall of Clark University, and echoed widely throughout the educational establishment. Just a few decades after the controversy occasioned by Clarke's attack on women's education, it appeared that a new consensus was building to change female schooling once again (Rury, 1991; Tyack & Hansot, 1990).

At the same time that some educators, mostly men, were fretting about the perceived feminization of American schools, others were working to devise new forms of education for young women. Ellen Richards, a chemist and the Massachusetts Institute of Technology's first female faculty member, helped to launch a distinctive academic field called *home economics* in the first decade of the 20th century. The home-economics movement eventually sought to define an entire academic discipline around the study of problems related to women and their roles as mothers and housekeepers, embracing everything from nutrition to consumer behavior (often called *family and consumer studies* today). For educators in the high schools, however, home economics became a way of defining women's roles through training in accepted forms of work, and socialization in prescribed standards of conduct. In this regard it represented a way of differentiating the education of young women from that of males, at the same time that it proposed to ready them for their "true" calling in life: preparing to become a wife, mother, and homemaker. In a relatively brief period, home economics would become one pillar of a distinctively female segment of the high-school curriculum (Kliebard, 1999; Rury, 1991).

There were other areas of change in women's education too, most of them connected to shifts in female employment. As suggested earlier, thousands of young women took new jobs in stores, offices, and other settings where they performed clerical tasks for the burgeoning corporate and governmental sectors of the economy. This led to a boom in enrollments for programs in commercial education, where women received training in stenography, typing, bookkeeping, and other subjects that could help them obtain clerical positions. It was not long before these classes became dominated by women, helping to typecast such forms of training and employment as feminine. The same tendency was evident in programs to train students in sewing and other skills suitable for the garment trades. The earliest programs of this sort were conducted in private trade schools that specialized in commercial and vocational education, but eventually most students who wanted such training opted for programs in the public high schools, where they were free and easily accessible. The development of a sizeable portion of the public high-school curriculum devoted primarily to preparing young women for "female" jobs in the labor force was yet another aspect of gender differentiation in education. As the high school became increasingly concerned with vocational preparation for its students, and young men and women were trained for different careers, the institution's course of study came to be divided along the lines of gender (Powers, 1992).

Although these developments probably did not result in a dramatic change in the schooling of many young men and women, the impact was far-reaching. Most schools continued to be coeducational, and girls and boys still took most of their academic classes together. The process of change occurred at the margins, in a relatively small number of vocational subjects, but it would be wrong to underestimate their importance. The very fact that several classes in most large, comprehensive high schools were almost exclusively populated by women—home economics, typing, stenography, sewing, and similar subjects—while others were considered the domain of the boys—shop, drafting, mechanics, and the like—sent a definite message: Gender was still a powerful determinant of a person's ultimate role in society. Unlike the 19th century, when the high school was dominated by academic subjects and there were few differences between the sexes, by the 1920s it was clear that boys and girls were destined to occupy distinct positions in the social division of labor. There is evidence, moreover, that it was at about this time that the academic performance of young women in certain subjects, particularly mathematics and science, began to fall behind that of the men. Just as the labor market dictated that young women were best suited to assume roles as secretaries and filing clerks, many educators came to believe that female students were not as analytically keen as their male classmates, at least in specific classes. A subtle but insidious set of gender distinctions slowly began to take hold, and it would be several decades before they would eventually come to light in public discussions (Rury, 1991; Tyack & Hansot, 1990).

The movement toward gender distinctions in American high schools was embraced enthusiastically by progressive educators of every stripe. For administrative progressives it represented an axiomatic case of curricular differentiation. After all, they reasoned, few areas of life exhibited a more striking set of distinctions than gender, and the urban industrial economy clearly called for men and women to fulfill different occupational roles. For pedagogical progressives, on the other hand, subjects like home economics for girls and shop for boys represented a healthy connection between the school and the wider world of work and living that students were preparing for. What better way to introduce them to their likely future positions in society? Few educators posed questions about the inequities inherent in this pattern of curricular specialization. Instead, the appearance of new courses such as home economics and the commercial subjects was widely hailed as the dawn of a new era in secondary education. Some fervent reformers made fantastic claims: Ellen Richards, for instance, predicted that home economics could save American civilization, as women learned to be better mothers and housekeepers. This was the ideology of "republican motherhood" taken to a new extreme. Such an assertion may seem silly today—historians David Tyack and Elisabeth Hansot labeled it "social salvation with white sauce"—but it helped obscure the sexist quality of the reforms being proposed. For educators in the early 20th century, the concept of differentiation was too logical to resist, even if it sharply delimited the options that their students would enjoy in the future (Powers, 1992; Tyack & Hansot, 1990).

A similar set of issues confronted African Americans in school at this time, but the pattern of discrimination and ideological classification that they encountered was even more pronounced. As noted in Chapter 4, Black schooling was decidedly inferior to that provided to Whites in the South in the later 19th century. This pattern of unequal education continued into the progressive era, with Black schools hobbled by shorter terms, lower pay for teachers, and fewer supplies than similar institutions for Whites. More than 90% of the African American population lived in the South and were forced to scratch out a meager living in the region's agricultural economy. Although the North experienced large-scale industrialization and urban development, the pace of economic change was considerably slower in the land of Dixie, despite claims of a "New South." In the years following 1910, hundreds of thousands of Blacks moved to the rapidly expanding cities of the North, to take industrial jobs and escape the Jim Crow mentality of Southern society. For the vast majority of the African American population that remained, however, life in the South did not improve appreciably. The poor condition of Black education was an important aspect of the region's continuing legacy of servitude (Cremin, 1988; Bond, 1966).

Despite the grotesque inequalities that characterized Southern education, there were some signs of progress. Spurred by the activities of Northern philanthropies, Southern states invested more resources in public education, including Black schools. The vast majority of this new funding for African Americans, however, was spent on primary schooling. New schools were built, additional teachers hired, and supplies purchased, but mainly to provide education in the elementary grades. This furnished Black Southerners with basic literacy skills but little else. In the meantime, it gave Whites some political cover when they were accused of depriving Black taxpayers of essential services, and it also helped to mask inequities in other areas of the educational system (Margo, 1990; Werum, 1997).

Perhaps the biggest source of racial disparity in Southern schooling appeared in secondary education. During the progressive era fewer than 5% of high-school-aged Black students were enrolled at the secondary level, most of them in private schools supported by tuition, local donations, and Northern philanthropy. In the meantime, public high schools were established throughout the South for White children, particularly in the region's larger towns and cities. Even if Southern school systems lagged behind the rest of the country in terms of facilities and attendance patterns, public secondary schools for the White population became available quite rapidly. Between 1905 and 1920 more than 500 of these institutions were established, making secondary schooling widely accessible. By contrast, in 1916 only 58 public high schools for African Americans existed in 14 Southern states, with just 25 in the former Confederate states. These institutions existed in major cities, where a small but active Black middle class helped to sustain them. In the rural areas where most Blacks lived, however, secondary education was virtually nonexistent. Even though the numbers of teenagers in each race were about the same in the states of the "Deep South," White public high schools outnumbered those for African Americans by more than a 10:1 ratio. For the Blacks, secondary education remained an elusive goal, a bitter reminder of their subservient status in the regional culture (Anderson, 1988; Fultz, 2008).

Even when public high schools did exist for local Black communities, there were questions about their academic quality. Reflecting the influence of Booker T. Washington, some Black public secondary institutions featured a manual-training curriculum. This meant that the male students spent most of the school day in shops and tool rooms, learning carpentry, other trades, or simple handicrafts. For Black women, there was an emphasis on home economics, with an eye to working as domestic servants, the largest category of employment for Black women at the time. These schools offered only a smattering of academic classes, and certainly were not equivalent to the highly scholastic quality of the best White high schools. Not everyone was enamored of manual training, however, and many Black communities struggled to maintain strong academic secondary institutions for their children. Historians have identified examples of outstanding Black secondary institutions during the latter stages of this era (Anderson, 1988; Siddle-Walker, 1996). But such efforts often faced an uphill struggle. In the minds of Southern Whites, secondary education was simply not appropriate for most African Americans, and when offered it was most suitably focused on vocational subjects. Southern congressmen led the way in drafting the first federal legislation to support vocational education, the Smith–Hughes Act in 1918, arguing that it would benefit the region's African American population. Like other education funds, most of this money eventually went to White schools, but the link between manual training and Black schooling was firmly established. It would take time and struggle to change (Werum, 1997).

These differences in the availability and quality of secondary schooling held enormous implications for African Americans. If indeed the opening decades of the 20th century marked the age of the high school, and secondary education became increasingly important to economic advancement, the nation's Black population missed out on this crucial step in the human capital revolution. As certain skills and knowledge became essential to economic growth, Blacks were denied access to them. This meant that an entire generation—or more—of them were deprived of the capacity to compete for employment in the expanding white-collar and managerial sector of the labor market. They could not hope to get jobs as clerks or typists, much less as accountants or office managers, without the critical credential represented by a high-school diploma. What is more, they could not pass the knowledge and insights gained from such positions—human and cultural capital—on to their own children. The withholding of secondary education from Black Southerners thus caused this large segment of the American population to fall even farther behind the rest of the nation in educational attainment and everything that accompanied it. As seen in Chapter 6, this would prove to be a difficult legacy to overcome.

Similar challenges faced the Hispanic population in the Southwestern and Western states, where segregated, inferior schools had become widespread by the early 20th century. Even in places where Mexican Americans were permitted to attend the same schools as Anglos, they were often required to take separate classes and focus on vocational subjects. Because of language barriers, they often scored poorly on standardized tests and were excluded from academic courses. Consequently, many did not remain in school, and their rates of secondary graduation were far below the norm. Millions of Mexican workers came to the U.S. in the opening decades of the century, and many were forcibly deported during the Great Depression. Outright discrimination and uncertainty about their status as full-fledged members of the U.S. polity made it difficult for those who remained to focus on improving educational attainment for their children. Despite some notable challenges to segregated schooling, conditions did not improve much during this period. Upon leaving school, Mexican American children and youth took jobs as agricultural workers, in factories or as domestic servants, low-paying positions that reinforced stereotypes about their menial status in American society. With a few exceptions, progressive educators did not concern themselves with the plight of these children, and school leaders ignored the problems of unequal achievement in their communities (Donato, 1997; Gonzales, 1990; MacDonald, 2004).

The experiences of young women, African Americans and Hispanics in this period should be considered a part of the legacy of progressivism. As suggested earlier, the treatment of these groups in secondary schools can be thought of as yet another aspect of differentiation. Indeed, David Snedden and other devotees of administrative progressivism probably would find little cause for concern in the foregoing account. The schools, in their view, were simply supposed to efficiently reproduce the existing social division of labor, not eradicate it—hence their term *social efficiency*. If African Americans or Mexican Americans occupied a servile position in the social order, it was not the educational system's task to change that. The work of the new testing professionals seemed to confirm this. Differences attributable to race and gender were often seen as biologically based, and thus taken to be God-given and not subject to human or institutional intervention. Indeed, the most zealous testers believed that inherent mental abilities separated all working-class children from those of more educated parents, regardless of race or ethnicity. Thus, the educational system was seen as a grand selection mechanism, certifying inequality as it chose certain students for success and others for failure.

The purpose of schooling, in that case, was to prepare each group for its inevitable social destination, and not to raise thorny questions about equality and fairness along the way (Drost, 1967; Kliebard, 1999).

If it is simple to comprehend the position of a conservative such as Snedden, it is harder to understand the view of the pedagogical progressives on questions of race and gender. John Dewey was a giant among American liberals of his day, a staunch opponent to the idea of racial inferiority and a founding member of the National Association for the Advancement of Colored Persons (NAACP) (Alridge, 2008). Yet he was strangely quiet on these issues—especially concerning race through much of his career. On occasion he acknowledged the problem, such as in a 1930 article on illiteracy where he noted the sharp racial discrepancies in Southern school funding (Dewey, 1930). But it was not a major theme in his writing. Perhaps the battle against traditional forms of education was too demanding, along with other philosophical debates, and pedagogical progressives feared that addressing yet other questions could jeopardize their fragile movement. It is possible that Dewey and other progressive thinkers did not feel compelled to confront racial issues explicitly, simply because relatively few Blacks lived in the North at the time. Although his Columbia University office was close to Harlem, a growing Black community by 1930, Dewey may have felt that the question of race was part of the larger issue of inequality in American democracy, a matter he devoted much time and energy to addressing in expansive terms (Westbrook, 1991). Whatever the cause, issues of race and ethnicity appear to have been something of a blind spot in the progressives' humanitarian campaign to transform the school. It was not a set of problems that they devoted very much time and energy to, and the movement—not to mention the nation's education system—was the poorer for it (Rury, 1991b).

## The University Enters an Age of Human Capital

As noted in Chapter 3, institutions of higher education underwent an important set of changes in the later 19th century. The old-time college, with its emphasis on classical study and mental discipline, slowly gave way to the modern research university. These new institutions were governed by an ethic of investigation and discovery, along with engagement with the problems of society. The leaders of this movement were elite Eastern private institutions and the flagship state universities of the Midwest and California. By the early 20th century it had become fashionable for middle-class youth, women and men alike, to attend these schools, both for the lively social scene and to gain credentials that would be useful in the labor force. Enrollments mounted quickly, as students found that higher education promised pathways to employment in the large corporations, government, and the professions. Even though overall attendance remained a small fraction of the number of high-school students, these developments were a harbinger of the future (Fass, 1977; Veysey, 1965).

The shift from the traditional college of the 19th century to the modern university was a gradual process, even if the differences between the two types of institutions were rather dramatic. Religion had played a prominent role in the colleges, and although it continued to be an important element in the life of the university, its dominance of the cultural ethos in higher education declined markedly with time. A new generation of faculty members was trained in Europe, mostly in Germany, where principles of scientific research held sway over traditional concerns with classics and religious morality. Many of these professors also believed that the university should be more intimately involved in improving society, whether through social reform or simply improving the efficiency of existing institutions and practices. By and large, they found a receptive audience. Increasingly, the classes that students took were grounded in the new research-based academic disciplines, and not classical languages or Biblical scholarship. Although large numbers of the graduates of the old-time college had become ministers in the 19th century, after 1900 more university graduates began to take jobs in business and the professions. All of this contributed to a new atmosphere of secularism and a quest for individual advancement through higher education. While many students still went to college for purposes of piety and scholarly growth, they were joined by a new type of student, one interested in having fun and getting a good job (Marsden, 1994; Reuben, 1996; Rodgers, 1998).

These changes were correlates of growth. Overall enrollment climbed from about a quarter million in 1900 to more than 1 million in 1930, representing more than 10% of the age 18 to 21 population at the time. This was a significant fraction of American youth, even if it still constituted something of a social and cultural elite. These growing enrollments were a direct reflection of expansion in secondary education, and improved linkages between the nation's high schools and colleges. The College Board, an association of schools and colleges established in 1900, became a key agency for coordinating admission examinations on a national basis. This made it much easier for students to consider a range of colleges, in all parts of the country. As more young people graduated from secondary school, after all, it was natural for some of them to seek even higher status or better career prospects than their peers, or even study far from home. Whether it was these concerns or simply an interest in learning more, increasing numbers considered going off to college.

Higher education in this era also began to have an important impact on American culture. Large concentrations of college students at the leading state universities, particularly those in the Midwestern and Western states, began to develop their own cultural identity. Enrollments grew into the thousands at these campuses, and an elaborate social life began to flourish. The number of female students grew even faster than the male collegiate population, expanding from less than 40% of the student body in the 1890s to almost half by the 1920s. These developments infused new energy into campus life. A brisk dating scene sparked an atmosphere of sexual openness and experimentation, the so-called flapper era, characterized by drinking, dances, and "necking." Although only a minority of students participated routinely in such behavior, these students represented a sharp break with the past. Fraternities and sororities also became very popular, especially after 1920, along with spectator sports such as football. All of this marked a new era in campus cultures. College life was emerging as a distinctive phase in the experience of middle- and upper-class youth, even if many still skipped college altogether. For those who participated, the social side of the university often constituted the start of a career in business or the professions: Many students formed friendships and associations that extended well into their adult and professional lives (Bledstein, 1976; Horowitz, 1987). This was a particular form of social capital, developed and nurtured on university campuses.

In case there was any doubt about these shifts, the utilitarian cast of the university was certified with the appearance of a host of new professional schools and institutes. In the 19th century legal and medical training had been conducted by private schools or individuals; around 1900 the universities began acquiring these institutions, or developing their own, and awarding degrees to students who completed professional courses of study. Similar arrangements were made for the preparation of engineers, social workers, and other professionals. It was also in this period that the first university programs to provide training for business were established, offering courses in accounting, finance, management, marketing, and similar subjects. These developments proved to be a substantial boost to enrollments, as students were drawn to the campuses to obtain the credentials that they would need for entry into work life. With the advent of professional study, it was harder to cast the university as an isolated academic ivory tower. For better or worse, higher education was being drawn ever closer to the practical worlds of business, government, and the major professions. In this way it was providing human capital, critical knowledge and skills, for the nation's future leaders (Geiger, 1986; Goldin & Katz, 1999b; Levine, 1986).

The growth of higher education also led to a proliferation of different types of institutions. This was yet a new kind of differentiation, as the demand for various forms of higher learning met with an institutional response. In addition to elite Eastern private schools and the big state flagship universities, along with other largely residential institutions, a number of new colleges and universities appeared in this era. Among the most important was a two-year institution designed to offer the most basic courses as a preparation for higher study, the junior college, later called the community college. These institutions first appeared in the West and the Midwest, numbering some 200 by the latter 1920s but enrolling less than one-tenth of all undergraduates. Other more popular forms of higher education also flourished, among them municipal colleges in the larger cities and private urban universities. These institutions served commuter students, providing baccalaureate education along with a variety of professional programs. Career-minded students in New York, Cincinnati, or Detroit thus could attend local public colleges, whereas those in Chicago went to DePaul, Loyola, or the Armour Institute (today's Illinois Institute of Technology). This was higher education for the new aspiring middle class, especially the children of immigrants, students who could not afford more elite schools or who were unable or less inclined to live away from home. Producing legions of lawyers, engineers, accountants, and teachers, these institutions embodied the new pragmatic ethos of American higher education (Brint & Karabel, 1989; Levine, 1986).

The early 20th century was a time of significant growth and change in higher learning. Responding to the demand for new knowledge and skills, the human capital requirements of the urban industrial age, the nation's colleges and universities shifted their mission to furnishing students with credentials that they could use in the rapidly evolving economy. As enrollments grew steadily, and coeducation became a national norm, a distinctive collegiate culture came to characterize the lives of students at these institutions. These changes highlighted the increased prominence that higher education was coming to assume in American civilization. They were also a portent of the future development of the university as a singular and critical feature of the nation's educational system. As striking as these events may have seemed at the time, they were just the beginning of the emergence of the modern system of higher education.

## Education and Social Change in an Urban Industrial Era

The progressive era was a period of transformation in the United States. The industrial revolution unleashed powerful forces of change. The economy expanded at an unprecedented rate, the nation's transportation and communications systems evolved rapidly, and the cities underwent booming growth. All of this demanded significant changes in the educational system, enabling it to supply both basic education to the masses of industrial workers and higher forms of instruction to the emerging white-collar labor force. As the nation's population expanded—a result of both natural increase and immigration—thousands of new schools were needed. With the educational system's growth, more sophisticated forms of management and organization were required to address these conditions. Along with this, fresh educational ideas were debated as educators struggled to fashion a new system of schooling for the 20th century.

As regards the direction of change, it seems clear that the schools responded to shifts in the economic and social organization of the nation.

The rational, bureaucratic reforms of the administrative progressives were in part a response to the development of large, complex, urban school systems, and to the problems of maintaining consistent standards of conduct for students and school employees alike, not to mention board members and politicians. In the countryside, the logic of efficiency and bureaucratic control led to campaigns to consolidate rural schools, although these efforts also met with a great deal of resistance. At the same time, high schools proliferated, in large part because of the demand for clerical workers, managers, and other white-collar workers needed to record and process information for the age's new large corporate firms and the governmental agencies established to monitor them. Demand for professional service, from legal advice to accountants and engineers, spurred new levels of interest in higher education, as colleges and universities created degree programs to serve their expanding clientele. At the same time, education helped to demarcate status distinctions between people performing different types of work. As society became increasingly differentiated, social class distinctions were exemplified by varying levels of schooling. In this respect, education also helped to accentuate inequality. If the industrial revolution was transforming American society, the education system was responding in kind. A new age was dawning, and modern schools evolved to meet its varied needs, and to reflect an emerging status hierarchy.

Did schools change society in this period as well? Clearly, they produced the skilled and knowledgeable workers needed for the growth of the urban industrial economy. This was no small matter, as Claudia Goldin and others have argued, for without an educated workforce it is unlikely that the U.S. economy would have developed as rapidly as it did. But what about other types of change? Did the pedagogical progressives succeed in creating a renewed sense of community by making schools more humane and "child-centered"? Did John Dewey and his followers establish an ethic of democracy for the nation's schools, militating against industry's tendency to make people "appendages of machines?" Here the impact of school reform appears to have been considerably more modest. Although the pedagogical progressives did create a number of exemplary schools, and conducted a number of inspired local reform experiments, such as in Gary and Winnetka, their impact on the larger educational system appears to have been modest at best. Driven by the rationalistic and efficiency-minded reforms of the administrative progressives, most teachers and administrators in American schools were not influenced much by the likes of Parker, Kilpatrick, or other pedagogical reformers. Instead, their lives were probably more immediately and deeply affected by the growing educational bureaucracy, by the testing movement, and by the sheer growth of the educational system than by any new ideas about how to improve or humanize instruction. As a result, the legacy of pedagogical reform in this period is an ambiguous one. It produced many zealous reformers, passionate experiments, and idealistic principles, but it is an open question whether it created lasting change in most of the nation's classrooms.

The impulse toward greater differentiation and "social efficiency" in American education is one area where the effect of school reforms does indeed appear to have had a significant impact on social change. As noted earlier, the desire to make the schools respond more effectively to the "needs" of various social groups helped to perpetuate and widen existing patterns of social inequality. In particular, women, African Americans, and Hispanics suffered as a consequence of efforts to design schools to fit them to sub-servient social roles. The development of vocational education, home economics, and manual arts schools was a part of this process. It would take decades before the effect of these "reforms" was recognized and remedied, and even then it would require considerable debate and struggle.

Education and social change were thus clearly linked during the progressive period of American history. The schools responded to the demands created by the nation's rapidly developing economy. As growth increasingly led to demand for highly educated workers, the "human capital revolution" gave certain forms of schooling new prominence, especially secondary and higher education. This would be a sign of developments to come. In other respects, however, educational reform does not seem to have succeeded in accomplishing the lofty aims that its spokespersons articulated for it. This was perhaps the great disappointment of a period of considerable ferment in American education, one that has left a legacy of advocacy for change that continues to echo today.

# 6

# The Human Capital Revolution
## *Postwar America to the End of the 20th Century*

There can be little doubt that the decades following World War II marked a time of extensive transformation in American life, and in the nation's schools. It was a period of astounding technological advances in many realms, an age of jet travel, television, and electric guitars. Equally dramatic shifts affected social policy issues and the relationships of various groups in American society. This was especially true in major metropolitan areas, where the vast majority of Americans had come to reside in the latter 20th century. Altogether, it was a period comparable in significance to the industrial revolution. It is against this backdrop of societal change that recent events in American education probably can be best understood.

From the standpoint of this book, however, perhaps the most striking feature of this period was the growing importance attached to formal education, both as a matter of public policy and as a private concern. It was during these years that the human capital revolution finally came to full bloom in the United States. As in earlier times, schools continued to be seen as engines of commercial development, but after World War II they increasingly were acknowledged as a primary factor in national economic growth. Reflecting this, economists coined the term "human capital" to denote the growing role of education in the economy. At the same time, schools also became instruments of federal social policy. In this connection, the role of education expanded further, to attempt the redress of seemingly intractable social inequity. The federal government became a major source of funding and policy initiatives, and schooling developed into an important issue in national politics. At the same time, more Americans attended schools than in any previous period. Enrollments climbed at all levels of the educational system, but especially in the nation's high schools and colleges. Everyone, it seemed, was interested in going to school, and educational attainment became a far-reaching public preoccupation.

This also was a time of change in the nation's intellectual life, and in the major ideological currents that shaped thinking about the schools. Progressive education fell out of favor with much of the public. Opposition to these ideas and practices came to a peak in the 1950s, abetted by a conservative ethos fostered by the anti-communist sentiments of the Cold War. At the same time, however, there was a gradual liberalization of racial ideas, partly influenced by wartime aversion for Nazi theories of Aryan supremacy and Cold War concerns about the American image abroad. The 1954 Supreme Court decision in *Brown* v. *Board of Education*, declaring segregated schools to be inherently unequal, was a milestone of national educational policy and in popular conceptions of social justice. It was also a defining moment for the modern civil rights movement, an event that eventually altered the ideological tenor of public life in the United States. Struggles for women's equality and students' rights eventually took inspiration from the battle over racial justice, and these too had an important effect on the schools. As a consequence of these changes, American education would never be the same (Ravitch, 1983).

In addition to these developments, several major social trends in the postwar period had an impact on American schools. The first of these was the changing racial and ethnic composition of the nation's principal metropolitan areas. As noted earlier, most African Americans lived in the South prior to World War II. Demand for cheap labor in the war industries, however, combined with the mechanization of agriculture in the South, led to a massive shift in the nation's Black population to urban areas in the North and upper Midwest. With the migration of millions of poorly educated Blacks during the late 1940s, 1950s, and 1960s, big-city public schools systems became highly differentiated along racial lines. Despite the principles of integration and equity embodied in the 1954 *Brown* decision, and the efforts of liberal-minded educators across the country, growing inequalities in the type and quality of education came to characterize metropolitan life (Kantor & Brenzel, 1993). If policymakers and large segments of the public believed that one purpose of the public school was to bring students from different backgrounds—and with differing social destinations—together, the process of racial and social/economic differentiation made it less tenable as time passed, something educators quickly came to recognize (Conant, 1961).

Another major event in the postwar era was the appearance of a vibrant, pervasive, and commercially expansive youth culture. This was partly a consequence of demographic numbers. Following the war, birth rates soared, as men (and women) returning from the military began to settle into family life. This was the beginning of the historically large "baby boom" generation, which created a large cohort of teenagers by the later 1950s and the 1960s (Hawes & Hiner, 1985; Macunovich, 2002). This was the leading edge of the new youth culture. Teens also shaped the evolution of courtship practices, especially as they became interested in sexuality and relationships, building an elaborate set of rituals and social practices around these concerns (Modell, 1989). With growing high-school attendance in the 1950s and 1960s, followed by rising college enrollments, educational institutions became the location in which these emerging forms of adolescent culture would develop most rapidly (Coleman, 1965).

Finally, there was the evolution of the American economy in the postwar period, particularly the changing occupational structure, and rising educational requirements for different types of jobs. This was perhaps the clearest manifestation of the new significance attached to human capital in American economic life. The high school dramatically expanded its purview, but its economic significance diminished. As the number of jobs requiring a high-school diploma or less declined, particularly in the years following 1980, rates of college enrollments began to increase significantly. American employers raised their educational expectations, and so did students and their parents (Buchman, 1989; Murphy & Welch, 1989). The result was a sea change in the way Americans came to view higher education.

Each of these issues is examined in greater depth in this chapter. The postwar years marked a time when the relationship between education and social change became quite complex. As a matter of social policy, schools increasingly were called on to address questions of economic and social inequality. At the same time, the nation's educational system was itself profoundly affected by ideological shifts, and by underlying patterns of economic and demographic change. Even as schooling assumed greater importance, the questions of its availability and quality became vital concerns. Given these dynamics, determining the relationship between education and social change in this period is a challenging task. First, however, it is important to consider one of the central issues of this era in American civilization: changing patterns of family life and the emergence of a teenage subculture that eventually swept the nation.

## FOCAL POINT: REBELS IN SEARCH OF THEMSELVES

In many respects the postwar period marked the beginning of the era of the teenager in the United States. Even though the teenage population was comparatively small in the 1950s, due to low birth rates during the Depression and war, changing occupational patterns gave teens a great deal more free time, and national prosperity meant that they had money to spend too. Shifts in industrial employment, along with labor laws enacted during the 1930s and 1940s, sharply reduced the number of factory workers under age 19, and growing high-school enrollments meant that large numbers of teens found themselves clustered together in classrooms and hallways for hours on end each day. All of this contributed to the development of a distinctive teenage society, a national subculture marked by particular patterns of behavior, fashion, and values.

Youth cultural identities had existed in earlier decades, but in the postwar years the emerging teenage social world seemed more pervasive and troubling. It was not long before a wide range of commentators began remarking on the problems of American youth, and terms such as *juvenile delinquent* and *high-school dropout* began to become commonplace. Teenagers seemed to be rejecting the values of their parents, listening to new music, and experimenting with tobacco, alcohol, and sex. It was a phenomenon that adults struggled to understand, even as many found the problems of the nation's youth quite alarming (Gilbert, 1986).

A series of books, magazine articles, television reports, and movies appeared in the 1950s and 1960s focusing on questions of teenage behavior. Perhaps the most famous of the movies was the 1955 film *Rebel without a Cause*, best known today for the role of its principal actor, the charismatic James Dean. *Rebel* is widely regarded as one of Dean's best film performances, but it also featured Natalie Wood and Sal Mineo in roles that helped to launch their careers. What made the film especially interesting, however, was its portrayal of the troubles teenagers experienced, and the role of adults—especially parents—in the creation and resolution of these problems. It was a dramatic story, but not one that exploited public fears by depicting base stereotypes. Unlike other films of the era, it was not a tale of demonic youth, crazed by music, sex, and alcohol, bent on self-destruction. Instead, it offered a portrait of misunderstood teens in search of parental love and guidance, forced into the bizarre social world of their peers by the selfishness and inhibitions of their elders. In these fundamental terms, *Rebel* was something of a morality play about the shortcomings of modern civilization and ways in which the larger society had neglected the nation's youth. As such, it offers a compelling glimpse into many of the concerns of its time, especially the feelings of many Americans about problems related to education and growing up in the modern world (Doherty, 1988).

*Rebel without a Cause* was a tale of alienation, violence, and love. It was set in Los Angeles, and represented the problems of moral confusion that many Americans associated with Southern California. Loosely based on the true story of a juvenile criminal, the script was developed from a storyline by the film's director, Nicholas Ray. Some critics noted that it bore certain Shakespearian characteristics, and loosely resembled Romeo and Juliet. All three of its central characters, Jim Stark (James Dean), Judy (Natalie Wood), and John or "Plato" (Sal Mineo), were teenagers struggling with different forms of parental neglect or rejection, and coping with this loss in ways that ultimately turned out to be quite self-destructive. In the case of Jim (Dean), his indecisive father was unable to provide a clear and admirable role model, filling the young man with self-doubt and insecurity. These traits caused him to lash out at adversaries, and to engage in aberrant behavior (such as binge drinking) to get the attention of his parents. Natalie Wood's character, Judy, was a young woman feeling rejected by her father, who was insecure about his daughter's budding sexuality and her yearning for his approval and affection. And John (Mineo), known mostly by his nickname Plato, was a social misfit whose wealthy parents had abandoned him altogether, leaving him in the care of an

African American maid. Judy sought solace in the in the fast company of other young malcontents, while John drifted at the margins of teen society until he met Jim, who became his friend and something of a father figure. It was these conditions that framed the movie's storyline, and revealed its principal message about the way adult society was disregarding the nation's youth.

Perhaps the most telling relationship in the movie is that between Jim and his father, played by Jim Bacchus (later the millionaire on the TV show *Gilligan's Island*). Bacchus's character is morally vacuous, and he appears unable to take a firm stand on anything. He is intimidated by his wife, who seems preoccupied with observing social conventions and maintaining appearances. These were familiar themes in the 1950s, when many commentators worried that weak or distracted fathers and obsessive, controlling mothers were psychologically harming children. While describing his troubles to a sympathetic police detective, young Jim complains that his parents are always bickering and that his father cannot stand up to his mother. "How can a guy grow up in a circus like that," he declares. "Boy, if I had one day when I didn't have to be all confused ... if I felt I belonged someplace, you know." Later in the movie, when Jim is faced with a moral dilemma and asks for guidance, the father can only mumble platitudes, urging him to be careful and not to do anything risky. This leads directly to the movie's violent climax, wherein two characters die, one of them Plato. The message was clear: Adults abdicating their responsibility for moral leadership can have dire consequences for the country's teens (Mintz, 2004; Cohen, 1997).

Given the quality of the actors' performances and the story's dramatic impact, the movie painted a forceful picture of adolescence at mid-century. It also helped to document changes in the ways that Americans thought about childhood and adolescence. The contrast between the image of Jim's father in *Rebel* and that encountered almost 40 years earlier in Anzia Yezierska's *Bread Givers* could hardly be more striking. As noted in the previous chapter, Sarah Smolinsky's father was domineering and manipulative. He imposed his values onto his daughters, and took payments from men who wanted to marry them. Jim Stark's father, on the other hand, was almost wholly inaccessible to him. Emotionally distant, he offered his son no clear sense of values and little guidance. While young Sarah yearned to escape her father's dominion, Jim hungered to be closer to his father, to have a clear sense of identity that they could share. Like Sarah he took flight, but because he had no distinct set of values to draw on, he drifted into trouble. The two characters reflected differing times and circumstances, and contrasting commentaries on youthful experience.

To some extent the differences in these two stories reflect culturally distinctive modes of childrearing and adolescence in 20th-century America. The families depicted in *Rebel* were decidedly middle and upper class, and the problems depicted in the movie were supposed to be those of the affluent. But childrearing practices had changed in the

United States for many families by the 1950s. Several decades of progressive critiques of authority and discipline had contributed to a new regime of parental behavior, at least in the middle class. At the same time, family size had dropped steadily, so that the average number of children among Whites was only around three (it had been as high as eight in the 18th century). Moreover, these families began to offer their children greater freedom. Following progressive models of education, self-expression came to be seen as more critical than obedience and conformity to traditional values. The famous baby doctor Benjamin Spock helped to revolutionize childcare by telling mothers to heed and fulfill their infants' needs and desires. Freudian psychology, reaching its popular peak in the 1950s, warned against the dangers of repression and overt control. Like teachers in many "progressive" classrooms, parents were told that they were not supposed to be authority figures. Instead they were to strive to relate to their children as individuals, or even as friends. In a logical extension of this line of thought, some parents abstained from moral judgments altogether, letting their children freely discover their own point of view. This was the pattern of parental involvement that came under scrutiny *in Rebel without a Cause*, and it represented a telling break with past traditions in American culture (Engelhardt, 1995; Graff, 1995).

Historians and other social observers have noted this pattern change in family life in the 20th century. Some, like Viviana Zelizar, suggested that middle-class Americans came to view children as extensions of themselves, and not as sources of support for their families—as in the case of Sarah Smolinsky—or as a religious and moral obligation—as Francis Wayland believed. In the new family, offspring became a form of self-expression, a way for parents to demonstrate and enhance their social status. This is not to say that parents did not care for their children, but it often meant that they placed different obligations or expectations on them, and greater psychological demands. This new outlook raised a host of questions, however, some of them voiced in *Rebel* and other social commentaries. If children were simply manifestations of a consumer ethic, allowed to inherit the materialism of their parents, there remained the issue of how they would learn the lessons of personal and social responsibility. Like many critics of the new progressive mode of childrearing, the producers of *Rebel* suggested that a lack of discipline and authority lay at the root of the new problems with American teenagers. Some believed that the very fate of the nation hung in the balance (Graebner, 1993; Mintz & Kellogg, 1988; Zelizer, 1985).

The teenage problem, in that case, was a thorny one. If indeed the critics of progressive education were correct in suggesting that it was a lack of traditional values in families and schools that contributed to teen misbehavior, nothing less than a sweeping change in these institutions could suffice to change things. This was precisely the solution that some observers recommended. More realistic voices, however, recognized that the problem was considerably more complicated than suggested by either the makers of *Rebel without a Cause* or other critics of progressivism. The development of the nation's youth subculture was in fact just getting underway, and would gain even greater force in the decades ahead. James Dean died at age 24, but his memory lived on in a teen society that became ever larger and more pervasive. The rise of this adolescent culture would become one of the major developments of the postwar period (Mintz, 2004; Modell, 1989).

## Ideological Currents in the Postwar Era

The 1930s and 1940s marked a significant change in the way Americans thought about a number of social issues. The experience of the Great Depression and World War II caused many to question prevailing theories of social superiority, especially those based on race and social class exclusion. During the 1930s, millions of people had lost their jobs, shattering illusions about the stability of social status and the security of a middle-class lifestyle. Socialists and communists were quite active at this time, and helped to spread radical ideas about equity and social justice. More important, the rapid growth of industrial trade unions, particularly those affiliated with the Congress of Industrial Organizations (CIO), propagated ideals of brotherhood, unity, and fairness, and militated against exclusionary practices and divisiveness. In certain respects, the world was turned topsy-turvy, and many traditional ideas became subject to question. It was the start of an important shift in popular thinking about a wide range of social issues (Engelhardt, 1995; Patterson, 1996).

World War II also left an indelible impact on the United States. The very fact of millions of men and women leaving the country to fight abroad, and the mobilization of millions more to work in the war industry, made a lasting impression on the public mind. All of this movement and uncertainty also affected the lives of children, including those who lost a parent in the conflict (Tuttle, 1993). Japanese Americans were moved to internment camps for fictitious security concerns, where their children received powerful lessons in racial prejudice, and minority youth were violently attacked in Los Angeles and other cities as racial tensions escalated (Mintz, 2004; Cogan, 2000). But the war also did much to diminish intolerance among many Americans. It was widely considered a good fight, intended to save democracy and to turn back the forces of avarice and hatred. The enemies were contemptible, especially the Nazi regime in Germany. Consequently, it was a war that helped Americans to feel good about themselves and their nation's egalitarian traditions. Many thought of the conflict as a struggle of democracy against totalitarianism, and this lent new significance to pleas for greater equity and social justice in American society. These themes extended into the postwar period, as the United States entered into a protracted ideological and political confrontation with the communist Soviet Union. Labeled "the Cold War," this conflict contributed to feelings of vulnerability in the U.S., but also lent credence to the idea that Americans should set a democratic example for the world to follow (Patterson, 1996; Terkel, 1997).

The war and its aftermath changed the mindset of many Americans. If the United States was opposed to dictatorships abroad, how could it morally sanction inequity and intolerance at home? The struggle against Nazi Germany had given a racial dimension to the question. For once, Americans were confronted with an explicit ideology of racial superiority that was used to justify a quest for world domination. This was more than a little ironic, given the long history of racial oppression in this country and the brutal experience of violence against Blacks in the South. Indeed, many of the most xenophobic Nazi ideas had been influenced by the American eugenics movement. The battle against Nazism helped to turn the tide of popular opinion against outright theories of racial predominance, perhaps for the first time in U.S. history. It was the dawn of a new era in American ideas about such questions (Kuhl, 2002; Polenberg, 1980; Sitkoff, 1993).

These tendencies were abetted by advances in the thinking of leading social scientists and other prominent public observers. Swedish sociologist Gunner Myrdal published his classic work on American race relations, *An American Dilemma*, in 1944, suggesting that racism was an anachronistic holdover from the 19th century, an ugly remnant of slavery. Myrdal noted that practices of discrimination stood in stark contrast to American ideals of liberty and equality, and predicted that they would eventually be changed for the better. In the same year, President Franklin Roosevelt issued an executive order banning discriminatory behavior in the nation's war industries, opening a wide field of industrial employment to the Black population. The ensuing demand for workers helped to start a new movement of African Americans out of the South, into the large industrial cities of the North and West, where they came to enjoy new freedoms and higher income. This too represented a step forward in race relations (Chafe, 1986; Lemann, 1991).

Such developments helped to set the stage for a remarkable shift in American opinion about questions of race and discrimination. The Truman administration's decision to desegregate the armed forces soon after the war reflected this, as did new federal civil rights measures in the areas of housing and employment. Meanwhile, the NAACP, described in Chapter 5, undertook a series of legal challenges to segregation in education, most of them at the university level. Its legal team, led by Thurgood Marshall, adopted a stance implicit in Myrdal's analysis of racism: that such discrimination was inherently inconsistent with the basic principles of American life, including the legal system. An important precedent was set in 1947, when Mexican Americans successfully challenged Southern California's segregated school policies in *Mendez* v. *Westminister*, decided by a federal district court. At about the same time, NAACP lawyers began attacking similar policies requiring Black children to attend separate schools, a practice still widespread in the South and certain other parts of the country. It was a difficult legal strategy, requiring an expensive and time-consuming process of confronting individual districts in the hope that the federal courts would establish clear precedents, extending beyond a particular school system or state. With this in mind, the judicial challenges pushed forward (Gonzales, 1990; Klinkner & Smith, 1999; MacDonald, 2004; Sitkoff, 1978).

As an immediate consequence of these actions, Southern states began to undertake substantial improvements in Black education, a strategy intended to make the legal doctrine of "separate but equal" appear more defensible. Many states launched "equalization" campaigns, improving pay for Black teachers and building new schools, including modern high schools in many districts. Beginning in the latter 1940s and extending through the following decade, Black enrollments surged upwards, especially at the secondary level. By 1960 a majority of Black teenagers were attending school, a historic level of attainment and a portent of future accomplishments. Altogether, it was a time of significant gains in Black education, but the most astounding advances were achieved in the courts (Bolton, 2000; Donohue, Heckman, & Todd, 2002; Margo & Finegan, 1993).

As it turned out, the NAACP approach to attacking segregation through the judicial system proved to be dramatically effective. When the case its lawyers had launched against the public schools in Topeka, Kansas, and other districts was decided by the Supreme Court in 1954, in *Brown* v. *Board of Education*, it marked a landmark in American social policy. The Court ruled that policies of formal segregation in public schools were contrary to the equal protection clause of the 14th Amendment of the Constitution, directly challenging prevailing practices in most of the educational systems of the South. There was an immediate outcry against the decision, with political leaders across the South declaring their determination to fight the ruling. But elsewhere in the country there was a broad sentiment of support for the Court's action. Many Americans were ready to end the Jim Crow practices of formal segregation, even if most still were not yet ready to embrace full residential and educational integration in their own communities. Additionally, federal authorities were reluctant to oppose racial equity in light of Cold War conflicts abroad, while the U.S. sought alliances with newly developing countries in Africa and Asia. Even so, progress was slow. In the years following *Brown*, steps to end the segregation of public education were difficult and halting, and often accompanied by dramatic—even violent—confrontations. But the 1954 Supreme Court ruling marked a decisive change in the prevailing ideology of racial exclusion in the United States. The pace of change in years to follow would often be incremental, but once the Supreme Court had ruled there could be no turning back (Borstelmann, 2003; Kluger, 1976; Patterson, 2002; Wilkerson, 1979).

*Brown* also gave added momentum to the development of the civil rights movement, a broad-based, collective effort by opponents of racism and discrimination to confront and end practices of segregation and racist oppression in the South and elsewhere. Although it embraced a wide cross-section of Americans, the long civil rights campaign was led by African Americans, and it was Blacks who constituted the vast majority of its participants. An expansive and diverse movement, it eventually embraced leaders as disparate as Martin Luther King and Malcolm X, and organizations extending from the integrationist NAACP to the militant and separatist Black Panthers. Some hoped to achieve a desegregated America, whereas others ultimately pursued a nationalist agenda, campaigning for Black control of their own communities and institutions. Although there was a good deal of debate and conflict between these various groups, the common thread that held the movement together was the struggle for equal rights. With an unusually creative and resourceful leadership, and many dedicated volunteers, the civil rights movement eventually succeeded in pointing out the contradiction between American ideals and the ugly reality of racist discrimination. Its impact was monumental (Cook, 1998; Klinkner & Smith, 1999).

Education remained a critical focal point for civil rights agitation during the 1950s and through the following decade. Other issues eventually took the limelight, such as housing and voting rights, but schooling continued to be a major concern. If the promise of democracy and social equality was to be extended to the nation's Black population, after all, most African Americans believed that equitable access to educational opportunities was an essential step. In this spirit, battles were waged to compel school systems to end policies and practices of segregation and educational inequality, first in the South—where compliance with the 1954 *Brown* decision was most controversial—and later in the North, where de facto patterns of segregation represented the principal barrier to improved schooling for African Americans. Gradually, *de jure* (or "by law") policies of educational segregation were ended, but de facto ("by fact" of other conditions) segregation proved much harder to change (Patterson, 2002). The most dramatic changes were achieved in the South, where integrated schools eventually became most widespread. It was in the North and West, on the other hand, where entrenched patterns of residential segregation made the integration of education an even bigger challenge (Orfield et al., 1996)

Despite the success of struggles waged in this period, the problem of racial inequality in education has continued to be a critical problem facing the United States up to the present. Historically, however, the ideological climate in the United States changed dramatically in the postwar years. The civil rights movement placed the question of social and educational equality squarely on the national agenda, and it could no longer be overlooked. Open espousal of racial segregation and discriminatory practices of any kind had ceased to be intellectually acceptable or politically tolerated. And educators everywhere, at least in principle, became conversant with the ideals of equity and social justice. Altogether, it represented a remarkable shift in the nation's egalitarian disposition (Eskew, 1997; King, 1996; Orfield, 1983).

At the same time that the quest for civil rights exposed many Americans to more liberal ideas on certain social questions, more conservative tendencies came into play also. One of the issues that garnered the most traditionalist response in these years was education, especially the way schools and classrooms were run by educators. In particular, the ideas and practices of progressive education came under sharp attack.

By the 1940s progressivism had become an important intellectual force in professional thinking about schools and learning, even if it still predominated in a relatively small segment of the nation's educational system. Although most Americans may have been suspicious of progressive ideas about education, they were seldom openly hostile to them. This changed in the years following 1950, as a number of prominent academics and journalists took aim at progressive education, linking it in the public mind with failure in the schools. This was partly due to the climate of the "Cold War" and ideological misgivings that progressive educators were "soft-headed" or left-leaning and therefore susceptible to communist influence. Heightened anxieties about national security, fueled by Senator Joseph McCarthy and other fanatical politicians, contributed to an atmosphere of intolerance for social policies and practices seen as unduly permissive. Critiques of progressivism also reflected widespread concerns about the lack of discipline in American students, particularly teenagers, and fears of juvenile delinquency, sex, and violence. Like the producers of *Rebel without a Cause*, many commentators suggested that a return to authority and traditional values was necessary, especially in the classroom. Consequently, there were calls for return to conventional teaching methods, and a renewed emphasis on core academic subjects such as history, mathematics (especially algebra and geometry), English, and the sciences. Above all, moreover, there was a demand for more order and control in the daily lives of children (Hofstadter, 1963; Ravitch, 1983).

This general tendency was bolstered by widespread public concern about the nation's schools in the wake of the Soviet Union's successful launch of the Sputnik spacecraft in 1957. The first man-made satellite, and the opening incident in the much-anticipated "space age," Sputnik's success was a major source of embarrassment for those who believed the U.S. to be scientifically superior. It also aggravated fears about national defense for many Americans. The apparent pre-eminence of Russian scientists directed attention to the need for higher standards of academic achievement, especially in mathematics and the sciences, leading to passage of the National Defense Education Act (NDEA) in 1958. This was a major step in expanding federal aid to schools, although it was generally limited to math and science programs and preparation for teachers (Kaestle, 2001). Meanwhile, the National Science Foundation and other agencies began to support programs to improve instruction and curricular materials, focusing on conventional approaches to teaching and learning. At about this time anti-progressive sentiments reached a peak. The Progressive Education Association, long an advocate of progressive school reform, dissolved itself in 1955, and two years later the magazine *Progressive Education* ceased publication. Although proponents of the ideas of Dewey and other progressive educators still existed, especially in colleges of education, the tide of national opinion had clearly taken a conservative turn with regard to schooling and childrearing practices. While it is questionable whether these attacks on progressive ideas had any immediate effect on the actual conduct of educators, it does appear that the influence of certain progressive ideas was weakened as a consequence, at least for a time (Cremin, 1961; Spring, 1976).

By the start of the 1960s, in that case, the nation's schools were buffeted by the influence of widely divergent ideological trends. Although there was a dramatic liberalizing of attitudes about race and discrimination, there was also a pronounced turn toward traditional ideas concerning instructional practices. In certain respects, both of these tendencies reflected a repudiation of progressive ideas. The civil rights movement, after all, attacked the principle of differentiation so dear to the administrative progressives. The cry for greater integration and equal education was, at least in part, the very antithesis of the progressive era preoccupation with highlighting distinctions of background and achievement. At the same time, conservative critics assailed the pedagogical progressivism of Dewey and his many disciples. At the very moment that certain matters of educational policy grew more equitable, in principle if not completely in practice, other aspects of educational practice may have marked a return to conventional methods and standards. Such was the state of ideas about education in the decade following World War II, a curious legacy of progressivism indeed.

### Race, Equity, and Education

In the years following World War II, race became an overriding issue in the nation's major urban school districts. This did not happen overnight, but it eventually became an inexorable question as larger numbers of African Americans moved to the North during and after the war. Because of changes in Southern agriculture and the reduced demand for farm workers, nearly four million Blacks moved from the South in the two decades after 1945. Most of these migrants came to the largest urban areas of the Northeastern, Midwestern, and Western states. Once there, they generally settled into existing inner-city racial ghettos, or working-class neighborhoods being deserted by Whites. By the 1960s, cities such as New York, Chicago, and Los Angeles, and scores of others, had developed sprawling Black settlements, typically areas marked by higher population density, greater poverty, and more crime than other neighborhoods. The degree of racial segregation in these cities was usually even greater than in the South. As a result of these sharp patterns of residential separation, public-school enrollments became highly segregated in the nation's major cities as well (Lemann, 1991; Wilkerson, 1979; Wolters, 1984).

Given these dynamics, race came to affect the spatial organization of cities in ways that other facets of social organization, such as ethnicity or social class, had not in earlier periods. Blacks often were forcefully kept separate from Whites, a feature of urban life that was maintained by violence, as well as with legal and quasi-legal measures (Massey & Denton, 1993). African Americans who attempted to leave the ghettos were met with hostility, wherein "redlining" mortgage-lending practices, and legally binding restrictive covenants attached to deeds barred large numbers of them from settling in certain neighborhoods. Educational resources, of course, were also spatially distributed, a point that eventually became a matter of great controversy. The schools in Black neighborhoods tended to be overcrowded, with larger classes and fewer experienced teachers than schools in White areas. Graduation rates were lower in these parts of the city, and fewer students went on to college after graduating. In many respects, there were clear and well-documented differences in the quality of schooling along racial lines. This, as critics noted, posed a great challenge to the very principle of public education as a fundamental institution of American civilization. If public schools were supposed to treat children equivalently, how could such disparities be reconciled with egalitarian national ideals? These concerns led to a great deal of conflict over remedies for inequities in education during the 1960s and 1970s and beyond. In big cities across the country, the question of school desegregation became a key matter of contention, a flashpoint of political conflict (Rury, 1993, 1999b).

There were other facets of city life that exacerbated these issues. Social and technological trends made the spatial organization of urban areas a major policy question in this period. At the same time that millions of African Americans began pouring into the central cities, other residents had just started to leave. World War II had barely ended when a grand migration to suburbia began in most of the nation's largest cities. Pressured by housing shortages in the central cities, and encouraged by public policies that stimulated road building and guaranteed inexpensive private transportation, building interstate highways, and maintaining cheap gas, Americans began flocking to newly opened developments on the fringes of the urban core areas. Between 1940 and 1960, the country's suburban population grew by some 27 million, more than twice the increase in major cities during the same period. As a result, the share of the metropolitan population living in central cities dropped from nearly 63% in 1940, to 59% in 1950, and to 51% in 1960. The decline continued thereafter, and by 1980 only 40% of metro residents lived in core cities, with the rest in surrounding suburbs (Fox, 1985; Jackson, 1985;

Teaford, 1990). This was a dramatic change in the spatial organization of the nation's principal urbanized areas.

Migrants from the big cities were disproportionately young, middle class, and upwardly mobile. The availability of Veterans Administration (VA) and Federal Housing Authority (FHA) loans in the decades immediately following World War II, along with housing shortages in central cities, made the suburbs especially attractive to new families. The expanding economy provided a stable source of employment, particularly in downtown office complexes but also in rapidly developing suburban retail and manufacturing centers. These families could afford to buy housing in the suburbs, and held jobs that allowed them to spend the time and incur the costs involved in daily commuting. A postwar "marriage boom" added more than 10 million new households within a decade. And a corresponding rise in births, the "baby boom," made relatively cheap homes in comfortable, spacious suburban subdivisions difficult to resist (Fox, 1985; Palen, 1997).

Suburban migrants were also overwhelmingly White. By 1960, when suburban population exceeded that of the central cities, fewer than 5% of suburbanites were African American (Goldsmith & Blakely, 1992). Thirty years later they were less than 10%, and suburban Blacks were largely segregated in separate communities. This was partly because of discriminatory real-estate practices that discouraged Blacks from buying homes in White suburban areas. As a group, Whites were allowed to move into these new, burgeoning, affluent communities on the edge of the expanding metropolitan area. And as they moved to suburbia, the populations of the country's central cities became older, poorer, and darker in complexion (Jackson, 1985; Massey & Denton, 1993; Teaford, 1990).

These historic developments dramatically affected public perceptions of the big cities. The proportion of central-city residents that were White diminished each decade after 1950, falling from more than 80% to about one-third in the 1990s. The Black population increased rapidly in the 1950s and 1960s, leveling off at about one-third of central-city residents, and the number of Hispanics increased significantly after 1970. As sociologist William Julius Wilson noted, poverty levels increased sharply among all groups of city residents in the closing decades of the 20th century, but particularly among Blacks. This was a consequence of discrimination, poor education and declining economic opportunities in the cities, but it also sprang from what Wilson and other social scientists described as "concentration effects," the fact that many Black city residents were crowded into poor ghettos. Although some 11% of central-city residents were impoverished by the mid-1970s, and 18% of central-city Blacks were poor, by 1990 the figures had jumped to almost 20% and 34%, respectively (Goldsmith & Blakely, 1992; Wilson, 1987). This is a large part of what had become known as the "urban crisis" by the latter 1960s, and it has continued up to the present.

It was the early stages of this process of change that educators confronted at the end of the 1950s. The decades following World War II witnessed a profound transformation of American metropolitan areas, creating a new cultural geography defined by race and income. This had a dramatic effect on many aspects of life in the nation's major urban centers. It meant that for large numbers of urban and suburban residents there were few shared public spaces and social experiences. Stereotypical images, increasingly fostered by the development of mass media, created an atmosphere of mistrust and fear (Dougherty, 2008; Fox, 1985). It was a situation ripe for escalating conflict and misunderstanding.

In the 1960s and 1970s, these problems grew worse as the Black population of urban school districts approached a majority, especially in large Northern cities. Despite protests, schools remained highly segregated, closely mirroring patterns of residential segregation in urban areas (Mirel, 1993; Orfield et al., 1996; Rury, 1999b). Examining the racial composition of Chicago public high schools in 1963, for example, along with a variety of other school characteristics, Robert Havighurst (1964) found in all but four schools the student body was 90% or more Black or White, despite the fact that the district's population was almost evenly divided between these groups. The vast majority of predominantly Black schools, moreover, reported low achievement scores and high dropout rates. This pattern was evident in other large cities (Harrison, 1972). In general, high levels of segregation—or "racial isolation"—marked the movement of Blacks into Northern urban school districts, along with big Black–White differences in educational outcomes (Mirel, 1993; Stolee, 1993; Wells & Crain, 1997). It was a situation that did not bode well for the traditional vision of the American public school.

Inevitably, questions of equity in Black and White schooling became major policy issues facing urban school districts. In public education, the question of race came to be a source of great political dissension, a point of differentiation that defined the institution in new ways. The 1954 *Brown* decision had helped to put schools at the very center of the emerging national civil rights movement. In large metropolitan areas this led to conflict over desegregation and equality, initially in the South but eventually in other regions also (Hochschild, 1985). In the major cities, the impact of these issues was decisive. In the late 1950s and 1960s the NAACP and other civil rights organizations began to agitate around the question of equity in urban education. Massive demonstrations and school boycotts were staged against segregated and inferior schools in the nation's major cities. In Chicago, for instance, during the fall of 1963 nearly 300,000 children stayed home from school, and tens of thousands of parents marched to the downtown offices of the Board of Education to protest de facto school segregation. Similar events occurred elsewhere, sometimes focusing on a single school and in other instances an entire district. In California and Texas, Hispanic students and teachers launched their own boycotts and protest marches, demanding curricular reform and improved facilities. It was a time of confrontation and struggle, when tensions over questions of equity and social justice were running very high (Anderson & Pickering, 1986; Donato, 1997).   (1950's + 1960's)

One of the principal civil rights strategies was to issue legal challenges to de facto patterns of school segregation, most of them holding urban school districts culpable for upholding segregation to avoid aggravating Whites. This, of course, was a continuation of the tradition of activist litigation that had led to the *Brown* decision, and civil rights organizations were determined to achieve equity in the major cities. Consequently, a series of federal court decisions in the later 1960s and early 1970s established a new legal doctrine in barring de facto segregation as a cause of segregated schooling, the root of educational inequities in many urban districts outside the South. This was a major extension of the logic employed in *Brown*, which had focused mainly on *de jure* practices of segregation. In the 1971 landmark *Swan* v. *Charlotte-Mecklenburg* case, a federal district court established mandatory bussing of students as a legitimate remedy to entrenched patterns of residential segregation. With this, school districts could be expected to redress inequalities due to segregation by moving children from one part of the city to another (Orfield et al., 1996) As parent groups on both sides of the issue began to organize in response to these developments, an already tense situation became even more politically explosive (Dougherty, 2003).

The controversy over de facto segregation, in fact, had been smoldering for some time, and drew national attention to the dilemma of urban education. In 1961 former Harvard president James Conant published the book *Slums and Suburbs*. He was hardly a proponent of desegregation, and when he visited Chicago to collect data, the schools were already embroiled in controversy over racial disparities in resources (Hampel, 1986). Even though Conant overlooked such disputes in his study, Chicago offered a telling example of trends in urban education, one that would only grow more disquieting in the years to come. By the late 1960s massive "White flight" to the suburbs and to private schools had caused the city's public school system to be limited largely to minority students. When the district was ordered by a federal judge to implement a desegregation plan in the 1970s, there were hardly enough White students in the system to make such a proposal viable. Non-Hispanic Whites were less than 20% of the public schools' student body by 1980, and in 1990 they were barely one-tenth. This made meaningful integration, particularly in the system's 60 large high schools, a virtual impossibility (Kleppner, 1984; Rury, 1999b). The ideal of the public school functioning as a microcosm of American society was inconceivable under these circumstances.

The story elsewhere was similar. By the time the 1973 *Keyes* decision finally established the principle of federally mandated desegregation in Northern and Western urban school districts, the term "White flight" had already become a part of the national lexicon. Just a year later the *Milliken I* decision blocked a massive inter-district integration plan in Detroit, foreclosing the possibility of legally mandated desegregation plans across urban–suburban boundaries. As a result, the racial profile of schools on either side of the big-city district lines became increasingly dissimilar, and segregation became even more entrenched in many places. In the 1980s only a small minority of public school students was White in the nation's largest cities, and an even smaller—although growing—segment of suburban students was Black (Orfield et al., 1996). Meanwhile, the portion of the nation's population living outside metropolitan areas continued to decline (Goldsmith & Blakely, 1992). If some observers had hoped that schools in non-metropolitan communities would provide the model for others to follow, this ideal became less tenable with time.

These changes had a particularly big impact on the culture of American high schools. As secondary education in major metropolitan areas became characterized by a sharp pattern of racial segregation, it was closely associated in the public mind with perceptions about the quality of schooling (Wells & Crain, 1997). This was evident in the early 1960s in large Northern cities, and became ever more pronounced as the desegregation struggles in public education reached a peak in the 1970s (Hochschild, 1985; Orfield, 1978). Of course, Conant had examined extant patterns of segregation in the early 1960s, but the differences between urban and suburban high schools grew even more striking in the decades that followed. By the end of the 1980s there were relatively few public high schools in large cities with a significant number of White students, and few schools that could be classified as academically excellent. Location came to be a significant factor in the life chances of children (Bettis, 1996; Mora, 1997; Sexton & Nickel, 1992). Schooling, of course, was a big part of this. Urban and suburban school districts became ever more distinct in the years following the protracted struggle over desegregation (Stone, 1998). In the realm of public perception, urban education became linked to poor academic performance and the problems of crime and violence. These images inevitably were influenced by questions of race.

In the decades since 1950, the ideal of a common-school experience for American youth appears to have become increasingly elusive, at least as regards questions of equity in metropolitan areas. Residential segregation, which changed little with the growth of large minority populations in the cities, historically led to even less heterogeneity in many urban high schools' student bodies (Rumberger & Willms, 1992). As metropolitan areas have grown in size and complexity, these patterns of differentiation have maintained their salience, despite the effort of generations of civil rights agitation and successive waves of litigation. If the public school system was supposed to bring students from different backgrounds together, it has not succeeded in accomplishing this goal in much of the country, at least concerning the issues of race and social class (Mora, 1997; Wells & Crain, 1997). In this respect, and in these settings, the traditional vision of American education certainly has not been fulfilled. At the start of the 21st century, this remains a vital question for future generations of American educators to ponder and resolve.

## Schools as Instruments of Social Change

As already suggested, when the nation grappled with questions of inequality and social justice, many looked to the schools as a means of overcoming these problems. Earlier generations of reformers had called on the schools to address social problems too, but this time the impetus came from the highest levels of the nation's political system. For the first time since Reconstruction, the federal government adopted policies to utilize public schools to resolve long-standing patterns of inequality. This was a sign of both the added significance assigned to education in the wake of the human capital revolution, and the increasingly popular idea that education alone would be sufficient to end poverty and discrimination. An important precursor to this was the establishment of the Peace Corps in 1961, following a call by John F. Kennedy to enlist education and the idealism of American youth to assist developing nations. Education also came to be viewed as a means to promote economic development and self-determination for American Indian communities (Senese, 1991; Szasz, 1974). As the United States struggled with ways to address its own growing crisis over social inequality, and race discrimination in particular, schooling of one sort or another appeared to be a practical and appropriate policy mechanism. This reasoning would eventually lead to the schools becoming even more embroiled in the new politics of inequality that came to dominate the closing decades of the 20th century (Hoffman, 1998; Kantor & Lowe, 1995; Nelson, 2008; Skrentny, 2004).

In certain respects, this new thinking about education was a logical outgrowth of the arguments made by Thurgood Marshall and his associates in the 1954 *Brown* Supreme Court case. Marshall maintained that education was a vital resource, critical to the future success of African Americans, both individually and as a group. Segregated schooling was inherently unequal, he argued, and therefore constitutionally questionable. This was an argument that the Supreme Court accepted. But if schooling was an indispensable public service, segregation was not the only problem; there were other sources of inequality in the way it was distributed to different social groups. Perhaps the most telling cause of educational inequity was the nation's historic commitment to local control and funding of public schools. This geographical approach to school finance meant that institutional resources varied enormously from one community to the next, depending on the general wealth of the population and taxation levels. As many observers quickly came to realize, this was a cause of school inequality nearly as great as formal systems of segregation, even if disparities were considerably less than had existed in the past (Wise, 1968).

One arena in which substantial progress towards greater equity had been made was the nation's many rural school districts. Consolidation campaigns that had been launched earlier in the century picked up steam in the postwar era, as the population of many rural areas declined. These efforts benefited from the widespread availability of motorized busses, but were driven by the administrative and instructional costs of small schools, a growing burden to state governments. As a result, tens of thousands of rural districts were combined into larger administrative units across the country. At the same time, new facilities were constructed, teacher certification standards were upgraded, and after-school programs were expanded, particularly sports. James Conant and other reformers gave voice to a push for larger high schools that could accommodate greater curricular diversity. The result was cost savings in many states, and greater equity among districts. In the rural South, African American schools received some of the greatest enhancements in this era. Despite resistance from local residents who valued the many small country schools of the past, the consolidation campaigns of the 1950s and 1960s helped to bring the country's rural schools into line with policies and practices observed in more urbanized areas (Rosenfeld & Sher, 1977; Sher & Tompkins, 1977; Strang, 1987).

At the same time, however, inequality became increasingly evident in the nation's larger metropolitan regions, impacted by suburbanization and social differentiation. The financial disparity between urban and suburban school districts was a major theme of Conant's *Slums and Suburbs*, and many other studies in the years that followed. The relative fiscal standing of the largest urban school districts actually declined in the 1960s and 1970s, as millions of middle- and working-class Whites left for the suburbs. This great exodus helped to erode the local tax base at the same time that it proved a tremendous boon to the suburban schools. As the relative numbers of poor city dwellers increased, the condition of public schools in many cities deteriorated significantly. By the end of the 1960s it was commonplace for observers of city schools to refer to a growing financial crisis in urban education (Dougherty, 2008; Katzman, 1971; Rury, 1993).

It did not take long for the federal authorities to recognize this problem, led by Commissioner of Education Francis Keppell and other reform figures in the Democratic Party. In 1965, following enactment of sweeping civil rights and antipoverty legislation, President Lyndon Johnson oversaw passage of the nation's most comprehensive federal education bill to date, the Elementary and Secondary Education Act (ESEA). This was an integral part of Johnson's "War on Poverty" campaign, a defining policy initiative of his presidency. The ESEA went far beyond other measures dictating federal involvement in the schools, such as the NDEA with its focus on science, mathematics, and related issues (Kaestle, 2001). In supporting this legislation, many Democrats were seeking ways to grant assistance to the cities, long a stronghold of support for the party, whereas other politicians were concerned about growing inequality and the rise of urban poverty. A critical element of ESEA spoke directly to the problem of financial inequity that Conant and other observers had noted. Title 1 of the Act allocated federal dollars to schools serving significant numbers of students from poverty backgrounds. This proved a sizeable benefit to many central-city school districts, as it constituted a source of income apart from local property tax revenues, which had been depressed by White flight and the movement of business out of the cities (Nelson, 2008; Ravitch, 1983; Silver & Silver, 1991).

Title 1 of ESEA addressed the problem of inequality, implicitly acknowledging the importance of equity in educational resources. It also established an important precedent for additional sources of school funding. In the later 1960s and 1970s, many state legislatures adopted similar financial formulas for assigning state aid to urban public schools. Although these new elements of funding did not completely erase the differences in support between city and suburban schools, they eventually came to narrow the spending gap by as much as half. Even if there continued to be significant disparities between urban and suburban schools, in that case, federal and state laws made the differences considerably less severe than they might have been. This was a major step in the development of liberal social policy in the postwar era. It helped to restore the principle that public education ought to be equal everywhere, a critical step if the American credo of equal opportunity was ever truly to be realized (Hummel & Nagle, 1973; Nelson, 2005; Silver & Silver, 1991).

Title 1, however, was just the beginning: there were still other educational initiatives begun under the Johnson Administration's War on Poverty. Perhaps the best known was Head Start, a federally funded preschool program aimed at boosting the achievement of children from poor families. Conceived as a broad social welfare intervention, Head Start was intended to help children overcome the developmental disadvantages that they may have faced in urban and rural areas with many social problems. It also was designed as a source of support for poor families. The program started with a great deal of fanfare and grew quickly to serve more than half a million children in its first year. Critics noted that Head Start often did not feature much educational content, focusing instead on social, medical, and psychological services that families in high-poverty areas may have needed. The President, they charged, had launched the program too fast, hoping to boost support for his antipoverty initiatives. Head Start proved popular from the very beginning, however, and eventually began to employ certified teachers to staff its various centers and classrooms. By the 1970s more than one million children were enrolled in the program each year, and assessments showed that it delivered a significant boost to achievement in the early grades, although long-term effects were harder to document. Like Title 1, Head Start represented a historically new approach to addressing inequality in education: providing compensatory programs and funding to make the impact of schooling more equitable (Vinovskis, 1999, 2005; Zigler & Muenchow, 1992).

Despite widespread support for Head Start and similar initiatives in urban communities, such programs also became a source of controversy. In the wake of the civil rights movement, public sensitivities to questions of race and inequality were running especially high. Critics objected to the very term *compensatory*, arguing that it implied that the clients of these programs were somehow deficient or deviant. Social scientists also came under fire for using the term *culturally deprived* to describe the poor and minority residents of the inner city, who typically were the recipients of these services. The very notion of cultural deprivation seemed to suggest that these people lacked certain values and productive habits, and that they needed to imitate the conventions of the White middle class. Not surprisingly, such suggestions proved offensive to many inner-city residents, especially activists who had struggled fiercely against racism, segregation, and discrimination. In addition to this, new research challenged the deprivation perspective, demonstrating the resourcefulness and resiliency of different sorts of city dwellers. By the 1980s the terms *culturally deprived* and *compensatory* had generally fallen out of favor, and social scientists eventually turned to the concepts of social and cultural capital to account for differences in the educational backgrounds of various groups. Meanwhile, federal and state programs providing urban schools with additional resources for their impoverished students were expanded, becoming even more critical sources of funding (Ravitch, 1983; Schram, 1995; Tucker, 1994).

Regardless of how these programs were described, however, it was clear to everyone that they were intended to do more than simply equalize school-funding levels. They were also supposed to offset inequities in the social and cultural backgrounds of different groups of students. When it came to achievement, after all, the playing field of life was not always level. As seen in the previous chapter, an entire generation of African Americans had been denied the opportunity of attending high school just when secondary education was becoming widely available in American history. Coming from the South, with its long and violent experience of discrimination and educational inequity, Blacks were at a disadvantage compared to most Whites, at least as regarded formal schooling. Mexican American children and others from non-native language groups faced similar challenges, especially those with little or no disposable income to devote to education. In this respect, Head Start and similar policy initiatives were born of recognition that poor families lacked educative resources that more affluent parents were able to offer to children. These included prior educational experiences, but also certain informal educational factors, ranging from books and magazines to music lessons and summer camps. When sociologist James Coleman completed a massive federal government survey of student achievement in 1966, he found that family background factors were more important determinants of academic outcomes in children than school resources. This was a very controversial discovery, but it was upheld in countless additional studies. This eventually led Coleman, along with others, to develop and articulate the concepts of cultural and social capital. To understand why some children were successful in school and others were not, it was necessary to look outside of the schools, to the social and economic environments in which children acquired their formative experiences (Coleman, 1990; Lagemann, 2000; Vinovskis, 2005).

As indicated earlier, theories of social and cultural capital were formulated to capture these very dimensions of life. Although these ideas did not seem to render judgments about the people's way of living, they certainly suggested that various socially valued abilities and behavior are more readily evident in some communities than in others. This was close to the concept of deprivation, but it was also different. Given agreement about the existence of such productive attributes, it was possible to see the task of schools as compensating individuals who lacked social and cultural capital by enabling them to develop these capacities and to learn the requisite forms of behavior. In other words, schooling would supply poor children with information and skills that their families and communities could not. It was possible, in that case, to preserve the basic purpose of compensatory education without declaring particular communities culturally deficient or deviant. The schools were simply a way to learn about the larger world, and to acquire the attributes necessary for success in life. And this is what many students in city schools wanted, as much as anyone else. Given their backgrounds, and their families' historic lack of formal education, some children simply needed more schooling than others to achieve these ends. Even though academic theories of social and cultural capital did not appear until later, this view became a cornerstone of liberal government social policy in the 1960s and 1970s (Coleman, 1990; Schram, 1995; Ravitch, 1983).

Lyndon Johnson's War on Poverty was relatively short-lived, but its imprint extended far beyond his departure from the presidency in 1969. In the 1970s and 1980s the compensatory logic of Title 1 and Head Start was extended to many other educational programs, including an array of job-training initiatives intended to help the poor find stable sources of employment. One example was the Comprehensive Employment Training Act (or CETA), passed in the mid-1970s. CETA was designed to train the unemployed for new jobs as the occupational structure of the economy changed. It paid stipends to individuals from poor backgrounds, and emphasized the importance of developing skills through various forms of vocational and basic academic education. Passed in response to changes in the economy, this measure and others like it represented yet another step in the new federal strategy of deploying education provision as a means to help people break the chains of poverty (Franklin & Ripley, 1984).

A parallel but somewhat different initiative in this period revolved around special education. As noted in the previous chapter, special classes for blind, deaf, and "slow" children had been established in many American schools earlier in the century. In the postwar period, as the school population expanded and enrollment through the high-school years became a societal norm, and as new ways of classifying learning problems were discovered, enrollments in these classes mushroomed. Between 1948 and 1968 special-education students increased from fewer than 400,000 to more than two million, and their numbers continued to grow in the years that followed. In the early 1960s new research had led to development of the concept of *learning disabilities*, contributing to a growing body of professional knowledge to inform the field. At the same time, educators and parent groups began to push for broader support of special education and for integration of special-needs students with the rest of the school population. In the later 1960s a series of court cases challenged the principle of separate classes for special-education students, employing basically the same logic that had informed the *Brown* decision. The plaintiffs in these instances held that separate education was unequal, and that students in such classes suffered a stigma that was difficult to overcome. Although these challenges did not result in a landmark Supreme Court decision regarding special-needs children, they did contribute to a growing movement to bring special education into the mainstream (Safford & Safford, 1996; Skrentny, 2004; Scotch, 2001).

The field of special education continued to grow in the closing decades of the century. In 1975 the Education for All Handicapped Children Act was passed by Congress and signed into law by President Gerald Ford. With this measure, the federal government required school districts to provide special-education students with free and appropriate schooling in the least restrictive environment possible (Winzer, 1993). The idea of compensatory education, backed by federal authority, now extended to children with learning disabilities and other special needs. By the early 1990s the number of children in federally mandated special-education programs exceeded 12% of the population of the public schools, nearly half of them labeled "learning disabled." The goal of special education was to supply the extra training and resources necessary to help these students keep up with the other children in the schools. This was redemptive schooling of a different kind, requiring a massive investment of financial resources and professional expertise, but it also reflected the national preoccupation with using schools to achieve greater levels of social and economic equity (Carrier, 1986; Turnbull, Stowe, & Huerta, 2006).

Perhaps the most ambitious program of compensatory-education measures, however, was directed at the issue of gender. Inspired by the civil rights movement, feminist activists began to criticize the treatment of women in schools during the late 1960s and early 1970s. Although girls had exhibited high levels of academic achievement since the later 19th century, these critics felt that schools reinforced sex discrimination in many other areas of life. They noted numerous problems: textbooks that perpetuated invidious gender stereotypes, counselors who urged students toward sex-typed courses and career options, curricular differentiation with boys excelling in math and science and girls in humanities, teachers who favored boys over girls in class discussions, and school athletic programs that heavily favored male sports and often glorified the accomplishments of boys who participated. They also pointed out that the administration of schools was dominated by men, a situation that subtly taught students that males should occupy positions of authority. Reflecting these concerns, the National Organization of Women (NOW) included a provision in its 1967 women's bill of rights calling for "equal and unsegregated education" (Skrentny, 2004).

Continued agitation and lobbying around these questions eventually led to the passage five years later of Title IX as an amendment to federal education legislation. A rather simple provision, Title IX declared that "no person … shall, on the basis of sex, be excluded from participation in, be denied the benefits of, or be subjected to discrimination under any education program or activity receiving federal financial assistance." Because federal aid to schools had become widespread, it was a measure with potential teeth, as noncompliance could lead to the loss of funding. It took several years for regulations governing the implementation of the legislation to be articulated, as Republican opponents created obstacles to them, but by the later 1970s activists were able to enlist Title IX to challenge sex discrimination in education across the country (Tyack & Hansot, 1990).

The problem of sexism in the schools turned out to be troublesome and difficult to remedy. Title IX could be considered as compensatory in the sense of correcting past inequities, but its impact was mixed. There continued to be battles over Title IX regulations in Congress, but many states had adopted similar provisions by the 1980s. School districts eventually began to respond, especially in the area of women's athletics. The 1970s witnessed a fivefold increase in female participation in competitive sports. By the end of the decade, more than one-third of all high-school athletes nationally were girls, although there was a great deal of variation across states and districts. This, of course, directly affected only a small portion of the student body, even though it held significant symbolic value. There were halting advances in additional areas too. Textbooks were revised to feature fewer stereotypes, and the number of women administrators slowly increased. Other aspects of the educational system proved more difficult to change, however. Curricular differentiation was stubbornly persistent despite efforts to boost female enrollments in math and science. Vocational education classes remained highly segregated by gender, even though the number of girls in technical courses more than doubled. Powerful norms continued to govern the behavior of teachers and students in schools and classrooms, making it difficult to change historic patterns of gender-linked behavior and communication patterns. Research showed teachers continuing to call more on the boys, and many girls still did not want to challenge social conventions for fear of becoming unpopular. In the case of gender, consequently, compensatory education proved to be a frustrating and elusive goal, although a number of important advances were made (Sadker & Sadker, 1994; Tyack & Hansot, 1990). Even with the best of intentions, it turned out to be very difficult to legislate certain changes in the schools, especially if large groups of students and educators were ambivalent about altering the status quo.

In spite of such dilemmas, the effect of all these programs was a virtual sea change in American education. By the end of the 1970s compensatory-education programming of one kind or another had become nearly a cradle-to-grave enterprise, extending from the very young (Head Start) to the adult population (job training), to children excluded by gender or special needs, and to bilingual education (discussed below). It represented a view of education as a mechanism for reducing inequality—defined in myriad ways—that had become firmly entrenched as a vital element of social policy. A substantial research and evaluation enterprise was established by the federal government to monitor these programs, and to address a host of other educational questions. As a matter of course, schooling had become a way of overcoming all kinds of social problems. A seemingly indispensable feature of the American political landscape in the late 20th century, it had become virtually inviolable in the public mind. Then, as never before, education of one sort or another was seen as profoundly influencing an individual's social standing. As such, it was too important to be left simply to the local authorities, especially the overburdened school bureaucracies of the nation's large urban areas (Lagemann, 2000; Silver & Silver, 1991).

## FOCAL POINT: CHICANO PROTEST AND BILINGUAL EDUCATION

On March 1, 1968, hundreds of Chicano (Mexican American) youth burst out of Lincoln High School in Los Angeles, protesting the school's lack of sensitivity to their cultural heritage and its weak academic curriculum. This was the first in a series of dramatic walkouts, or "blowouts," in LA's public secondary schools that would escalate in scale and notoriety that spring, eventually involving some 12,000 students. These events were significant both for the anger and frustration that they reflected, but also because they represented a movement for equity in education that would eventually impact the nation (Escobar, 1993).

The 1960s were years of demonstrations and controversy, and most people associate them with the civil rights movement and Black protests. But there was also a forceful movement among Mexican Americans, and much of its attention was focused on the issue of education. In the same tradition as Black youth who staged walkouts to demand better instruction and culturally relevant classes, Chicano students saw themselves as fighting for respect and honor, a sense of dignity that the schools had historically denied them. For decades the public institutions in Los Angeles and other cities across the Western states had denigrated the Spanish language and the traditions of these students' families. They were not permitted to study their own history, and were told by teachers and counselors that they were best suited for menial jobs as laborers, factory operatives, or domestic servants. In the latter 1960s, walkouts like those in Los Angeles occurred in cities across the region, with Chicano youth demanding new curricula and a faculty that reflected the cultural backgrounds of the community (Donato, 1997; Sanchez, 1993; Valenzuela, 1999).

These were hardly the first protests conducted by Mexican American youth. Sporadic battles against discrimination had occurred in earlier decades, particularly the 1940s. As noted earlier, the historic *Mendez v. Westminister* case against school desegregation served as an important precedent to the *Brown* decision. But the 1960s were a different time, and in the wake of the broader civil rights movement this was a coherent response to the grievances endured by Chicano students. In the case of the protesters in Los Angeles, it took a long and difficult struggle to win any concessions from the city's Board of Education, and the police subjected protesters to a grueling process of harassment. Elsewhere progress occurred much quicker. In Texas, local school boards instituted reforms and began hiring Chicano teachers. Similar changes were undertaken in New Mexico, Arizona, and Colorado. At the same time, new curricula in Mexican American history and culture were initiated, just as courses appeared in Afro American studies and allied fields (Escobar, 1993; Gonzales, 1990; San Miguel, 1987).

These events helped to set the stage for even more momentous changes. One important area of curricular controversy was bilingual education, as protesters demanded instruction in Spanish to address the needs of students with limited English proficiency. This was not a new issue, however, as various forms of bilingual education had flourished in American schools at earlier points in history. In the 1890s, for instance, German communities across the Midwest successfully campaigned to include instruction in their native language as a part of public-school curricula. Thousands of children participated in these programs, but they ended abruptly with World War I and the anti-German sentiments that it occasioned. After the war, patriotic fervor gripped the nation in the wake of federal legislation to restrict immigration, and there was little effort to revive non-English instruction in the schools. Even so, the idea of multilingualism lingered in the minds of various immigrant groups throughout the decades that followed. Bilingual schooling gained new life in the late 1950s, when Cuban refugees flooded into South Florida, fleeing Fidel Castro's regime. Consequently, the first bilingual education programs of the era were launched in Miami. Agitation by the very effective Cuban refugee lobby, and community protests elsewhere, led to passage of the Bilingual Education Act of 1968, which authorized the federal government to allocate support to local bilingual education programs. In the 1970s continued agitation by local advocates and actions taken by the U.S. Office of Civil Rights expanded the purview of bilingual instruction in public schools. Finally, the 1974 Supreme Court ruling in *Lau* v. *Nichols* required the schools of San Francisco to offer bilingual instruction to Chinese students, establishing a broad precedent for arguing the necessity of such programs. This led to a proliferation of state and local actions to support bilingual schooling, marking a historic shift in educational policy. While bilingualism had a long record in American schools, it had never been undertaken on a scale such as this. Now language became a variable element of public education, a fact that drew considerable controversy to the schools (Gann and Duignan, 1986; Portes and Bach, 1985; Skrentny, 2004; Zimmerman, 2002).

Driven by the rapid growth of the nation's foreign-born population in the 1960s and 1970s, bilingual education quickly became a large-scale element of the school systems serving immigrant children. Tens of thousands were enrolled in bilingual classes, at a cost of hundreds of millions of dollars, and demand for bilingual teachers soon outstripped the supply. At the same time, the expense of bilingual education, along with the idea of teaching in a language other than English, began to stir debate. Critics charged that bilingual classes only slowed the process of assimilation, and did not contribute to academic achievement. Researchers also clashed on these questions, at least at the outset. Eventually, these issues found their way into the political arena, as certain politicians in California made opposition to bilingual education a topic of debate and strife. All of this came to a head in 1998, with the passage of Proposition 227, which mandated an English-only approach in California's schools. The approval of this measure by popular vote indicated the extent of controversy that bilingualism had aroused in the public mind, fueled by decades of opposition from conservative political interests. Even with an emerging consensus among researchers on the importance of bilingual education in promoting achievement among immigrant children, public suspicions about its value continued to be widespread. In the end, it seems that the idea that public schools should support cultural diversity, or even ease the passage from a foreign culture into the mainstream, has been difficult for many Americans to accept. No doubt this was partly a legacy of the assimilationist history of the common school, the long-standing purpose of public education depicted as helping to forge a single national culture (Garcia 2001; Portes and Rumbaut, 1996; San Miguel, 2002).

The irony of these developments is that bilingual education may very well be more important now than ever before in recent history, as new waves of non-native students have inundated the schools in many American cities in recent decades. By the year 2000, immigrants and their children represented more than one in five Americans, and were especially concentrated in major metropolitan areas. In particular, Mexican Americans have become one of the nation's largest ethnic groups, representing nearly 10% of the population, and other Spanish-speaking immigrant groups have grown substantially as well. As a number of scholars have pointed out, this has led to a new diversity evident in American education, with important implications for the success of the schools. While children from certain immigrant groups appear to be doing better than others, those from Mexican families still suffer low achievement levels and higher rates of dropping out of school. While large numbers of them have prospered in the United States, others still struggle with persistent poverty. This is a dubious legacy for the protesters of 1968, and the fight that they waged for respect of their cultural heritage. Despite the immediate success of their struggles, many of the problems that they identified still exist. Overt cultural discrimination may have been reduced, but it still exists and the schools that many Mexican American students attend today suffer chronic underfunding, high teacher turnover, and a shortage of personnel in critical positions. Even if measures as extreme as California's Proposition 227 have been few, support for bilingual education has diminished in many parts of the country. This has created a great challenge for the new generation of American children born to the immigrants of the last several decades. Theirs is a task of assimilating in an increasingly diverse national culture, while pursuing ever-higher standards of academic achievement. Given their growing numbers, insuring the success of schools in meeting their needs must be seen as a critical issue for the nation's future (Olneck, 2008; Perlmann, 2005; Portes and Rumbaut, 2001).

**Political Controversies over Education as Social Policy**

Federal measures to ensure provision of compensatory education of one form or another enjoyed a high degree of public support, as they seemed to extend the benefits of schooling to new groups in the population at relatively little cost. But they also engendered vocal opposition, and were depicted as intrusive, overly liberal elements of social policy. Some Americans worried that initiatives such as bilingual education, Title IX and special education were causing the schools to lose their focus on academic achievement. Others believed that increasing diversity posed a threat to scholastic standards, a position with discriminatory overtones. These were sentiments that readily found expression in the political arena.

Not surprisingly, a good deal of public concern focused on the role of federal courts in school desegregation, a major point of intervention in the educational system during this era. As noted earlier, the Swan case in 1971 established a critical precedent for the use of bussing to desegregate public schools. In the years that followed, desegregation plans requiring some form or another of bussing for students attending segregated schools were implemented in scores of cities, most of them by order of federal or state authorities. These decisions followed the reasoning of the 1954 *Brown* decision in holding that separate schools represented a singular harm to students, and that school districts had a moral and educational duty to actively resist segregation in any form. This view was abetted by Coleman's 1966 survey, which found that integrated schooling produced higher achievement levels, particularly in minority students. With this, equality in education became linked firmly to the idea of desegregation, and bussing became the primary mode of achieving this goal (Orfield et al., 1996; Wilkerson, 1979).

Millions of schoolchildren were affected by the bussing plans established in the 1970s, which moved students from one area of a city to another to achieve levels of integration established by the courts. In many instances, this approach to ending inequity was met with anger and conflict, as parents, most of them White, protested the end of "neighborhood schools." In certain cities, such as Boston and Chicago, these battles turned violent and confrontational (Lukas, 1985). Politicians, especially the Republicans, seized on these sentiments, blasting federal intervention into schooling as being unnecessary and intrusive. Others defended it but found themselves fighting a losing battle in the realm of public opinion. If separate schools truly were unequal, the reasoning of arguments made in 1954 necessitated solutions of the kind being implemented in the 1970s. But local groups of citizens, especially in the North and West, had not imagined that the *Brown* decision applied to their own communities, and they eventually began to question the wisdom of the judiciary. The logic underlying the desegregation movement was clear-cut. If indeed education was a critical determinant of an individual's future, and access to it was a right guaranteed by the state, then some measure of equality in its provision had to be ensured. For opponents of segregation, this was true even if it meant disrupting the lives of millions of families and pitting neighbors against one another in the conflicts that ensued. For others, the bussing controversy became a growing source of irritation and anger, one that would ultimately help to usher in a new era in American politics (Hochschild, 1985; Stolee, 1993; Wolters, 1984).

A parallel controversy arose in connection with yet another federal initiative in this era: a policy standpoint widely known as *affirmative action*. This idea employed the compensatory logic of desegregation and the educational programs described above, but applied it to the politically sensitive arenas of higher education and employment. Basically, the principles of affirmative action held that groups that had been the objects of discrimination in the past should be permitted first consideration for opportunities in the present and future. This was deemed a necessary step to overcome the accumulated weight of past exclusion, and to permit members of these groups to develop the human and cultural capital that historically had been denied them. In the domain of education, affirmative-action policies primarily affected postsecondary institutions, particularly regarding entrance to professional and graduate programs, as well as hiring practices. These initiatives concerned both gender and race, but it was the latter question that inevitably proved most controversial (Skrentny, 2004).

In the mid-1970s a White medical-school applicant named Allan Bakke sued the University of California, arguing that he had been denied admission to the Davis campus in favor of less-qualified minority students. In 1978 the U.S. Supreme Court ruled that the school's admissions policies had established rigid racial categories or quotas that were deemed discriminatory and therefore unconstitutional, and Bakke was subsequently admitted. On the other hand, the Supreme Court also ruled that universities could use race or other background characteristics as one criteria—among many—in making admission decisions. Thus, affirmative action remained a viable option in admissions under certain conditions. It was a case that spoke to both sides of the dispute (Wilkerson, 1979).

While the *Bakke* case did not fully resolve the legality of affirmative-action policies, it did become a focal point for public debate of the issue, and in this way fanned the flames of dissension over race and inequality in American life. Recent research suggests that the *Bakke* case and the attending furor came to exert little long-term influence on admission practices, but the question of race and higher education continues to be a turbulent issue today. A 2003 Supreme Court decision regarding affirmative action at the University of Michigan upheld the central idea that race can be considered as a factor in admissions, but that strict quotas cannot be applied. This case also occasioned a good deal of public outcry, even though the basic principles of *Bakke* were upheld (Gruhl & Welch, 1990; Skrentny, 2004; Stohr, 2006). Because the court was closely divided in the Michigan case, as it had been in *Bakke*, it is likely that the issue will be revisited in future disputes.

By the end of the 1970s, the political storm that had gathered over desegregation and affirmative action helped to establish a conservative tenor in debates about education. These concerns became a part of an anti-big-government movement that propelled Ronald Reagan into the presidency in 1980. A degree of public cynicism about other measures also resulted, particularly job-training programs, as many of them seemed to do little to boost employment, especially among the chronically poor. CETA, for instance, had come under sharp attack on these grounds. These issues were linked in the minds of many to the extensive Reagan campaign against antipoverty programs and welfare, and his stated goal of shifting responsibility for such services to the states. Vowing to end federal involvement in education as a part of his program to reduce the size of government bureaucracy, Reagan proposed to close the U.S. Department of Education, or at least remove it as a cabinet position. It was a promise that he was never able to fulfill, however. The federal role in education had simply grown too large, and the government's commitment to deploying schools to address issues of social inequity had become too thoroughly entrenched as a matter of policy and public expectations. Urban communities, civil rights groups, teachers' unions, and other special interests lobbied heavily against curtailment of various federal education programs. Hundreds of millions of dollars were at stake in these decisions, representing thousands of jobs and services to millions of students. A new politics of education had emerged at the national level, with various forms of schooling representing a partial transfer of wealth from the upper and middle classes to the urban poor. This made it very difficult to change many of the federal education policies that had been started under Lyndon Johnson and subsequent administrations (Haynes, 1991; Nelson, 2008).

The Reagan years presented a clear demonstration of just how firmly entrenched the idea of compensatory programming in education had become as a matter of American social policy. Had Reagan decided arbitrarily to end the various programs established in the 1960s and 1970s, especially such popular ones as Head Start or Title 1, the political fallout would have been enormous. Indeed, if other aspects of Reagan's conservative political program were to be realized, such as massive reductions in welfare budgets and a big tax cut for the wealthy, he could hardly afford the political cost of attacking education as well.

In addition to this, conservative opposition to education measures was not as forceful as it was to other social programs. Mainstream public opinion had long been more sympathetic to expenditures for education than for welfare payments, reflecting a traditional American belief in the power of self-improvement. If the federal government was going to tax the wealthy to help the poor, providing compensatory education was a politically palatable way to do it. What was more, there was also growing evidence that these policies had made a difference. After lagging for most of the 20th century, rates of Black graduation from high school began to catch up to those for Whites in the 1970s and 1980s, eventually closing the gap significantly. Black college enrollments also climbed dramatically, ultimately amounting to about two-thirds of the White attendance rate. Although important differences in academic achievement continued to exist, these trends helped to establish a growing Black middle class, including a number of people who entered the major professions with high-status university credentials (Jencks, 1998). This was a significant development in itself, but the role of education in the process helped to highlight the importance of federal policies designed to attack problems of discrimination and inequity. These circumstances helped to make the major federal education programs relatively secure politically, even in an age of retrenchment (Farley, 1997; Levitan, Johnston, & Taggart, 1975; Peterson, 2006; Stockman, 1986).

Perhaps even more significant, conventional wisdom had come to hold schooling as very important for the country as a whole. Americans of nearly every social strata believed that education was a vital national interest, necessary for competing on a global scale with such rising economic powers as the Japanese and Europeans. This was a position even the most ardent Reaganite could hardly take issue with. It was perhaps best expressed in a 1983 report issued by a special commission appointed by U.S. Secretary of Education Terrance Bell, *A Nation at Risk*. Noting problems of declining achievement in American schools, the report called for a massive reform of education, focusing on higher standards of performance. *A Nation at Risk* also served to deflect attacks on the Department of Education, but its overall impact was momentous. National polls showed a widespread public concern that education was slipping in quality, and that this was linked to American economic strength. In short, schooling had simply become too important a part of the nation's social and economic life for the federal government not to play a leading role in formulating policy questions, and in funding key elements of the educational system. It became a political imperative that leaders of both parties could not ignore, yet another dimension of the human capital revolution. Not only was schooling indispensable as an agent of economic growth and individual earning power, it was also a critical instrument of social policy. As the significance assigned to education by the public increased, its political importance grew as well (Ginsberg & Plank, 1995; Harris, Wong, & Guthrie, 2004).

At the time Reagan's successor, George H. Bush, was elected in the late 1980s, public schooling had changed significantly since World War II. The role of education had broadened to include rectifying social inequities, supplying a variety of social services, and promoting national economic development. Once concerned primarily with providing instruction in a variety of subjects, the schools had become vital instruments of social policy. Federal funding for education registered in billions of dollars, with programs ranging from Head Start to special-education funds to Pell grants for needy college students. State governments added billions more, especially following waves of litigation over equity in school finance, which have helped to increase spending as well as reduce geographic inequity (Bosworth, 2001; Odden & Picus, 2007). Despite debate, public support for these initiatives was so strong that Bush campaigned by describing himself as the "education president," even though he eventually proposed little meaningful change in school policies. It was the dawn of a new era in the history of American education, the cresting of the human capital revolution, and a time when schooling was clearly becoming a principal national concern (Greene, 2000).

## High Schools and the Youth Culture

At the same time that American culture became more divided along racial and urban/suburban lines, and was increasingly preoccupied with education, it also became split along generational lines. As suggested in the earlier discussion of *Rebel without a Cause*, the postwar period saw the development of a national youth culture, much larger and more pervasive than the collegiate culture that began to flourish in the 1920s. One of the keys to this development was the rise of the high school as a truly mass institution (Angus & Mirel, 1999; Haubrich, 1993).

As the size and numbers of high schools grew after 1950, they ultimately included a larger proportion of the total teenage population. This meant that a broad cross-section of adolescents was brought together in one institution for the first time in history. This was an upshot of the comprehensive vision promulgated by reformers dating from the Kingsley Commission, the idea of a secondary institution that brought youth from various social classes and groups together. Educators believed that the high school should be a universal American tradition, even if they did not feel that everyone should study the same subjects. Statistical evidence points to the prescience of these views. As the number of adolescents grew in the 1950s and 1960s, especially after the first baby-boomers became teenagers, high-school enrollments climbed dramatically. This was a consequence of both demographic increases and improved rates of high-school attendance (West, 1996). By the end of the 1950s, more than 80% of American teenagers attended high school, making it practically a universal experience for the first time in American history (Angus & Mirel, 1999). This had a number of important consequences.

One effect of the high school's growth was the fact that adolescents as a social group were segregated from the rest of society for a significant amount of time each week, throughout most of the year, in institutions where they constituted the vast majority of the populace. Because of age-grading, and the differentiated structure of most secondary schools, they did not even have systematic contact with youth in different age groups, such as young adults over 18 or 19. This contributed to the development of what James Coleman described as the "adolescent society," an array of social relations with its own behavioral norms and cultural artifacts. From the very start it was a phenomenon rooted largely in the high school (Coleman, 1961, 1965). This was an important component of what many observers at the time began to refer to as the "youth culture" (Cohen, 1997).

The institution of schooling, in that case, was a critical component of the development of this distinctive aspect of modern American civilization. Coleman argued that the social world of high-school adolescence was defined by status groups associated with different sorts of school activities. In general, he found that athletics played an especially important role in the lives of high-school students, especially boys. Academic performance was less important, although it may have gained significance as students progressed through school (Coleman, 1961). Other studies examined the influence of the larger youth culture, mostly existing outside the schools, which was commercially exploited by record companies, the radio, television, and print media, and a host of other enterprises. Adolescents had preferred distinctive forms of music for several decades, and dancing had been popular with the rise of dating as a distinctive teenage activity in the 1920s and 1930s (Modell, 1989; Palladino, 1996). But in the 1950s and 1960s, these aspects of the youth subculture assumed larger proportions.

In the 1950s new forms of teenage entertainment burst into view, especially with the rapid rise of rock-and-roll music as a popular idiom. More working-class youth were involved, as teen employment dropped and large numbers of them remained in school for the first time in history (Rury, 2004). New dances came into play also, reflecting the growing diversity of "adolescent society," and teenagers became enamored of a variety of distinctive forms of consumption. In this regard, they were influenced by the development of an expansive consumer culture in postwar America, but their behavior was quite different from that of previous generations (Cohen, 2003). The influence of working class experience and mores was evident in a number of respects. Fast cars, cigarette smoking and alcohol, and the hint of sexual promiscuity came to represent the new youth culture, and to distinguish it from the clean-cut images of youth from earlier decades. Despite attempts at censorship, these images were spread through the media, including radio, the movies, and the increasingly ubiquitous influence of television. It is doubtful that any more than a minority of teens actually engaged in such activities routinely, but even for those who did not, the idea of rebellion against adult mores exerted a powerful appeal (Mintz, 2004; Gilbert, 1986). This was an impulse that would exert even greater influence in the decades to follow.

If music and movies were important features of youth culture, clothing may have been equally significant. High-school students in earlier decades had often dressed like miniature adults, with boys wearing coats and ties and girls dresses or skirts. As the number of students in school increased, particularly those from the working class, these standards of dress came to be considered outmoded. As one study of students in Milwaukee found, by the later 1950s high-school students there had shed coats, ties, and dresses in favor of slacks, shirts, and sweaters (Haubrich, 1993). With time, standards of dress became even more informal. In the 1960s high-school dress codes became a subject of student protests and were eliminated in schools across the country. By the 1970s jeans and T-shirts were the norm in many schools, even among younger faculty members, and adolescent tastes were becoming a major force in the world of adult fashion (Davis, 1992; Grant, 1988; Palladino, 1996).

At about the same time there was a dramatic shift in sexual mores, with a corresponding change in teenage behavior. Rates of non-marital sex among teenagers had increased significantly by the early 1970s, jumping from less than 20% to more than one-third in less than a decade. This revived the movement to make sex education a major element of the secondary curriculum, a long-standing concern of many reformers, but even this moderate response helped to fuel new anxieties about teenage sexuality. In the end, no single coherent national response could be agreed upon, apart from politically motivated calls for "abstinence only" policies (Moran, 2000; Zimmerman, 2002). By the latter 1980s a clear majority of teens had reportedly engaged in one form or another of significant consensual sexual activity. This represented a sharp break from the past, as recently as the 1950s. At the same time, the number of single-parent households increased dramatically and teen pregnancy became a primary concern of national policymakers. By the 1990s nearly one-quarter of all children were born to single mothers, the majority of them teenagers. At the close of the 20th century, traditional forms of family life had been dramatically altered by these changes, with only about half of American households representing the nuclear family that had predominated in earlier times. Sexuality had become a prominent feature of popular culture, and a central aspect of the rapidly evolving high-school-based adolescent society (Chilman, 1978; Esman, 1990; Palladino, 1996; Vinovskis, 1995). It remains a critical educational and social issue.

It is important to acknowledge the role of the school in contributing to these developments. The rise of a youth culture coincided with the movement to consolidate and expand high schools across the country, plans that educators endorsed enthusiastically following World War II. The average size of public secondary schools more than doubled between 1950 and 1970, both because of school consolidation in rural areas and the building of new institutions in the rapidly expanding suburbs. Average figures, however, tend to understate the size of institutions most students attended because of the many small rural districts that still existed. Ernest Boyer, writing in the early 1980s, put the number of high schools at about 16,000, which made the average enrollment at that point nearly 900 (Boyer, 1983). Survey data collected in the 1970s and 1980s indicate that the typical public high school at that time had some 875 students, and more than 40% had over 900 (Bryk, Lee, & Holland, 1993). It was the latter schools, of course, that enrolled the majority of the nation's secondary students, and continue to do so today. These larger high schools have historically been concentrated in urban areas, but many suburban districts also established massive secondary institutions as their teenage populations expanded in the postwar years. For metropolitan youth, the institutional norm became a large, differentiated public secondary school.

School size, it turns out, appears to have contributed significantly to the formation of a distinctive youth culture. Research suggested the development of bigger high schools, with greater numbers of students and psychological distance between adolescents and adults. Psychologists Barker and Gump (1964), in their analysis of high-school size in the 1960s, found that greater numbers of students were excluded from school activities in larger schools, a condition that contributed to more widespread alienation from the institution and its goals. This appears to have been particularly true among working- or lower-class students. More recent research has associated a loss of adult control in big schools and a reduction in the degree of personalism in contact between students and adults (Bettis, 1996; Eckert, 1989). A number of studies have argued that greater school size inhibits student learning, especially when it makes it difficult for adolescents and adults to communicate meaningfully (Bracy, 1998; Haller, 1992; Lee & Smith, 1997). This point was made emphatically by scholars comparing private—particularly Catholic— and public high schools. These authors reported that school size was a significant factor in accounting for the superior academic performance and school climate of private institutions (Bryk et al., 1993; Coleman, Hoffer, & Kilgore, 1982; Greely, 1982). Bigger, it turned out, was not always better.

A general movement to expand students' rights in high schools across the country added force to these developments. In 1969 the U.S. Supreme Court handed down a decision in the case *Tinker* v. *Des Moines Independent School District*, wherein it ruled that a suspension of two students for wearing black armbands to protest the Vietnam War represented a violation of their 1st Amendment rights (Zirkel, 1999). *Tinker* set off a wave of litigation that soon broadened the definition of self-expression to include everything from dress to hairstyles to displays of affection on school premises. Although not all such challenges to conventional authority were successful, educators soon found themselves on the defensive, forced to justify traditional rules, policies, and practices that had existed for generations. The new legal standard became one of requiring an educational rationale for policies governing the behavior of students, and many school districts chose to minimize such measures rather than risk additional protests and potential litigation (Arum et al., 2003; Olson, 1972). Developments such as these helped to usher in a new era of uncertainly and permissiveness in the nation's high schools.

This set of problems was complicated by changes in the culture of schools during the 1960s and 1970s. There was a resurgence of interest in the ideas of progressive education and curricular experimentation at this time, and a movement to radically alter disciplinary practices. Many schools attempted to make courses more relevant to the interests of students, dropping core requirements in mathematics, history, and the sciences in favor of new experiential learning approaches or interdisciplinary units. In the same spirit, student conduct codes were changed—sometimes in response to protest—to allow greater freedom, especially with regard to dress and deportment. These shifts in adult supervision added even greater momentum to the development of an independent youth culture, in all of its colorful variety. In some big, impersonal high schools, the infrequency of contact between teens and adults eventually led to youth subcultures that appeared to militate actively against the academic purposes of the institution. In such instances, the schools may have lost control of student socialization altogether, and merely provided a place for teens to meet and plan their own events and activities (Angus and Mirel, 1999; Eckert, 1989; Grant, 1988; Willis, 1977).

As Coleman and other observers have noted, youth culture often took the immediate community and its values as a point of departure. This accounted for a heavy value placed on athletics in most high schools (Coleman, 1961). But with the social and economic differentiation of the metropolitan landscape, this has resulted in a variegated adolescent culture, or—alternatively— a set of different youth subcultures (Coleman, 1965). In the large and impersonal secondary institutions of metropolitan America today, differing networks of peers seem to conduct much of the socialization for teens. Particularly in the larger schools, adolescent society seems to reign supreme. This may be yet another aspect of how the comprehensive high-school ideal, handed down from an earlier time, has contributed to challenges facing secondary education today.

## FOCAL POINT: WOODSTOCK NATION

Late in the summer of 1969 over half a million young people gathered near Woodstock, New York, just an hour north of New York City, to hear a remarkable variety of musical performers brought together for a three-day festival. The turnout far exceeded even the most optimistic projections, as many had learned about the event through word of mouth and did not even buy tickets. The festival organizers struggled with the logistics of providing food, toilet facilities, and medical services, but all observers remarked on the peaceful temper of the gathering and the extraordinary spirit of brotherhood and sharing that prevailed. Plagued by rain and the absence of shelter and basic services, the event was marked by sentiments of opposition to the U.S. military campaign in Vietnam, and a winking consent to the use of hallucinogenic drugs, sexual freedom, and unbridled nonconformity. For many, the Woodstock experience came to represent a moment when the values and distinctive cultural tastes of American youth achieved their most singular form of expression. Going well beyond the high-school world of the adolescent society that Coleman and others described, Woodstock seemed to demonstrate that young people could discard the norms of the larger society and establish their own social and political identities. It was, in the words of Theodore Roszak, a key instance in the making of a counterculture (Gitlin, 1987; Roszak, 1969).

As noted earlier, a striking increase in fertility during the 15 years following World War II produced a historically large cohort of Americans who shared the experience of growing up in the 1950s and 1960s. Numbering nearly 50 million, these "baby boomers" came of age during a time of great prosperity. Theirs was the first generation of Americans to realize near universal high-school attendance, and they reveled in the various forms of adolescent socialization then taking form across the country. Unlike previous cohorts of youth, they had a common set of social and cultural reference points, ranging from music to a prevailing sense of communal hope for a better future. They also shared a healthy suspicion of older generations (Patterson, 1996).

When the baby-boom students graduated from high school, they moved on to college in record numbers. Although American post-secondary institutions enrolled just two million students in 1946, by 1970 the numbers had quadrupled to more than eight million. There had been an early increase due to the GI Bill, which provided tuition benefits to veterans, but that group of students had largely left by the mid-1950s. The major source of these new students was the relatively affluent baby-boom generation, as many as one-third of whom went to college. The number of colleges and universities did not increase nearly as much, but the average size of campuses grew dramatically. By the end of the 1960s it was not uncommon for large state institutions, which grew most rapidly, to enroll tens of thousands of students. Under these circumstances, the universities dropped any pretense of governing the daily living habits of their students, even those residing on campus. Apart from a limited number of basic rules, students were left largely to their own devices outside of class. This created a fertile field for the development of unconventional lifestyles and alternative cultural norms. It also opened the door to widespread sexual freedom. It was a new age on American campuses, and record numbers of youth were determined to go to college. By the early 1970s many of the nation's post-secondary institutions were veritable hotbeds of radical sentiments of one sort or another (Heineman, 1993; Kim and Rury, 2007; Roszak, 1969).

The baby-boom phenomenon started its decline in the 1970s, and fertility levels began to dip substantially, but the nation's schools and colleges already were nearly bursting with students. It was the largest cohort of youth in American history, and its members had experienced much of their lives in institutional settings where they constituted a vast majority. It was little wonder, in that case, that they began to question the adult world that demanded their obedience and conformity. Given their numbers, and collective buying capacity, the postwar youth generation also wielded great social and economic power. This was a new element in the development of a national consumer culture. Whether it was intended or not, their influence was pervasive, and it ultimately changed the face of American life (Owram, 1996).

It would be wrong to suggest, of course, that the people who attended the Woodstock festival represented the entire baby-boom generation. Like any historically large group, the postwar generation included individuals of all kinds, including many who identified strongly with traditional values and American nationalism. But a significant portion of the baby boomers grew to become quite suspicious of authority figures and institutions, especially mainstream politicians, the police, and the military. Two major historical events account for much of this sentiment: the civil rights movement and the war in Vietnam. Both blatantly seemed to contradict the professed ideals of American civilization, albeit in different ways. As noted earlier, the civil rights movement confronted racism and discrimination in a dramatic and often forceful manner. It revealed the inconsistency between traditional principles of equality and freedom and the reality of cruel oppression and injustice. Thousands of college students volunteered to participate in civil rights campaigns, and witnessed firsthand the brutal response of reactionary racists in the South and elsewhere. Millions of others followed these struggles in the press and on television, wondering just how the nation's professed standards of democracy could be reconciled with the events unfolding before their eyes. This was an important lesson in the realities of American politics, and it affected many of them profoundly (Halberstam, 1998).

The Vietnam War represented a different kind of learning experience, one that proved considerably more divisive among both American youth and the nation as a whole. The war began as an operation to support the flagging pro-West regime in South Vietnam, a process that led to full-scale U.S. military involvement by the late 1960s. The armed services had relied on a modest draft from the beginning of the conflict, one that permitted college students to defer their service while attending school. This, of course, proved a substantial boon to enrollments, and at the same time focused the impact of the draft on those too poor or unprepared to make it to college. Some saw the injustice in this early on, but many youth did not become concerned about the war until it threatened to affect their own lives directly. When the Nixon Administration began to dramatically escalate the war in the later 1960s and early 1970s, and changed the draft to a lottery without exemptions, antiwar protests surged in magnitude. Even though Nixon succeeded in polarizing public opinion about the war, drawing heavily on lingering Cold War sentiments, the ensuing national debate helped to radicalize millions more youth who had grown up believing the United States to be a defender of democracy. The war's widely publicized atrocities, the corruption and cruelty of the South Vietnamese regime, and the fact that no formal declaration of hostilities was ever made, all contributed to a growing impression that U.S. involvement in the conflict was ill advised or just plain wrong. To many it appeared as yet another instance of traditional adult authority figures manipulating the levers of power simply to maintain the status quo (Brokaw, 2007; Gitlin, 1987; Ravitch, 1983).

The historical experience of the civil rights struggles and the antiwar movement contributed to a rising level of skepticism among many youth about adult institutions and their values. The largest universities had become important centers of research, much of it funded by the government or large corporations and foundations. These activities offered convenient targets for student protests. Demonstrations against university complicity in war-related research, and about curricular reform issues, rocked the campuses. Berkeley (California), Madison (Wisconsin), Ann Arbor (Michigan), Lawrence (Kansas) and other large academic centers became the sites of immense struggles between students and college administrators. In 1970 the announcement of U.S. bombing in Cambodia led to massive protests and to the killing of four students by the Ohio National Guard at Kent State University. The sense of moral outrage that this engendered was compounded by the release of the so-called "Pentagon Papers" just a short time later, revealing the manipulative plots that lay behind the Nixon Administration and its war effort. The Watergate scandal and Richard Nixon's dramatic fall from power in 1974 were the final blows, along with the sudden collapse of the South Vietnamese government shortly afterward. Public confidence in the government and other traditional institutions came to a low ebb, particularly among the young. "Never trust anyone over 30" became a popular slogan among high-school and college-aged youth. The experiences of the previous decade had taught them to be inherently suspicious of existing social and economic arrangements. A strong "antiestablishment" ethic had taken hold of many in the baby-boom generation by this time, and before long its influence was quite pervasive. This too became a critical aspect of the counterculture (Heineman, 1993; Monhollon, 2004; Roof, 1993).

The very size of the baby-boom generation magnified the effects of these developments and gave them added cultural force. American youth represented a massive market for alternative music, clothing, and other cultural artifacts, and in each of these realms its tastes set new standards and fashion sensibilities. Alternative tastes in food, footwear, jewelry, and a host of other forms of expression flourished. Rock music had entered the mainstream by the 1970s, and garments made of such casual cotton fabrics as denim, gingham and chambray were ubiquitous. In the words of sociologist Fred Davis, "antifashion" became the new mainstream taste in clothing, as the anti-formalism of the young grew to be a dominant force in the apparel industry. T-shirts and jeans became signature fashion articles, eventually drawing the attention of name designers. Organic crops also became popular, prompting new companies to enter the industry in order to serve the expanding market for alternative products. In these and countless other ways, the postwar generation began to change the shape of popular culture (Davis, 1992; Jones, 1980; Russell, 1982).

The impact on politics was equally palpable. The left-of-center presidential campaigns of Eugene McCarthy (1968) and George McGovern (1972) were fueled by the antiestablishment opinions of the baby boomers, as was much of the most virulent opposition to Nixon and his policies. After Nixon's demise, politicians ignored baby-boomer concerns at their peril, and the election of the slightly offbeat and unconventional Jimmy Carter as president in 1976 was partly a reflection of their influence, as was the rejection of traditionalist Gerald Ford. By the 1980s, however, the political momentum of the postwar generation had become fragmented. Without a clear moral cause such as civil rights or an unjust war, its energy was divided between a spectrum of smaller movements: antiracism, feminism, gay rights, and the concerns of other special interests. This eventually allowed the conservative revolution led by Ronald Reagan to prevail, attacking many of the social values the postwar generation had fought to uphold (Owram, 1996).

In the end, it appears, the Woodstock nation asserted its will with considerable authority, but it also became part of a changing set of American traditions. Because of their prevalence, the baby boomers eventually found themselves in the mainstream of a shifting national culture especially as they entered early adulthood. This came as something of a shock to many, but it too was partly a function of numbers. The postwar generation was large enough to impose many of its tastes on the country and, indeed, the world. Given its size and economic power, advertisers catered to the preferences of this group and its often nontraditional and diverse tastes. But the shift to a new cultural mainstream may also have been simply a matter of aging. No generation can remain radical forever. Inevitably, even the most revolutionary ideas can become conventional wisdom. Consequently, members of the baby-boom generation ultimately became less enamored of change, and started looking for sources of stability in their lives. As the oft-cited cartoon character Pogo once said, "We have seen the enemy and they are us!" At the same time that they matured, the boomers began to grow somewhat more cautious, especially as they started having children of their own. With this it was left to the next generation to discover the vitality and ferment of the Woodstock nation—and as the continuing popularity of the music, movies, and other artifacts of that age has suggested, some have.

The experience of the baby-boom generation represented an unusual process of learning, one conducted on a grand historical scale. As already noted, its members were products of the schools, the first generation of Americans to attend high schools and colleges in exceptionally large numbers. While there, they developed a distinctive set of social relationships, values, and customs that became collectively known as the "youth culture" of the time. This eventually became a vast and variegated social landscape in itself, embracing a wide range of different subcultures, but it was bound together in a pervasive distrust of traditional sources of authority and the mores of adult society. Eventually, the youth culture, in all of its variety, entered the mainstream, establishing itself as a new set of norms or traditions, and impressing its values and customs on the rest of American culture. Partly a creation of the schools, many elements of the Woodstock nation have become integrated into the dominant culture of education today. And perhaps it is against this new set of "traditional" cultural forms that the next generations of students now find themselves rebelling.

## Schools, Youth, and the Changing Economy

Yet another critical issue in the postwar period was the changing American economy, especially the decline of industrial employment, and the importance of a well-trained workforce. Despite the proclivities of baby boomers for alternative lifestyles, the human capital revolution continued to gain momentum. Perhaps the most important manifestation of this was the shifting role of education in the labor market. Ever higher levels of formal schooling became an expectation for American employers, and this was reflected in the monetary returns paid to individuals with different kinds of educational credentials. As the economy evolved from one based on manufacturing to one dominated by services and technological development, the significance of education increased accordingly. It was the dawning of a new era, a time when brute strength and commonsense know-how were no longer sufficient to secure a good job. Suddenly, thinking and analytical skills were considered important, and schooling was the most reliable way of cultivating and documenting such abilities (Murnane & Levy, 1996).

Early in the 20th century most American youth started to work before the age of 20, even if only on a part-time basis (Kett, 1977). Employment rates for high-school-aged youth contracted dramatically in the 1930s, however, as a consequence of the Great Depression. This ended during World War II, as demand for labor skyrocketed. By the postwar period the job market for youth had been restored somewhat, but patterns of enrollment established during the Depression also returned. The fact that more youth enrolled in high school meant that fewer took jobs than in earlier times, and it was more difficult to acquire work experience in such fields as manufacturing and office work (Angus & Mirel, 1999). In particular, it became uncommon for teenagers to be employed in factories, a sharp break from the pre-Depression era. Consequently, the transition from school to work became a little more complicated than it had been in the past. It was no longer possible for many youth to simply find a job; education and training gained new significance (Rury, 2004).

The nation's economy also changed profoundly in the decades following World War II. In the immediate postwar period, industrial jobs were plentiful, and it was the prospect of employment in the booming factories of the great Northern cities that drew African Americans out of the South in the 1950s. Despite minor periodic downturns, the urban industrial economy was flush during the 1950s, but it began to show signs of change in the following decade (Teaford, 1990). By the mid-1960s some observers already were warning that the demand for unskilled labor would be limited in the future, although even these projections underestimated the rate of long-term change (Harrison, 1972; Havighurst, 1966). No one, however, anticipated the shifting relationship of education and employment that came to characterize the closing decades of the century.

As noted earlier, of course, the rapid growth of American secondary education was premised on the principle of differentiation: the idea that high-school youth were destined to enter a variety of different occupational fields on graduation. This was in large part a legacy of the progressive era and of the social efficiency rationale for the vocational-education movement. The Cardinal Principles held that the high school should be preparation for life, and vocational-education advocates argued that there were many different roads that students could take in their working careers. This was certainly true in the 1920s, when only a fraction of the teen population attended school, even in the cities (Krug, 1972). And it continued to hold in the immediate postwar period. Industrial employment remained quite robust, and even if many high-school graduates did not find jobs as manual laborers, the rationale for vocational training was still clearly preparation for blue-collar occupations (Coleman, 1965). As the urban economy changed, however, and industrial jobs contracted, the relevance of vocational training weakened. Before long, vocational education became supplanted with a variety of other curricular options, particularly a somewhat watered down academic curriculum called the "general course." Youth taking this plan of study were not being prepared for any particular future employment; nor were they trained for additional schooling. Instead, they simply were given a broad, unfocused education, one intended to prepare them for life. Some historians have referred to this as "warehousing," or simply keeping youth out of the labor force and off the streets (Angus & Mirel, 1999; Sedlak et al., 1986).

Changing curricular patterns were partly a response to shifts in the economy. Even if most jobs did not change in the short term, the labor market was evolving rapidly and demanding new skills of entry-level workers. Literacy requirements in the workplace began to rise, especially in the 1960s and 1970s, at about the same time that the academic quality of many urban high schools began to be questioned (Ginzberg, 1975; Levine & Zipp, 1993). This was a major element of the crisis in urban education that emerged in the 1970s and 1980s. Youth unemployment in the cities climbed to new heights, especially among African American youth. Employers complained that many were not well prepared for jobs in the new economy. And these concerns became linked to the rising national interest in education reflected in the publication of *A Nation at Risk* in the early 1980s. Employers specifically expressed concern about the poor quality of inner-city high schools and the difficulties that they faced in finding capable workers. Such questions became more commonplace in the latter 1980s, as employment opportunities in downtown offices expanded rapidly, fueled by the burgeoning banking, financial services, and insurance industries (Levine & Trachtman, 1988). It was the dawn of a new era, but the city schools did not appear to be well prepared for the challenges that lay ahead (Kahlenberg, 2000).

These changes were related to a set of larger shifts in the American economy that have received much attention in recent years. During the 1950s more than one-quarter of all U.S. workers were employed in manufacturing. When employees in industry were added to other sectors of the economy requiring similar skills, over 40% of the labor force could be classified as "bluc collar," both skilled and unskilled. Another 35% were clerical workers, most of them employed in urban offices. On the other hand, managerial and professional employment accounted for less than one-quarter of overall employment (Levy, 1987; Long, 1958). Given this, it appeared quite reasonable for Conant and others to surmise that the majority of American youth would not require education beyond the secondary level. For these students, vocational or commercial training would be considered most appropriate. Only a minority of the "brightest" youth was thought to need preparation for postsecondary education, perhaps 20% at the most (Conant, 1959, 1961).

The basic occupational structure of the American labor force changed slowly through the 1960s, with a gradual shift away from employment in manufacturing and toward greater numbers of workers in the "service sector." In 1970 more than one-quarter of the nation's workers were employed in manufacturing, and the number of positions requiring higher education had changed relatively little. But the years that followed witnessed a dramatic transformation that continues to unfold today. Beginning in the 1970s, and accelerating in the decades afterward, the number of manufacturing jobs began to plummet (Levy, 1987). Nationwide, the proportion of the labor force employed in manufacturing fell from about one-quarter to 18% between 1970 and 1990, and it continued to drop thereafter (Murphy & Welch, 1993). The impact of this was evident first in the cities, as noted earlier, but it eventually affected all areas of the country. Economists speculate that it was due both to technological change and to the movement of jobs to other countries (Abramovitz & David, 1996). Whatever the causes, it was a set of changes that came to have important implications for schools. The number of jobs for which relatively little formal education was necessary had started to contract sharply (Grubb, 1995).

Jobs in manufacturing were replaced by positions in offices, and by growth in management and technical and professional employment. This was slow to develop, but beginning in the 1980s a shift toward jobs requiring progressively higher levels of education had become evident (Cohn & Hughes, 1994; Murphy & Welch, 1989). This was reflected in wage rates for workers with different levels of education. At the start of the 1970s the hourly earnings for employees with less than a high-school education and those for college graduates were about $7 apart, and high-school graduates earned only about $1.50 more per hour than non-graduates. Because of the large cohort of college graduates produced in the 1960s and 1970s, the advantage of college actually shrank appreciably in the 1970s, and in 1979 only about $6 separated the hourly wages of high-school dropouts and college graduates. But soon afterward the gap began to widen, and by the mid-1990s college graduates earned nearly $10 more per hour than those lacking a secondary diploma, and $7 per hour more than high-school graduates (Datazone, 1999). In other words, the labor market began to pay even bigger returns to students who went to college.

These developments appear to have reflected two trends. First, dollar returns to college education increased slightly across the 1980s and 1990s, by roughly 7%. At the same time, however, the wages of high-school dropouts fell by more than one-quarter, and those of high-school graduates declined by about 8%. The impact on high-school dropouts was particularly dramatic (Stern et al., 1989). Thus, by the 1990s, the earnings premium for attending college was greater than at any time in the postwar period. This, not surprisingly, helped to spur a significant jump in college enrollments.

Beginning in the mid-1980s, ever-larger numbers of American high-school graduates entered college. In the late 1970s less than half of high-school seniors continued on to college, but 20 years later the figure approached 70% (Murphy & Welch, 1993). These figures reflect, of course, reasonable decisions on the part of students, given the decline of employment opportunities for workers lacking higher education and the growing wage differentials. By 1990 it was calculated that a college degree, on average, was worth $0.5 million dollars more than a high-school diploma in lifetime earnings. Figures such as these helped to make the idea of attending college attractive to a much broader range of American youth than had been the case just two decades earlier (Hunt, 1995).

A dramatic rise in female laborforce participation in the 1970s and 1980s also contributed to this general trend. Among the most rapidly growing areas of female employment were the professions, and other jobs requiring some measure of higher education. This was partly the consequence of the women's movement of the 1960s and 1970s, an offshoot of the civil rights era that itself became a major force in American life. It also reflected the self-conscious effort of young women to challenge the existing sexual division of labor. These tendencies may have been augmented by the sex-equity reforms achieved in the 1970s and 1980s under the auspices of Title IX, discussed earlier. As a result of these changes in outlook, female enrollments in college also climbed sharply, particularly in the 1980s and 1990s. This was the case despite a lower responsiveness in female enrollments to wage dividends for college (Averett & Burton, 1996; Geiger, 1993). By the 1980s, women outnumbered men among undergraduates for the first time in American history, and their numbers continued to grow. This development contributed to the rapid rise in high-school graduates continuing on to college in the 1990s; indeed, the rate of college entry among women was about 10% greater than among men.

Across the country, educational expectations were rising in the later 20th century. In an analysis of White high-school graduates in 1960 and 1980,

Marlis Buchman found that students' expectations of the highest degree they would earn changed significantly between these two cohorts. Altogether, the number expecting to simply end their education at high school fell from more than a quarter to just 18%, almost a 30% drop. At the same time, those expecting to earn graduate or advanced professional degrees increased from about 12 to over 21% (Buchman, 1989). More youth at the latter date planned to graduate from college than to simply end their education at high school. This was a remarkable shift in the educational plans of American youth, evident in a relatively short span of two decades. These trends would only accelerate in the years to follow.

Such changes in students' educational plans can be interpreted as a rational response to the changing job market. As Buchman and other observers noted, the earning power of high-school diplomas declined in the 1980s, at the same time that returns to college education began to increase significantly. This was partly due to shifts in the occupational structure, especially the decline in manufacturing employment. But it was also due to the growing preference of employers to hire workers—especially beginning employees—with higher levels of education (Carnevale & Desrochers, 1997). In a thoughtful analysis of federal statistics, economists Kevin Murphy and Finis Welch pointed out that the employment of workers with college education increased in all industrial sectors in the 1980s, contributing to a broad rising demand for higher levels of educational attainment. These changes helped to fuel a continuing expansion of higher education through the later 1980s and early 1990s, despite a drop in the number of high-school graduates as the baby boomers aged (Murphy & Welch, 1993). By the middle of the 1990s, consequently, a large majority of high-school graduates across the country were planning to undertake some form or another of higher education.

The changing economy also helped to underscore the importance of educational differences between inner-city and suburban communities. Although the latter kept pace with the new expectations of the economy, the former fell farther behind (Harrison, 1972; Sexton & Nickel, 1992). For inner-city neighborhoods, and the students who live in them, the prospect of vocational education providing a means of economic development had faded. This was evident as early as the late 1970s, and was reported by educational researcher and leader Earnest Boyer in 1983 (Boyer, 1983). Jobs calling for these manual skills were in short supply. In the 1980s and 1990s this fact contributed to improved rates of college enrollment for African Americans, but not everyone responded in the same way. Postsecondary participation rates for Hispanic students, for instance, have lagged behind the gains of other groups. As the new service economy has continued to develop, these patterns of educational differentiation posed a significant problem. They have been linked to a widening income gap separating workers with higher-education credentials from those who lack them, contributing to patterns of persistent poverty for inner-city minority communities (Bishop, 1989; Katz, 2000; Neckerman, 2007).

All of these changes reflect the impact of the human capital revolution. The emphasis in the closing decades of the 20th century, as never before in recent history, was on academic skills. This was evident in the behavior of employers (Sexton & Nickel, 1992; Stern et al., 1989; Wilson, 1995). The growing educational mismatch between the expectations of downtown employers and the preparation of city high-school students was a major impetus behind urban-school reform campaigns of the 1980s and 1990s. In Chicago it led to Mayor Richard M. Daley assuming control of the public schools and instituting a series of changes aimed at restoring public confidence in the system, chiefly by focusing on test scores (Shipps, 1998, 2006; Wong & Moulton, 1998). Leaders in other cities have undertaken similar interventions, even though it is not clear that long-term gains in academic achievement will result from such a reform strategy (Stone et al., 2001). The fates of hundreds of thousands of poor and minority central-city youths hang in the balance. In the meantime, urban children often lack the social and cultural capital to compete for higher-education opportunities. Families living in poverty are concentrated in the larger cities, as are single-parent households and children from minority ethnic and racial groups. These are all factors associated with lower levels of academic achievement, and city schools may well require additional resources to help their students to succeed scholastically (Alexander, Entwisle, & Olson, 1997; Rury, 1993).

James Conant and other proponents of the comprehensive high school believed that the allocation of students to various types of curricula would correspond to the demand for various skills in the labor market. The historical development of the economy and corresponding changes in high-school enrollments have proven this view to be correct in certain respects. The picture that has emerged in the last 15 years of the century, however, is quite different from the one that educators envisioned in the latter 1950s. The changing occupational structure, with the resulting demand for stronger educational credentials, has shifted the manner in which students make educational plans. Today, more than ever, the emphasis is on getting into college and on using formal education to find a secure niche in the rapidly evolving world of employment. Academic skills carry a premium, and educators at all levels of the school system are struggling with the challenge of improving achievement. As the nation's interest in schooling has grown, the stakes of success and failure in the schools have gone way up. For better or worse, the development of the economy is driving the educational system in new directions. Finding ways to address the social and economic needs of the 21st century will constitute the next major challenge for American education.

## An Era of Dramatic Changes

There can be little question that American society has changed profoundly since the 1940s and 1950s. As seen earlier, shifts in ideology, government policies, the social and demographic organization of cities, and in the economy all have contributed to the ways that Americans live their daily lives and relate to one another. In the course of these changes, education has become an increasingly important aspect of the national culture, and the economy. Today, as never before, where one goes to school—and what is learned there—carries profound implications for the likelihood of success in the future.

A number of historical developments converged in the decades following World War II to shape the relationship between education and social change. First, ideological currents in the immediate postwar period helped to set a new tone for social and political events in the years to follow. The 1954 *Brown* decision marked a historic shift in American thinking about questions of race and social equity. At the same time, however, racial segregation and the movement of Southern Blacks to Northern cities divided urban and suburban school districts, creating sharp disparities in educational resource allocation, curricular orientation, perceptions of school success. Although educators dating back to Horace Mann had imagined the school as an instrument of democratic socialization, by the 1970s it had evolved into an agency of racial isolation and alienation in much of metropolitan America. Rather than bringing students from the nation's principal social/ethnic groups together, in many respects the schools helped to highlight their differences in a new era of social and cultural segregation.

At the same time, however, schools became instruments of federal social policy, intended to help alleviate the very problems that they had come to reflect. Education grew to be thought of as a form of compensation for social and cultural inequities, and a way of helping individuals to pull themselves into the mainstream of society. In the South particularly, segregation declined for a time, and levels of Black educational attainment increased dramatically. The creation of a sizeable African American middle class was one critically important outgrowth of these developments. Schools also have been considered sources of economic development, and in this respect they have become a vital aspect of national policy. Expenditures on education have increased steadily as a result. In addition to this, the interest of federal and state governments in schooling has escalated in recent decades. The age when education was purely a local concern has long passed. Now education is considered a tool to promote certain types of social change. Whether it has been successful in that regard, on the other hand, is an open question.

Meanwhile, some very difficult problems have become associated with the schools, largely because they have become such a critical feature of modern life. One is the development of a pervasive youth culture, often working at cross-purposes to the institutions that play host to it. Educators' insistence on the importance of large schools in the 1950s and 1960s may have helped to compromise adult authority in the face of the growing influence of the "adolescent society." The relaxation of rules and changing standards of conduct helped make the schools into centers of an elaborate social world for teenage youth, often diverting energy and enthusiasm away from academic interests. Even if educational leaders were not proponents of many of these reforms, the campaign for larger schools helped to set the stage for other developments in the evolution of a school-based and media-promoted youth culture. As noted in discussing the Woodstock nation, this came to have wide ramifications in postwar America. The impact of this generation of young people on all facets of American history at this time was palpable.

Finally, changes in the economy altered the very premise of a differentiated curriculum for the nation's schools and colleges. Observers like Conant already had noted the heavily academic orientation of some high schools in the 1960s. In the 1980s this tendency became even more pronounced, as ever-larger numbers of high-school graduates prepared to enter college of one sort or another. The rationale for vocational secondary education became weaker as the manufacturing sector of the economy stagnated or even disappeared, as it had in many larger cities by the 1980s. In the last decade of the century, schools across the country were attempting to offer stronger academic programs to all students. In the face of significant change in the economy, and the rapidly rising value of academic skills, the academic curriculum was no longer considered suitable for only the most gifted students. The old comprehensive-school ideal inherited from the progressive era has acquired an increasingly academic demeanor in the face of these changes. This represented a significant shift in the purposes of schooling

But some things have been lost too. At the end of the 20th century few observers bother to discuss the high school as an instrument for bringing students from different backgrounds together. The common-school ideal, espoused by Horace Mann, has rarely been invoked in this new age of higher standards and economic predominance. Smaller schools are now being urged to give adults greater authority and diminish the influence of the youth culture, in all of its varied manifestations, and the differentiated curriculum is giving way to a greater interest in academic preparation. These developments have been driven in large part by changes in the economy and public perceptions about the importance of education, especially at the postsecondary level. But concern with children learning about democracy from the schools, acquiring an appreciation for diversity of backgrounds and viewpoints, and the process of democratic decision-making appears to have faded from view. Government policies are focused increasingly on boosting achievement, but the other purposes of schools—articulated by Dewey and his many students and colleagues—seem to receive little attention today. And nearly 50 years after the *Brown* decision, as suburbanization has polarized most large urban areas into Black and White enclaves, the federal government has largely abandoned the aggressive pursuit of desegregation. Given this, it appears that the vision of the public school as an instrument of egalitarian social policy may have almost slipped from view. It might be time for members of the public to begin questioning some of the current directions of American schools, and to ask policymakers how education could effectively address new patterns of inequity now becoming manifest in virtually all parts of the country.

# Epilogue
## *Recent Developments and Looking to the Future*

At the stroke of midnight, January 1, 2000, festivities around the world marked the beginning of a new millennium. Despite quibbles about the apposite celebration of this epochal moment, there was little disagreement about its significance. As television images reflected a heightened sense of global consciousness in the midst of these events, feelings of amity and optimism ran especially high. Among the themes touched upon in innumerable public forums about the new millennium was the importance of education. If people were to live in peace and prosperity, and humankind were to move forward, schooling of one sort or another was seen as critical. As never before, education had become an expression of hope for the future.

Historians are often reluctant to write about their own times. Many claim it is difficult to gain a sense of perspective, to put events in order, and to identify probable lines of influence from one development to another. It is with some trepidation, then, that one undertakes a chronicle of the last decade or so of American education. It has been a time of seemingly momentous development in all sectors of the nation's school system, involving a series of events that has led directly to its present set of circumstances. Given that it is still largely underway, finding words to characterize this dynamic period is fraught with difficulty. Still, certain trends are clearly evident. These developments provide an outline of the age, and offer some immediate historical evidence for comprehending the factors affecting schools today.

At the same time, it is also true that all of the various forces discussed in the preceding six chapters continue to play a role, one way or another, in the current state of American education. The weight of history is not carried lightly. National polls show that Americans continue to believe in the principle of free and universal public education, both as an instrument of assimilation and a way of promoting national unity, and as a means of economic advancement, personal and collective. Race, gender, and social class still produce invidious distinctions within the schools, and across the larger society that sustains them. Despite the growing role of the federal government in education, schooling remains a highly localized affair, and differences in the provision and quality of instruction from one place to another, sometimes in close proximity to one another, can be quite dramatic. And finally there is the economy. As seen earlier, education has been linked in various ways to economic activity since the very first schools, but in the past several decades the influence of the labor market has been especially striking. To understand American schools today, one must consider the collective impact of all these elements and decide which of them are especially salient at this particular time.

## Accountability for Schools

Among the major developments of the 1990s, few events in education were as important as the so-called *standards movement*, an outgrowth of what became known as *systemic reform* undertaken by state governments at the urging of national political figures. The basic idea behind these developments was that the curricula of the schools ought to be "aligned" with systems of assessment, so that reliable estimates could be made of what children were learning and of how well the schools were fulfilling their instructional mission. Marshall Smith, undersecretary of education in the Clinton Administration, is sometimes credited with originating this idea, but by the later 1990s the impact of systemic reform could be felt across the country. By that time, most of the states had identified learning standards in the major subject areas for each grade level. These were goals and objectives that teachers were expected to aim for in classroom practice; in practical terms they often amounted to a state-mandated curricular framework. More importantly, however, most of the states then instituted standardized tests to assess the effects of these measures. Although the tests varied a great deal in their sophistication and degree of difficulty, the effect was to produce a new atmosphere of accountability and recrimination in public education, wherein schools and teachers were increasingly judged on the basis of student performances on these examinations. With these developments, public concern with education, already historically significant, began to reach even higher levels (Smith & Scoll, 1995; Vinovskis, 1996).

In certain cases the emphasis on testing was taken to new extremes. In Chicago, for instance, Mayor Richard M. Daley announced in the late 1990s that public-school children in certain grades would be required to achieve a predetermined score on the Iowa Test of Basic Skills (ITBS), a nationally normed achievement test, before they could proceed to the next grade level. Among the children tested each year were 8th graders, so that a passing score was needed for promotion into high school. As one might imagine, this placed enormous pressure on teachers and students to succeed, but progress was slow and uneven. One problem was that the ITBS was not designed to assess how much children had learned from a particular curriculum. Instead, it compared their overall achievement against that of a national sample of students in the same grade. This meant that the children in Chicago's public schools, with the vast majority from poor, minority households, were being asked to perform at the same levels in reading and math as students from affluent and traditionally mainstream backgrounds.

Not surprisingly, children from more prosperous neighborhoods in the city tended to perform better on these exams than students from poverty-affected areas. Historically, differences in social and cultural capital appear to have accounted for great disparities in the school performance of children from different backgrounds, and this has continued to be true into the 21st century. On top of this, the public schools in Chicago suffered by comparison to those elsewhere. They had greater numbers of students from poor or otherwise disadvantaged backgrounds, many Chicago teachers taught without full credentials, and class sizes were large. Consequently, the challenge of raising scores on this sort of test was enormous. Only through massive investment in extra instructional time, summer school, and special sessions were advances made possible. Still, thousands of schoolchildren suffered through mind-numbing test-preparation exercises that probably contributed little to their overall education. For those who did not succeed, some of them good students who simply did not test well, there was the humiliation of failing a grade and falling behind one's peers. It was a policy that engendered considerable controversy but it also received a great deal of public support (Bryk et al., 1998; Lipman, 2003).

Assessment policies like those employed in Chicago became known as *high-stakes testing*, and were an increasingly popular feature of American schooling as the 20th century drew to a close. President Bill Clinton touted Chicago as a model for the nation to follow in combating "social promotion," and his successor in the White House, George W. Bush, campaigned on an education platform that focused on increasing the amount of testing required of American schoolchildren. Unlike his father, the younger Bush made education a high priority in his Administration, and proposed significant increases in federal spending on schools. But he also contributed to a growing national preoccupation with standardized tests to measure the results of schooling. These ultimately found expression in the 2001 reauthorization of ESEA, known popularly as "No Child Left Behind" (NCLB for short), a name given the legislation by the White House (DeBray, 2006; Rury, 1999a).

NCLB was intended to strengthen Title I accountability by requiring States to implement statewide testing systems covering all public schools and students. These systems were to be based on the state standards in reading and mathematics, annual testing for all students in grades 3–8, and annual statewide progress objectives ensuring that all groups of students reach proficiency within 12 years. Assessment results and state progress objectives were required to be reported by poverty, race, ethnicity, disability, and limited English proficiency. Districts and schools that failed to make adequate yearly progress (AYP) toward proficiency goals were subject to corrective action and restructuring measures, while those that met or exceeded AYP objectives were eligible for academic awards. Altogether, it was an ambitious proposal, designed to compel teachers and schools to take the education of all children seriously, and to boost academic achievement dramatically (Mcguinn, 2006).

It was not long, however, before educators in all parts of the country began to cry out against the new accountability system represented by NCLB. Schools in impoverished urban neighborhoods like those in Chicago found it challenging to meet annual improvement goals, and even institutions in more affluent communities were hard-pressed to address achievement gaps in the performance of critical subgroups, such as minority students or the learning disabled. Educators complained that gains were difficult to realize with limited additional funding, a situation made worse by the recession of 2002 and steep cuts in state and local budgets. Increased testing and data-management requirements for the states also raised costs, sometimes well beyond the additional funding provided by NCLB. Federal education officials vigorously defended the new law, arguing that strict accountability was neces-sary to insure change in the schools and that funding levels were adequate to the task. But as the 2008 presidential election approaches, the intensity of debates over these questions seems to be building ever higher. The NCLB reauthorization legislation has been vigorously debated in Congress, with opponents demanding greater flexibility for states and local districts in meeting standards. While public support for educational reform remains high, and considerable bipartisan support for elements of NCLB still exists, especially for the concept of accountability, it is likely that important changes will be made in the federal role in education in the years ahead (Abernathy, 2007; Poetter, Wegwert, & Haerr, 2006).

Taking a somewhat longer perspective, it is possible to see the rush to insti-tute new regimes of accountability in American education as a corollary of the human capital revolution, and a correspondingly narrow way of viewing the function of schools. The point of systemic reform, after all, was to make schooling more productive in terms of specific curricula, and most of the attention of the testers was focused on mathematics, science, and reading. These, of course, were the subject areas most frequently linked to the new service and professional sectors of the economy and to the higher demand for advanced educational credentials. Standardized tests were simply a form of technology well suited to the task of identifying individuals who had developed these abilities, and schools that successfully imparted them. Making schools accountable for producing more such skilled individuals was thus a strategy for strengthening the national capacity for economic growth and at the same time improving the productivity and earning power of indi-vidual Americans. In other words, education was increasingly seen as just another factor of production, subject to measurement and improvement like sources of energy, new machinery, raw material, and waste management (Hillocks, 2002).

Ultimately, historians may look back at this era as testimony to the power of the human capital revolution as it approached its logical apogee. If education is to be viewed primarily as an economic resource, after all, it makes perfect sense to use tests to insure that schools turn out uniformly and optimally acceptable products. There also are international manifestations of this way of viewing schools, as evidenced by the high level of public interest in the Third International Mathematics and Science Study (TMSS), a comparison of performance on a single standardized test given to samples of students in more than 30 countries. The relatively poor performance of Americans in this assessment exercise became a point of national concern in the mid-1990s, and no doubt fueled interest in intensified testing policies in the United States. Even so, the ideology of the human capital revolution, framing schools in narrowly economic terms, probably would have produced the same result, if perhaps a little less expeditiously. For the moment, in that case, the other purposes of schools appear to have been made subsidiary to their economic function, at least as regards national policy. Just when and how this era will eventually change, of course, is beyond the ken of a historian (Rury, 2002).

**Equity and Privatization**

At the same time that the federal government has become a growing presence in the schools, a number of other developments have shaped educational policies at the state and local levels. Court battles over equity of funding in a number of states have partially reduced financial differences across districts, at least with respect to support from legislative sources. Wealthier districts, particularly in suburban areas, have often been able to maintain an advantage by increasing local taxes or finding other ways of raising funds, such as private donations. But the additional resources that urban and poor rural schools have received in the wake of these actions have been quite helpful in meeting the manifold needs of their students. The impact of these judicial battles over state financial support has proven very controversial, but it has helped to raise awareness of the question of systematic inequity in schooling among a large segment of the public (Bosworth, 2001; Evers et al., 2006).

Whether simply allocating equal funding is enough to address the significant achievement gaps that exist between students in wealthy and poor districts is a question often debated by educational researchers and policymakers. There is considerable evidence, for instance, that smaller classes and more experienced teachers can have a positive impact on the performance of poor and minority students, but these are measures that require additional funding. Students from more affluent backgrounds, on the other hand, do not always appear to gain as much from smaller classes. Their relatively high stocks of social and cultural capital, it seems, enable more privileged children and youth to achieve success with somewhat fewer school resources. Many of them are able to attend private schools as well. Given this, it may be the case

234 • Education and Social Change

that one way to realize better equality in educational outcomes would be to grant children from less-advantaged backgrounds greater funding than their more affluent counterparts. This, of course, could prove politically difficult to accomplish, as it would almost inevitably entail a transfer of resources from the wealthiest communities in most states to the poorest ones, a step that many politicians from affluent areas would certainly resist forcefully. But the very fact that these questions are currently being debated is a positive sign that problems of educational inequality are being considered seriously. A significant and sustained effort to address learning gaps that are linked to inequities in school resources would be a historic development indeed (Heckman and Kreuger, 2005; Kreuger et al., 2002; Rothstein, 2004).

Yet another development that has affected education in recent years has been an abiding movement to remove children from the public schools, which many parents believe have been compromised by materialistic, secular values and the pervasive influence of the youth culture. This impulse has found expression in long-standing criticisms of the public institutions for lack of discipline and a willingness to tolerate a wide range of student behavior, especially in the years following the *Tinker* decision and the student rights movement. Families with strong religious beliefs have always objected to the secularist stance of the public schools, but this line of criticism gained extra impetus with the rise of evangelical churches in the years following 1960. In the South, private schools multiplied in number following desegregation of public institutions, and many of these White institutions have persisted to the present. Together, all of these elements have contributed to a historically new degree of criticism aimed at the public schools. Private education, although serving little more than one-tenth of the nation's children, has been routinely held up as an alternative.

Sentiments such as these helped to foster the development of a movement advocating school vouchers, campaigning to permit children to attend private institutions with the government paying tuition. The idea of school vouchers dates from the early postwar era, and the writing of conservative economist Milton Friedman. Vouchers also have long been backed by the Catholic Church, which supports the nation's largest network of private schools, dating back to Bishop John Hughes in the 19th century. In recent years, inner-city residents have also spoken in favor of vouchers, as they sought alternatives to failing public institutions. Large-scale experimental voucher programs have been undertaken in Milwaukee and Cleveland and, despite legal challenges, have managed to gain a loyal following. Research reports indicate that students in the voucher programs do not perform significantly better than those in the public schools, once background factors such as income and parental education are considered. But the supporters of vouchers have been persistent in calling for more such programs across the country. Republican politicians have expressed considerable sympathy for voucher schemes, but to this date have not proposed a national program for their adoption. While popular sentiment, as measured in polls, appears to view the idea with considerable skepticism, the voucher movement continues to push for new initiatives. Time will tell if these efforts will eventually bear fruit (Carnoy, 2001; Witte, 1999).

The debate initiated by the proponents of vouchers in the 1990s quickly led to the formation of a broader educational reform impulse, widely captured by the expression "school choice." Acknowledging criticisms of the public schools with regard to academic achievement, defenders of the public schools fashioned the idea of an alternative form of publicly supported education, outside the traditional organizational structure of many districts. These new institutions became widely known as "charter schools," as they typically were authorized (or "chartered") by state legislatures in agreement with local authorities. Generally located in cities and serving larger districts, many of these schools were sponsored by universities, neighborhood groups, or other organizations concerned with improving education. At the same time, conventional district schools in many cities were opened to a wider selection of students, whether for special programs or particular groups of students. In many respects, these different institutions fostered by the charter movement were similar to the magnet schools developed during the desegregation era, especially those organized around a particular theme or serving children with special needs. Predictably, a vigorous debate soon unfolded about the strengths and weaknesses of this version of "school choice" as an approach to educational reform, and as a political response to critiques of the public schools. As the dust has settled, however, it appears that there is relatively little systematic evidence that charter schools perform much better than ordinary public schools in raising educational achievement. The school finance and class-size debates have demonstrated, after all, that there are few effective policy alternatives to smaller classes and highly effective teachers when it comes to improving the performance of most urban students. Increasing school choice, whether in the form of vouchers or charters, has not yet proven to be a "magic bullet" for transforming American education (Carnoy et al., 2005; Miron & Nelson, 2002).

Finally, perhaps the most severe critics of the public schools, and educational institutions in general, have been those who support the idea of withholding children from school in order to educate them at home. This notion dates from the 1960s and author John Holt, who wondered if schools were the most effective venue for the education of many children. In the following decade a nascent movement to educate children at home took form, principally comprised of evangelical Christians and others who objected to the secular and youth-centered environment that public schools often engendered. As criticisms of the schools mounted in the 1980s and 1990s, the home-schooling movement began to expand rapidly. Following early battles with state and local authorities over compulsory attendance laws and other regulations, home-school advocates succeeded in marshalling enough political support to gain passage of legislation supporting the rights of parents to educate their own children. Provisions varied from one state to another, but by the start of the 21st century it was possible in most parts of the country to conduct schooling within a home environment. Meanwhile, a national network of support groups and organizations sprang up to assist the movement, providing resources and advice for parents, including extensive materials on the internet (Knowles, Marlow, & Muchmore, 1992; Rudner, 1999).

On the whole, the home-school movement has not cooperated with researchers, making it difficult to gauge its size, but estimates in 2005 put the number of children receiving an education in this way at more than one million nationwide. The majority of these students appear to be religiously motivated, and most come from larger families headed by parents who are avowedly conservative in political orientation. Others see the local schools as academically weak, or unable to serve the special needs of their children, among other concerns. Their degree of detachment from the schools varies somewhat as well. Tensions sometimes occur between parents and home-schooled children who would like to participate in sports or other activities, and many districts have made arrangements to accommodate such requests. Some districts have experimented with virtual schools, featuring extensive online instruction, as a way to count home schoolers as enrolled and allow access to a more complete curriculum than they might otherwise receive.

Despite its growth in recent years, however, concerns about the quality of this form of formal education persist. Lately, there have been questions about the ability of parents to provide a balanced and effective program of studies, especially those lacking a college education. In an age of increased apprehension about academic achievement, it is hardly surprising that such issues have arisen. Perhaps even more important, many educators and researchers have raised concerns about the long-term effect of home-schooling on American society, and its historic commitment to democracy. If the public school is supposed to function as a commons or meeting ground for all of the various elements of the polity, the home-schooling movement would appear to be ideologically opposed to the democratic principles that Horace Mann, John Dewey, and other educational leaders have long espoused. This, of course, strikes at the most fundamental purposes of schools in modern society. It is an issue that will have to be addressed in the years to come, as Americans consider the role of education in the continuing evolution of the country's democratic traditions (Reich, 2002).

Given the foregoing, it is clear that the challenges facing American schools in the immediate future are manifold. By any historical standard, the last decade or so of educational reform measures and policy debates has been unusually tumultuous. Perhaps this too reflects the momentous influence of the human capital revolution, and a consequential narrowing of educational purposes to economic questions in the minds of many people. From this perspective, the appeal of privatization—and even home-schooling—is explicable. If education is primarily seen as a financial good, a basic commodity, it may be reasonable to turn away from the public schools if they seem unable to boost academic achievement. Even the disputes over school funding are driven primarily by concerns for boosting achievement, as a means to greater economic opportunity. In the meantime, there seems to be considerably less concern about the egalitarian purposes of education, especially the role of public education in fostering democratic values and behavior. In other words, education is increasingly seen as a personal or private benefit rather than a public good (Labaree, 1999; Rury, 2002).

Without doubt, the current debates are yet further testimony to the great significance that education has come to assume in our society, and the divisions that characterize it, but fundamental questions about the goals of schooling remain unanswered. For many Americans, schools today are considered an avenue to individual advancement rather than a means of civic and social integration. This has always been true to one extent or another, and in this respect the current controversies over education are hardly new. They are the latest incarnations of debates that have shaped American education in the past. But the quality and intensity of current policy disputes seems historically distinctive. This raises the question of context: How do we assess these concerns in view of history? One means of weighing their significance is to consider them in light of the larger process of transformation that has shaped the course of American education through more than two centuries.

### Education and Social Change: A Long View

Perhaps the best way to put current issues into perspective is to begin with the problem of education and social change, the question posed at the beginning of this book. How are these two facets of modern life related, and how has their interaction shifted throughout history? And what bearing does this have on the current problems facing the schools? Given the many historical events discussed in the preceding chapters, perhaps it is now possible to offer some answers.

As suggested in the book's opening chapter, the interrelationship of education and social change is quite complex. Clearly, the schools and educational practices observed throughout history have been shaped by larger social forces, just as have other social institutions and practices. Many of the major processes of social transformation discussed earlier were economic: the search for labor in the New World, the rise of the factory system, the onset of full-scale industrialization, and the human capital revolution. Each of these events bore significant implications for education, and led to changes in the schools. The factory system provided models for creating more orderly and uniform schools; industrialization helped inspire the social efficiency movement, the celebration of differentiation, and the rise of testing during the progressive era. The human capital revolution has focused attention on the economic value of education and on the role of schooling in national development. In each of these instances, the institution of schooling responded to social change dictated by the process of economic expansion and development. Given this historical record, there can be little doubt that the shifting economy has exerted a powerful influence over the schools.

But social change is not simply economic. As suggested in Chapter 1, ideology has been an important component of the shifting relations between major social and political groups in American history, and this too has affected the schools. Ideology has been informed by underlying economic relationships, but religion, the development of science and a host of other influences have also shaped it. Racist and sexist ideology has operated historically to restrict the educational opportunities available to African Americans and women. Other minority groups suffered similar patterns of discrimination in the schools as a consequence of beliefs that held all non-White or non-Protestant students to be inferior in motivation or ability. As noted in Chapter 6, these attitudes were slow to change, despite breakthroughs such as the 1954 *Brown* decision and the rise of the civil rights movement. In certain respects, women have achieved greater progress in the continuing struggle against the ideological forces of restriction and exclusion, but sexism continues to exert a powerful influence in the schools today. In these respects, and perhaps in countless others, it is possible to say that ideology has been a major element of social change that has served to shape the course of American education throughout its history.

At the same time, families have changed. As observed in earlier discussions of childhood experiences, at different points in American history, patterns of socialization—rearing the young—and relationships between family members have evolved significantly. Families became smaller over the course of American history, demographic episodes like the baby boom notwithstanding, and this has contributed toward greater intimacy and affection in household relations. It has also meant that parents have even greater resources to devote to the education of their children, and this has played a role in the growth of schooling, especially postsecondary enrollment in the postwar period. In this regard, the baby boomers and the generations that followed them have been among the most privileged children in history. On the other hand, changes in family structure have created new problems. In particular, the number of single-parent households has increased dramatically during the past several decades, especially in the nation's larger cities. These families typically have fewer resources, both psychological and financial, to contribute to their children's education. Students from poor, single-parent households pose a great challenge to the schools today.

The disparity in family experiences can be seen in the discussion of current issues above. Families with greater resources, both in terms of income and parental availability, are more likely to assist their children in achieving educational success. This even extends to the home-schoolers, who may have average income levels but are more likely to reside in two-parent households than other children. Single-parent households are more common in the larger cities, a set of circumstances highly correlated with low income or household poverty. As we have seen, because of sharp differences in social and cultural capital, these conditions are also associated with lower likelihood of success in school. The growing division between children living in these circumstances and those with greater resources, including the home-schoolers, is one of the great challenges of our time. But it too can be linked to the social and economic changes described above. As certain segments of society have benefited from the human capital revolution, attaining ever-higher levels of education, others have been left behind. The widening gulf between those families and children who have experienced success in school and those who have not could eventually pose a major dilemma for our democratic society. The school funding debates have pointed to some promising ways to overcome these differences, but the idea of devoting greater resources to the education of poor children will undoubtedly prove to be politically charged.

Differences in the educational accomplishments of children from different family backgrounds have been pointed to as a key consideration in social inequality since Coleman's national survey of educational opportunity in the 1960s. They have undoubtedly been an important element of human relations throughout modern history. The importance of family-background factors such as poverty and household structure in Coleman's findings and countless studies since points to the significance of cultural and social capital as factors affecting the fates of children today. The ability of some parents to provide their offspring with valuable knowledge and insight about the dominant cultural forces that they must negotiate to succeed, and to offer relationships with influential people who can assist with problems and advance careers, cannot be underestimated. This is true of home-schoolers as well as students attending public or private institutions. As a general rule, children who lack these family advantages will face greater difficulty in achieving success. Research has shown that schools often reinforce the advantages associated with social and cultural capital, especially when students who possess them receive even greater institutional resources than those who do not. This is evident in the superior test scores and other accomplishments of students in wealthy suburban school districts, who routinely outperform their inner-city counterparts. These disparities make the idea of additional funding for schools serving the most disadvantaged children even more imperative, particularly as educational credentials become historically more important. Without reform of this sort, inequality may very well grow even more severe in the years ahead (Lareau, 2003; Lareau & Horvat, 1999).

Finally, there is yet another element of social change, closely related to the question of inequity, which can perhaps best be described simply as community. As noted in Chapter 3, it was the cohesiveness of early rural settlements that accounted for much of the success of the 19th-century common schools. Families knew one another, and a sense of shared values and goals in life served to reinforce the role of the school in imparting academic skills, social norms, and culturally sanctioned knowledge. This process reflected the influence of social capital at the community level, the stock of shared relationships and resources that children in these settings could draw upon to succeed in acquiring relevant values, skills, and knowledge. As noted earlier, the level of social capital in these settings probably was quite high. Most people felt generally equal in status, and thus had few reservations about helping one another in times of need.

Then came urbanization. This too was a corollary of economic growth, but it exerted a particular type of influence on social relations and the schools. The rapid growth of cities in the 19th and early 20th centuries altered familiar patterns of social interaction among Americans. With people continually on the move, it became more difficult to know and trust one's neighbors, and shared values were not always evident. As a result, the stock of social capital available to children in such circumstances was diminished. They had fewer relationships and social resources to rely upon as they struggled with the demands of school and learning enough to contend with the future. Schools and other institutions struggled to fill this void, providing a growing range of services and resources to help students succeed, and to create a sense of community in the midst of seemingly constant urban change. With the development of massive, complicated metropolitan regions in the later 20th century, however, the challenges of creating a sense of community that spanned the divisions of race, ethnicity, and social class became even greater. The scale and complexity of modern life had made it increasingly difficult to establish the sense of shared values and goals that had once held communities together. Education, as a consequence, became a source of public concern, and schools found the task of imparting essential skills and knowledge a formidable one. Today the challenge of establishing a sense of community to support the nation's schools continues to be an important problem facing American democracy. Many social scientists have commented on the historic loss of social capital in recent decades (Putnam, 2001, 2004). The absence of an awareness of collective responsibility, aggravated by the manifold divisions that characterize our lives, makes the prospect of political solutions to the question of educational inequity even more remote.

Such developments have figured prominently in the evolution of American society, particularly in recent decades. In these respects social change has clearly influenced the schools. Society has become a good deal more complicated, and as a result the demands that it has placed on the educational system have grown. At the same time, the ability of the schools to meet the challenges of growing social inequality in recent years has been diminished. But what about the reverse question? How have the schools affected society? Here too there are definite patterns that history reveals to the attentive observer. Education has clearly influenced the direction of social change, in both dramatic and rather subtle ways.

It has become a central tenet of American civilization that schooling is a vehicle of social betterment. In the past, education was considered a way of improving the moral condition of the common folk and contributing to the greater stability of the social order. This was seen in the case of the New York Manumission Society in Chapter 2, and their compatriots in the New York Public School Society in Chapters 3 and 4. It was also depicted as a means of self-improvement, and as an instrument of social mobility for talented and industrious members of society dissatisfied with their lot in life. As noted earlier, schooling became a powerful instrument of social mobility for the off-spring of European immigrants to the United States, albeit in varying degrees. Education thus contributed to social change by simply making society better and by vouchsafing alternative pathways to success for those individuals and groups who were able to utilize it toward such purposes. However incremental, this too was a part of social change.

Perhaps more significant was the role of education in affording groups and individuals a means of challenging dominant forms of ideology and the social norms and practices that accompanied them. This was explored in Chapter 4, which contrasted the experiences of women and African Americans in the later 19th century. Following the Civil War, Blacks eagerly embraced school-ing as a way to escape the degradation and ignorance of slavery, only to see their hopes frustrated by the resurrection of White supremacy following Reconstruction. Dramatic advances in literacy among African Americans were made, despite the meager support that Southern states extended to Black schools. By and large, however, schooling was not a means to social advance-ment for the nation's Black population in this era, despite the success of a few individuals such as W. E. B. DuBois. For White women, on the other hand, schooling was a potent—if delimited—instrument of social improvement. Young women flocked to the newly established public high schools in the decades following the Civil War, soon outnumbering the young men by as much as two to one. Relatively high levels of formal education helped women to move into such new occupations as clerical employment and social work, along with the expanding fields of nursing and teaching. Female labor-force participation grew significantly, partly because of the growing numbers of educated women entering offices, classrooms, and hospitals across the country. Old barriers erected in the name of sexism were falling and, even if new ones were being built, it was clear that American women would continue to march forward in the quest for yet new opportunities in the future.

The lessons to be drawn from these historical experiences are manifold. On the one hand they demonstrate both the power and limitations of education as a means of ameliorating the effects of ideology. One might say that the schools were strong enough to overcome certain aspects of sexist ideology, but not so powerful that they could fully resist the forces of racism in the 19th century. It was not until the following century that the educational system became a means to confront and defeat racism, as demonstrated in the NAACP campaign to end segregated and unequal schooling. Then the results were quite dramatic, even though it eventually took decades for meaningful changes to occur in many school systems. In most of metropolitan America today the quest for desegregated and equal education remains a source of frustration for activists still seeking social justice and equity. Even when the schools have successfully challenged the dominant ideology, the process of change is often slow and halting, and new barriers often appear just beyond the point where old obstacles had been cleared away. Still, recent advances in Black education have been significant, and the development of a sizeable Black middle class of university-trained professionals is an important historical achievement. It is a step in the right direction and a foundation on which further progress can be made.

The history of the schools working to change society is also marked by well-intended failures and unplanned instances of success. The many progressive experiments at using the schools to help build community and to impart stronger social values do not appear to have exerted much lasting effect. One by one, the major centers of these reforms—Gary was among the most prominent—reverted to traditional models of school organization and instructional practice. Dewey's call to make the school into an agency of democratic values and practices, it appears, had relatively little effect on the larger social order. This certainly does not mean that his ideas were wrong, just that the power of schools as social institutions to effect such changes is limited. On the other hand, rapidly rising enrollments in high schools and colleges during the decades following World War II helped to foster the rise of a pervasive youth culture, an event that continues to shape the nation's culture in ways that could hardly have been foreseen some 50 years ago. This was an unintended consequence of the growth of modern school systems, but it nonetheless came to exert a powerful social influence. As places where large numbers of children, adolescents, and young adults meet together on a daily basis—a vast portion of the nation's population—schools have become incubators of unplanned social change. It is difficult to predict just what new influences will emerge from this aspect of the nation's educational system in the future.

Then there is the human capital revolution. Simply put, education has become a major source of economic productivity in the 20th century, particularly during the years following World War II. Economic historians have found that a high-school education added significantly to the earnings of both men and women early in the 20th century, and more recently economists have determined that the relative income of college graduates is at an all-time high. This certainly was good for the individuals possessing these educational credentials, but it also meant that the U.S. economy could enjoy the benefits of their enhanced skills and productivity. Enrollments in American schools surged upward across the 20th century, first in the high schools and after World War II in the nation's colleges and universities. This represented an enormous investment in resources, but it helped to fuel a postwar period of general economic prosperity that has continued to the present. At the same time, education came to be seen as a means of ameliorating social and economic inequality. As a matter of social policy, education and training programs have been designed to combat poverty and unemployment. Education has thus become both a source of economic development and an instrument of social policy. This is a dramatic change from the start of the century, and perhaps a suggestion of its future importance as an agent of societal transformation.

Today the challenge is one of helping the schools to revisit that historic mission of redressing the social and economic divisions that have become so apparent in recent years. The abiding disenchantment with public education, evident in both the home-school movement and the call for vouchers, seems to represent an inward turn on the part of many families and communities, away from a sense of responsibility for the rest of society that has resided in the ideals of public education since the time of Horace Mann. If this is the case, it is an unfortunate development, and one that deserves to be met with a vigorous reaffirmation of the role of schooling in fostering a truly democratic society. To do this, it is necessary to convey a clear sense of the history of education, and the possibilities that it holds for social transformation. Without such a shift in orientation, we are likely to see inequality grow into an even more important problem in the future.

These have been some of the broad contours of change in the history of American education. Over the course of American history, it is clear that society has changed the schools, at the same time that the schools have exerted a telling influence on the shape of social change. The major social forces that have affected the schools—industrialization, urbanization, ideological change—were deeply rooted in the American historical experience. Most of these forces originated in the 18th or 19th centuries, and they helped to give shape to the foundational elements of the nation's educational system. It seems to be only more recently, as the schools became an ever-larger factor in American life, that they have started to exert a telling influence themselves. Enrolling the vast majority of American youth from ages 5 until 18 and beyond, today they embrace more than 80 million people. This alone would seem to represent a capacity for social change unparalleled in American history, and it is already possible to see evidence of the power of schools to influence the direction of social and economic development. If there is a general historical trend, it is that schooling has become an ever-more significant factor in modern life, and a potent force in the process of social change. This development alone would seem to cast a bright light on the prospects for education exerting a positive influence on the future development of American civilization, and the larger world.

# References

Abernathy, S. (2007). *No child left behind and the public schools.* Ann Arbor: University of Michigan Press.

Abramovitz, M., & David, P. A. (1996). Technological change and the rise of intangible investments: The U.S. economy's growth-path in the twentieth century. In *OECD documents, Employment and growth in the knowledge-based economy* (pp. 35–60). Paris: Organization for Economic Cooperation and Development.

Abrams, P. (1982). *Historical sociology.* Ithaca, NY: Cornell University Press.

Adams, D. W. (1995). *Education for extinction: American Indians and the boarding school experience, 1875–1928.* Lawrence: University Press of Kansas.

Aghion, P., & Williamson, J. G. (1998). *Growth, inequality, and globalization: Theory, history, and policy.* New York: Cambridge University Press.

Alexander, K., Entwisle, D., & Olson, L. S. (1997). *Children, schools, and inequality.* Boulder, CO: Westview Press.

Alridge, D. (2008). *The educational thought of W.E.B. Dubois: An intellectual history.* New York: Teachers College Press.

Anderson, A. B., & Pickering, G. W. (1986). *Confronting the color line: The broken promise of the civil rights movement in Chicago.* Athens: University of Georgia Press.

Anderson, E., & Moss, A. A., Jr. (1999). *Dangerous donations: Northern philanthropy and Southern Black education, 1902–1930.* Columbia: University of Missouri Press.

Anderson, J. D. (1988). *The education of Blacks in the South, 1860–1935.* Chapel Hill: University of North Carolina Press.

Angus, D., & Mirel, J. (1999). *The failed promise of American high school, 1890–1995.* New York: Teachers College Press.

Archdeacon, T. J. (1983). *Becoming American: An ethnic history.* New York: Free Press.

Arum R., Beattie I., Pitt R., Thompson, J., & Way, S. (2003). *Judging school discipline: The crisis of moral authority.* Cambridge, MA: Harvard University Press.

Ashton, T. S. (1948). *The industrial revolution, 1760–1830.* New York: Oxford University Press.

Averett, S. L., & Burton, M. I. (1996). College attendance and the college wage premium: Differences by gender. *Economics of Education Review, 15*(1), 37–49.

Axtell, J. (1974). *The school upon a hill: Education and society in colonial New England.* New Haven, CT: Yale University Press.

Axtell, J. (1985). *The invasion within: The contest of cultures in Colonial North America.* New York: Oxford University Press.

Ayers, E. L. (1992). *The promise of the new South: Life after reconstruction.* New York: Oxford University Press.

Babson, S. (1999). *The unfinished struggle: Turning points in American labor, 1877–present.* Lanham, MD: Rowman & Littlefield.

Bailyn, B. (1960). *Education in the forming of American society: Needs and opportunities for study.* New York: Random House.

Bailyn, B. (1967). *The ideological origins of the American Revolution.* Cambridge, MA: Belknap Press of Harvard University Press.

Bannister, R. C. (1979). *Social Darwinism: Science and myth in Anglo-American social thought.* Philadelphia, PA: Temple University Press.

Barker, R. G., & Gump, P. V. (1964). *Big school small school.* Stanford, CA: Stanford University Press.

Barton, J. J. (1975). *Peasants and strangers: Italians, Rumanians, and Slovaks in an American city, 1890–1950.* Cambridge, MA: Harvard University Press.

Beadie, N. (1999). From student markets to credential markets: The creation of the regents examination system in New York state, 1864–1890. *History of Education Quarterly, 39*(1), 1–30.

Beadie, N. (2008). Tuition funding for common schools: Education markets and market regulation in rural New York, 1815–1850. *Social Science History, 32*(1) (Spring), pp. 107–134.

Beadie, N., & Tolley, K., Eds. (2002). *Chartered schools: Two hundred years of independent academies in the United States, 1727–1925.* London and New York: Routledge/Falmer.

Becker, G. S. (1964). *Human capital: A theoretical and empirical analysis, with special reference to education.* New York: National Bureau of Economic Research; distributed by Columbia University Press.

Berkhofer, R. F. (1965). *Salvation and the savage: An analysis of Protestant missions and American Indian response, 1787–1862.* Lexington: University of Kentucky Press.

Bernard, R. M., & Vinovskis, M. A. (1977). The female school teacher in ante-bellum Massachusetts. *Journal of Social History, 10*(3), 332–345.

Bettis, P. J. (1996). Urban students, liminality, and the postindustrial context. *Sociology of Education, 69*(2), 105–125.

Binder, F. M. (1974). *The age of the common school: 1830–1865.* New York: Wiley.

Binder, F. M., & Reimers, D. M. (1995). *All the nations under heaven: An ethnic and racial history of New York City.* New York: Columbia University Press.

Bishop, J. (1989). Occupational training in high school: When does it pay off? *Economics of Education Review, 8*(1), 1–15.

Blackwelder, J. K. (1997). *Now hiring: The feminization of work in the United States, 1900–1995.* College Station: Texas A & M University Press.

Blassingame, J. W. (1972). *The slave community: Plantation life in the ante-bellum South.* New York: Oxford University Press.

Bledstein, B. (1976). *The culture of professionalism: The middle class and the development of higher education in America.* New York: Norton.

Blount, J. M. (1998). *Destined to rule the schools: Women and the superintendency, 1873–1995.* Albany: State University of New York Press.

Blumin, S. M. (1976). *The urban threshold: Growth and change in a nineteenth-century American community.* Chicago: University of Chicago Press.

Bolton, C. C. (2000). Mississippi's school equalization program, 1945–1954: "A last gasp to try to maintain a segregated educational system." *Journal of Southern History, 66*(4), 781–814.

Bond, H. M. (1966). *The education of the Negro in the American social order.* New York: Octagon Books.

Borstelmann, T. (2003). *The Cold War and the color line: American race relations in the global arena.* Cambridge, MA: Harvard University Press.

Bosworth, M. H. (2001). *Courts as catalysts: State Supreme Courts and public school finance equity.* Albany: State University of New York Press.

Bourdieu, P., & Coleman, J. S. (1991). *Social theory for a changing society.* Boulder, CO: Westview Press.

Bowles, S., & Gintis, H. (1976). *Schooling in capitalist America: Educational reform and the contradictions of economic life.* New York: Basic Books.

Boyer, E. L. (1983). *High school: A report on secondary education in America.* New York: Harper & Row.

Boyer, P. S. (1978). *Urban masses and moral order in America, 1820–1920.* Cambridge, MA: Harvard University Press.

Bracy, G. E. (1998). An optimal size for high schools? Research. *Phi Delta Kappan, 79*(5), 406.

Brint, S., & Karabel, J. (1989). *The diverted dream: Community colleges and the promise of educational opportunity in America, 1900–1985.* New York: Oxford University Press.

Brokaw, T. (2007). *Boom!: Voices of the sixties: personal reflections on the '60s and today.* New York: Random House.

Brown, E. E. (1902). *The making of our middle schools: An account of the development of secondary education in the United States.* New York: Longmans, Green.

Brown, J. A. (1992). *The definition of a profession: The authority of metaphor in the history of intelligence testing, 1890–1930.* Princeton, NJ: Princeton University Press.

Brown, R. D. (1989). *Knowledge is power: The diffusion of information in early America, 1700–1865.* New York: Oxford University Press.

Brown, R. D. (1996). *The strength of a people: The idea of an informed citizenry in America, 1650–1870.* Chapel Hill: University of North Carolina Press.

Brownlee, W. E. (1979). *Dynamics of ascent: A history of the American economy.* New York: Knopf.

Bryk, A., Lee, V. E., & Holland, P. B. (1993). *Catholic schools and the common good.* Cambridge, MA: Harvard University Press.

Bryk, A., Sebring, S., Bender, P., Kerbow, D., Rollow, S., & Easton, J. Q. (1998). *Charting Chicago school reform: Democratic localism as a lever for change.* Boulder, CO: Westview Press.

Buchman, M. (1989). *The script of life in modern society: Entry into adulthood in a changing world.* Chicago: University of Chicago Press.

Bullock, H. A. (1967). *A history of Negro education in the South: From 1619 to the present.* Cambridge, MA: Harvard University Press.

Bulmer, M. (1984). *The Chicago School of Sociology: Institutionalization, diversity, and the rise of sociological research.* Chicago: University of Chicago Press.

Burke, C. B. (1982). *American collegiate populations.* New York: New York University Press.

Bushman, R. L. (1967). *From Puritan to Yankee: Character and the social order in Connecticut, 1690–1765.* Cambridge, MA: Harvard University Press.

Butchart, R. E. (1980). *Northern schools, Southern Blacks, and reconstruction: Freedmen's education, 1862–1875.* Westport, CT: Greenwood Press.

Butler, J. (2000). *Becoming American: The revolution before 1776.* Cambridge, MA: Harvard University Press.

Calam, J. (1971). *Parsons and pedagogues: The S.P.G. adventure in American education.* New York: Columbia University Press.

Callahan, R. (1962). *Education and the cult of efficiency: A study of the social forces that have shaped the administration of the public schools.* Chicago: University of Chicago Press.

Carnevale, A. P., & Desrochers, D. M. (1997). The role of the community college in the new economy: Spotlight on education. *Community College Journal, 67*(5), 26–33.

Carnoy, M. (2001). *School vouchers: Examining the evidence.* Washington, DC: Economic Policy Institute.

Carnoy, M., Jacobsen, R., Mishel, L., & Rothstein, R. (2005). *The charter school dust-up: Examining the evidence on enrollment and achievement.* Washington, DC: Economic Policy Institute.

Carrier, J. G. (1986). *Learning disability: Social class and the construction of inequality in American education.* New York: Greenwood.

Chafe, W. H. (1986). *The unfinished journey: America since World War II.* New York: Oxford University Press.

Chilman, C. S. (1978). *Adolescent sexuality in a changing American society: Social and psychological perspectives.* Washington, DC: Government Printing Office.

Chudacoff, H. P. (1975). *The evolution of American urban society.* Englewood Cliffs, NJ: Prentice Hall.

Clarke, E. H. (1873). *Sex in education: Or, a fair chance for the girls.* Boston: J. R. Osgood and Company.

Clinton, C. (1984). *The other Civil War: American women in the nineteenth century.* New York: Hill & Wang.

Cochran, T. C. (1981). *Frontiers of change: Early industrialism in America.* New York: Oxford University Press.

Cogan, F. B. (2000). *Captured: The Japanese internment of American civilians in the Philippines, 1941–1945.* Athens: University of Georgia Press.

Cohen, L. (2003). *A consumers' republic: The politics of mass consumption in postwar America.* New York: Vintage.

Cohen, P. C. (1982). *A calculating people: The spread of numeracy in early America.* Chicago: University of Chicago Press.

Cohen, R. D. (1990). *Children of the mill: Schooling and society in Gary, Indiana, 1906–1960.* Bloomington: Indiana University Press.

Cohen, R. D. (1997). The delinquents: Censorship and youth culture in recent U.S. history. *History of Education Quarterly, 37*(3), 251–270.

Cohen, R. D., & Mohl, R. A. (1979). *The paradox of progressive education: The Gary plan and urban schooling.* Port Washington, NY: Kennikat.

Cohn, E., & Hughes, W. W. (1994). A benefit–cost analysis of investment in college education in the United States, 1969–1985. *Economics of Education Review, 13*(2), 109–123.

Coleman, J. (1961). *The adolescent society: The social life of the teenager and its impact on education.* New York: Basic Books.

Coleman, J. (1965). *Adolescents and the schools.* New York: Basic Books.

Coleman, J., Hoffer, T., & Kilgore, S. (1982). *High school achievement: Public, Catholic and private schools compared.* New York: Basic Books.

Coleman, J. S. (1988). Social capital in the creation of human capital. *American Journal of Sociology, 94*(S), 94–121.

Coleman, J. S. (1990). *Foundations of social theory.* Cambridge, MA: Belknap Press of Harvard University.

Coleman, M. C. (1993). *American Indian children at school, 1850–1930.* Jackson: University Press of Mississippi.

Conant, J. B. (1959). *The American high school today: A first report to interested citizens.* New York: McGraw-Hill.

Conant, J. B. (1961). *Slums and suburbs: A commentary on schools in metropolitan areas.* New York: McGraw-Hill.

Cook, R. (1998). *Sweet land of liberty? The African-American struggle for civil rights in the twentieth century.* New York: Longman.

Cowan, R. S. (1997). *A social history of American technology.* New York: Oxford University Press.

Cravens, H. (1993). *Before Head Start: The Iowa station and America's children.* Chapel Hill: University of North Carolina Press.

Cremin, L. A. (1951). *The American common school: An historic conception.* New York: Bureau of Publications, Teachers College, Columbia University.

Cremin, L. A. (1961). *The transformation of the school: Progressivism in American education, 1876–1957.* New York: Knopf.

Cremin, L. A. (1970). *American education; The colonial experience, 1607–1783.* New York: Harper & Row.

Cremin, L. A. (1980). *American education: The national experience, 1783–1876.* New York: Harper & Row.

Cremin, L. A. (1988). *American education: The metropolitan experience, 1876–1980.* New York: Harper & Row.

Crunden, R. M. (1982). *Ministers of reform: The Progressives' achievement in American civilization, 1889–1920.* New York: Basic Books.

Cuban, L. (1984). *How teachers taught: Constancy and change in American classrooms, 1890–1880.* New York: Longman.

Curry, L. P. (1981). *The free Black in urban America, 1800–1850: The shadow of the dream.* Chicago: University of Chicago Press.

Curti, M. E. (1959). *The social ideas of American educators, with new chapter on the last twenty-five years.* Totowa, NJ: Littlefield, Adams.

Dalzell, R. F. (1987). *Enterprising elite: The Boston Associates and the world they made.* Cambridge, MA: Harvard University Press.

Datazone, The. (1999). *Average real hourly wages of all workers by education, 1973–1997.* http://epinet.org/datazone/wagebyed_all.html.

Davies, M. W. (1982). *Woman's place is at the typewriter: Office work and office workers, 1870–1930.* Philadelphia, PA: Temple University Press.

Davis, F. (1992). *Fashion, culture and identity.* Chicago: University of Chicago Press.

Dawley, A. (1976). *Class and community: The industrial revolution in Lynn.* Cambridge, MA: Harvard University Press.

DeBray, E. (2006). *Politics, ideology and education: Federal policy during the Clinton and Bush administrations.* New York: Teachers College Press.

Degler, C. N. (1980). *At odds: Women and the family in America from the Revolution to the present.* New York: Oxford University Press.

Demos, J. (1970). *A little commonwealth: Family life in Plymouth colony.* London: Oxford University Press.

Demos, J. (1986). *Past, present, and personal: The family and the life course in American history.* New York: Oxford University Press.

Dewey, J. (1930). Our literacy problem. Reprinted in Jo Ann Boydston, Ed. *John Dewey, The later works, 1925–1953, Volume 5: 1929–1930* (pp. 311–318). Carbondale: Southern Illinois University Press, 1988.

Dewey, J. (1938). *Experience and education.* New York: Macmillan.

Dewey, J., & Dewey, E. (1915). *Schools of to-morrow.* New York: E. P. Dutton & Co.

DiMaggio, P. (1982). Cultural capital and school success: The impact of status culture participation on the grades of U.S. high school students. *American Sociological Review, 47*(2), 189–201.

Doherty, T. (1988). *Teenagers and teenpics: The juvenilization of American movies in the 1950s.* Boston: Unwin Hyman.

Donato, R. (1997). *The other struggle for equal schools: Mexican Americans during the civil rights era.* Albany: State University of New York Press.

Donohue, J. J. III, Heckman, J. J., & Todd, P. E. (2002). The schooling of Southern Blacks: The roles of legal activism and private philanthropy, 1910–1960. *Quarterly Journal of Economics* (Feb.) *117*(1), 225–268.

Dougherty, J. (2003). *More than one struggle: The evolution of Black school reform in Milwaukee.* Chapel Hill: University of North Carolina Press.

Dougherty, J. (2008). Bridging the gap between urban, suburban, and educational history. In W. J. Reese & J. L. Rury, Eds. *Rethinking the history of American education* (pp. 248–260), New York: Palgrave Macmillan.

Douglas, A. (1977). *The feminization of American culture.* New York: Knopf.

Drost, W. (1967). *David Snedden and education for efficiency.* Madison: University of Wisconsin Press.

Dublin, T. (1979). *Women at work: The transformation of work and community in Lowell, Massachusetts, 1826–1860.* New York: Columbia University Press.

DuBois, W. E. B. (1935). *Black reconstruction: An essay toward a history of the part which black folk played in the attempt to reconstruct democracy in America, 1860–1880.* New York: Harcourt, Brace and Company.

Dykhuizen, G. (1973). *The life and mind of John Dewey.* Carbondale: Southern Illinois University Press.

Eckert, P. (1989). *Jocks and burnouts: Social categories and identity in the high school.* New York: Teachers College Press.

Eddy, E. D. (1957). *Colleges for our land and time: The land-grant idea in American education.* New York: Harper.

Engelhardt, T. (1995). *The end of victory culture: Cold War America and the disillusioning of a generation.* New York: Basic Books.

Escobar, E. (1993). The dialectics of repression: The Los Angeles police department and the Chicano movement, 1968–1971. *Journal of American History, 79*(4), 1483–1514.

Eskew, G. T. (1997). *But for Birmingham: The local and national movements in the civil rights struggle.* Chapel Hill: University of North Carolina Press.

Esman, A. H. (1990). *Adolescence and culture.* New York: Columbia University Press.

Evers, W. M., Clopton, P., Hirsch, E. D., & Lindseth, A. A. (2006). *Courting failure: How school finance lawsuits exploit judges' good intentions and harm our children.* Cambridge, MA: Education Next Books.

Fairclough, A. (2007). *A class of their own: Black teachers in the segregated South.* Cambridge, MA: Harvard University Press.

Faler, P. G. (1981). *Mechanics and manufacturers in the early industrial revolution: Lynn, Massachusetts, 1800–1860.* Albany: State University of New York Press.

Farley, R. (1997). Racial trends and differences in the United States 30 years after the Civil Rights decade. *Social Science Research, 26*(3), 235–262.

Fass, P. S. (1977). *The damned and the beautiful: American youth in the 1920s.* New York: Oxford University Press.

Finkelstein, B. (1989). *Governing the young: Teacher behavior in popular primary schools in nineteenth-century United States.* New York: Falmer Press.

Fischer, D. H. (1989). *Albion's seed: Four British folkways in America.* New York: Oxford University Press.

Fisher, B. M. (1967). *Industrial education: American ideals and institutions.* Madison: University of Wisconsin Press.

Fishlow, A. (1966a). The American common school revival: Fact or fancy? In H. Rosovsky, Ed. *Industrialization in two systems* (pp. 40–67). New York: Wiley.

Fishlow, A. (1966b). Level of nineteenth century investment in education. *Journal of Economic History, 26,* 418–436.

Fliegelman, J. (1982). *Prodigals and pilgrims: The American revolution against patriarchal authority, 1750–1800.* New York: Cambridge University Press.

Foner, E. (1988). *Reconstruction: America's unfinished revolution, 1863–1877.* New York: Harper & Row.

Foner, E., & Mahoney, O. (1995). *America's reconstruction: People and politics after the Civil War.* New York: HarperCollins.

Fox, K. (1985). *Metropolitan America: Urban life and urban policy in the United States, 1940–1980.* New Brunswick, NJ: Rutgers University Press.

Franklin, B. M. (1994). *From "backwardness" to "at-risk": Childhood learning difficulties and the contradictions of school reform.* Albany: State University of New York.

Franklin, G. A., & Ripley, R. B. (1984). *CETA: Politics and policy, 1973–1982.* Knoxville: University of Tennessee Press.

Franklin, J. H. (1961). *Reconstruction: After the Civil War.* Chicago: University of Chicago Press.

Franklin, V. P. (1979). *The education of Black Philadelphia: The social and educational history of a minority community, 1900–1950.* Philadelphia: University of Pennsylvania Press.

Fredrickson, G. M. (1971). *The Black image in the white mind: The debate on Afro-American character and destiny, 1817–1914.* New York: Harper & Row.

Fuchs, E., & Havighurst, R. (1972). *To live on this earth.* Garden City, NY: Doubleday.

Fuller, W. E. (1982). *The old country school: The story of rural education in the Middle West.* Chicago: University of Chicago Press.

Fultz, Michael (2008). "As is the teacher, so goes the school": Future directions in the historiography of African American teachers." In W. J. Reese & J. L. Rury, Eds. *Rethinking the history of American education* (pp. 73–102). New York: Palgrave Macmillan.

Gabaccia, D. (1994). *From the other side: Women, gender, and immigrant life in the U.S., 1820–1990.* Bloomington: Indiana University Press.

Gann, H. L. and Duignan, P. J. (1986). *The Hispanics in the United States: A history.* Boulder, Co.: Westview Press.

Garcia, E. (2001). *Hispanic education in the United States: Raíces y alas.* Lanham, MD: Rowman & Littlefield.

Geiger, R. L. (1986). *To advance knowledge: The growth of American research universities, 1900–1940.* New York: Oxford University Press.

Geiger, R. L. (1993). *Research and relevant knowledge: American research universities since World War II.* New York: Oxford University Press.

Getz, L. M. (1997). *Schools of their own: The education of Hispanos in New Mexico, 1850–1940.* Albuquerque: University of New Mexico Press.

Gilbert, J. B. (1986). *A cycle of outrage: America's response to the juvenile delinquent of the 1950s.* New York: Oxford University Press.

Gilmore-Lehne, W. J. (1989). *Reading becomes a necessity of life: Material and cultural life in rural New England, 1780–1835.* Knoxville: University of Tennessee Press.

Ginsberg, R., & Plank, D. N., Eds. (1995). *Commissions, reports, reforms, and educational policy.* Westport, CT: Praeger.

Ginzberg, E. (1975). *The manpower connection: Education and work.* Cambridge, MA: Harvard University Press.

Giroux, H. (1996). *Fugitive cultures: Race, violence and youth.* New York: Routledge.

Gitlin, T. (1987). *The sixties: Years of hope, days of rage.* New York: Bantam.

Gleason, P. (1992). *Speaking of diversity: Language and ethnicity in twentieth-century America.* Baltimore, MD: Johns Hopkins University Press.

Goldin, C. (1990). *Understanding the gender gap: An economic history of American women.* New York: Oxford University Press.

Goldin, C. (1998). America's graduation from high school: The evolution and spread of secondary schooling in the twentieth century. *Journal of Economic History, 58*(2), 345–374.

Goldin, C. (2001). The human capital century and American leadership: Virtues of the past. *Journal of Economic History, 61* (June), 263–292.

Goldin, C., & Katz, L. F. (1999a). Human capital and social capital: The rise of secondary schooling in America, 1910–1940. *Journal of Interdisciplinary History, 29*(4), 683–723.

Goldin, C., & Katz, L. F. (1999b). The shaping of higher education: The formative years in the United States, 1890 to 1940. *Journal of Economic Perspectives, 13*(1), 37–62.

Goldin, C., & Katz, L. F. (2000). Education and income in the early twentieth century: Evidence from the prairies. *Journal of Economic History, 60*(3), 782–818.

Goldman, E. E. (1952). *Rendezvous with destiny: A history of modern American reform.* New York: Knopf.

Goldsmith, W. W., & Blakely, E. J. (1992). *Separate societies: Poverty and inequality in U.S. cities.* Philadelphia, PA: Temple University Press.

Gonzales, G. (1990). *Chicano education in the era of segregation.* Philadephia, PA: Balch Institute Press.

Gonzalez, G. & Fernandez, R. A. (2003). *A century of Chicano history: Empire, nations, and migration.* New York: Routledge.

Goodwyn, L. (1978). *The populist moment: A short history of the agrarian revolt in America.* New York: Oxford University Press.

Gordon, L. D. (1990). *Gender and higher education in the Progressive era.* New Haven, CT: Yale University Press.

Gould, S. J. (1981). *The mismeasure of man.* New York: Norton.

Graebner, W. (1993). *Coming of age in Buffalo: Youth and authority in the postwar era.* Philadelphia, PA: Temple University Press.

Graff, H. J. (1995). *Conflicting paths: Growing up in America.* Cambridge, MA: Harvard University Press.

Graham, P. A. (1967). *Progressive education from Arcady to academe: A history of the Progressive Education Association, 1919–1955.* New York: Teachers College Press.

Graham, P. A. (1974). *Community and class in American education, 1865–1918.* New York: Wiley.

Grant, G. (1988). *The world we created at Hamilton High.* Cambridge, MA: Harvard University Press.

Greeley, A. (1982). *Catholic schools and minority students.* New Brunswick, NJ: Transaction Books.

Greene, J. P. (1988). *Pursuits of happiness: The social development of early modern British colonies and the formation of American culture.* Chapel Hill: University of North Carolina Press.

Greene, J. R. (2000). *The presidency of George Bush.* Lawrence: University Press of Kansas.

Greven, P. J. (1977). *The Protestant temperament: Patterns of child-rearing, religious experience, and the self in early America.* New York: Knopf.

Grubb, N. (1995). Postsecondary education and the sub-baccalaureate labor market: Corrections and extensions. *Economics of Education Review, 14*(3), 285–299.

Gruhl, J., & Welch, S. (1990). The impact of the *Bakke* decision on Black and Hispanic enrollment in medical and law schools. *Social Science Quarterly, 71*(3), 458–473.

Gulliford, A. (1991). *America's country schools,* 2nd ed. Washington, DC: Preservation Press.

Halberstam, D. (1998). *The children.* New York: Random House.

Haller, E. J. (1992). High school size and student indiscipline: Another aspect of the school consolidation issue? *Educational Evaluation and Policy Analysis, 14*(2), 145–156.

Hampel, R. L. (1986). *The last little citadel: American high schools since 1940.* Boston: Houghton Mifflin.

Harlan, L. R. (1958). *Separate and unequal.* Chapel Hill: University of North Carolina Press.

Harlan, L. R. (1972). *Booker T. Washington: The making of a Black leader, 1856–1901.* New York: Oxford University Press.

Harlan, L. R. (1983). *Booker T. Washington: The wizard of Tuskegee, 1901–1915.* New York: Oxford University Press.

Harris, B. J. (1978). *Beyond her sphere: Women and the professions in American history.* Westport, CT: Greenwood Press.

Harrison, B. (1972). *Education, training and the urban ghetto*. Baltimore, MD: Johns Hopkins University Press.

Harzig, C., Ed. (1997). *Peasant maids—city women: From the European countryside to urban America*. Ithaca, NY: Cornell University Press.

Haubrich, P. (1993). Student life in Milwaukee high schools, 1920–1985. In J. L. Rury & F. A. Cassell, Eds. *Seeds of crisis: Public schooling in Milwaukee since 1920* (pp. 193–228). Madison: University of Wisconsin Press.

Havighurst, R. (1964). *The public schools of Chicago: A survey for the Board of Education of the City of Chicago*. Chicago: Board of Education of the City of Chicago.

Havighurst, R. (1966). *Education in metropolitan areas*. Boston: Allyn and Bacon.

Hawes, J. M., & Hiner, N. R. (1985). *American childhood: A research guide and handbook*. Westport, CT: Greenwood Press.

Hawkins, H. (1962). *Booker T. Washington and his critics: Black leadership in crisis*. Lexington, MA: Heath.

Hawkins, H. (1972). *Between Harvard and America: The educational leadership of Charles W. Eliot*. New York: Oxford University Press.

Hawkins, M. (1997). *Social Darwinism in European and American thought, 1860–1945: Nature as model and nature as threat*. New York: Cambridge University Press.

Hawley, A. H. (1950). *Human ecology: A theory of community structure*. New York: Ronald Press.

Haynes, J. (1991). *Sleepwalking through history: America in the Reagan years*. New York: Norton.

Hays, S. P. (1964). The politics of reform in municipal government in the Progressive era. *Pacific Northwest Quarterly, 55*(4), 157–169.

Hays, S. P. (1995). *The response to industrialism, 1885–1914*. Chicago: University of Chicago Press.

Heckman, J. J., & Krueger, A. B. (2005). *Inequality in America: What role for human capital policies?* Cambridge, MA: MIT Press.

Heimert, A. (1966). *Religion and the American mind, from the Great Awakening to the Revolution*. Cambridge, MA: Harvard University Press.

Heineman, K. J. (1993). *Campus wars: The peace movement at American state universities in the Vietnam era*. New York: New York University Press.

Henretta, J. A. (1973). *The evolution of American society, 1700–1815: An interdisciplinary analysis*. Lexington, MA: Heath.

Henriksen, L. L. (1988). *Anzia Yezierska: A writer's life*. New Brunswick, NJ: Rutgers University Press.

Herbst, J. (1989). *And sadly teach: Teacher education and professionalization in American culture*. Madison: University of Wisconsin Press.

Herbst, J. (1996). *The once and future school: Three hundred and fifty years of American secondary education*. New York: Routledge.

Hershberg, T., Ed. (1981). *Philadelphia: Work, space, family, and group experience in the nineteenth century. Essays toward an interdisciplinary history of the city*. New York: Oxford University Press.

Higgs, R. (1971). *The transformation of the American economy, 1865–1914: An essay in interpretation*. New York: John Wiley and Sons.

Higgs, R. (1977). *Competition and coercion: Blacks in the American economy*. New York: Cambridge University Press.

Hillocks, G. (2002). *The testing trap: How state writing assessments control learning*. New York: Teachers College Press.

Hiner, N. R. (1979). Cotton Mather and his children. In B. Finkelstein, Ed. *Regulated children/liberated children: Education in psychohistorical perspective* (pp. 24–43). New York: Psychohistory Press.

Hochschild, J. (1985). *The new American dilemma: Liberal democracy and school desegregation*. New Haven, CT: Yale University Press.

Hoffman, E. C. (1998). *All you need is love: The Peace Corps and the spirit of the 1960s*. Cambridge, MA: Harvard University Press.

Hofstadter, R. (1955a). *Academic freedom in the age of the college*. New York: Columbia University Press.

Hofstadter, R. (1955b). *The age of reform: From Bryan to F. D. R.* New York: Knopf.

Hofstadter, R. (1963). *Anti-intellectualism in American life.* New York: Vintage.

Hofstadter, R. (1971). *America at 1750: A social portrait.* New York: Knopf.

Hogan, D. (1985). *Class and reform: School and society in Chicago, 1880–1930.* Philadelphia: University of Pennsylvania Press.

Hogan, D. (1989). The market revolution and disciplinary power: Joseph Lancaster and the psychology of the early classroom system. *History of Education Quarterly, 29*(3), 381–417.

Hogan, D. (1990). Modes of discipline: Affective individualism and pedagogical reform in New England, 1820–1850. *American Journal of Education, 99*(1), 1–56.

Hogan, D. (1992). Examinations, merit, and morals: The market revolution and disciplinary power in Philadelphia's public schools, 1838–1868. *Historical Studies in Education, 4*(1), 31–78.

Hogan, D. (1996). "To better our condition": Educational credentialing and "the silent compulsion of economic relations" in the United States, 1830 to the present. *History of Education Quarterly, 36*(3), 243–270.

Horowitz, H. L. (1987). *Campus life: Undergraduate cultures from the end of the eighteenth century to the present.* New York: Knopf.

Horsman, R. (1981). *Race and manifest destiny: The origins of American racial Anglo-Saxonism.* Cambridge, MA: Harvard University Press.

Hoxie, F. E. (1984). *A final promise: The campaign to assimilate the Indians, 1880–1920.* Lincoln: University of Nebraska Press.

Hummel, R. C., & Nagle, J. M. (1973). *Urban education: Problems and prospects.* New York: Oxford University Press.

Hunt, E. (1995). *Will we be smart enough? A cognitive analysis of the coming workforce.* New York: Russell Sage Foundation.

Hunter, J. (2002). *How young ladies became girls: The Victorian origins of American girlhood.* New Haven, CT: Yale University Press.

Ignatiev, N. (1995). *How the Irish became White.* New York: Routledge.

Jackson, K. (1985). *The crabgrass frontier: The suburbanization of the United States.* New York: Oxford University Press.

Jacobson, M. F. (1998). *Whiteness of a different color: European immigrants and the alchemy of race.* Cambridge, MA: Harvard University Press.

Jencks, C. (1998). The Black–White test score gap: An introduction. In C. Jencks, & M. Phillips, Eds. *The Black–White test score gap* (pp. 1–9). Washington, DC: Brookings Institution.

Joncich, G. M. (1968). *The sane positivist: A biography of Edward L. Thorndike.* Middletown, CT: Wesleyan University Press.

Jones, L. Y. (1980). *Great expectations: America and the baby boom generation.* New York: Coward, McCann & Geoghegan.

Kaestle, C. F. (1973a). *The evolution of an urban school system: New York City, 1750–1850.* Cambridge, MA: Harvard University Press.

Kaestle, C. F. (1973b). *Joseph Lancaster and the monitorial school movement: A documentary history.* New York: Teachers College Press.

Kaestle, C. F. (1983). *Pillars of the republic: Common schools and American society, 1780–1860.* New York: Hill and Wang.

Kaestle, C. F. (2001). Federal aid to education since World War II: Purposes and politics. In J. Jennings, Ed. *The future of the federal role in elementary and secondary education* (pp. 13–35). Washington, DC: Center on Education Policy.

Kaestle, C. F., & Vinovskis, M. (1980). *Education and social change in nineteenth-century Massachusetts.* New York: Cambridge University Press.

Kahlenberg, R., Ed. (2000). *A notion at risk: Preserving public education as an engine for social mobility.* New York: Century Foundation Press.

Kalmijn, M., & Kraaykamp, G. (1996). Race, cultural capital, and schooling: An analysis of trends in the United States. *Sociology of Education, 69*(1), 22–34.

Kantor, H. A. (1988). *Learning to earn: School, work, and vocational reform in California, 1880–1930.* Madison: University of Wisconsin Press.

Kantor, H., & Brenzel, B. (1993). Urban education and the "truly disadvantaged": The historical roots of the contemporary crisis, 1945–1990. In M. B. Katz, Ed. *The underclass debate: Views from history* (pp. 366–401). Princeton, NJ: Princeton University Press.

Kantor, H., & Lowe, R. (1995). Class, race, and the emergence of federal education policy: From the New Deal to the Great Society. *Educational Researcher, 24*(3), 4–11.

Karier, C. J. (1972). Liberalism and the quest for orderly change. *History of Education Quarterly, 12*(1), 57–80.

Karier, C. J. (1979). The quest for orderly change: Some reflections. *History of Education Quarterly, 19*(2), 159–177.

Kasson, J. F. (1999). *Civilizing the machine: Technology and republican values in America, 1776–1900*. New York: Hill and Wang.

Katz, L. (2000). Technological change, computerization, and the wage structure. In E. Brynjolfsson & B. Kahin, Eds. *Understanding the digital economy* (pp. 219–243). Cambridge, MA: MIT Press.

Katz, M. B. (1968). *The irony of early school reform: Educational innovation in mid-nineteenth century Massachusetts*. Cambridge, MA: Harvard University Press.

Katz, M. B. (1971). *Class, bureaucracy, and schools: The illusion of educational change in America*. New York: Praeger.

Katzman, M. T. (1971). *The political economy of urban schools*. Cambridge, MA: Harvard University Press.

Katznelson, I., & Weir, M. (1985). *Schooling for all: Class, race, and the decline of the democratic ideal*. New York: Basic Books.

Kaye, K. (1973). Reappraisal of Jencks's inequality: Some clarity on inequality. *School Review, 81*(4) (August), 634–641.

Kenny, K. (2000). *The American Irish: A history*. New York: Longman.

Kerber, L. K. (1980). *Women of the Republic: Intellect and ideology in Revolutionary America*. Chapel Hill: University of North Carolina Press.

Kessler-Harris, A. (1982). *Out to work: A history of wage-earning women in the United States*. New York: Oxford University Press.

Kessner, T. (1977). *The golden door: Italian and Jewish immigrant mobility in New York City, 1880–1915*. New York: Oxford University Press.

Kett, J. (1977). *Rites of passage: A history of youth and adolescence in America*. New York: Harper.

Kim, D., and Rury, J. L. (2007). The changing profile of college access: The Truman Commission and enrollment patterns in the postwar era. *History of Education Quarterly* (August 2007), 302–327.

King, R. H. (1996). *Civil rights and the idea of freedom*. Athens: University of Georgia Press.

Kleppner, P. (1984). *Chicago divided: The making of a Black mayor*. DeKalb: Northern Illinois University Press.

Kliebard, H. M. (1986). *The struggle for the American curriculum, 1893–1958*. Boston: Routledge & Kegan Paul.

Kliebard, H. M. (1999). *Schooled to work: Vocationalism and the American curriculum, 1876–1946*. New York: Teachers College Press.

Klinkner, P. A., & Smith, R. M. (1999). *The unsteady march: The rise and decline of racial equality in America*. Chicago: University of Chicago Press.

Kluckhohn, C. (1949). *Mirror for man: The relation of the anthropology to modern life*. New York: McGraw-Hill.

Kluger, R. (1976). *Simple justice: The history of Brown v. Board of Education and Black America's struggle for equality*. New York: Knopf.

Knowles, J. G., Marlow, S. E., & Muchmore, J. A. (1992). From pedagogy to ideology: Origins and phases of home education in the United States, 1970–1990. *American Journal of Education, 100*(2) (February), 195–235.

Kozol, J. (1991). *Savage inequalities: Children in America's schools*. New York: Crown.

Krueger, A. B., Hanushek, E. A., Rice, J. K., & Mishel, L. (2002). *The class size debate*. Washington, DC: Economic Policy Institute.

Krug, E. A. (1964). *The shaping of the American high school, 1880–1920*. New York: Harper & Row.

Krug, E. A. (1972). *The American high school, 1920–1940*. Madison: University of Wisconsin Press.

Kuhl, S. (2002) *The Nazi connection: Eugenics, American racism, and German National Socialism.* New York: Oxford University Press.

Kuper, A. (2000). *Culture: The anthropologists' account.* Cambridge, MA: Harvard University Press.

Labaree, D. F. (1988). *The making of an American high school: The credentials market and the Central High School of Philadelphia, 1838–1939.* New Haven, CT: Yale University Press.

Labaree, D. F. (1999). *How to succeed in school without really learning: The credentials race in American education.* New Haven, CT: Yale University Press.

Lagemann, E. C. (1979). *A generation of women: Education in the lives of progressive reformers.* Cambridge, MA: Harvard University Press.

Lagemann, E. C., Ed. (1985). *Jane Addams on education.* New York: Teachers College Press.

Lagemann, E. C. (2000). *An elusive science: The troubling history of educational research.* Chicago: University of Chicago Press.

Lamont, M., & Lareau, A. (1988). Cultural capital: Allusions, gaps and glissandos in recent theoretical developments. *Sociological Theory, 6,* 153–168.

Landes, D. S. (1969). *Unbound Prometheus: Technological change and industrial development.* New York: Cambridge University Press.

Landes, D. S. (1998). *The wealth and poverty of nations: Why some are so rich and some so poor.* New York: W. W. Norton.

Lannie, V. P. (1968). *Public money and parochial education: Bishop Hughes, Governor Seward, and the New York school controversy.* Cleveland, OH: Press of Case Western Reserve University.

Lannie, V. P., Ed. (1974). *Henry Barnard, American educator.* New York: Teachers College Press.

Lareau, A. (2003). *Unequal childhoods: Class, race, and family life.* Berkeley: University of California Press.

Lareau, A., & Horvat, E. M. (1999). Moments of social inclusion and exclusion: Race, class, and cultural capital in family–school relationships. *Sociology of Education, 72*(1), 37–53.

Larkin, J. (1988). *The reshaping of everyday life, 1790–1840.* New York: Harper & Row.

Lasch, C. (1991). *The true and only heaven: Progress and its critics.* New York: Norton.

Laslett, P. (1965). *The world we have lost.* New York: Scribner.

Laurie, B. (1997). *Artisans into workers: Labor in nineteenth-century America.* Urbana: University of Illinois Press.

Lee, V., & Smith, J. (1997). High school size: Which works best and for whom? *Educational Evaluation and Policy Analysis, 19*(3), 205–227.

Leloudis, J. L. (1996). *Schooling the New South: Pedagogy, self, and society in North Carolina, 1880–1920.* Chapel Hill: University of North Carolina Press.

Lemann, N. (1991). *The Promised Land: The great Black migration and how it changed America.* New York: Knopf.

Lemann, N. (1999). *The big test: The secret history of the American meritocracy.* New York: Farrar, Straus and Giroux.

Levine, D. O. (1986). *The American college and the culture of aspiration, 1915–1940.* Ithaca, NY: Cornell University Press.

Levine, M., & Trachtman, R. (1988). *American business and the public schools: Case studies of corporate involvement in public education.* New York: Teachers College Press.

Levine, M., & Zipp, J. F. (1993). A city at risk: The changing social and economic context of public schooling in Milwaukee. In J. L. Rury, & F. A. Cassell, Eds. *Seeds of crisis: Public schooling in Milwaukee since 1920* (pp. 42–73). Madison: University of Wisconsin Press.

Levitan, S. A., Johnston, W. B., & Taggart, R. (1975). *Still a dream: The changing status of Blacks since 1960.* Cambridge, MA: Harvard University Press.

Levy, F. (1987). *Dollars and dreams: The changing American income distribution.* New York: Russell Sage Foundation.

Lewis, D. L. (1993). *W. E. B. Du Bois: Biography of a race, 1868–1919.* New York: Holt.

Lipman, Pauline (2003). *High Stakes Education: Inequality, Globalization, and Urban School Reform.* New York: Routledge/Falmer.

Lipset, S. M. (1979). *The first new nation: The United States in historical and comparative perspective.* New York: Norton.

Litwack, L. F. (1961). *North of slavery: The Negro in the free States, 1790–1860.* Chicago: University of Chicago Press.

Litwack, L. F. (1999). *Trouble in mind: Black Southerners in the age of Jim Crow.* New York: Knopf.

Lockridge, K. A. (1974). *Literacy in colonial New England: An enquiry into the social context of literacy in the early modern West.* New York: Norton.

Long, C. D. (1958). *The labor force under changing income and employment.* Princeton, NJ: Princeton University Press.

Lucas, C. J. (1994). *American higher education: A history.* New York: St Martin's.

Lukas, J. A. (1985). *Common ground: A turbulent decade in the lives of three American families.* New York: Alfred A. Knopf.

Luker, R. E. (1991). *The social gospel in Black and White: American racial reform, 1885–1912.* Chapel Hill: University of North Carolina Press.

McCluskey, N. G. (1958). *Public schools and moral education: The influence of Horace Mann, William Torrey Harris, and John Dewey.* New York: Columbia University Press.

MacDonald, V.-M. (1999). The paradox of bureaucratization: New views on Progressive era teachers and the development of a woman's profession. *History of Education Quarterly, 39*(4) (Winter), 427–453.

MacDonald, V.-M. (2004). *Latino education in the United States: A narrated history from 1513–2000.* New York: Palgrave Macmillan.

Mcguinn, P. J. (2006). *No child left behind and the transformation of Federal Education policy, 1965–2005.* Lawrence: University Press of Kansas

McLoughlin, W. G. (1985). Evangelical child rearing in the age of Jackson: Francis Wayland's views on when and how to subdue the wilfulness of children. In N. R. Hyner, & J. M. Hawes, Eds. *Growing up in America: Children in historical perspective* (pp. 87–108). Urbana: University of Illinois Press. (Original work published 1975.)

Macunovich, D. L. (2002). *Birth quake: The baby boom and its aftershocks.* Chicago: University of Chicago Press.

Main, J. T. (1965). *The social structure of revolutionary America.* Princeton, NJ: Princeton University Press.

Margo, R. A. (1990). *Race and schooling in the South, 1880–1950: An economic history.* Chicago: University of Chicago Press.

Margo, R. A., & Finegan, T. A. (1993). The decline in Black teenage labor-force participation in the South, 1900–1970: The role of schooling. *American Economic Review, 83*(1) (March), 234–247.

Markowitz, R. J. (1993). *My daughter, the teacher: Jewish teachers in the New York City schools.* New Brunswick, NJ: Rutgers University Press.

Marsden, G. M. (1994). *The soul of the American university: From Protestant establishment to established nonbelief.* New York: Oxford University Press.

Marx, L. (1964). *The machine in the garden: Technology and the pastoral ideal in America.* New York: Oxford University Press.

Massey, D., & Denton, N. (1993). *American apartheid: Segregation and the making of the underclass.* Cambridge, MA: Harvard University Press.

May, E. R. (1964). *The Progressive era: 1901–1917.* New York: Time, Inc.

Meier, A. (1963). *Negro thought in America, 1880–1915: Racial ideologies in the age of Booker T. Washington.* Ann Arbor: University of Michigan Press.

Messerli, J. (1972). *Horace Mann: A biography.* New York: Alfred A. Knopf.

Meyer, J. W., Tyack, D., Nagel, J., & Gordon, A. (1979). Public education as nation-building in America: Enrollments and bureaucratization in the American states, 1870–1930. *American Journal of Sociology, 85*(3), 591–613.

Miller, P. (1956). *Errand into the wilderness.* Cambridge, MA: Belknap Press of Harvard University Press.

Miller, P. (1959). *Orthodoxy in Massachusetts, 1630–1650* (with a new preface by the author). Boston: Beacon Press.

Minton, H. L. (1988). *Lewis M. Terman: Pioneer in psychological testing.* New York: New York University Press.

Mintz, S. (2004). *Huck's raft: A history of American childhood.* Cambridge, MA: Harvard University Press.

Mintz, S., & Kellogg, S. (1988). *Domestic revolutions: A social history of American family life.* New York: Free Press.

Mirel, J. (1993). *The rise and fall of an urban school system: Detroit, 1907–81.* Ann Arbor: University of Michigan Press.

Miron G. J., & Nelson, C. D. (2002). *What's public about charter schools? Lessons learned about choice and accountability.* San Francisco, CA: Corwin Press

Modell, J. (1989). *Into one's own: From youth to adulthood in the United States, 1920–1975.* Berkeley: University of California Press.

Mohl, R. A. (1971). *Poverty in New York, 1783–1825.* New York: Oxford University Press.

Mohraz, J. J. (1979). *The separate problem: Case studies of Black education in the North, 1900–1930.* Westport, CT: Greenwood Press.

Monhollon, R. L. (2004) *This is America?: The sixties in Lawrence, Kansas.* New York: Palgrave Macmillan.

Monkkonen, E. (1988). *America becomes urban: The development of U.S. cities and towns, 1790–1980.* Berkeley: University of California Press.

Moore, J. R. (1979). *The post-Darwinian controversies: A study of the Protestant struggle to come to terms with Darwin in Great Britain and America, 1870–1900.* Cambridge: Cambridge University Press.

Mora, M. T. (1997). Attendance, schooling quality, and the demand for education of Mexican Americans, African Americans, and non-Hispanic Whites. *Economics of Education Review, 16*(4), 407–418.

Moran, G. F., & Vinovskis, M. (1992). *Religion, family, and the life course: Explorations in the social history of early America.* Ann Arbor: University of Michigan Press.

Moran, G. F., & Vinovskis, M. (2007). Literacy, common schools and high schools in colonial and antebellum America. In W. J. Reese & J. L. Rury, Eds. *Rethinking the history of American education.* (pp. 17–46). New York: Palgrave Macmillan.

Moran, J. P. (2000). *Teaching sex: The shaping of adolescence in the 20th century.* Cambridge: Harvard University Press.

Morgan, E. S. (1966). *The Puritan family: Religion and domestic relations in seventeenth-century New England.* New York: Harper & Row.

Morgan, E. S. (1975). *American slavery, American freedom: The ordeal of colonial Virginia.* New York: Norton.

Morris, R. C. (1981). *Reading, 'riting, and reconstruction: The education of freedmen in the South, 1861–1870.* Chicago: University of Chicago Press.

Moss, A. A., Jr. (1981). *The American Negro Academy: Voice of the talented tenth.* Baton Rouge: Louisiana State University Press.

Moss, H. (2006). Education's inequity: Opposition to Black higher education in antebellum Connecticut. *History of Education Quarterly, 46*(1) (Spring), 16–35.

Murnane, R. J., & Levy, F. (1996). *Teaching the new basic skills: Principles for educating children to thrive in a changing economy.* New York: Free Press.

Murphy, K. M., & Welch, F. (1989). Wage premiums for college graduates: Recent growth and possible explanations. *Educational Researcher, 18*(4), 17–26.

Murphy, K. M., & Welch, F. (1993). Industrial change and the importance of skill. In S. Danziger, & P. Gottschalk, Eds. *Uneven tides: Rising inequality in America* (pp. 101–132). New York: Russell Sage Foundation.

Myrdal, G. (1944). *An American dilemma: The Negro problem and modern democracy.* New York: Harper & Bros.

Nasaw, D. (1979). *Schooled to order: A social history of public schooling in the United States.* New York: Oxford University Press.

Nash, G. B. (2000). *Red, White, and Black: The peoples of early North America.* Upper Saddle River, NJ: Prentice Hall. (Original work published 1974.)

Nash, M. A. (2001). "Cultivating the powers of human beings": Gendered perspectives on curricula and pedagogy in academies of the new republic. *History of Education Quarterly, 41*(2), 239–249.

Nash, M. A. (2005) *Women's Education in the United States, 1780–1840.* New York: Palgrave Macmillan.

Nash, M. A. (2008). The historiography of education for girls and women in the United States. In

W. J. Reese & J. L. Rury, Eds. *Rethinking the history of American education*, pp. 143–160. New York: Palgrave Macmillan.

Neckerman, K. (2007). *Schools betrayed: Roots of failure in inner-city education.* Chicago: University of Chicago Press.

Nelson, A. (2005). *The elusive ideal: Equal educational opportunity and the Federal role in Boston's public schools, 1950–1985.* Chicago: University of Chicago Press.

Nelson, A. (2008). The Federal role in American education: A historiographical essay. In W. J. Reese and J. L. Rury, Eds. *Rethinking the history of American education*, pp. 261–280. New York: Palgrave Macmillan.

Nevins, A. (1938). *The gateway to history.* New York: D. C. Heath.

Norton, M. B. (1980). *Liberty's daughters: The Revolutionary experience of American women, 1750–1800.* Boston: Little, Brown.

Nybakken, E. (1997). In the Irish tradition: Pre-Revolutionary academies in America. *History of Education Quarterly, 37*(2), 163–183.

Odden, A. O., & Picus, L. O. (2007). *School finance: A policy perspective.* New York: McGraw-Hill.

Ogren, C. (2008). Sites, students, scholarship, and structures: The historiography of American higher education in the post-revisionist era. In W. J. Reese, & J. L. Rury, Eds. *Rethinking the history of American education* (pp. 187–222). New York: Palgrave Macmillan.

Olneck, M. R. (2008). American public schooling and European immigrants in the early twentieth century: A post-revisionist synthesis. In William J. Reese and John L. Rury, Eds. *Rethinking the History of American Education* (pp. 103–142). New York: Palgrave Macmillan.

Olson, R. K. (1972). Tinker and the administrator. *School & Society, 100*(2339), 86–89.

Omi, M., & Winant, H. (1994). *Racial formation in the United States: From the 1960s to the 1980s.* New York: Routledge & Kegan Paul.

Orfield, G. (1978). *Must we bus? Segregated schools and national policy.* Washington, DC: Brookings Institution.

Orfield, G. (1983). *Public school desegregation in the United States, 1968–1980.* Washington, DC: Joint Center for Political Studies.

Orfield, G., Eaton, S., & the Harvard Project on School Desegregation. (1996). *Dismantling desegregation: The quiet reversal of Brown v. Board of Education.* New York: New Press.

Owram, D. (1996). *Born at the right time: A history of the baby-boom generation.* Toronto: University of Toronto Press.

Palen, J. J. (1997). *The urban world.* New York: McGraw-Hill.

Palladino, G. (1996). *Teenagers: An American history.* New York: Basic Books.

Parkerson, D., & Parkerson, J. A. (1998). *The emergence of the common school in the U.S. countryside.* Lewiston, NY: Edwin Mellen.

Patterson, J. T. (1996). *Grand expectations: The United States, 1945–1974.* New York: Oxford University Press.

Patterson, J. T. (2002). *Brown v. Board of Education: A Civil Rights Milestone and Its Troubled Legacy.* New York: Oxford University Press

Perkinson, H. (1968). *The imperfect panacea: American faith in education, 1865–1965.* New York: Random House.

Perlmann, J. (1988). *Ethnic differences: Schooling and social structure among the Irish, Italians, Jews, and Blacks in an American city, 1880–1935.* New York: Cambridge University Press.

Perlmann, J. (2005). *Italians then, Mexicans now: Immigrant origins and the second-generation progress, 1890 to 2000.* New York: Russell Sage.

Perlmann, J., Siddali, S. R., & Whitescarver, K. (1997). Literacy, schooling, and teaching among New England women, 1730–1820. *History of Education Quarterly, 37*(2) (Summer), 117–139.

Perlmann, J., & Margo, R. (2001). *Women's work? American teachers, 1750–1920.* Chicago: University of Chicago Press.

Peterson, P. E. (1985). *The politics of school reform, 1870–1940.* Chicago: University of Chicago Press.

Peterson, P., Ed. (2006). *Generational change: Closing the test score gap.* New York: Rowman & Littlefield.

Poetter, T. S., Wegwert, J. C., & Haerr, C. (2006). *No child left behind and the illusion of reform: Critical essays by Educators.* Washington, DC: University Press of America.

Polenberg, R. (1980). *One nation divisible: Class, race, and ethnicity in the United States since 1938.* New York: Viking.

Pollard, S. (1965). *The genesis of modern management: A study of the industrial revolution in Great Britain.* Cambridge, MA: Harvard University Press.

Portes, A. (1998). Social capital: Its origins and applications in modern sociology. In J. Hagan, & K. S. Cook, Eds. *Annual review of sociology* (Vol. 24, pp. 1–24). Palo Alto, CA: Annual Reviews.

Portes, A., & Bach, R. L. (1985). *Latin journey: Cuban and Mexican immigrants in the United States.* Berkeley: University of California Press.

Portes, A., & Rumbaut, R. (1996). *Immigrant America: A portrait.* Berkeley: University of California Press.

Portes, A., & Rumbaut, R., Eds. (2001). *Ethnicities: Children of immigrants in America.* Berkeley: University of California Press and Russell Sage Foundation.

Powers, J. B. (1992). *The "girl question" in education: Vocational education for young women in the Progressive era.* New York: Falmer Press.

Pred, A. R. (1966). *The spatial dynamics of U.S. urban-industrial growth, 1800–1914.* Cambridge, MA: MIT Press.

Prucha, F. P. (1976). *American Indian policy in crisis: Christian reformers and the Indian, 1865–1900.* Norman: University of Oklahoma Press.

Putnam, R. D. (2001). *Bowling alone: The collapse and revival of American Community.* New York: Simon & Schuster.

Putnam, R. D., Ed. (2004). *Democracies in flux: The evolution of social capital in contemporary society.* New York: Oxford University Press.

Rabb, T., & Rotberg, R., Eds. (1981). *Industrialization and urbanization: Studies in interdisciplinary history.* Princeton, NJ: Princeton University Press.

Rabb, T., & Rotberg, R., Eds. (1982). *The new history, the 1980s and beyond: Studies in interdisciplinary history.* Princeton, NJ: Princeton University Press.

Ravitch, D. (1974). *The great school wars: 1805–1973. A history of the public schools as a battlefield of social change.* New York: Basic Books.

Ravitch, D. (1978). *The revisionists revised: A critique of the radical attack on the schools.* New York: Basic Books.

Ravitch, D. (1983). *The troubled crusade: American education, 1945–1980.* New York: Basic Books.

Ravitch, D. (2000). *Left back: A century of failed school reforms.* New York: Simon & Schuster.

Rawls, J. and Bean, W. (2003). *California: An interpretive history.* New York: McGraw-Hill.

Reese, W. J. (1986). *Power and the promise of school reform: Grassroots movements during the progressive era.* Boston: Routledge & Kegan Paul.

Reese, W. J. (1995). *The origins of the American high school.* New Haven, CT: Yale University Press.

Reese, W. J. (2001). The origins of progressive education. *History of Education Quarterly, 41*(1), 1–24.

Reich, R. (2002). *Bridging liberalism and multiculturalism in education.* Chicago: University of Chicago Press.

Reiss, A. J., Ed. (1964). *Louis Wirth on cities and social life: Selected papers.* Chicago: University of Chicago Press.

Rendall, J. (1985). *The origins of modern feminism.* London: Macmillan.

Reuben, J. A. (1996). *The making of the modern university: Intellectual transformation and the marginalization of morality.* Chicago: University of Chicago Press.

Reynolds, D. (1999). *There goes the neighborhood: Rural school consolidation at the grass roots in early twentieth-century Iowa.* Iowa City: University of Iowa Press.

Rodgers, D. T. (1978). *The work ethic in industrial America, 1850–1920.* Chicago: University of Chicago Press.

Rodgers, D. T. (1998). *Atlantic crossings: Social politics in a progressive age.* Cambridge, MA: Belknap Press of Harvard University Press.

Roof, W. C. (1993). *A generation of seekers: The spiritual journeys of the baby boom generation.* New York: HarperCollins.

Roscigno, V. J., Ainsworth, D., & Race, J. W. (1999). Cultural capital, and educational resources: Persistent inequalities and achievement returns. *Sociology of Education, 72*(3), 158–178.

Rosenberg, R. (1982). *Beyond separate spheres: Intellectual roots of modern feminism.* New Haven, CT: Yale University Press.

Rosenfeld, S. A., & Sher, J. P. (1977). The urbanization of rural schools. In Jonathan P. Sher, Ed. *Education in rural America* (pp. 11–40). Boulder, CO: Westview Press.

Roszak, T. (1969). *The making of a counter culture: Reflections on the technocratic society and its youthful opposition.* Garden City, NY: Doubleday.

Roszak, T. (1994). *The cult of information: A neo-Luddite treatise on high tech, artificial intelligence, and the true art of thinking.* Berkeley: University of California Press.

Rotberg, R. I., Ed. (2001). *Patterns of social capital: Stability and change in historical perspective.* New York: Cambridge University Press.

Rotella, E. J. (1981). *From home to office: U.S. women at work, 1870–1930.* Ann Arbor, MI: University Microfilms International.

Rothman, S. M. (1978). *Woman's proper place: A history of changing ideals and practices, 1870 to the present.* New York: Basic Books.

Rothstein, R. (2004). *Class and schools: Using social, economic, and educational reform to close the Black–White achievement gap.* Washington, DC: Economic Policy Institute.

Rousmaniere, K. (1997). *City teachers: Teaching and school reform in historical perspective.* New York: Teachers College Press.

Rudner, L. (1999). Scholastic achievement and demographic characteristics of home school students in 1998. *Education Policy Analysis Archives, 7*(8), 23 March 1999, online publication.

Rudolph, F. (1962). *The American college and university, a history.* New York: Knopf.

Rudolph, F. (1965). *Essays on education in the early republic: Benjamin Rush, Noah Webster, Robert Coram, Simeon Doggett, Samuel Harrison Smith, Amable-Louis-Rose de Lafitte du Courteil, Samuel Knox.* Cambridge, MA: Belknap Press of Harvard University Press.

Rudolph, F. (1978). *Curriculum: A history of the American undergraduate course of study since 1636.* San Francisco, CA: Jossey-Bass.

Rumberger, R., & Willms, J. D. (1992). The impact of racial and ethnic segregation on the achievement gap in California high schools. *Educational Evaluation and Policy Analysis, 14*(4), 377–396.

Rury, J. (1983, September). The New York African Free School, 1825–1835: Conflict over community control. *PHYLON, 44*(3), 187–198.

Rury, J. (1985, September). Philanthropy, self help and social control: The New York Manumission Society and free Blacks, 1785–1810. *PHYLON, 46*(3), 231–241.

Rury, J. L. (1988a, Summer). Imagining gender in educational history: Themes from the lives of colonial women. *Educational Foundations,* 45–60.

Rury, J. (1988b, Spring). The variable school year: Measuring differences in the length of American school terms in 1900. *Journal of Research and Development in Education,* 29–36.

Rury, J. (1988c). Race, region and education: An analysis of Black and White Scores on the 1917 Army ALPHA Test (Winter 1988). *Journal of Negro Education,* 51–65.

Rury, J. (1989). Who became teachers: The social characteristics of teachers in American history. In D. Warren, Ed. *American teachers: Histories of a profession at work* (pp. 9–48). New York: Macmillan and AERA.

Rury, J. L. (1991a). *Education and women's work: Female schooling and the division of labor in urban America, 1870–1930.* Albany: State University of New York Press.

Rury, J. (1991b). Transformation in perspective: A retrospective review of Lawrence Cremin's transformation of the school. *History of Education Quarterly* (Spring), 67–76.

Rury, J. L. (1993). The changing social context of urban education: A national perspective. In J. L. Rury, & Frank A. Cassel, Eds. *Seeds of crisis: Public schooling in Milwaukee since 1920* (pp. 10–41). Madison: University of Wisconsin Press.

Rury, J. L. (1999a). Historians and policy making. *American Journal of Education, 107*(4), 321–327.

Rury, J. (1999b). Race, space and the politics of Chicago's public schools: Benjamin Willis and the tragedy of urban education. *History of Education Quarterly, 39*(2).

Rury, J. (2002). Democracy's high school? Social change and American secondary education in the post-Conant era. *American Educational Research Journal* (Summer), 307–336.

Rury, J. (2004). Social capital and secondary schooling: Inter-urban differences in American teenage enrollment rates in 1950. *American Journal of Education* (August), 293–320.

Rury, J. (2006). Social capital and the common schools. In D. Warren, & J. J. Patrick, Eds. *Civic and moral learning in America* (pp. 69–86) New York: Palgrave Macmillan.

Rury, J., & Harper, G. (1986). The trouble with coeducation: Mann and women at Antioch, 1853–1860. *History of Education Quarterly, 26*(4), 481–502.

Russell, L. B. (1982). *The baby boom generation and the economy.* Washington, DC: Brookings Institute Press.

Russett, C. E. (1976). *Darwin in America: The intellectual response, 1865–1912.* San Francisco, CA: W. H. Freeman.

Rutman, D. B., Ed. (1970). *The Great Awakening: Event and exegesis.* New York: Wiley.

Rutman, D. B. (1977). *American Puritanism.* New York: Norton.

Ryan, A. (1995). *John Dewey and the high tide of American liberalism.* New York: Norton.

Sadker, M., & Sadker, D. (1994). *Failing at fairness: How America's schools cheat girls.* New York: C. Scribner's Sons.

Safford, P. L., & Safford, E. J. (1996). *A history of childhood and disability.* New York: Teachers College Press.

San Miguel, G. (1987). *"Let all of them take heed": Mexican Americans and the campaign for educational equality in Texas, 1910–1981.* Austin: University of Texas Press.

San Miguel, G. (2001). *Brown, not White: School integration and the Chicano movement in Houston.* College Station: Texas A&M University Press.

San Miguel, G. (2002). *Contested policy: The rise and fall of federal bilingual education in the United States, 1960–2001.* Denton: University of North Texas Press.

San Miguel, G., & Valencia, R. (1998). From the Treaty of Guadalupe Hidalgo to "Hopwood": The educational plight and struggle of Mexican Americans in the southwest. *Harvard Educational Review, 68*(3), 353–412.

Sanchez, G. J. (1993). *Becoming Mexican American: Ethnicity, culture and identity in Chicano Los Angeles, 1900–1945.* New York: Oxford University Press.

Sanders, J. W. (1977). *The education of an urban minority: Catholics in Chicago, 1833–1965.* New York: Oxford University Press.

Schnore, L. F. (1965). *The urban scene: Human ecology and demography.* New York: Free Press.

Schnore, L. F., Ed. (1974). *The new urban history: Quantitative explorations by American historians.* Princeton, NJ: Princeton University Press.

Schram, S. F. (1995). *Words of welfare: The poverty of social science and the social science of poverty.* Minneapolis: University of Minnesota Press.

Schultz, S. K. (1973). *The culture factory: Boston public schools, 1789–1860.* New York: Oxford University Press.

Scotch, R. (2001). *From good will to Civil Rights: Transforming Federal disability policy,* 2nd ed. Philadelphia, PA: Temple University Press.

Scott, A. F. (1978). What, then, is the American: This new woman? *Journal of American History, 65*(3), 679–703.

Scott, A. F. (1979). The ever widening circle: The diffusion of feminist values from the Troy Female Seminary, 1822–1872. *History of Education Quarterly, 19*(1), 3–25.

Sedlak, M., Pullian, D., & Wheeler, C. (1986). *Selling students short: Classroom bargains and academic reform in the American high school.* New York: Teachers College Press.

Selden, S. (1999). *Inheriting shame: The story of eugenics and racism in America.* New York: Teachers College Press.

Sellers, C. (1991). *The market revolution: Jacksonian America, 1815–1846.* New York: Oxford University Press.

Semel, S., & Sadovnick, A., Eds. (1999). *"Schools of tomorrow," schools of today: What happened to progressive education.* New York: P. Lang.

Senese, G. (1991). *Self-determination and the social education of Native Americans.* Westport, CT: Praeger Publishers.

Sexton, E., & Nickel, J. F. (1992). The effects of school location on the earnings of Black and White youths. *Economics of Education Review, 11*(1), 11–18.

Sharpless, J. B. (1977). *City growth in the United States, England and Wales, 1820—861: The effects of location, size and economic structure on inter-urban variations in demographic growth.* New York: Arno Press.

Sher, J. P., & Tompkins, R. B. (1977). Economy, efficiency, and equality: The myths of rural school and district consolidation. In J. P. Sher, Ed. *Education in rural America* (pp. 43–75). Boulder, CO: Westview Press.

Shipps, D. (1998). Corporate influences on Chicago school reform. In C. Stone, Ed. *Changing urban education* (pp. 161–183). Lawrence: University Press of Kansas.

Shipps, D. (2006). *School reform, corporate style: Chicago, 1880–2000.* Lawrence: University Press of Kansas.

Siddle-Walker, V. (1996). *Their highest potential: An African American school community in the segregated South.* Chapel Hill: University of North Carolina Press.

Silver, H., & Silver, P. (1991). *An educational war on poverty: American and British policy-making, 1960–1980.* New York: Cambridge University Press.

Silverman, K. (1984). *The life and times of Cotton Mather.* New York: Harper & Row.

Sitkoff, H. (1978). *A new deal for Blacks: The emergence of civil rights as a national issue.* New York: Oxford University Press.

Sitkoff, H. (1993). *The struggle for Black equality, 1954–1992.* New York: Hill and Wang.

Sklar, K. K. (1973). *Catharine Beecher: A study in American domesticity.* New Haven, CT: Yale University Press.

Sklar, K. K. (1993). The schooling of girls and changing community values in Massachusetts towns, 1750–1820. *History of Education Quarterly, 33*(4), 511–542.

Sklar, K. K. (1995). *Florence Kelley and the nation's work: The rise of women's political culture, 1830–1900.* New Haven, CT: Yale University Press.

Skocpol, T., Ed. (1984). *Vision and method in historical sociology.* New York: Cambridge University Press.

Skrentny, J. (2004). *The minority rights revolution.* Cambridge, MA: Harvard University Press.

Smith, D. B. (1980). *Inside the great house: Planter life in eighteenth century Chesapeake society.* Ithaca, NY: Cornell University Press.

Smith, D. (1991). *The rise of historical sociology.* Philadelphia, PA: Temple University Press.

Smith, M. S., & Scoll, B. W. (1995). The Clinton human capital agenda. *Teachers College Record, 96*(3), 389–404.

Solomon, B. M. (1985). *In the company of educated women: A history of women and higher education in America.* New Haven, CT: Yale University Press.

Solomon, L. C. (1970). Estimates of the costs of schooling in 1880 and 1890. *Explorations in Economic History. 2nd Ser., 7*(4), 531–581.

Soltow, L., & Stevens, E. (1981). *The rise of literacy and the common school in the United States: A socioeconomic analysis to 1870.* Chicago: University of Chicago Press.

Spindler, G. D. (1963). *Education and culture: Anthropological approaches.* New York: Holt, Rinehart and Winston.

Spring, J. H. (1976). *The sorting machine: National educational policy since 1945.* New York: McKay.

Stern, D., Paik, I. W., Catterali, J. S., & Nakata, Y. F. (1989). Labor market experience of teenagers with and without high school diplomas. *Economics of Education Review, 8*(3), 233–246.

Stockman, D. A. (1986). *The triumph of politics: Why the Reagan revolution failed.* New York: Harper & Row.

Stohr, G. (2006). *A Black and White case: How affirmative action survived its greatest legal challenge.* New York: Bloomberg Press.

Stolee, M. (1993). The Milwaukee desegregation case. In J. L. Rury, & F. A. Cassell, Eds. *Seeds of crisis: Public schooling in Milwaukee since 1920* (pp. 229–246). Madison: University of Wisconsin Press.

Stone, C. N. (1998). Introduction. In C. Stone, Ed. *Changing urban education* (pp. 1–23). Lawrence: University Press of Kansas.

Stone, C., Henig, J. R., Jones, B. D., & Pierannunzi, C. (2001). *Building civic capacity: The politics of reforming urban schools.* Lawrence: University Press of Kansas.

Stowell, D. O. (1999). *Streets, railroads, and the great strike of 1877*. Chicago: University of Chicago Press.

Strang, D. (1987). The administrative transformation of American education: School district consolidation, 1938–1980. *Administrative Science Quarterly, 32*(3) (September), 352–366.

Szasz, M. (1974). *Education and the American Indian: The road to self-determination, 1928–1973*. Albuquerque: University of New Mexico Press.

Szasz, M. C. (1977). Federal boarding schools and the Indian child: 1920–1960. *South Dakota History, 7*(4), 371–384.

Szasz, M. C. (1988). *Indian education in the American colonies, 1607–1783*. Albuquerque: University of New Mexico Press.

Takaki, R. T. (1979). *Iron cages: Race and culture in 19th-century America*. New York: Oxford University Press.

Tamura, E. (2001). Asian Americans in the history of education: An historiographical essay. *History of Education Quarterly, 41*(1), 58–71.

Tanner, L. N. (1997). *Dewey's laboratory school: Lessons for today*. New York: Teachers College Press.

Taylor, G. R. (1968). *The transportation revolution, 1815–1860*. New York: Harper.

Teaford, J. C. (1990). *Rough road to renaissance: Urban revitalization in America, 1940–1985*. Baltimore, MD: Johns Hopkins University Press.

Terkel, S. (1997). *The good war: An oral history of World War II*. New York: New Press.

Thernstrom, S. (1964). *Poverty and progress: Social mobility in a nineteenth century city*. Cambridge, MA: Harvard University Press.

Thernstrom, S. (1973). *The other Bostonians: Poverty and progress in the American metropolis, 1860–1970*. Cambridge, MA: Harvard University Press.

Tolley, K. (2002). *Standing at the portals: The science education of American girls*. New York: Routledge/Falmer.

Trent, J. W., Jr. (1994). *Inventing the feeble mind: A history of mental retardation in the United States*. Berkeley: University of California Press.

Tropea, J. L. (1987). Bureaucratic order and special children: Urban schools, 1890s–1940s. *History of Education Quarterly, 27*(1) (Spring), 29–53.

Tuchman, B. W. (1978). *A distant mirror: The calamitous 14th century*. New York: Knopf.

Tucker, W. H. (1994). *The science and politics of racial research*. Urbana: University of Illinois Press.

Turnbull, H. R., Stowe, M. J., & Huerta, N. E. (2006). *The Individuals with Disabilities Education Act as amended in 2004*. Columbus, OH: Merrill/Prentice Hall.

Tuttle, W. (1993). *"Daddy's gone to war": The Second World War in the lives of America's children*. New York: Oxford University Press.

Tyack, D. B. (1967). *George Ticknor and the Boston Brahmins*. Cambridge, MA: Harvard University Press.

Tyack, D. (1974). *The one best system: A history of American urban education*. Cambridge, MA: Harvard University Press.

Tyack, D. B. (1978). The spread of public schooling in Victorian America: In search of a reinterpretation. *History of Education [Great Britain], 7*(3), 173–182.

Tyack, D. B., & Cuban, L. (1995). *Tinkering toward utopia: A century of public school reform*. Cambridge, MA: Harvard University Press.

Tyack, D. B., & Hansot, E. (1982). *Managers of virtue: Public school leadership in America, 1820–1980*. New York: Basic Books.

Tyack, D. B., & Hansot, E. (1990). *Learning together: A history of coeducation in American schools*. New Haven, CT: Yale University Press.

Tyack, D. B., James, T., & Benevot, A. (1987). *Law and the shaping of public education, 1785–1954*. Madison: University of Wisconsin Press.

Tyler, A. F. (1962). *Freedom's ferment: Phases of American social history to 1860*. New York: Harper & Row.

Valenzuela, A. (1999). *Subtractive schooling: U.S.-Mexican youth and the politics of caring*. Albany: State University of New York Press.

VanOverbeke, M. (2008). *The standardization of American schooling: Linking secondary and higher education.* New York: Palgrave Macmillan.

Veysey, L. R. (1965). *The emergence of the American university.* Chicago: University of Chicago Press.

Vine, P. (1976). The social function of eighteenth-century higher education. *History of Education Quarterly, 16*(4) (Winter), 409–424.

Vinovskis, M. A. (1970). Horace Mann on the economic productivity of education. *New England Quarterly, 43*(4), 550–571.

Vinovskis, M. A. (1972). Trends in Massachusetts education, 1826–1860. *History of Education Quarterly, 12*(4), 501–529.

Vinovskis, M. A., Ed. (1979). *Studies in American historical demography.* New York: Academic Press.

Vinovskis, M. A. (1995). *Education, society, and economic opportunity: A historical perspective on persistent issues.* New Haven, CT: Yale University Press.

Vinovskis, M. A. (1996). An analysis of the concept and uses of systemic educational reform. *American Educational Research Journal, 33*(1), 53–85.

Vinovskis, M. A. (1999). *History and educational policymaking.* New Haven, CT: Yale University Press.

Vinovskis, M. A. (2005). *The birth of Head Start: Preschool education policies in the Kennedy and Johnson administrations.* Chicago: University of Chicago Press.

Vinovskis, M. A., & Bernard, R. M. (1978). Beyond Catharine Beecher: Female education in the antebellum period. *Signs, 3*(4), 856–869.

Vinyard, J. E. M. (1976). *The Irish on the urban frontier: Nineteenth century Detroit, 1850–1880.* New York: Arno Press.

Violas, P. C. (1978). *The training of the urban working class: A history of twentieth-century American education.* Chicago: Rand McNally.

Wainwright, N., Weigley, R., & Wolf, E. (1982). *Philadelphia: A 300-Year History.* W.W. Norton & Company.

Waltershausen, A. S. von (1999). *The workers' movement in the United States, 1879–1885.* Cambridge: Cambridge University Press.

Ward, D. (1975). *Cities and immigrants: A geography of change in nineteenth-century America.* New York: Oxford University Press.

Warren, D. R. (1974). *To enforce education: A history of the founding years of the United States Office of Education.* Detroit, MI: Wayne State University Press.

Webber, T. L. (1978). *Deep like the rivers: Education in the slave quarter community, 1831–1865.* New York: Norton.

Weber, M. (1930). *The Protestant ethic and the spirit of capitalism* (T. Parsons, Trans., with foreword by R. H. Tawney). New York: Scribner.

Wells, A. S., & Crain, R. L. (1997). *Stepping over the color line: African American students in White suburban schools.* New Haven, CT: Yale University Press.

Welter, B. (1966). The cult of true womanhood: 1820–1860. *American Quarterly, 18*(2), 151–174.

Welter, R. (1962). *Popular education and democratic thought in America.* New York: Columbia University Press.

Werum, R. (1997). Sectionalism and racial politics: Federal vocational policies and programs in the predesegregation South. *Social Science History, 21*(3), 399–453.

West, E. (1996). *Growing up in twentieth-century America: A history and reference guide.* Westport, CT: Greenwood Press.

Westbrook, R. B. (1991). *John Dewey and American democracy.* Ithaca, NY: Cornell University Press.

Westbrook, R. B. (1994). On the private life of a public philosopher: John Dewey in love. *Teachers College Record, 96*(2), 183–197.

Wiebe, R. H. (1967). *The search for order, 1877–1920.* New York: Hill and Wang.

Wilkerson, J. H. (1979). *From Brown to Bakke: The Supreme Court and school integration.* New York: Oxford University Press.

Williamson, J. (1984). *The crucible of race: Black–White relations in the American South since emancipation.* New York: Oxford University Press.

Willis, P. (1977). *Learning to labor.* New York: Routledge.

Wilson, W. J. (1987). *The truly disadvantaged: The inner city, the underclass, and public policy.* Chicago: University of Chicago Press.

Wilson, W. J. (1995). *When work disappears: The world of the new urban poor.* New York: Alfred A. Knopf.

Winzer, M. A. (1993). *The history of special education: From isolation to integration.* Washington, DC: Gallaudet University Press.

Wise, A. E. (1968). *Rich schools, poor schools: The promise of equal educational opportunity.* Chicago: University of Chicago Press.

Wishy, B. W. (1967). *The child and the Republic: The dawn of modern American child nurture.* Philadelphia: University of Pennsylvania Press.

Witte, J. (1999). *The market approach to education: An analysis of America's first voucher program.* Princeton, NJ: Princeton University Press.

Wolters, R. (1984). *The burden of Brown: Thirty years of school desegregation.* Knoxville: University of Tennessee Press.

Wong, K., & Moulton, M. (1998). Governance report cards: Accountability in the Chicago public school system. *Education and Urban Society, 30*(4), 459–478.

Wong, K., Guthrie, J., & Harris, D. (2004). *A nation at risk: A 20-year reappraisal.* Mahwah, NJ: Lawrence Erlbaum.

Wood, P. H. (1974). *Black majority: Negroes in colonial South Carolina from 1670 through the Stono Rebellion.* New York: Knopf.

Woodward, C. V. (1974). *The strange career of Jim Crow,* 3rd rev. ed. New York: Oxford University Press.

Woody, T. (1923). *Quaker education in the colony and state of New Jersey.* Philadelphia: University of Pennsylvania.

Woody, T. (1929). *A history of women's education in the United States.* New York: Science Press.

Yezierska, A. (1925). *Bread givers: A struggle between a father of the old world and a daughter of the new.* Garden City, NY: Doubleday, Page.

Zelizer, V. A. (1985). *Pricing the priceless child: The changing social value of children.* New York: Basic Books.

Zhou, M., & Bankston, C. L., III. (1994). Social capital and the adaptation of the second generation: The case of Vietnamese youth in New Orleans. *International Migration Review, 28*(4), 821–845.

Zigler, E., & Muenchow, S. (1992). *Head Start: The inside story of America's most successful educational experiment.* New York: Basic Books.

Zilversmit, A. (1967). *The first emancipation: The abolition of slavery in the North.* Chicago: University of Chicago Press.

Zilversmit, A. (1993). *Changing schools: Progressive education theory and practice, 1930–1960.* Chicago: University of Chicago Press.

Zimmerman, J. (2002). *Whose America?: Culture wars in the public schools.* Cambridge, MA: Harvard University Press.

Zimmerman, J. (2008). *Small wonder: The little red schoolhouse in history and memory.* New Haven, CT: Yale University Press.

Zirkel, P. A. (1999). The 30th anniversary of "Tinker." *Phi Delta Kappan, 81*(1), 34–40, 58.

Zschoche, S. (1989). Dr. Clarke revisited: Science, true womanhood, and female collegiate education. *History of Education Quarterly, 29*(4), 545–569.

Zunz, O. (1982). *The changing face of inequality: Urbanization, industrial development, and immigrants in Detroit, 1880–1920.* Chicago: University of Chicago Press.

# Index